Charles Manson Coming Down Fast

Also by Simon Wells

Your Face Here: British Cult Movies Since the 1960s
The Beatles: 365 Days
The Rolling Stones: 365 Days

Charles

A Chilling Biography

Manson

Coming

Down

SIMON WELLS

Fast

HODDER

First published in Great Britain in 2009 by Hodder & Stoughton.
An imprint of Hodder & Stoughton
An Hachette UK company

First published in paperback 2010

9

Copyright © Simon Wells 2009

The right of Simon Wells to be identified as the Author
of the Work has been asserted by him in accordance with
the Copyright, Designs and Patents Act 1988.

A CIP catalogue record for this title is available from the British Library

ISBN 9780340977033

Typeset in Sabon by Hewer Text UK Ltd, Edinburgh
Printed and bound by CPI Group (UK) Ltd, Croydon, CRO4YY

Hodder & Stoughton policy is to use papers that are natural, renewable
and recyclable products and made from wood grown in sustainable
forests. The logging and manufacturing processes are expected to
conform to the environmental regulations of the country of origin.

Hodder & Stoughton Ltd
338 Euston Road
London NW1 3BH

www.hodder.co.uk

Contents

Contents

Ah Sunflower, weary of time,
Who countest the steps of the sun;
Seeking after that sweet golden clime
Where the traveller's journey is done;

Where the Youth pined away with desire,
And the pale virgin shrouded in snow,
Arise from their graves, and aspire
Where my Sunflower wishes to go

William Blake, 1794

Introduction

As a child, I remember watching the film *Whistle Down the Wind*, which was about a gaggle of children who'd discovered an escaped convict hiding out in a barn. In their innocence, the kids believed that the escapee was Jesus Christ; a persona the fugitive was more than happy to adopt. At the film's end, the children's secret is made public and the criminal is recaptured. No more Jesus in the barn.

Years later, when I became interested in the Manson case, I was reminded of that odd British film. Whilst the concept of a criminal posing as Christ seems like a celluloid fantasy, I was shocked to find some startling similarities with the real-life case of Charles Manson. It's hard to make parallels with someone as infamous as Manson. In the criminal hierarchy he stands alone, towering over all other pretenders. Furthermore, he's become the perverse flip side to the joyous optimism of the 1960s: the worm in the ointment, the bogeyman, the rotten apple in the barrel.

Anyone who is interested in the 1960s and popular culture will have heard about Charles Manson; he's become as synonymous with the decade as the Beatles and flower-power, Vietnam and psychedelic drugs, hippies and free love. In fact, it's impossible to avoid this mad, crazy lunatic with a swastika carved deep into his forehead. It's equally hard to ignore the man's followers, his

'Family' of drugged-up, sexed-up, delusional maniacs, slavishly obedient to Manson's every whim. As history informs us, these were once good kids from middle-class backgrounds, but they ended up fighting for him, stealing for him, even killing for him. And when they finally ended up facing the full retribution of law and state, their love for Manson remained unabated.

Intrigued by the stories I'd heard about Manson, I began to look deeper. I soon uncovered a disturbing picture of what really occurred during those last days of the sixties. As I pored over the reams of material that have been written about him over the last forty years, I found it impossible not to be deeply intrigued by the man. As original trial prosecutor Vincent Bugliosi puts it: 'Next to Jack the Ripper, Manson is probably the most famous serial killer ever. His name has become a metaphor for evil, and evil has its allure.' Yet, there is no proof that Manson was a serial killer; he was more than fifteen miles away from the scene the night that the most notorious murders took place – in this and in so many other ways, Charles Manson was unique.

As my research took me deeper and deeper into my subject, it became clear that drugs, sex, ritualistic murders and mind-control were by no means the whole story; throw in the Beatles, the Beach Boys, Hollywood A-List celebrities, black magic, the Mafia and even two presidents of America, and you are still only halfway there. The relatives of the Family's victims may still be grieving their losses, but it's fascinating to think how future generations will come to view Manson and his followers. Will they be romanticised like Jesse James, Bonnie and Clyde, or 1930s Prohibition mobsters? Or will they be seen as Jack the Ripper is: the enduring symbol of the evil of their age?

From the day he was born in 1934, Charles Manson certainly had the right credentials to qualify as an outlaw. With an absent father and prostitute mother, he easily gravitated towards a life of petty crime and wayward behaviour. Despite being superficially charming, his taste for mixing with society's underbelly ensured he spent most of his early years in America's state institutions. Without the framework of family, it's not really that surprising that Manson grew to enjoy prison; its regime and criminal fraternity offered a structure to his life. Rather than rehabilitation, Manson put together a sizeable list of contacts and an encyclopaedic knowledge of criminal methodology.

During a ten-year term for fraud at the beginning of the early 1960s, Manson began to actively study mind control and psychology. He became highly adept at manipulating certain personalities for his own ends. He also developed a considerable ability for song writing, which he blended with the esoteric philosophies he'd picked up from Scientology, Buddhism and even Masonic folklore. Seen as little more than a freak by fellow inmates, Manson was left alone to read, write and fester. The racial divides that existed within the microcosm of jail helped lay the foundation for the Family's unbridled racism.

When Manson emerged from jail in 1967, he found the monochrome world that he left behind had turned Day-Glo in his absence. Even at thirty-two, he easily picked up this new vibe, the revolution driven by America's youth. A desire to search and explore for a new, shared experience, and rebellion in whatever shape or form it took, had become *de rigueur*. Luckily for Manson, any expression of this freedom, however extreme, was welcomed in these new communities, many of them based in California.

Heading swiftly to San Francisco in March 1967, Manson was greeted by the peace and love brigade with open arms and legs. His guitar slung round his shoulder, he started to accrue a large retinue of followers; principally young kids looking for a saviour. These weren't your regular failures and dropouts; most were high achievers and homecoming queens; girls and boys 'most likely to'. They were also intelligent, instinctive, and looking for someone to soothe their angst and answer all their questions. Manson's caring smile and heart-felt manifesto enchanted many an impressionable mind into following him, allowing their past to be erased, and their future to be rewritten.

How did Manson manage to wield such influence over his followers? Perhaps it was the strange ambience of the mid-1960s that was to blame. Freedom, oft talked about in America, was now being demonstrably exercised for the first time in modern history. Equally groundbreaking, dissent had become exciting, new – a craze, even. With the war in Vietnam vividly showing their elders' corruption, opposition to anything that represented the past caught on like wildfire. As a result, a deep schism separated young people from conventional society. Being totally mercurial, Manson was hip to what was going down on the streets and in the gutter. At the other side of thirty, and seasoned by life in the clink, Manson was savvy enough to use this dissent for his own ends.

Hallucinogenic drugs became an obligatory rite of passage into this new world, while for Charles Manson they were an important device for unlocking troubled minds, and bending them his way. Furthermore, LSD's ability to desensitise the psyche to every imaginable horror was hugely appealing to Manson's darker side.

Manson soon found that he had collected a small, but dedicated band of devotees. Manson made sure to instil a cocky assurance in his followers that went far beyond the open-minded attitude of the broader hippie movement. Despite the flowers and flares, his new breed weren't hippies; they were 'slippies', a term Manson coined for the kids who hung on his every word.

And for a short while in 1967, the party looked as though it would never have to end. Like many other communes on a road to nowhere, Manson's band formed their home aboard an old school bus. Soon, they would find a more permanent sanctuary in an old movie set on the fringes of Los Angeles. Like a psychedelic version of *Little House on the Prairie*, Manson's Family began to gel together into one unit, aided by their leader's teachings. At this early point in their history, the talk was not of murder, but of love, community, brotherhood and music – as long as it was Manson's or the Beatles. By the mid-1960s, the Beatles' massive success pointed out a route for others to follow, Manson included. Despite coming from the bluegrass of Kentucky, he identified with their own humble beginnings. He was eager to follow in their footsteps and secure some of the enormous success that seemed there for the taking.

To aid their search for a record deal, Manson and his followers settled in Los Angeles at the end of 1967. Manson soon collected a number of admirers – Dennis Wilson of The Beach Boys, Neil Young and plenty of others were taken in by Manson and his girls. In these early halcyon days, Manson looked set for stardom, and yet just eighteen months after his first recording session, all Manson had left was the devotion of his tiny flock of admirers. The music industry he so wanted to enchant was by now turned off by his crazed antics. With his musical career on a steep decline, Manson fell back on his two constants: petty criminality and pseudo-religious proclamations. He announced an impending Armageddon, and took his followers out to the Californian desert. There, he acted out his increasingly bizarre fantasies for his small audience of believers. Meanwhile, the world he so desperately wanted to infiltrate back in Los Angeles was moving on without him. Isolated and forgotten by the glitterati, Manson's frustrations boiled over; and the stage was set for what was soon to come.

The dreadful crimes that occurred in California in August 1969 rocked the whole of America, and threw up a raft of witness reports, testimonies and court documents, as well as countless first-hand interviews and source material. However, in the end, one of the forgotten associates of the Family presented me with the most intriguing material and gave me my most difficult task.

Joel Pugh was an enigmatic, peripheral personality in the Manson saga, whose story ties the Family's commune in the permanent sunshine of the Los Angeles desert to grey old England, and more specifically to Joel's death in London in 1969 – the year of the Sharon Tate murders. Initially, any paperwork relating to his demise was impossible to trace. Remarkably, Scotland Yard had destroyed all their notes that pertained to his death, and there was no trace of them in police archives in Los Angeles, despite much speculation at the time. Eventually, through a labyrinth of enquiries and informants, a folder of information relating to Joel Pugh and Manson Family activities in the UK was discovered in a college archive in Nevada, California. Much of the contents of this file has never been publicly revealed before, and gives an amazing insight into the Manson family's activities outside of America.

It's not only Joel Pugh's tragic death that tied Manson's Californian murders to Swinging Sixties Britain. In this book,

I make no apologies for delving into the world of the Beatles, and how it mapped on to the strange territory Charles Manson occupied. Although the chances of any of the Fab Four actually meeting Manson appear remote, in the Neverland of the 1960s, suggestion was often more powerful than reality. Whereas the Beatles might have seen their 1968 'White Album' project as little more than collecting songs together for a contractually required album, outside the group, every nuance was interpreted as meaning something. Most tragically, the Beatles' signals were wholly misinterpreted by Charles Manson, and ended up forming part of the Family's twisted mythology.

In putting the book together there were other, even more contentious decisions to be made. For example, I have chosen to include a series of photos that were taken following the murders at Cielo Drive. Whilst I apologise for any distress they may cause, they offer an insight into the madness that no words could ever convey. Equally, they present a necessary shot of brutal reality. Whatever the rhetoric, the Family was always something darker than the happy, shambling caravan of dissenters they sometimes appear to be. While many would prefer to keep the photographs out of the public domain, their horrendous detail are one of the factors that ensure the continued incarceration of those guilty of one of the twentieth century's most sensational crimes.

Charles Manson knows only too well that the chances of his own freedom are less than zero. At the time of writing, Manson is kept in a protective unit at Corcoran prison in southern California. He is seventy-four. The protective unit is more for his own safety than for those of his fellow inmates. Whilst Manson will take any opportunity to take a swipe, both verbal and otherwise, at his warders, the authorities are more concerned about the opportunist jailbird who might want his scalp. Manson's days are long, and he fills the hours making speeches to anyone who'll listen. But outside the world has changed, and time has long overtaken the prisoner and his pretensions.

The saga of the Family is a mad, wayward story that fulfilled no other purpose than to magnify the notoriety of Charles Manson. Looking at the facts in the cold light of day, everything Charles

Manson set out to achieve failed dismally. Music, relationships, crime, putative attempts at world domination – all ended in abject catastrophe. While there are still many people who would wish to elevate him to near deity status, the fact remains that Manson achieved little other than carnage. If he did succeed in sending America a wake-up call, it was by chance – a by-product of the wreckage that built up around him. Others with similarly fractured childhoods have gone on to forge great and extraordinary futures for themselves. Charles Manson's inability to rise above the knocks and the barbs of life prompts little sympathy.

The great irony is that the joyous optimism and boundless love of the 1960s was responsible for allowing Manson a voice in the first place. That really is the sad, fascinating truth at the heart of Manson and the Family's story.

Simon Wells, April 2009
Sussex, England

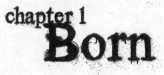

chapter 1
Born

'I am only what you made me. I am only a reflection of you. I have ate out of your garbage cans to stay out of jail. I have wore your second-hand clothes . . . I have spent twenty-three years in tombs that you built.'

Charles Manson, 20 November 1970

CHILDHOOD. Infancy. Youth. These are not words that sit easily with someone once depicted as 'the most evil person alive'. When, at the age of thirty-five, Charles Manson was held responsible for some of the most horrific murders of modern times, his humble, formative years were of little consequence. It's not hard to see why. What's one man's hard-luck story compared to the sea of bloodstained bodies left strewn across affluent Los Angeles? The legend of Charles Manson has emerged as the twentieth century's prime metaphor for unspeakable horror, but his formative days have remained a mystery.

While Charles Manson, the 'mass murderer', the 'serial killer', the 'mind controller', has been fully seared into popular history, the more mundane circumstances of his arrival in 1934 are less sensational. Five years after Wall Street's spectacular collapse, the ripple effects of the Great Depression were still being felt by ordinary Americans. As stockbrokers and businessmen pondered their diminishing fortunes, the working-class in hinterlands such as Kentucky were faced with the choice between survival and death.

It was into this tough, austere arena that young Charles Manson would first emerge. We don't know much about sixteen-year-old Kathleen Maddox, or how aware she was of the desperate times she was living through. However, it's certain that 12 November 1934 would be the most momentous day of her early years.

Kathleen was the youngest of Nancy and Charles Maddox's three children, following her brother Luther and older sister Alene into the world. The family were based in Ashland, Kentucky, a modest industrial town nestling on the banks of the Ohio river. Charles Manson's family tree reveals an unremarkable litany of short lives and nondescript vocations; Kentucky people, who stuck to ideals of endurance and self-sufficiency. Charles, like Kathleen before him, seemed to be cut from a different cloth.

The Maddoxes were devout Christians, and were dominated by the matriarch of the household, Nancy Loraine. So formidable was Nancy in her religious convictions that she barred her two daughters from any overt show of femininity. Kathleen's father Charles was a hard-working man, who'd carved out a long career on the Baltimore & Ohio railways as a conductor. Somewhat in the shadow, Charles Senior didn't have the religious vehemence of his wife, but would fall quietly in line with her in order to keep the peace. This uneven atmosphere made the Maddox house a brittle environment for the children to grow up in. As puberty approached, and hormones ran wild, the constraints evidently proved too overwhelming.

As a teenager, Kathleen rebelled against the regime. Although her mother had forbidden any form of dating, once Kathleen got a taste for the enticing world of adult sexuality, she leapt in head first. Her sister and brother had been eager to break the bonds of their austerity but Kathleen's youthful exuberance meant she took to secular pleasures with even more zeal. On reflection in 1970, Charles's mother Kathleen was matter-of-fact about it: 'My mother was a very strict woman, very religious, so when me and my sister got a few years older, I guess we had a tendency to be a little wild, the way kids will.'

Kathleen soon fell in with a dismal assortment of suitors from the wrong side of the tracks. They revelled in the favours she was more than happy to share.

At the age of fifteen, Kathleen started seeing Colonel M. Scott, a man eight years her senior. Despite received wisdom suggesting otherwise, 'Colonel' was his Christian name, rather than his rank. The youngest of Walker and Gladys Scott's four children, Colonel was in fact a freewheeling itinerant, maintaining himself with a host of menial jobs. According to the sketchy reports, he spent time as a cook, a labourer and an assistant in a dry-cleaning laundry – not the most auspicious match for a member of the respectable, God-fearing Maddox clan.

It's unlikely that anyone would have remembered the couple's relationship if Kathleen hadn't become pregnant. Given her early penchant for the wild side, it wasn't that much of a surprise to the neighbourhood, but, in the pious setting of her family, it was a terrible scandal, and Kathleen was forced to move out. At the age of fifteen, with her mother's admonishments echoing in her ear, she took off, shacking up in a string of seedy boarding houses and flats in downtown Cincinnati.

Here truth begins to differ from legend. Much has been said about Charles Manson being the product of a paid encounter. But while many observers of the case have spoken of Kathleen as a prostitute, there is no tangible evidence to suggest that she was selling herself for money at this point. Although Manson has since conceded that his mother may have been forced to engage in paid sex later in life, it's more likely that baby Charles was an unplanned teen pregnancy, rather than anything more sensational. Those around Kathleen at the time describe her personality as 'loose' and that she 'ran around a lot, drank, got in trouble'.

Following the announcement of her pregnancy, Colonel Scott took off to avoid having to support the child. Kathleen didn't seem overly perturbed by her lover's abandonment. During the later stages of her pregnancy, she started seeing William Manson, a twenty-four-year-old labourer. William was evidently enamoured enough with her to see the pregnancy through, and to maintain a presence in Kathleen's life after the birth. In return his name was to go down in history.

At 4.40 p.m. on 12 November 1934, Kathleen's baby entered into the world at Cincinnati's main hospital on Pike Street. As befits the chaos that has surrounded little Charles's life ever since, the child got off to a confused start. Initially, hospital paperwork recorded him as 'no-name Maddox', on account of the father's absence, and Kathleen not yet having a name for her son. Evidently mother and daughter had patched up their differences because Kathleen waited for a few days until her mother's arrival in Cincinnati before deciding on a suitable moniker. Together, they chose the name Charles Milles. To give the child some semblance of a family, Kathleen married her beau, William Manson. The marriage would allow for the bona-fide registration of Charles Manson to be properly filed three weeks after the little boy's birth, with 'William Manson' clearly stated on the certificate as the father.[1] Later, Kathleen would later make her own, more ad hoc, alteration to her little boy's name. Charles was shortened to Charlie, the name that he would carry with him for the rest of his life.

According to official reports, in 1936 Kathleen pursued the errant Colonel Scott through the courts for child support for Charlie. Despite a ruling in April 1937 ordering a one-off payment of $25, and $5 weekly maintenance, Kathleen claims she never received any money. By 1940 she was applying to the courts to have the money siphoned from his wages. Many years later, after Manson was happily revelling in his own bastard status, Kathleen reported that his absent father had apparently taken some interest in his young son before his death from cancer in 1954. '[Colonel] Scott used to come and pick Charlie up and take him home for weekends with his own child,' she claimed in an interview following Manson's arrest in 1969. 'He just loved him.'

When Manson achieved global notoriety in 1969, there were suggestions that the enigmatic Colonel Scott had actually been of black origin.[2] As Charlie doesn't appear to have any African-American features, and without convincing photographic or genetic evidence, it remains, like much connected with the case, part of the lore of Manson's enigma. Little is recorded of Colonel Scott's future movements, other than a conviction for assault and battery, and a sustained conviction of malicious shooting and wounding in November 1941. Census reports cite that he died aged just forty-four on 30 December 1954.

Regardless of the arguments concerning Charlie's paternal origin, the little boy was very close to his mother in his formative years. She later claimed she was overly generous in her feelings towards him: 'Maybe it was because my own mother had been so strict, but if Charlie wanted anything, I'd give it to him.'

Although Kathleen would later claim to have spoilt her little Charlie, by her own admission, she was regularly out of the house for a variety of reasons. This left the boy to be cared for by a legion of carers, friends, and anyone else who happened to be around. Court records of the time reveal that Kathleen used a variety of aliases to ease her passage through debt and other scrapes. Legend has it that once, when she was short of cash for a drink, she traded the little boy for a flagon of beer to a childless waitress in a bar, only to have the child later reclaimed by a concerned relative. While this and other rumours were embellished over the years, Kathleen was evidently having a difficult time juggling child-rearing, work and her hectic social life.

In 1939, Kathleen, along with her older brother Luther and his wife, took part in a robbery of a service station in Charleston, West Virginia. The crime, despite having all the glamour of a 'Bonnie and Clyde' style adventure, was a messy affair; Kathleen, armed with Coke bottles, knocked out the attendant during the robbery. She ended up taking the rap and was sentenced to five years' imprisonment. Kathleen later claimed that her brother's wife told her that they could all escape if she took the bulk of the charge. With six-year-old Manson now without any primary carer, he was placed in the temporary custody of his grandparents. The environment was as strict as when his mother Kathleen had left it, and the little boy was browbeaten into a quiet subservience. Nonetheless, Charlie appears to have held his grandmother in high regard: 'My grandmother was a mountain girl from Kentucky up in the mountains ... She never did drink or smoke or cuss or lie. She used to cook for the Salvation Army and was a human being, a good one. I'd go to the church down there and sweep the floor for her.'³

While austerity reigned supreme in the Maddox household, the failing health of Charlie's grandmother made it impossible for her to care adequately for him. Additionally, the child's bastard status would have been severely at loggerheads with her pious doctrine. At that point, it was deemed more appropriate for Charlie to be in the care of his aunt Alene and her husband Bill. While sister Kathleen and brother Luther had gone seriously off the rails, Alene had evidently settled down to married life. She and her husband were based in the leafy environs of McMechen, a modest mining town in West Virginia, which had a rich churchgoing tradition running through its seams. They were living a comfortable life in a riverside property with a large garden. It was a long way from the disordered, money-strapped life Kathleen could offer.

While Alene and Bill's relationship had been rocky at first, they'd overcome any obstacles through their shared belief in Christianity. This soon turned into a devout obsession. As McMechen prided itself on its religious traditions, young Charlie was expected to attend a variety of services on Sunday. While others might have been dismissive of the bundle dumped on their doorstep, his uncle and aunt were proactive in shaping the young boy up to the rigours of the Christian world.

Manson has since claimed that he was placed under a strict regime at McMechen, living a devout and disciplined life, working his way through a long list of chores during the day. However, his mother begged to differ in an interview she gave in 1980. 'He never had to do a thing to earn what he wanted. Those stories about him earning his own living selling newspapers when he was seven or eight, those aren't true. He didn't even have to do things around the house, like rake or mow lawns.'

Charlie's innate sensitivity to his plight ensured that he often cried for his mother. Soon the young boy would be, in his own words, 'the sissy of the neighbourhood'. His Uncle Bill – evidently a graduate of the Johnny Cash School of sensitivity – threatened the young boy that if he didn't start shaping up and stop acting like a woman, he would make him wear a dress. Uncle Bill was sincere in his threat, and one Sunday the hapless Charlie was made to don a skirt to church in an attempt to 'learn to fight and be a man'. For the community of McMechen, lined up meekly in their pews, the sight of the little boy wearing a dress caused much amusement. The following week at school, Charlie had to fight off a barrage of teasing about the event – eventually, he snapped, and started attacking anyone who dared taunt him. From a shrinking violet to ultra-violence, Manson's uncle had certainly succeeded in shaping up young Charlie.

Dolores Longwell was a classmate of Charlie's during his

years at McMechen. She noted that the 'new boy in class' caused a flutter of interest among the girls, due to his 'lovely eyes', having little reason to believe that he would eventually become synonymous with evil. While Charlie was negative about his new home, Dolores saw it somewhat differently. 'He had just about anything he wanted,' she recalled. 'His aunt and uncle and grandmother took him to church. He didn't like going. The only thing he really liked was the singing. He really loved to sing.'

Despite Charlie's reticence, these church services proved pivotal in the way he developed both musically and spiritually. Although a tearaway waiting in the wings, he instantly warmed to the sonic vibrations of the hymns and the obedient spirituality they evoked in the attendees. This would be a power he would later harness for his own ends.

While academia was never going to be his strongest point, Charlie was nonetheless possessed with an instinctive intelligence. He was sensitive and creative, and only too aware of his social shortcomings – his illegitimacy and his mother's status – and he never fulfilled his academic potential.

The close-knit, close-minded community did its best to remind young Charlie of his dubious parentage. Phrases such as 'the little bastard', and 'your mother's a jailbird' were shouted across park and playground. In return, Charlie would attempt to stand his ground; his short stature was no obstacle to his fierce self-preservation. Predictably, Charles's first brush with the law would soon follow.

Given the extreme Christian values dominant in his guardians' house, Charlie's formative Christmases were spartan affairs. While the other children of McMechen enjoyed their festive gifts, young Charlie didn't have much to look forward to at Yuletide. Manson recalled one particular Christmas where all he received was a hairbrush; albeit one with a *Superman* transfer. Unsurprisingly, the other children in the neighbourhood took great pleasure in showing off their bigger and better presents once school recommenced. In a fit of pique, Charlie took action. While the other children were studying, Charlie rounded up their prized Christmas gifts, and set off towards a desolate stretch of land. Once there, he built a fire and ceremoniously burnt the lot. Charlie's involvement was soon discovered, and the local police called in. While too young to be charged, the seven-year-old was soundly reprimanded for his misdemeanours. It was to be Manson's first taste of infamy.

Before Charlie could establish any further criminal credentials, fate intervened. In 1942, his mother Kathleen was granted parole. She camped out for a while at her sister's house in McMechen, but family circumstances made a long stay at the house awkward. With Uncle Bill suffering from respiratory problems, and Charlie causing something of a stir around McMechen's quiet environs, it was considered best for Kathleen and her young son to move on. Equally pleased to be free from the parochial mindset of McMechen, the pair moved onwards towards Cincinnati. While their reunion had been warm, within weeks Kathleen returned to her peripatetic, slacker lifestyle. Soon, a succession of carers would resume foster duty for the little boy while his mother was occupied elsewhere. She even made steps to have him fostered.

If Kathleen's business required Charlie to be away for longer than an afternoon or an evening, he'd be shunted up to Kentucky to spend time with his 'uncle' Jess and his family. Jess was every part the hillbilly relative, living a lawless life in a log cabin with his wife, four daughters and a variety of animals. While there, Charlie got exposed to the sharp end of family life. At the mercy of the elements, Manson learnt a lot from his uncle Jess about survival and blood kinship. Jess was also a firm opponent of schooling, telling the young boy, 'We ain't surrendered, we're still rebels, and we'll be rebels until the end of time, because I ain't accepting any Yankee school. Don't go to those schools, boy.' As a sideline, Uncle Jess ran an illicit 'moonshine' business. Charlie has claimed that later, on being confronted by police about his activities, Uncle Jess blew himself and his family sky high.

While Manson was learning tough family values in Kentucky, mother Kathleen's taste for the seamy side of life continued unabated. With Charlie back in tow, she'd take on a variety of temporary jobs in pubs and bars, constantly in search of some sort of sanctuary. More often than not, she'd be on the move, usually prompted by a break-up with one of her numerous lovers. Needless to say, it wasn't the most stable upbringing for a sensitive young boy.

Sometime in late 1947, Kathleen stepped up her attempts to have twelve-year-old Charlie taken into care. Reportedly, a new lover found the youngster's presence an irritation. With no apparent places available, she sought help through the local courts. Eventually, she succeeded in having Charlie made a ward of court, and placed in the secure quarters of Gibault School for Boys at Terre Haute on the fringes of Indiana. The school, still there to this day, boasted an extensive range of programmes and services to aid children with all manner of issues and disorders. As is still part of their credo, Gibault was 'the last opportunity for our clients to receive treatment before they find themselves involved with the Department of Corrections'.

At last, Charlie's life had some form of stability, largely thanks to the Catholic monks who ran the school. According to Manson, despite their altruistic intentions they could also be stern, treating any misdemeanour, such as Manson's bedwetting, with corporal punishment. His experiences with his strict uncle and aunt in McMechen had equipped him well for this sort of religious authoritarianism. Equally, he swiftly fended off any initial challenges to his height and diminutive frame from potential bullies keen to exploit the new runt of the litter. Despite being just twelve years old, and one of the youngest in the institution, Manson soon fell in with the most hardened of the youthful criminals. With expert tutelage from fellow inmates, he soon learnt a legion of scams and tricks that would inform his nefarious activities later in life. School reports of the twelve-year-old describe him as a 'pleasant' and 'likeable boy' while noting he had, 'a tendency toward moodiness and a persecution complex'.

Although Manson coped fairly well at Gibault, his past soon began to catch up with him. Desperately missing his mother, he became withdrawn and remote. 'I was lonelier, lonelier than I had ever been in my life,' he reflected many years later. 'I wanted to live with her, under any conditions. Not in some school locked away from everything.'

Occasionally Charlie's mother Kathleen would visit. Mostly, though, she made her excuses and stayed away. Although Charlie would eagerly await these brief audiences, it hit him hard when she didn't show up. To make matters worse, Kathleen would make constant promises that she would sort them both out a place to live in Cincinnati, promises that never seemed to materialise.

On the scant occasions when Manson has spoken of his mother, the most telling was to Diane Sawyer of ABC news in 1994: 'The only thing my mother taught me was that everything she said was a lie. And I learned never to believe anyone about anything.'

After ten months, tired of waiting for his mother to come and get him, Charlie left Gibault and ran back home to Cincinnati to be with her. While making the long and lonely 180-mile trip on foot, he imagined her reaction, and hoped that she would welcome him with open arms. Nothing, it appears, could be further from the truth. When Charlie did finally make contact with his mother in Cincinnati, she swiftly called the police and had her son taken back to Gibault. Within hours of returning, he was out of the school again. However, this time any thoughts of meeting up with his mother were gone.

Instead, Charlie headed towards Indianapolis; although still some seventy miles away from Gibault, it was the closest major city to the school. Manson had reckoned on finding anonymity amongst Indianapolis's population, something he claims he was desperately seeking. For a few days, young Charlie yomped through fields and roads that led towards the city. En route, he fell in with a mass of drifters, who were happy to share their meagre meals with a youngster on his travels.

Manson soon entered the city limits of Indianapolis, and for the first few nights he bedded down wherever he could find shelter. With no cash available, he robbed a few shops for food. On one such occasion, he discovered to his delight that the store had left out their day's takings in a cigar box. With over $100 now in his possession, young Charlie managed to persuade someone to rent him a room in one of the city's less salubrious quarters. Although the money soon dried up, he now had a base to operate from, and he took on any task that paid. One of his jobs was for Western Union delivering messages around town. This was about as close as Manson ever got to playing the respectable citizen.

However, one slip-up led to Charlie's new life coming to an abrupt halt. He'd stolen a bike, more as a necessity than anything else, but the police soon spotted it and he was apprehended. After some time in the cells, Charlie's identity was determined, and he was returned to court. As a formality, Charlie's mother was called to help decide his fate. She declined to get involved. Manson was placed in a young offenders' institution in Indianapolis – but he promptly escaped. The following day he was recaptured and was swiftly put up before the courts.

On this occasion, the judge was sympathetic to young Manson's case, and he passed him over to Boys Town, 'a non-sectarian, non-proselytising home for young boys.' The school catered for disadvantaged and challenged children and had been established some thirty years previously by the altruistic Father Edward Flanagan. A Catholic minister, Flanagan dedicated his life to the cause. With his visionary ethos that, 'There are no bad boys. There is only bad environment, bad training, bad example, bad thinking', the establishment flourished. Word of its achievements soon spread, inspiring a couple of films, notably the 1938 Academy Award-winning movie, *Boys Town*, starring Spencer Tracy and Mickey Rooney. Instrumental in placing Charlie at the school was one Reverend George Powers. He recalled Manson as 'very lonesome, just craving attention and affection. He looked like an innocent altar boy, and he was so ashamed of his mother.' It seemed that Charlie was playing up to them somewhat when remarking to officials, 'I didn't want to stay where Mother lived in sin.'

In March 1949, at the age of fourteen, Charlie Manson's arrival at Boys Town created something of a minor buzz. In an attempt to garner some attendant publicity for the school, a reporter and photographer from the *Indianapolis Today* paper were dispatched to record young Manson's induction into the institution. The resulting photograph captured a smart, agreeable young man shaking hands with the school's administrator over a desk. If the headline 'Boy Leaves Sinful Home for New Life in Boys Town' was upbeat, the text of the feature promised good times ahead. 'A dead-end kid who has lived in an emotional blind alley is happy today; he's going to Boys Town.'

Four days later, with the ink barely dry on the page, Manson ran away from Boys Town. This time, he hooked up with a fellow inmate by the name of 'Blackie' Nielson, and together they headed off to Peoria, Illinois; firstly on a motor scooter, and then in a stolen car. When they arrived, they laid low at an uncle of Nielson's. A World War Two vet, Nielson's uncle had been involved in petty crime before disability had sidelined his activities. Despite his handicap, the uncle was happy to be playing the role of Fagin, furnishing the boys with information on various establishments that he reckoned they could squeeze their small frames into. As a result, the pair embarked on an enormous crime spree, netting huge amounts of cash. For a while things looked good, although – as Manson would later note – the uncle was creaming off the majority of their spoils.

Not surprisingly, Manson and his friend soon fell foul of the law. A bungled grocery-store robbery put them in police custody and, despite implicating Nielson's uncle, the pair met guilty charges. With his chances at Boys Town blown, and with the knowledge that it would take some time to decide his fate, Manson was placed in the Indianapolis City Juvenile Hall for processing. He promptly escaped, taking over thirty fellow inmates with him through a hole he'd cut in the wire fence. Once free, Manson quickly hot-wired a car and drove off. He was soon picked up, though; the sight of the miniature Manson barely visible above the dashboard ensured a swift capture.

It was little surprise that the local press picked up on the story. With no reference to the glowing appraisal they'd handed Manson a few weeks earlier, the paper labelled Charlie as 'ringleader' of the pack of escapees. After such an audacious affront to authority, the courts demanded a heavy sentence. While reports were being collated, Charlie was placed in Indiana's county jail – an adult institution. History was made that day, as Charlie Manson, aged fourteen, became the youngest offender ever to sit behind the jail's stone walls. The incarceration was a temporary measure though, and authorities were soon required to find somewhere more appropriate for their young charge.

What they found was the Indiana School for Boys at Plainfield – in layman's terms, reform school. Established in 1867, Plainfield was a maximum-security institution, complete with high walls and razor wire fencing. Despite the sweeping lawn at the front, this was a hardline facility which existed to contain those with 'severe character disorders.'

Whilst Manson had been able to wheedle his way through his previous placements, life at Plainfield was to be a different story altogether. Even Manson, already well seasoned to harsh discipline, was shocked. If we are to accept Charlie's account, it might go some way to explaining the grudges he'd forever hold against authority. With an alleged litany of daily assaults, rape and other sordid forms of abuse, any semblance of innocence was summarily beaten from him. Like many adolescents faced with situations out of their own control, he began to self-harm on a regular basis. Manson's later hope that 'all the warped, sadistic bastards I met there are now dead' is a fair measure of his torment. He'd later rename the institution 'Painsville' in honour of the harshness of life there.

Charlie's resistance to the regime at Plainfield ensured that any easy integration back into society was highly unlikely. In the three years that he was registered at the institution, he attempted to escape at least eighteen times. This made it more than likely that he'd be transferred into an adult facility for an undetermined period. In February of 1951, and with nothing left to lose, Charlie absconded with two other inmates in a stolen car, with the aim of reaching California and swiftly absorbing themselves into the Golden State.

The journey west was somewhere in the region of 2,000 miles, and the trio were forced to steal a variety of motors en route. To sustain themselves, they held up numerous grocery stores and fuelling stations on their way. Manson himself suggests that the tribe robbed between 'fifteen to twenty' stores and garages on their trip. On approaching Utah, one of the many cars they'd stolen was reined in at a roadblock by police looking for a couple of robbery suspects. All three teen outlaws were swiftly apprehended. However, as they crossed into another state, they now fell within the stricter jurisdiction of the federal authorities. The seriousness of this meant that on 9 March 1951, Manson was transported up to Washington DC and into the care of the National Training School for Boys.

Charlie's reputation preceded him and he now held the dubious honour of being in the top league of young offenders, and he had become used to defending himself physically. With little contact with women, Charlie began to explore his sexuality with other inmates. Although not a homosexual by preference, he took every opportunity to engage in some relief from the obvious frustration a young man would feel at being locked up all day.

Following his transfer to Washington, Charlie's infractions involving prison guards would ensure that he'd see the detention halls of three further institutions over the next few years: the Natural Bridge Honor Camp in Virginia; the Federal Reformatory at Petersburg, and the Federal Reformatory of Chillicothe, in Ohio. During these spells inside, he acted up so much that any possibility of parole began to look increasingly remote.

It was during his time at the Natural Bridge Honor Camp that Manson underwent some long overdue psychiatric evaluation. These early tests were conducted by a Doctor Block, who considered that, superficially, Charlie was 'a slick institutionalised youth'. However, the doctor gauged that behind this front lay an 'extremely sensitive boy who has not yet given up in terms of securing some sort of love and affection from the world'. Others monitoring Charlie weren't that convinced of his apparent duality, noting that he 'only did good work for those from whom he figured he could gain something'. Additional evaluations were also undertaken to determine his character. Despite his lack of schooling, Charlie's creativity was noted, music remaining his constant interest.

While doctors were attempting to unravel Charlie's complex mind, records show that members of his family were working on the outside to obtain his freedom. His aunt, Alene, had visited the prison to petition the governor to consider a possible parole date. She'd vouched that McMechen's stable, if unremarkable environment would act as a suitable buffer to any temptation that might cause Charlie to veer off track. The approach worked, and Charlie was let out on temporary licence. The party was to be short-lived, though, and he was rearrested following an incident where he allegedly raped a youth while holding a razor blade to his throat. Manson would later claim that he had been the subject of a set-up, and that he'd initially believed that the encounter was mutually agreeable. Whatever the case, he'd blown his shot at freedom.

Yet again, Manson was hauled back into prison to be reassessed, any chance of parole now apparently gone. On 18 January 1952, he was transferred to the Federal Reformatory in Petersburg, Virginia. While there, he committed numerous violations, including homosexual acts and violent outbreaks. This meant further tests to determine Manson's mental state. The new evaluation declared Manson 'dangerous' and 'criminally sophisticated' and recommended that he spend time in a more secure institution. What the authorities found for him was the Federal Reformatory at Chillicothe, Ohio, and he was transferred there on 22 September 1952.

It was at Chillicothe that he'd make the acquaintance of Mafia mobster Frank Costello. Costello was every bit the gangster, cast fully in the mould of Al Capone and other Prohibition-era mobsters. In an eventful career spanning over eight decades, the Italian had overseen an enormous gaming empire. This had led to him being christened 'Prime Minister of the Underworld'. Charlie basked in the notoriety of Costello, observing the deference with which he was treated by the authority's prison guards and his fellow inmates. It made a powerful impression on him.

Despite fraternising with legendary criminals such as Costello, Manson's disciplinary record settled down. For the first time, he started engaging in gainful activities within the prison. On 1 January 1954, he earned himself a merit award for services to their transportation unit where he'd maintained several of the prison's vehicles. This led to a review date being considered, and with no further behavioural problems recorded, he was prepared for parole.

In May 1954, at the age of nineteen, Manson was finally granted a release date. Attached to his freedom however, were strict conditions; his appalling crime record demanded nothing less. Again, his aunt and uncle were instrumental in supporting his release and, in a receptive mood, Charlie returned back to McMechen.

With over seven years spent locked up in institutions, Manson enjoyed his freedom. Back in the lush greenery of McMechen, he spent the first few days walking and hiking, taking in the beauty of the surrounding area. While on these meditative jaunts across the neighbouring hills, he'd constantly muse on the time he'd lost inside, and how much of his formative development had been stunted. With his prison record preceding him, the opportunities for employment were slim. Still, he managed to occupy himself with some menial tasks, serving time as a gardener, cleaner and pump attendant. However, Charlie's lackadaisical approach to work meant these jobs were fleeting, employees noting his 'lateness, absence or general neglect'. His mother also reappeared at this time and, despite all their combined problems and issues, they managed to re-establish their relationship.

Given Manson's years inside, he'd had very little contact with women. As a young man in his prime, he'd stockpiled an enormous amount of unrequited interest in the fairer sex. Not surprisingly, Manson had few social skills when it came to the art of wooing. After a few disastrous attempts at relationships, Charlie ended up marrying the first girl he slept with. Her name was Rosalie Jean Willis, and he'd been smitten with her charms when he chanced upon her in a local café. A romance soon flourished and, on 17 January 1955, they were wed.

For a while things appeared promising, and Charlie enjoyed these early days together, where he got his first taste of domesticity. But with the couple both working, Charlie began to find the daily grind of gainful employment laborious and tiresome, and he began to drift back into petty crime, eventually engaging once again in his preferred activity of car theft. On one occasion, Manson took a car across state and down towards Fort Lauderdale, Florida.

With life in McMechen a stifling predictability, Charlie and Rosalie started to dream of California. These aspirations for sun, sea and sand were obviously something of a constant with Manson. With no realistic future outside of the drudgery of a workaday routine, Charlie stole a car, and Rosalie and he loaded up their possessions and once more headed west during July 1955. They had added incentive for starting again in the Golden State; Rosalie was now in the early stages of pregnancy with Manson's child.

Cutting through a landscape of small towns and dust-bowl farms, the couple road-tripped towards California. Stopping off wherever they fancied, and robbing for their needs, they stole a variety of vehicles to get them into Los Angeles. Once there, and with only a few dollars to their name, they rented a small apartment, and got to work in establishing a new life.

Manson's attempts at settling down soon hit a snag when, some three months later, local police did a routine check on the couple's car and discovered that it was stolen. Tracing back, they connected the stolen vehicle that Manson had taken to Florida. With Charlie taken into custody, and the case passed over to the FBI, things appeared bleak. In court, Manson begged for leniency, claiming; 'I was mentally confused, and stole a car as a means of mental release from the confused state of mind that I was in.'

The authorities listened to Charlie, and ordered a fresh psychiatric evaluation to determine the validity of his claim. The findings were ambivalent, and yet with Rosalie's fragile condition taken into consideration, the authorities took a sympathetic view. As a result, Manson was placed on five years' probation, with regular parole visits and rigid movement orders part of the conditions. Although the earlier case concerning the stolen car back in Florida was soon up for consideration, given the ruling in LA, Charlie was in a good position to escape a custodial sentence. For a while, the couple made the most of their freedom, exploring the funkier areas of sprawling Los Angeles, spending time among the bohemians in Venice Beach.

However, despite the leniency shown by the courts, five months later, Charlie would hit the road again, leaving a pregnant Rosalie behind; this time he went in the direction of his old stomping ground, Indianapolis. However, this life on the open road was short-lived and, on 14 March 1956, the police picked him up in violation of his probation order.

This time Charlie was placed in the secure quarters of Terminal Island penitentiary in San Pedro, Los Angeles, for a three-year stretch. With Manson's mother Kathleen moving to California to help Rosalie through the final stages of her pregnancy, Manson's women shared their visits to the jail. Although Kathleen's visits were typically infrequent, Rosalie kept up a regular attendance at the jail. Sometime in 1956, Rosalie would give birth to their first child, a son named Charlie Junior. With the promise of a family life awaiting him on release, Charlie knuckled down to the regimes of prison life. Knowing a good attitude would count towards an early release, Manson utilised every opportunity to impress his captors.

After a few months of frequent visits and regular letters, Rosalie dropped contact with Charlie. It didn't take her husband long to piece the scenario together: she had left him for someone else. It was Charlie's mother Kathleen who broke the news to him of Rosalie's departure.

Because of his compliant behaviour, Manson had just been transferred to a less secure area of Terminal Island. With the news that Rosalie had hooked up with a truck driver and was heading east, Charlie's solitary beacon in the outside world was extinguished. On one of his mother's occasional visits to the prison, she noted the change in Charlie's demeanour. Another woman had let him down. 'I think the business with Rosalie really hurt,' Kathleen recalled later. 'I think Rose was the only woman he ever really loved, and from then on, he never respected women.'

Within weeks of Rosalie's departure, Charlie had hot-wired a car in the prison yard. He was wearing civilian clothing and was in the process of absconding when he was captured. This escape attempt extinguished any hopes of parole. With no other evident incentive to lure him back to the outside, Manson gave up on any idea of rejoining conventional society. Adding to his upset, Rosalie filed for divorce, and went on to win full custody of the couple's son.

Manson responded by throwing his energy into working his way up the prison hierarchy. The authorities too, had noted his decline. A psychiatric report from the time revealed that Charlie was 'very unstable emotionally and very insecure. He tells about his life inside the institutions in such a manner as to indicate that he has got most of his satisfactions from institutions ... In my opinion, he is probably a sociopath personality with psychosis. Unfortunately, he's rapidly becoming an institutionalised individual.'

Among the broad range of criminals at Terminal Island, Charlie had fallen in with a pimp, who had considerable notoriety as a flash and successful operator. With tales of large cars, luxurious dwellings, huge amounts of ready cash, and of course, an endless stream of girls, he made pimping sound like an attractive prospect. In particular, Charlie was fascinated by the relationship between the pimp and the girls who earned money for him, and the allure of the attentive, all-powerful master. The major rejections in his life had come from women; here was a prospect of unconditional obedience that brought with it rich rewards. With dreams of a lavish lifestyle filling his head, Charlie buckled down to quietly seeing out his time in prison, and, despite many reservations, he was rewarded with a parole date.

On leaving Terminal Island on 30 September 1958, Charlie headed west to what he thought was the best place on earth to start his new career: Hollywood. 'I was in my element,' he'd later recall on his relocation. 'I was twenty-three years old, and my jail-house tutoring was going to go to work for me.'

Charlie soon made the acquaintance of a young, impressionable woman, and the pair quickly shacked up together. Using all of his many wiles, Charlie managed to persuade her to start sleeping with other men for money, and when she started handing over money to him, Charlie was overjoyed. In honour of his new status, Manson adopted a glamorous pseudonym, 'Chuck Summers'.

It was at this time that Charlie set up '3-Star Enterprises; Nite Club, Radio and TV Productions,' a wholly fraudulent operation designed to snare young wannabes and turn them into Manson's girls. Charlie had a partner in crime by the name of Tony Cassino, and together they operated out of a rented suite on Hollywood's Franklyn Avenue. Such was the apparent legitimacy of the business that they managed to convince many impressionable starlets to hand over their cash. Exploiting their wide-eyed innocence further, the pair would take a variety of suggestive shots which they'd then hawk on to glamour magazines. Soon Manson and partner were able to transfer their operations to Hollywood's swanky Roosevelt Hotel. However, with more than one aggrieved parent soon demanding the return their child's money, word of 3-Star Enterprises' dirty dealings soon made their way to Manson's parole officer, who was by then under pressure to revoke his probation.

A court hearing was convened to assess Charlie's parole status. In his defence, a young starlet by the name of Leona Rae Stevens was wheeled out, purporting to be his pregnant wife. Through a mist of tears and other emotional outbursts, she begged for Manson's freedom. It was later discovered that although Charlie had actually married her, she was a seasoned hooker who worked under the name of Candy. She was indeed pregnant with his child, which she bore later that year. Whatever their relationship, Charlie has never once spoken of Leona, or to his second son, Charles Luther Junior.

Outside of his fraudulent talent business, Charlie encountered few problems in soliciting new women into his pimping fold. Most were young, inexperienced and easily swayed. Although on strict parole conditions, Manson managed to sidestep the law on numerous occasions. He was finally caught trying to cash a $34.50 stolen government cheque at a supermarket on 1 May 1959. The cheque disappeared – believed to have been swallowed by Charlie – but the felony still stood. With the parole board looking for a custodial sentence, the judge nonetheless resisted the opportunity of jailing Manson, instead imposing a ten-year suspended sentence if he reoffended. If ever there was a last chance for Charlie, here it was. Undeterred by the threat, Manson duly set off to Laredo, Texas with his tribe of girls; they were aiming to work their way through a business convention.

Business in Laredo boomed for Charlie and the girls, so much so that Manson considered setting up a base there. However, spoiling the party, one of his women got booked for hustling, and immediately told police that she was working for Charlie Manson. With the threat of the deferred sentence coming back to haunt him, Charlie headed to Mexico. Once there, Manson got in with the local population of hoods and other unsavoury characters. Aside from his tour of local criminality, he dallied with some bullfighters, and was apparently praised for his adept manoeuvring. At some point, Charlie spent some time with the Yaqui Indians in their desert reserve. While there, he sampled some of the tribe's legendary psilocybin mushrooms as well as some particularly potent marijuana.

With word of Manson's infamy spreading between states, Manson was soon captured and transferred back to Laredo, Texas, to answer charges relating to the White Slave Traffic Act. Keen to avert a scandal, the Texan authorities shunted Manson back to LA on his broken parole conditions. Fate too would secure Charlie's future, as he was charged by the same judge that had originally deferred his sentence. The judge was keen to reverse his mistake, declaring: 'If ever there was a man who demonstrated himself completely unfit for probation, he is it.' While the pimping charge was eventually dropped, it was nonetheless decided that – courtesy of his string of minor offences – Manson had violated all of his parole conditions. Despite an appeal that dragged on for over year, Charlie's reservoir of opportunity had finally run dry. In July 1961, after spending a year languishing in a Los Angeles police cell, Manson found himself at McNeil Island off the coast of Washington State. Ten long years in jail now lay ahead of him.

Once again, Manson reacquainted himself with life behind bars. Assigned to a timetable of routine work, he settled quickly back into prison. It was only after he began to see some of his fellow inmates reach their parole dates that he began to think things through. At twenty-five years of age, with half his life already spent behind bars, and with ten years' further incarceration lying ahead of him, there was little to celebrate. With virtually no prospect of parole, even the prison authorities thought their resources would be better spent elsewhere.

While there was an in-house programme to equip inmates with trades to enhance their prospects in the workplace after release, Charlie was denied a place on the scheme. A prison note from this time confirms Manson's resignation to the inevitable: 'He has commented that institutions have become his way of life and that he receives security in institutions which are not available to him in the outside world.' Indeed, it appears the one constant that saw him through his early years at McNeil was his love of music, and he managed to get himself an old guitar, which he'd play almost continuously, despite its battered state.

At some point during his early tenure at McNeil, Manson had a reunion of sorts with his mother. She'd moved to Washington with her new husband so that, according to her, she would 'be near Charlie'. She began visiting, and had written to the prison authorities to stand surety for Charlie if he was ever likely to be considered for parole.

Any happiness that their rapprochement might have brought proved short lived. When Charlie had asked her if she could get him a new guitar, his mother told him that it wasn't possible, seeing that she was continually broke. They struggled through a few more visits but things came to a head later in 1961 when she arrived carrying a baby girl. With great excitement, she introduced Charlie to his little half-sister. Rather than celebrating the new addition to his family, Charlie flew into a rage. How could she afford to look after a new kid when she couldn't scrape the money together for a guitar? After his mother stormed out, he turned again to his old beaten-up instrument as his only form of escapism.

With his prospects looking increasingly dreary, Charlie became more and more introverted, and highly self-critical, as he explains in his memoirs. 'I saw myself as I really was; an immature, mixed-up person with nothing but a mouth going for him. I was without direction or a proper goal in life. In the following years, I ceased to be a flippant little fool. I was sincere in my search for self-understanding.'

Given the ten-year stretch ahead, soul-searching may well have been the only option available to him. Manson's lack of educational skills made things difficult, but with nothing to lose, he began the slow trail towards some sort of understanding of his own troubled psyche. At some point, Charlie looked closely at Christianity. Religion had featured heavily in his childhood, and he painstakingly explored biblical doctrines, becoming struck by the figure of Christ as a scorned individual and finding irresistible parallels to his own situation. Manson also began to dabble in the eastern doctrines of Buddhism and other belief systems that took deep self-examination as their basis. It was as though he was looking for a religion that would have Charles Manson at its very heart.

As prison presented a microcosm of society, it also magnified the personal beliefs usually practised behind closed doors. In his new role as observer, Charlie was intrigued at the way other inmates went about their daily religious practices with great integrity and commitment: 'I found them solid in their beliefs, so I watched them and began to appreciate their rituals and traditions.' In particular, Manson studied intently the unifying bond of Islamic traditions running deep through the community of Muslim inmates. By way of contrast, he also became familiar with right-wing white prison gangs, such as the Aryan Brotherhood, whose belief system was based around white supremacy.

With these contrasting creeds forming a vivid backdrop to his own soul-searching, Manson also delved into the prison library to read up on hypnotism, psychiatry and other mind-expanding techniques. During this dawn of his enlightenment, Charlie would take every opportunity to engage in group therapy, using the sessions to learn about any new psychiatric theory that was being tried out on the patients.

It was about this time that Charlie booked a place on a course based on Dale Carnegie's standard text, *How To Win Friends and Influence People.* Reportedly, he'd been impressed by its unilateral promise of self-improvement. Charlie also read psychiatrist Eric Berne's book, *Games People Play.* Published during the early 1960s, the book explored the three ego-states we go through in life, and how they affect our spiritual development; it became a key text for those involved in psychological study. Manson was evidently fascinated by Berne's ideas, especially by his theories concerning the innocence of the child's mind. Much of Berne's observations were drip-fed into his own proselytising around the prison yard. They would later inform some of Manson's later songs with titles such as, 'Look at Your Game Girl' and 'Ego'.

However, the belief system that truly captured his imagination was that of Scientology. Developed by leading science-fiction author L. Ron Hubbard in the 1950s, Scientology started life as Dianetics, a term Hubbard defined as a bridge between science and reality, or 'the study of truth'. In the 1950s, Dianetics was a new and fashionable mind-development technique (its religious status was a few years away). As a simple process to rid individuals of any inherent hang-ups and repetitive behaviour, Hubbard's technique swiftly accumulated an enormous worldwide audience.

Copies of his book, *Dianetics*, flew off the shelves on its release in May 1950, and legions of devotees were quick to champion Scientology's powers.

Lanier Ramer, a cellmate at McNeil Island, is credited with introducing Charlie to Scientology. Ramer had studied Scientology in California, before falling foul of the law following an armed raid. Ramer had reached the status of 'clear' – a Scientology term meaning that a person has become free of the influence of past traumatic and negative emotions; on the primary rung of the enlightenment ladder, achieving the status of 'clear' nonetheless required a couple of years' daily study. Reports suggest that Ramer studied under the auspices of none other than L. Ron Hubbard himself.

To help spread the word inside, Ramer ran special Scientology sessions in McNeil, and gathered together a circle of seven willing students to be 'audited'. This Ramar did from within the confines of his cell without prison approval. In the grim surroundings of McNeil, Ramer's talk of attaining a 'clear' state leading to 'the brilliant joy of spiritual existence' was evidently very attractive to Manson.

For a while, Charlie could talk of nothing else but his obsession with the discipline. When required to fill in prison forms, Manson would list 'Scientology' as his religion.

If reports are to be believed, Charlie received over 150 hours of 'auditing'; a Scientology term for one-to-one counselling. Once Manson was confident in his Scientology skills, he dispensed with Ramer, much to his tutor's annoyance. Apparently Ramer was so put out that he pursued Manson around the prison quarters, demanding an explanation; until, that is, Charlie asked to be put in solitary confinement. There, through the use of the mental exercises, Charlie managed to drag himself out of his depression and assume a new vitality. Prison officials also saw a change in Manson, noting that he 'appears to have developed a certain amount of insight into his problems through his study of this discipline'.

Manson's Scientology would become a rare constant in his life, and much of Hubbard's language became part of his own daily vocabulary. But whereas the elders of Scientology advised a carefully structured regime to their studies, Manson prefered to borrow whatever philosophy suited him, if and when the occasion demanded it.

Yet another esoteric angle that Manson explored during his time at McNeil was that of Freemasonry; its hierarchical and powerful subculture was very enticing to Charlie. It is evident that aside from the mystery attached to the cult, Manson was also fascinated by its most popular manifestation: the hand signal. Interviews with Manson throughout the years often include him displaying a variety of hand gestures. It might well have been pure theatre but, given his interest in the Masonic lore and traditions, there could have been more symbolism attached to these strange gesticulations than we realised. During one of the interviews he gave following his indictment for murder in 1969, Manson offered a unique insight into his take on Freemasonary: 'Masons have the power. It's a secret that's been handed down since the pharaohs. The secret wisdom. Jesus knew the symbols. The preacher and the judge got a hold of the symbols and kept them to themselves ... Every time I got into court, or have my picture taken, I use another Masonic sign. Like three fingers, two fingers outstretched. When the judge sees it, it really freaks him out because he can't say anything.'

As if this smorgasbord of influences wasn't enough, the doors to Charlie's perception were opened wider by the arrival of the book, *Stranger in a Strange Land*. This bestselling 1961 novel by Robert A. Heinlein told the story of Valentine Michael Smith, an Earth-born child left behind on Mars after the first manned mission to the planet. Raised on the planet by the indigenous Martians, Smith later returns to Earth possessed with unique powers and attributes acquired while on Mars. Through a series of adventures, he explores love and morality, and in turn, acquires a succession of young women – mainly on account of his insatiable sex drive. At Valentine's behest, these women learn to express themselves through free love and other ritualised behaviour. Later in the tale, Valentine Smith establishes his own church and attempts to share his fantastical talents with other earthlings. Eventually, like all messiahs, he meets his demise at the hands of a frightened group intimidated by Smith's unworldly talents and perceptions.

Manson, of course, found this tale of messianic power and suggestion gloriously attractive, and the book, like Hubbard's *Dianetics*, would remain one of Manson's key texts. Charlie wasn't alone in his fanaticism for Heinlein's work, and the book soon accrued an enormous cult following. With the hippie scene exploding across America, Heinlein's book became required reading for the 'now' generation.

Not surprisingly, as Charlie immersed himself in philosophical and psychology study, he became something of an curiosity in the prison yard. Phil Phillips, a cell-mate who was also serving a ten-year stretch explains how others saw him: 'I had this conception of Charlie as not a leader, he wasn't a leader, he was always a follower. At least he always conveyed this impression. I always felt that he was good. He was on what they called the "pay me no mind" list, that's the kind of list that everybody thinks you're crazy, but you're harmless nuts, so nobody bothers you. They'd say "Oh Charlie, get out of here! – Take your act somewhere else."'

Another inmate claims that the impression that Charlie gave was of a passive character, who'd cry off if things got heavy. If anything, he'd be happier to get other people to do his bidding for him. 'He had a certain smile that would always get to people,' the ex-con claims. 'He tried to hypnotise them. He always got other people to supply him with the necessities.'

It has been reported that some of these 'necessities' were books on Satanism and witchcraft, which he badgered outgoing inmates to mail to him on their release. Prison counsellors were equally baffled and intrigued by Manson, reporting on his 'fanatical interests' and 'tremendous drive to succeed'.

Aside from continued love of music, it also appears that Charlie began to immerse himself in the prison's amateur dramatic society, and happily joined in with their numerous productions. While he was trying to understand himself, he was also busy trying on different roles for size.

One of the most infamous inmates at McNeil during Charlie's tenure was Alvin 'Creepy' Karpis, who at fifty-two (twice Charlie's age) still cut an imposing figure. Karpis had been a part of the notorious Ma Baker gang of the 1930s, and one of the few to hold the dubious title of 'public enemy number one'. He'd been nicknamed 'Creepy' Karpis on account of his bizarre smile and had spent nearly thirty years in Alcatraz before being transferred to McNeil.

With a lengthy stretch still ahead of him, Karpis had taken to playing steel guitar to while away the long hours. With Charlie keen to improve his own guitar skills, Karpis had taken an interest in him and shown him a few of the chords that made up a couple of basic tunes. In his memoirs, *On the Rock*, the veteran inmate recalls Manson as a mostly peaceable, rather slothful character.

'This kid approaches me to request music lessons. He wants to learn guitar and become a music star. Little Charlie is so lazy and shiftless, I doubt if he'll put the time required to learn. The youngster has been in institutions all of his life – first orphanages, then reformatories, and finally federal prison. His mother, a prostitute, was never around to look after him. I decide it's time someone did something for him, and to my surprise, he learns quickly. He has a pleasant voice and a pleasing personality, although he's unusually meek and mild for a convict. He never has a harsh word to say and is never involved in even an argument.'

With Karpis's assistance, Manson began to get more creative on the guitar. With a strange synthesis of philosophy and pop metre, Charlie would soon be composing his own material. Heavily underpinned with his idiosyncratic thoughts and beliefs, it made for some unique compositions. Despite his offbeat material, Manson reportedly wowed audiences during the occasional inmates' concerts.

At 8 p.m. on Sunday 9 February, seventy-three million Americans tuned into the Ed Sullivan Show to see the Beatles' first network television appearance. The inmates of McNeil would undoubtedly have been among that number. America was stopped in its tracks; over the course of the forty-five-minute broadcast, crime figures fell to their lowest level since records begun; and even hardline preachers such as Billy Graham and his ilk abandoned their strict Sunday television embargo edict to look in on the phenomena. For Manson, the Beatles were a revelation. Like many others, he was aware that their potential lay well beyond their elementary tales of love, holding hands and 'yeah yeah yeahs'. To Charlie they were a 'hole in the infinite', offering him a Technicolor vision of his own future.

Inspired by the massive success of the band, Charlie, having figured that Karpis's criminal fraternity would have excellent contacts with the entertainment industry, took any opportunity to engage his 'celebrity' inmate.

Alvin Karpis remembered: 'He told me he knew I could make some contacts outside. He thought I could put him in touch with some of the men in the rackets. He always thought they controlled the show business in places like Las Vegas. I told him I couldn't do it, even if I did know someone. I tried to tell him that I couldn't give the world to someone and everything would be fixed up.'

Eventually, like many others before him, Karpis would tire of Charlie's attention. 'My decision in the end [was] to leave him on his own,' recalled Karpis later. 'The history of crime in the United States might have been considerably altered if "Little Charlie" had been given the opportunity to find fame and fortune in the music industry.'

By June 1966, the revolution in Manson's head had transformed this once violent, confrontational character into a more thoughtful and deliberate personality. Now free of the depression that had dogged his early years at McNeil, Manson set his sights on turning legitimate. At the same time, an unexpected lifeline came from a *pro bono* legal firm working on Manson's behalf. With scant interest from conventional lawyers, an alliance of ex-prisoners championing the interests of convicts inside McNeil had been established. With Manson's behavioural record vastly improved, and with this legal team's assistance, a transfer back to Terminal Island was proposed. While it was familiar territory for Charlie, it was a less restrictive environment than McNeil; a step closer to release. The proposal was successful, and on 29 June 1966, Manson was shipped back to Terminal Island jail, California.

The move back to Terminal Island brought him into contact with Phil Kaufman. A man of varied talents, Kaufman was doing time for importing marijuana from Mexico. With Charlie high on his musical dreams, it wasn't surprising that the two soon collided. Kaufman had already earned himself a respectable place in rock-and-roll mythology, and as a result had impeccable contacts in Los Angeles and Hollywood. At Terminal, he honed in on Charlie's voice, which to him sounded like a young Frankie Laine's, and his idiosyncratic, folksie compositions. This was enough for Phil to pass on Charlie's details to Gary Stromberg, a young impresario attached to Universal Studios in Hollywood. Suddenly it seemed as though the young jailbird might be destined for stardom.

Manson was finally up for release in March of 1967. While every day of a convict's life is spent leading up to this moment, Charlie begun to view his imminent release with trepidation. Staff preparing his release noted in their reports that Manson, 'has no plans for release as he says he has nowhere to go'.

Charles Manson: 'They were ready to let me out and I said, "Oh no, I can't go outside there. I can't, I'm not able to adjust to their world. I'd be a stranger." But they said, "No it's time. I had to go outside." But I wanted no part of the world outside . . . I knew that I couldn't adjust to that world, not after all my life had been spent locked up and where my mind was free. I was content to stay in the penitentiary, just to take my walks around the yard in the sunshine and play my guitar and sit and play in my cell, or do all the things that I'd been used to doing in prison.'

What would Manson do on the outside? Behind bars, he might have talked of world domination, but now the stark reality of fending for himself was staring him in the face. With Rosalie history, and mother Kathleen busy with her own adventures, Charlie would have to face the world alone, without any of the props he'd taken for granted within the prison system. Like most exiting prisoners, he was supplied with a few paltry resources: a money warrant for $35; a suitcase of used clothes, and the services of a parole officer. At 8.15 a.m. on 21 March 1967, after serving nearly seven years of a ten-year sentence, Charlie Manson was released from jail into the general population.

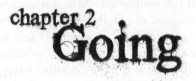
chapter 2
Going

'What we're thinking about is a peaceful planet, we're not thinking about anything else. We're not thinking about any kind of power; we're not thinking about any of those kind of struggles; we're not thinking about revolution or war or any of that. That's not what we want. Nobody wants to get hurt; nobody wants to hurt anybody. We would all like to be able to live an uncluttered life, a simple life, a good life, y'know, and think about moving the human race ahead a step, or a few steps.'

Jerry Garcia, March 1967

CHARLES Manson sat overlooking Long Beach bay. For the first time in over five years he was able to see a horizon unobscured by fences, brick walls, or watchtowers. It was a beautiful, warm spring day. For a few moments Charlie surveyed the vista and took stock of his situation. 'I'm free,' he'd reflect later. 'I'm on the outside. I can go where I want, I can do what I please. I don't have to get in line to eat, or get out of bed when a bell rings. Nobody's going to tell me, "Line up, Charlie."'

Eventually, Charlie stepped onto one of the waiting ferries and headed off towards the mainland. Once on solid ground, he was required to make immediate contact with a parole officer to discuss his plans for the future. At that meeting Charlie expressed a desire to go to San Francisco. With the request under consideration, Manson headed off into downtown Los Angeles.

The world Charles Manson emerged into that spring equinox day in 1967 had been completely transformed since he'd last tasted freedom. America in particular was in the middle of a seismic shift. Having emerged from the Cold War paranoia of the late

1950s, there was now a real clamour for change. At its centre was an ever-growing youth rebellion. These post-war baby boomers, now in their late teens and early twenties, were hungry for a new world. The assassination of John F. Kennedy in November 1963 had momentarily seemed to extinguish the hopes of this fledgling generation, leaving the nation in limbo. The election of Lyndon B. Johnson in 1964 spectacularly failed to capitalise on any of the optimism that Kennedy had so passionately evoked. Johnson's appointment ran totally against the aspirations of the nation's youth. At the core of this impasse was the spectre of the war in Vietnam. With the US government pouring vast sums of money into its drive against communism, American military intervention in Vietnam in 1965 elevated the ideological struggle to a new level. With over half a million US troops in South East Asia by 1967, opportunities for mass dissent back home were rife.

In the wake of Vietnam protests, other social issues began jostling for attention. The establishment, in whatever shape or form it manifested itself, was struggling to contain the escalating resentment it faced from every level of the social strata. To the world watching intently from the outside, America appeared to be a country at war with itself.

Despite the establishment's vain attempts to thwart any revolt, America's youth were bolstered by their newly found emancipation. Post-war affluence had trickled down through the generations and, by 1967, those under twenty-five had started to accrue enormous cultural and financial power. At the core of this rebellion was the music and arts industry, evidently more influential and attractive than anything the establishment had to offer. Dissent became compulsory for anyone who wanted to buy into the counterculture's ideals, and was spread via the globalisation of the media.

In an attempt to quell the rebellion, a series of draconian crackdowns were undertaken, usually in the full glow of the media's spotlight. In most cases, these only served to reinforce the ideology of the new order, enraging the authorities further. Infuriating their aggressors, the ethics of the proto-hippie movement decreed that any official opposition should be met with passive resistance. During 1967, putting a flower in the barrel of a gun was seen as the ultimate retaliation.

Driven by fear and paranoia, America's politicians were intent on weeding out dissenters right across the board. Anyone in a position of influence, be it college lecturer, teacher or social worker, who deviated from the prescribed 'norm', fell under intense scrutiny. As California was fast becoming the epicentre of radicalisation, Governor Ronald Reagan began to seriously consider locking up the hippie scene's chief protagonists in internment camps. The extent of Reagan's concern can be seen by a report he commissioned regarding a 'happening' at the University of California in 1967.

Ronald Reagan: 'The incidents were so bad, so contrary to our standards of human behaviour, that I couldn't possibly recite them to you here from this platform in detail. Three rock-and-roll bands were in the centre of the gymnasium playing simultaneously ... and during the dance, movies were shown on two screens at the opposite ends of the gymnasium. These movies were the only lights in the gym proper. They consisted of colour sequences that gave the appearance of different coloured liquids spreading across the screen, followed by shots of men and women, on occasion. Shots where the men and women's nude torsos, on occasion [sic]. And persons twisted and gyrated in provocative and sensual fashion. The smell of marijuana was prevalent throughout the building. Sexual misconduct was raging.'

It was this brave new world of psychedelia and 'sexual misconduct' that Charles Manson now had to negotiate. If Manson had caught sight of a newspaper on the day of his release, he probably wouldn't have seen much to spark his interest. Other than the interminable war in Vietnam, there was little on 21 March 1967 by way of news. Of considerably more interest to Charlie would have been the sounds coming from transistor radios. The airwaves were full of the jingle jangle of West Coast bands attempting to weld folk and electric pop together. Sharing radio space at the other end of pop's evolutionary scale were the Monkees; the pre-fab fakers who scored numerous hits in the wake of their successful TV show. For years to come, rumours would persist that Charlie had unsuccessfully auditioned for the show. As good a story as it is, his prison records show that he was incarcerated during their rise to fame.

Manson's immediate concerns were less rock-and-roll. He needed to find somewhere to stay until he had the means to support himself. Bearing the emotional scars from years of imprisonment, he also needed to ease himself back into civilisation. In an attempt to get his head straight, Manson took to riding buses around Los Angeles, studying humanity as it went about its mundane business. More often than not, he'd fall asleep en route, only to be thrown off at the journey's end.

Hitching also offered Manson a chance to meet up with kindred spirits, and quite by chance, a driver who worked at Terminal Island prison ended up giving him a lift. When he explained his homeless status, the driver offered to let him stay a few nights in his house. Unfortunately his wife wasn't best pleased to find an ex-con sharing their space so, not wishing to outstay his welcome, Manson bade his hosts goodbye and headed into the town. At another crossroads, Manson sat down at a nearby coffee house and scanned his options. With his $35 release allowance rapidly dwindling, he pulled out the phone numbers of a few old cohorts, to see if any of them might put him up.

Manson's initial idea was to head for Hollywood. He was keen to get in touch with the music industry contacts that Phil Kaufman had passed on to him in jail. However, at that point, no one would take his call. Manson had also hoped to hook up with some of the characters he'd hung out with in Hollywood during the late 1950s, but the passage of time had eroded memories and undermined promises. Eventually, Charlie was forced to take another look at his contact list to find more genuine prospects.

One prison contact that came good was based in Berkeley, on the outskirts of San Francisco. Manson soon made plans to make the journey up to the north of California and was able to okay his relocation with his parole officer. The offer of accommodation from 'a relative', and the possibility of work as an entertainer were convincing enough for the official to rubber-stamp the transfer. There were several conditions, though; mainly that Charlie's parole monitoring had to continue once he arrived in the city. Manson agreed, and a parole officer by the name of Roger Smith was alerted to Manson's imminent arrival in San Francisco.

While LA's sprawling streets were full of action, it was a city without any discernible centre or community. San Francisco's villagey ambience condensed the revolutionary frisson into a smaller area, making it more vital and accessible. All of this was highly appealing to Charlie, his sense of spatial awareness honed by the prison environment. With San Francisco's growing reputation as a place of infinite possibility, Manson set his sights on sharing in the many riches the city had to offer.

On arrival in San Francisco, Manson crashed at his contact's house, but finding his friend in very straitened circumstances, he soon took his leave. Without any place to stay, Charlie ended up sleeping rough. On the streets, Manson's feral sense of survival required him to arm himself, and he acquired a pistol. Once in the city centre, this 'stranger in a strange land' surveyed the kaleidoscopic scene at ground level. He'd later recall, "Frisco and the generation that now occupied its streets was something else.'

The San Francisco of the mid-1960s truly was 'something else'. Although the stories surrounding the so-called 'Summer of Love' have long been the stuff of legend, in reality, the scene had been brewing long before the media discovered it.

By early 1967, this vibrant flower-power movement was in full bloom. Though it was never official, everyone knew that the core of the counterculture was at Haight-Ashbury, the junction of Haight and Ashbury streets, in a run-down part of town.

Haight-Ashbury's role as the hippie capital occurred wholly by accident. For years, the majority of San Francisco's left-field had gravitated towards alternative action at North Beach, a funky neighbourhood just above the city. With literary luminaries like Jack Kerouac, Allen Ginsberg and Lawrence Ferlinghetti resident in the district, the area became an attractive hub for beatniks and other counterculture surfers. As the 1960s took hold, North Beach's celebrity meant a hefty rise in property prices as professionals began to move into the area. With spiralling rents, many of the original inhabitants were forced to look elsewhere for cheaper accommodation. As Haight-Ashbury was an affordable and underpopulated region, it soon found itself a convenient bolt hole for those looking to settle. The district's status became enshrined in the lyrics of bands such as the Grateful Dead, Janis Joplin and Jefferson Airplane, all of whom occupied houses around Haight.

With cheap and plentiful accommodation, it offered a superb base for anyone searching for bohemia. With a plethora of nineteenth-century three-storey pine-structured houses being decorated in colourful psychedelic paint, the Haight took on the appearance of a living hallucination. Soon, communal living would become the requisite lifestyle for anyone wishing to 'find themselves' on the cheap. With the concept of working for a living royally sneered upon by all, lack of food and money was by no means an obstacle to living the dream. The Diggers, a cheeky but highly organised group of good-natured anarchists, took the lead and set out to give practical help to those wishing to live by hippie ideals. Taking their lead from Gerrard Winstanley's seventeenth-century band of English agricultural rebels, the Diggers transformed the psychedelic dream into a sustainable reality. With enormous imagination, they began supplying the wageless, displaced and gentle warriors with the necessities for survival on the front line. Soon free food handouts, communal crash pads, legal and medical advice centres sprung up. The Diggers were, indisputably, the beating heart of Haight Ashbury.

As Manson had been signed off from Los Angeles' parole authorities, responsibility for his movements in San Francisco now fell to Roger Smith. A kindly altruist, Smith shared his time between parole duties and drug counselling at Haight-Ashbury's legendary Free Medical Clinic. Smith took responsibility for a large number of offenders who, like Manson, had flocked to the city in search of a new direction. While Roger Smith was fairly inured to all sorts of way-out behaviour, nothing – it seems – had prepared him for Charles Manson.

'Charlie was the most hostile parolee I've ever come across,' Smith recalled to *Life Magazine* in December 1969. 'He was totally upfront about it. He told me right off there was no way he could keep the terms of his parole, and that he was headed back to the joint and there was no way out of it.'

Whereas others saw a more genial Charlie around San Francisco, Manson's bombastic stance in front of Smith seemed designed to provoke a reaction. Although surprised by his first meeting with Manson, Smith felt that Charlie's behaviour was more theatre than anything else. 'In the back of my mind I felt he was a con man,' remembers Smith. 'Charlie's rap was a little too heavy . . . he was a little bit too polished.'

To the experienced Smith, Manson was nothing more than another unprepared ex-con, looking for a role to fill on the outside. 'There are a lot of Charlies running around, believe me,' recalled Smith. 'He's just one of several hundred thousand people who are released from prison after a shattering, soul-rendering experience; not prepared for anything except to go back on the streets and do more of the same, but bigger.'

Smith attempted to get Charlie somewhere better to stay than the floors and park benches he was crashing on. Given that San Francisco was awash with tens of thousands of runaways, spaces in the halfway houses were scarce. Smith also attempted to have his charge placed on a training scheme to help him back into work, but Charlie didn't meet the requirements. Although Manson met with Smith on a regular basis, he also tapped into the support structure on the streets of the Haight. Life had hardened Charlie to be suspicious of any unwarranted show of kindness, yet the unconditional display of genuine love around Haight-Ashbury made a deep impression on the ex-con. 'In a sense I think Charlie was really sort of shaken by it all,' recalled Roger Smith. 'People were friendly, willing and open to do things with him . . . They didn't care whether he had just gotten out of the joint. That was a real shocker for him.'

Despite Smith's efforts, Charlie still remained homeless. However, with the Diggers and other altruists attending to all his core needs, Charlie easily sustained himself, sussing out the best crash pads; with many other displaced seekers floating around, Manson was never short of like-minded company.

Charlie, at thirty-two, should have been at the twilight end of the youth explosion. However, the large swathes of time he'd lost inside jail meant he was really witnessing the world through a teenager's eyes. Manson's vast criminal record was of no hindrance to his ascendancy in the Haight. Indeed, it served to endear him further to the largely ungovernable community. Manson recalled one youngster, who early on in his stay in the Haight, acted as his guide and mentor. Even at fifteen, the young boy was savvy to the ins and outs of the district, and steered Charlie around the underground network. Like many drawn to San Francisco, the boy was a runaway. Fleeing from his aggressive stepfather, and with a little dealing and hustling on the side, the youth had kept the wolves from his door, and could pick and choose what he did with his day. Manson was impressed.

'I met this dude,' Charlie would later recall of his meeting with the teenager. 'He gave me something to eat, and [he] took me up to the Haight. I stayed up there with him, and we slept in the park in sleeping bags, and my hair got a little longer and I started playing my music and everyone was digging it ... and they're smiling at me and putting their arms around me and hugging me. Hey, I didn't know how to act, like it just grabbed me up man, that there were people who were real ... It was the young people walking up and down the street trading shirts with each other and throwing flowers and being happy, and I just fell in love.' Such was Manson's confidence in this new world, he threw his pistol off the Golden Gate Bridge.

Before long, Charlie had earned the title 'The Gardener' – wholly apt given the way he tended to young saplings – and it was around this time that Manson took his first tab of LSD. Charlie wasn't exactly new to chemical mind expansion; he'd had some experience of psychedelics while sharing psilocybin mushrooms with the Yuki Indians in Mexico some eight years before.

Manson would take his first trip at the Avalon Ballroom while the Grateful Dead played on stage. Situated in the Polk Gulch district of San Francisco, the modest-sized venue had become a popular gathering point. Run by the hippie 'impresario' Chet Helms, the venue hosted such psychedelic luminaries as Janis Joplin, Quicksilver Messenger Service and, of course, the Grateful Dead.

Without doubt, the Grateful Dead were San Francisco's 'house' band during 1966 and 1967. Since they occupied a house at 710 Ashbury Street, it was unsurprising that their early music was a total reflection of what was occurring on the streets of the Haight. By the summer of 1967, the band was fast outgrowing the district, and their fame was swiftly spreading across America and beyond. With a sizeable record deal from Warner Brothers, and a fast-expanding fan base, the Dead nonetheless found time to play at numerous venues in and around San Francisco.

Given the timeline, it's most likely that Charlie's LSD epiphany occurred on Sunday 11 June 1967. Whether Manson was high before he entered the hall is neither here nor there; the Dead's legendary light show would already have created a virtual reflection of the psychedelic experience. Nonetheless, once the drug had entered into his bloodstream, Charlie soon slipped through the thin veil of reality and into acid's swirling neverland.

'The people in all their strange clothing looked like they were at a costume party,' Charlie later recalled. 'I flipped over the completely uninhibited routines of the musicians. And though I had never danced to that style of music, I saw it that it was all motion and each person did their own thing ... Before I actually realised what I was doing, I was out there on the floor innovating to the beat of The Grateful Dead ... The acid, the music and the loss of inhibitions opened up a new world for me. I was experiencing rebirth. Finally, in the middle of one of my dances, I collapsed on the floor.'

During Manson's trip, he apparently saw a vision of the crucifixion, probably not an uncommon experience for a LSD user, but an earth-shattering one for Charlie nonetheless. This biblical vision was pivotal to Manson's understanding of the power of LSD, and, in later years, he'd bend the experience his way when guiding others through their first trips.

Still under parole observation, and with years of incarceration behind him, Manson was careful not to involve himself in any overt criminality, despite the obvious rewards that were there for the taking. With his guitar the sole moneymaking tool in his meagre bag of possessions, Charlie began to tout his songs across town. Despite his shabby appearance, he was remarkably successful across the bars, restaurants, and other venues who all took to his mix of song and banter.

In those early busking days, Manson often found himself with an admiring gaggle of followers, all enchanted with his repertoire and evident charisma. Many were keen to be a bigger part of Charlie's world, outside of the impromptu gigs. Still nursing the hurt of Kathleen and Rosalee's rejections, Manson's blatant chauvinism began to manifest itself frequently. An anonymous female acolyte from the Haight talked of one of these episodes in 1969. 'I was hitching to San Francisco once with Charlie,' recalled Manson's cohort, 'and we had these huge packs. He wanted me to carry both of them. I refused. I said I'd share, but I wouldn't carry both. He got more and more angry and finally said I had to carry both bags and walk ten steps behind him. When I wouldn't do that, he took my guitar from me and smashed it into little pieces against a post.'

Occasionally, Manson would wander outside the confines of San Francisco, and attempt to extend his influence beyond the hippie hangouts and squats of the Haight. One such location was Berkeley, just a few miles short of San Francisco Bay. A spot he soon came to favour was Telegraph Avenue, with its row of unattractive but upmarket shops and restaurants. The other was the University of California.

At the southern entrance to the university are the green iron arches of Sather Gate. To secure himself the best vantage point, Charlie would stand underneath the arches and, in what must have made for a fairly absurd sight, Manson would busk under the metal figures of eight naked men and woman, each representing a different academic discipline. As it was nearing the end of the working day, a steady stream of the university's clerical employees were making their way home. One of these white-collar workers was Mary Theresa Brunner, a blonde, twenty-three-year-old from Eau Clair, Wisconsin. A quiet, thoughtful personality, Brunner had been successful in following her ambition of becoming a librarian, and after graduating with a bachelor's degree in History from the University of Wisconsin in 1966, she took a job as an assistant librarian in the Humanities department based at the Berkeley Campus. With her modest salary, she'd acquired a flat at 1319 Milton Street, which she shared with her pet poodle.

Up until this point Brunner's life had been largely uneventful. One of her few quirks was to take her dog to work with her, its presence no doubt livening up the library. While walking along with her colleagues, Mary's poodle, intrigued by Charlie, bounded towards him to get a closer look. Confronted by the little dog, Manson feigned horror; and Brunner ran over to check things out.

Manson has since claimed that he wasn't that interested in Brunner's dowdy, collegiate appearance. What intrigued him more were her wry sense of humour and her evident kindness. If, as if has been reported, this first meeting was just a few minutes long, it's obvious that Charlie worked his magic spectacularly fast.

On hearing of his homeless status, Mary acted the good Samaritan, and offered Manson the use of her sofa. Although it may seem an extraordinary act of blind faith, Brunner was obviously looking for something extra in her life, which until then had revolved around her job, her dog and the odd trip to the movies.

Mary Brunner lived in downtown San Francisco and, as was his style, Manson made himself at home in a flash; although that night Brunner made sure Charlie slept on the couch. Within days, Charlie had registered himself at Brunner's address with his parole officer. Charlie assured her that he'd help her out with the rent and expertly smoothed over any of her worries.

With Mary busy with her librarian duties during the day, Charlie maintained his wanderings around San Francisco. As was fast becoming the norm, young people would congregate around him whenever he pulled out his guitar. Daily gatherings or 'happenings' were frequent within the city's parks and squares, and for hippies and drifters with many hours to fill, a talented and personable troubadour like Charlie made for a welcome diversion.

At those happenings, it was not only the music that the flower children were hungry for. It wasn't much of a surprise that the free love generation also freely indulged in casual sex. For a man caged up for nearly half his life, Charlie was more than ready to indulge whenever and wherever he could.

'Pretty little girls were running around every place with no panties or bras and asking for love,' recalled Charlie in 1989.

'Grass and hallucinatory drugs were being handed to you on the streets. It was a different world than I had ever been in and one that I believed was too good to be true. It was a convict's dream and after being locked up for seven solid years, I didn't run from it.'

One of the 'pretty little girls' was a sixteen-year-old who went by the name of Darlene. She was just one of the scores of runaways who gravitated to San Francisco during 1967 in search of some meaning to her life. For a while, she found that meaning in Charlie Manson.

When Charlie met her, Darlene was in the grips, both mentally and physically, of another overbearing male, and she didn't need much coaxing to change masters. Seizing the moment, Manson stepped in to rescue the girl from her controlling admirer, claiming he was an older relative. He then shepherded the girl back to Mary's small flat. Once there, Darlene's sorry tale was relayed to Brunner, who agreed to the girl spending some time with them until she sorted herself out.

With Mary out at work, Charlie and young Darlene were alone together for the best part of the day. While Manson has since claimed he had no plans to sleep with the teenager, within days the pair had had their first encounter. Whatever the dynamics at play, the relationship between Charlie and Darlene was to be short-lived; a former male contact of hers from the Haight made contact with her, and in Charlie and Mary's absence, she took him back to the apartment for a quick bit of catching-up. Shortly afterwards, Manson walked in on their lovemaking, and their nascent arrangement was over almost before it had begun. Despite the pervading atmosphere of free love, Charlie was not prepared to be forgiving when faced with Darlene's infidelity. Although the girl swore blind that she'd be faithful to Charlie, he turned his attentions towards Mary, and distanced himself from Darlene.

The night of Darlene's indiscretion, Charlie had penned a poem; a scribbled few lines about his feelings of rejection. When he passed it over to Brunner, she was enthralled, especially as he'd referenced her affectionately. As a bibliophile, Brunner was used to literary advances, and yet something in Manson's verse opened her up.

With little further prompting from Manson, Brunner offered herself over to him. It was a pivotal moment for the pair; for Mary, that first night with Charlie was nothing less than earth-shattering. After that she turned herself over to him completely and unconditionally; for Charlie, Mary's total subservience confirmed to him the depth of his power. His past had equipped him with animal instinct, but now he was seeing that, in the right circumstances, he could wield enormous influence.

With Brunner transformed into his first true acolyte, Charlie marvelled at how he'd managed so easily to conjure such subservience out of the previously self-contained Brunner. Confirming Manson's role as master, Brunner instantly assumed deference in his presence, tending to Charlie's every need. While she maintained her position at the college library, her mind was elsewhere. Patently, life under Manson's wing was far more rewarding and adventurous than stacking shelves and stamping books.

'He opened me up,' Brunner recalled during the making of the film *Manson* in 1973. 'I was living with my dog in a flat, and having just a real . . . go to work, go home, go to movies, go to bed, go shopping. You know, it was so routine, it was truly a drag . . . and it was getting to me, and when he came in, I just dropped it, whatever was happening.'

While Brunner was out at work, Manson had to cope with Darlene's scantily clad presence around the flat. Since she'd parted company with her last beau, she was at a loose end, and sensed Charlie's newly ignited libido. Despite nurturing some hurt over her prior indiscretion, Manson soon gave into temptation and reconnected with the teenager.

It was only a matter of time before Mary realised what was occurring under her roof. Although she hesitated slightly when confronted with the truth of Charlie's dalliances with a girl half his age, he easily talked her through her 'commitment issues' and explained how this wouldn't muddy their own relationship.

While the trust between the girls was broken, they eventually accepted their associate roles in Charlie's life. While Manson wasn't in the least bit shy about having his cake and eating it, maintaining the fraught love triangle soon became too much for

Darlene, and she headed back to the Haight and an uncertain future.

With his status confirmed as a sexual giant, Charlie decided to cast his net further and head off into the unknown, curious to see what was occurring on other points of the dial. As he was still under the rule of his parole officer, any trip that left the city limits had to be signed off and its purpose approved. With a tale about tracing his absent mother, he convinced Parole Officer Smith to sign off his trip. Leaving Mary Brunner waiting for him in San Francisco, Manson could set off, happy in the knowledge that he would have some security on his return.

Manson travelled along the Californian coastline, calling at Reno and Sacramento and other points on the hippie trail. Some two years before the movie *Easy Rider* was to reveal to the world the length and depth of the hippie imprint, scores of communities had already sprung up in and around California's remote hinterlands. According to a report commissioned in early 1968, there were over a hundred such communes operating in California alone – rich pickings for a charmer like Charlie.

While Manson had been at the core of this new explosion in San Francisco, the scene had been well supported by the likes of the Diggers and other altruistic agencies. These rural communes were, however, a far more radical experiment in survival and harmony. Many of the communes relied on nothing more than their wits to get by, while others produced drugs on a small scale to fund their operations.

Manson continued up through the northern regions of San Jose. As he relied on his thumb for transport, Charlie just pitched up on the side of a road and waited for a lift.

Charlie was soon picked up by a truck driven by a large balding man – the Reverend Deane Morehouse, or 'Baba' to his friends. The Reverend drove at a furious pace, and his fervent evangelism tripped just as speedily off his tongue. When Manson responded with his own philosophy diatribe, Morehouse became fascinated by the hitchhiker's turn of phrase. The Reverend invited Charlie back to meet his family, and to continue their conversation.

While the women of the Morehouse household attended to their domestic chores, Deane and Charlie spent the evening sparring over religious doctrine. The gathering was a major success, with prayers and hymns around the family piano, and Charlie the centre of attention.

The visitor's thoughts, however, were running on a more secular track. Between hymns, Charlie quickly honed in on the family's pretty teenage daughter, Ruth Ann. Although just fifteen, Charlie's charismatic presence clearly had a powerful effect on Ruth, and Manson vowed to take up the Reverend's offer of a return visit at the earliest opportunity.

Charlie soon returned to Mary Brunner's flat in San Francisco, where he regaled her with tales of his colourful adventures. When Manson suggested a joint trip, Brunner immediately took leave from the library and prepared to hit the road.

The pair was soon speeding off in Mary's car towards Seattle; aiming to hook up with some of the ex-cons Charlie had spent time with in jail. Taking off along the coast road that skirted the Pacific, they collected all manner of freewheelers and hitchhikers en route. Occasionally, the couple would accompany their passengers back to one of the communes hidden in the foothills of Northern California. Obligingly, Charlie and Mary involved themselves in any available action, although Manson was increasingly cynical of the flaky optimism that propped up these haphazard communities.

While the hippies were all looking for a brave new future, the ex-cons Manson met up with seemed locked in their own little histories. With Mary tending to all of Charlie's physical and spiritual needs, there seemed little to be gained from dwelling in the past tense.

Meanderings complete, the pair headed back to San Francisco, although Manson's homecoming was to be brief. Still keen to realise his musical dreams, Charlie told Mary that he was heading back to Los Angeles. Thanks to tales of supportive record executives ready to bank-roll his move into Hollywood, his parole officer allowed him yet another stay of leave. By this time, Charlie had taken possession of a 1949 Chevrolet, so he no longer had to worry about where he would sleep. By late summer of 1967, Manson was on the road again, itching to impress the Hollywood impresarios that prison pal Phil Kaufman had tipped him off about.

Not surprisingly, fame didn't exactly fall into Charlie's lap once in Los Angeles. With little else to do, Charlie headed over to Venice Beach. Although Charlie tried his best to join in with the many impromptu theatre productions being staged in the district, there was little reward for his efforts.

With his contacts exhausted and almost totally unreceptive to Charlie's musical offerings, and nowhere else to go, Charlie took to wandering down Venice's promenade. On one particular evening, twilight was descending over the Pacific, and the noisy cafés, lines of street buskers and legions of roller skaters made for a sweet cacophony as the light began to fade. Above this jangling, gypsy soundtrack came the sound of a whimper. There, sitting on the beach was a young redhead, crying into her handkerchief. Part of Charlie's strength was his willingness to make the most of others' weakness, and he made a beeline straight for her. As he approached he saw on her freckled face the teary trickles of stray mascara, and that she had a suitcase by her side. Her name was Lynette Alice Fromme. She was eighteen years old, and had nowhere left to run.

Lynette had been born on 22 October 1948, the oldest of the three Fromme children, who had all grown up in Westchester, a modest but respectable enclave of Los Angeles. While Lynette's mother, Helen, was a doting parent, her father William was a slightly more complicated individual. Although outwardly a regular working guy from Middle America, William Fromme viewed himself as a distinct underachiever. To compensate for his perceived inadequacies, he dominated Lynette, her younger brother and sister and his wife. Perhaps as a result of the strained atmosphere at home, Lynette's early years had been crammed with a whole host of after-school activities. Whilst she was good at sports, her extrovert personality meant she excelled at artistic and creative endeavours. She studied drama with Phil Hartman (who went on to star in *Saturday Night Live*). In addition to her dramatic prowess, Lynette's musical talents were also strong.

She'd joined an established singing troupe called the Westchester Lariats. Such was the group's blend of sweet tones and girlish charm they endeared themselves to all they met. At one point Lynette and her group were guests on the top-rated *Lawrence Welk Show* and were even invited to the White House. They also got to lay down some of their tracks in a recording studio, and overall the future looked bright.

Lynette's father, however, remained unimpressed. William had already deeply undermined his daughter's confidence, but he wasn't going to leave it at that. In the end, Lynette had to drop out of the group after her father refused to let her mother use the car to drive her daughter to rehearsals.

In 1963, just after she was forced to quit the Lariats, the Frommes moved to Redondo Beach, another Californian middle-class suburb. Lynette enrolled at Redondo Union High School, one of Los Angeles' largest public schools. There, it seems, she developed a talent for poetry, and was able to express herself with great emotional clarity. Immersing herself in verse, she became particularly enamoured with Dylan Thomas, modelling her style on his rich, deep observations. Indeed, such was her talent that she became a protégée of her English teacher, James Van Wagoner, who combined teaching with screenwriting. Wagoner encouraged Lynette's obvious literary talent, and was confident that she'd do well once things settled down at home.

However, William's bizarre attitude towards his daughter only escalated. Suddenly, without any explanation, he stopped talking to her. For the next three years this ridiculous state of affairs continued. For reasons Lynette couldn't understand, her father had written her out of his life, and from then on all dialogue had to be conducted through her mother. There are also reports that Fromme Senior started being physically as well as mentally abusive. Bill Siddons (later to manage Jim Morrison and the Doors) briefly dated Lynette during this period. In 1994, he described to the Biography Channel the peculiar ambience that surrounded the Fromme family. 'Her father just decided she was not worth talking to anymore, and he decided to exclude her from his life. She wasn't even a hundred per cent clear why ... If something had to come from her father, she spoke to her mother, and her mother asked her father and then answered Lyn. I mean, imagine being thirteen years old and not being able to talk to your father?'

In the local community, William Fromme became something of a pariah; neighbours recall a tyrannical figure whose attitude towards his children was well known by all. Lynette eventually decided enough was enough, and began immersing herself in alcohol and drugs to dull some of the pain. She also began a pattern of self-harm, burning herself with cigarettes.

Lynette took on an after-hours job in a picture framers to earn some extra cash, and it was here that her self-destructive behaviour began to manifest itself in public displays. On one shift, she took a staple gun and shot the metal into her right arm. As the tags embedded themselves in her flesh, she didn't flinch, continuing with her work to the amazement of her colleagues. The situation worsened with two botched suicide attempts – first she tried slitting her wrists, then she downed a bottle of barbiturates. Significantly, both attempts occurred following arguments with her father. Afterwards Lynette did receive some counselling, although ultimately it proved too little too late.

With her behaviour veering heavily off course, it was little surprise that Lynette was absent for much of her final year at high school. In a whirl of confusion, she decided to postpone any further studies, and in order to alleviate some of the pressure at home, she took off. Soon, she was bumming around the local coastline, bedding down with a number of friends who were happy to house her. She began experimenting with LSD, the effects of which shocked her deeply.

Despite her troubles, Lynette felt confident enough to resume her studies, and return to the family home. In late 1966, she enrolled in El Camino Junior College in the Santa Maria district of California. Here she signed up to a heavy schedule, undertaking French, theatre arts, psychology and modern dance. However, within weeks, the old animosity between first-born daughter and domineering father reared its head. On one night, the two had a blazing row over, of all things, the definition of a word. Lynette took it as a signal to leave. In a flash she'd packed her suitcase and headed off to Venice Beach.

Charlie approached Lynette; his smell a potent combination of tobacco, whisky and body odour. Of late, Charlie had taken to wearing an old cap which, together with his straggly beard, gave him the appearance of a wily old hobo; nevertheless he was able to engage her in conversation.[3]

'What's the problem?' Charlie asked.

'How did you know?' she replied, curiously.

'In the Haight they call me the Gardener,' Charlie offered, 'I tend to the flower children.'

Lynette was initially thrown off guard, and rather perturbed by Charlie's metaphor, feeling that 'gardening' evoked images of earthy things like seeds and planting that had obvious sexual connotations. Instinctively, she sensed a come-on rather than a genuine offer of help. However, Charlie's smile eventually reassured her that his intentions were wholly honourable and, as Manson gazed into her eyes, she sensed a deep warmth, something that she'd never experienced before. Manson's spell was working.

Slightly embarrassed by her tearful display, Lynette put her head down to compose herself. When she looked up again, Manson had vanished. Bemused, she looked around at the rocks and palm trees that surrounded her; then, from behind a pebble wall he reappeared. 'So, your father kicked you out?' He'd hit a nerve. Lynette nervously confirmed the fact, and from that they started talking. Although stilted at first, Charlie used the conversation to slowly draw out the teenager's sorry tale.

Once he'd figured out Lynette's predicament, Manson offered her a way out. With his peculiar double-speak and use of metaphor, he told her that he'd managed to free himself from what he painted as the worst environment imaginable – a life behind bars. 'The way out of a room,' he revealed, 'is not through the door. Just don't want out and you're free.' Charlie added that if she cared to join him, she too, could easily lose all of her inhibitions and worries.

Lynette looked at him, unable to come up with an immediate response. Battling against her instinct, and feverishly debating the offer in her mind, Lynette saw plenty of reasons why she shouldn't wander off with this New Age hobo; not least the fact that she was supposed to be returning to college.

Charlie waited patiently for an answer. Eventually, seeing as none was likely to be forthcoming, he shrugged his shoulders and smiled his beatific smile: 'Well, I can't make up your mind for you.' With that, he said goodbye, and sauntered off along the boardwalk, apparently untroubled by her rebuttal.

Whether Lynette was just one of many lost souls with whom Charlie had crossed paths that day, we will never know. However, for this lonely redhead, the seed that Manson had planted immediately began to germinate. A wave of emotions ran through her as home and school life began to dissolve into the ether. With her brightest hope for the future gradually fading into the landscape of Venice Beach, she made her decision and leapt off the stone wall. 'He cracked the shell that was trying to be so adult and so cut off from all feelings like we're trained to be,' she recalled. 'I definitely went after him when I saw that he wasn't pushing, and that he had spirit and he understood me . . . He had the most delicate, quick motion, like magic, as if glided [sic] along by air, and a smile that went from warm daddy to twinkely [sic] devil. I couldn't tell what he was . . . He got about halfway down the block, and I just grabbed everything and went after him . . . I don't know why, I didn't care . . . '

With her suitcase in hand, Lynette hurtled along Venice's promenade, drawn into Manson's magnetic slipstream. 'Wait!' she called out. 'Where are you going? Can I come along?'

chapter 3
Family

Sadder than a dream,
Is that he should pass us by
Sadder is the scheme,
In the dreams within the sky

From 'I once Knew a Man', by Charles Manson

CHARLIE and Lynette spent the next few hours wandering around Venice Beach swapping life stories. While Lynette's vocabulary dwarfed Charlie's modest lexicon, to her his words made perfect sense. Both of them felt as if they had been punished for crimes they didn't fully understand – Lynette with years of silence, and Charlie with a succession of reform schools. It was a liberating meeting of minds.

The couple hung around LA for a few days, but although they slept in Manson's car, it was still a purely platonic arrangement. Charlie, as was his custom, swiftly abridged her name to Lyn. Over the years, much like her mercurial personality, her name would change a further two times. Lyn loved to hear Manson's tales of San Francisco, and especially the kaleidoscope of activities that occurred in the Haight. Like most young people, she'd heard about the antics of the peace and love brigade, and Charlie's stories only served to heighten her desire to see it for herself. As Manson appeared to be getting nowhere in LA, he decided to postpone his plans and travel back to San Francisco with his new catch.

Along the way, Charlie opened up further, revealing more about himself and his current arrangement with Mary Brunner. He told Lyn about his dalliances with young Darlene, and how, as he saw it, he'd tried to protect her. Although starry-eyed when it came to Charlie's own tales of heroics, Lyn was savvy enough to know that the vibe in San Francisco had to have a darker side to it. Sadly, she was soon to be proved right.

On arrival in San Francisco, Charlie took Lyn back to Mary Brunner's flat. Such was Mary's delight at Manson's return that she raised no objection. While the newcomer made herself at home, she noted Mary's conventional, bookish lifestyle, finding it strangely at odds with Charlie's own freewheeling philosophy. However, under Manson's charismatic tutelage the women began to gel into a cohesive unit. Mary told Charlie that during his trip to LA, she'd given notice on her job at the university library, and similarly, the lease on her flat. It was a sign that she was putting herself entirely in Manson's hands.

Manson chanced upon an apartment at 636 Cole Street in the centre of Haight-Ashbury. The property was typical of the houses in the district, with a steep flight of steps up to its front door. With Mary Brunner stumping up the deposit, the trio got to work on transforming the interior, with tapestries and decorative animal skins, into what Brunner would describe as a 'luxurious hobo castle'. 'From our elegant and elevated flophouse,' Brunner relayed to a friend in a letter, 'we could look out into the yard and see dancing trees and smiling clover. We passed our time playing our plays, singing and beating our drums.'

Much has been said of Charlie's movements in some of the stranger quarters of San Francisco during that time, although little has ever been properly substantiated. However, it has been determined that Manson did indeed make the acquaintance of the occupiers of 407 Cole Street, just a few hundred feet away from their residence. The owner, Victor Wild, was ostensibly a leather-smith, but also operated under the name of 'Brother Ely', and was an active participant in the Process of the Church of the Final Judgement. The organisation would soon become one of the most important cogs in Manson's expanding psychology.

The Process Church was a quasi-scientific religious movement founded in 1963 by Englishman, Robert Moore, an early British proponent of Scientology. With his sympathetic partner, Mary Ann MacLean, they began to look beyond L. Ron Hubbard's mind science for more celestial goals. Through a mass of intellectualising, a concept was born that had as its core tenet a proposed alliance between Christ and Satan. Not surprisingly, this *entente cordiale* with the dark side pulled in a considerable crowd of disciples, and the organisation flourished. Moore changed his surname to DeGrimston, but such was his charisma and influence, devotees soon began referring to him as 'Jesus', 'God', and even 'Satan'.

While the Process movement was initially restricted to the affluent quarters of West London, it soon became a global ethos. As self-styled leaders of the pack, DeGrimston and his wife embarked on many a convoluted mission to spread the word. One such trip was in August 1966, when they found themselves in Yucatán in New Mexico. It is here that DeGrimston, his wife, and a party of around thirty believers found themselves in a small village called Xtul. There, it is said, the party survived a three-day hurricane that, in wholly biblical fashion, confirmed their commitment to this newly defined religion. Energised by this extraordinary experience, DeGrimston was propelled to write *The Xtul Dialogues*, the group's own Bible meets Bhagavad-Gita, by way of *Sergeant Pepper*.

Their faith confirmed by the experience in Xtul, Process disciples were instrumental in setting up churches in quarters receptive to their beliefs. With the mishmash of spiritual elements descending on San Francisco during 1967, it wasn't surprising that the Process Church were keen to get a piece of the action. Such was San Francisco's importance; DeGrimston reportedly sent thirty of his disciples to establish a base in the city.

Whereas early Process meetings were conducted quite plainly, the church's dark beliefs were soon reflected in their choice of fashion. Black polo-necks and capes became the Process's preferred uniform, and were a familiar sight around the Haight. The black would often be broken up by idiosyncratic items of jewellery – a variation of a swastika cast in silver, and a badge sporting the 'Goat of Mendes'.

The Process organisation would later move to 1820 Oak Street, and adopt a much more public face. The Oak Street dwelling hosted regular meetings and lectures on Processian theory, as well as selling sympathetic literature and other paraphernalia allied to its teachings. Given Charlie's fervent interest in anything that expanded upon presumed conventions, it's evident that he lapped up the doctrines of the Process movement, lifting and reshaping much of its core philosophy into his own rapidly developing world view. Dr David Smith of the Haight-Ashbury Free Medical Clinic clearly recalls Charlie's bus parked outside the Process's Oak Street base.

Manson was soon spouting the Process belief that an apocalyptic end was fast approaching, and that only selected cognoscenti would survive. Drawing on references from the New Testament's book of Revelation, these survivors would apparently travel through a labyrinth of caves and tunnels before arriving at a 'Bottomless Void' to sit out the turmoil occurring above ground. According to Process interpretations, motorcycle gangs, such as the Hell's Angels, would play an important role as 'shock troops' in this New World. In the higher echelons of the religion, there was ambivalence about Hitler and the Nazis, citing the Holocaust as some sort of karmic repercussion for the Jews.

Most attractively to Charlie, the Processions shared a belief that rock bands would also play a determining factor in this apocalypse. The pop angle was evidently important to the movement and, for a while, devotees of the church in London would manage the Voice, a psychedelic band featuring David Bowie's guitarist Mick Ronson. In an attempt to promote the Voice's talents, Process members would regularly show up at the Beatles' Apple offices, although like most of the oddballs that congregated around there, they were firmly shown the door. Over in Los Angeles, members of the church would form the Black Swan, a rock group made up entirely of church members, although their dark sound-scapes didn't win many fans.

Undeterred, Processian scouts would court the likes of Mick Jagger, Marianne Faithfull and even Paul McCartney to give support to their cause. Like a lot of these new 'religions', the Process was more than aware of the power of celebrity endorsements.

Of particular interest to Charlie was the Process's amalgam of Jesus and Satan into one working entity. As Manson saw both at work in his own persona, this theological duality would become a major source of inspiration. The following text, penned by DeGrimston under the banner of 'The Unity of Christ and Satan', became the church's clarion call. This passage also found its way into Charlie's own speeches over the following months.

'Christ said: Love your enemies. Christ's enemy was Satan and Satan's enemy was Christ. Through love, enmity is destroyed. Through love, saint and sinner destroy the enmity between them. Through love, Christ and Satan have destroyed their enmity and come together for the end: Christ to judge, Satan to execute the judgement. The judgement is wisdom; the execution of the judgement is love.'

Manson's continual references to the debilitating effects of fear appears also to have its roots in the Processian theory. As the cult began to expand, the group established an occasional publication to give wider coverage to their esoteric aims. One issue, entitled 'Mindbending', boasted an interview with Mick Jagger. Another, under the banner of 'Fear', included quotes from Paul McCartney. 'Fear. I'm not really afraid of people, nor of the world ending or anything like that. It's just fear really, a fear of fear. It's not fear of a lion, or of a man with a club – it's fear, a sort of abstract fear.' This small contribution from rock royalty gave the organisation immense kudos.

Manson also paid great attention to DeGrimston's views on spatial time and awareness. Long before 'the power of now' became a fashionable idea, DeGrimston had appropriated much from existentialist theory on the fragile borders to reality: 'I reduce everything to a common dominator that defies change and the passage of time. Time is an instrument of change, of flow, or evolution, of devolution. Time allows the pendulum to swing. I endeavour to prevent it.'

A later acolyte of Charlie's, Patricia Krenwinkel, would recall Manson's own obsession with letting go of anything that didn't relate to the present. 'The whole idea was to let time disappear; there was no time, we were all living "now". "Now" was the only time.'

Much has been said about Charlie's growing fascination with death and dying. The Process Church was equally absorbed with mortality. An edition of the Process magazine entitled 'Death', included a feature written by Charlie. Although published during the brouhaha of Manson's later court hearings, the text is indicative of how much the cult's teaching had rubbed off on his receptive mind. 'To fall off into endless dream, becoming the dream of total self . . . Death goes to where life comes from. Total awareness closing the circle, bringing the soul to now, ceasing to be, to become a world within yourself. Locked in your own totalness. Oh, fear my GOD, giving all to life as life falls into no thought pattern. Becoming the Sun, Moon and my mountains have breath, my oceans have feeling, my eyes cry rivers and blinking stars reflecting other suns, other worlds at peace in my calm night, becoming the wind and knowing all in my world is death . . . Death is peace from the world's madness and paradise in my own self. Death as I lay in my grave of constant vibration, endless now.'

One, more earthbound, element that Charlie took immediate notice of was the hierarchy that existed within the Process. As DeGrimston had decreed that conventional marriage was 'an abomination', a broader union was encouraged instead. Devotees were segregated into what they called a 'family' of 'messengers'. As a result, within Processian circles there were many a 'brother', 'father', 'mother' and 'sister'. It appears that Manson's views on love and loyalty may well have been formulated during his time with the organisation. Furthermore, just like those in the Process fold, Charlie would revere animals above all other life forms.

It was around this time in 1967 that Manson met a young man by the name of Robert 'Bobby' Beausoleil who, at just seventeen years old, was mostly distinguishable by his choice of costume: a large top hat, an intricately carved cane, and Snofox, the loyal white dog that was forever at his side. He'd earned the name 'Cupid' on account of his boyish, handsome features, and mercurial personality.

A native of Santa Barbara, south California, Bobby had followed the typical route of a teenage rebel. Despite having loving and attentive parents, Bobby was evidently not cut out for the narrow perimeters of conventionality. As a result of various run-ins with the law, he'd been made a ward of court and spent time in reform school. Possessing a powerful creativity, Bobby had concentrated his efforts in the field of music, becoming adept at a variety of instruments. Barely in his mid-teens, Beausoleil gravitated towards Los Angeles in search of fame and sensations. With his remarkable talents, Beausoleil soon gained considerable respect around town. This in turn led to brief stints with various bands; notably Arthur Lee's Grass Roots, an early incarnation of the celebrated band Love. Indeed, the band's name appears to have been inspired by Beausoleil's overwhelming charisma. Additionally, he'd impressed the counterculture's prime iconoclast, Frank Zappa, providing backing vocals on the track, 'Who Are The Brain Police?' from Zappa's 1967 album, *Freak Out*.

Although LA housed the bulk of California's music moguls, Beausoleil had moved to San Francisco to escape the superficiality of the industry. Once there, he fitted in seamlessly with the more organic, hassle-free vibe that permeated the Haight. Soon he became a permanent fixture at the Avalon and Fillmore West venues, checking out the new wave of psychedelic bands that were emerging. Within time he joined the Outfit, a group who were building a name for their experimental sound. Now with Bobby's multi-instrumental skills to the fore, the Outfit's quality lifted them above many of the district's other pretenders.

In his desire to strive for more esoteric sounds, Bobby eventually outgrew the limitations of the Outfit. Instead he set about forming his own group, better suited to his experimental vision of progressive music. He discovered David LaFlamme, a violinist, whose virtuoso talents straddled classical and rock music genres, and who'd later find greater fame with the group It's a Beautiful Day. With a few kindred minds on board, the Orkustra was born; its edict to weld classical and Middle Eastern sounds within the framework of the rock genre. Not surprisingly, the band really took off in the Haight, where experimentation was roundly welcomed. They became the Diggers' house band, and accompanied many of their free-food handouts with their symbiotic sounds, and sometimes even shared stage space with the doyens of the Haight, The Grateful Dead. With positive responses and impeccable contacts, the possibilities for the Orkustra seemed limitless.

Although the Diggers were busy feeding the hippie populace during daylight hours, they'd occasionally organise other events to satisfy their ravenous party instincts. One of these was a seventy-two-hour happening entitled 'The Invisible Circus'. This broad alliance of the tribes was planned for Friday 24 February 1967 in, of all places, the Glide Memorial Church Hall in downtown San Francisco.

With minimal planning, the mischievous coordinators had put the word out that 'The Invisible Circus' would be absolutely without limits or boundaries. Put simply, if there were something you wanted to do, but had never been offered a place to do it, 'The Invisible Circus' would allow it to take place. The posters too were idiosyncratic, inviting one and all to the 'environmental' event.

At its core, 'The Invisible Circus' was a celebration of all the elements that were energising the area. Space was given over to poetry readings, music, lectures, even left-field printing workshops, word soon spread that this was to be something quite out of the ordinary. When you consider the other happenings taking place around town that year, this would mean it had to be truly something else. Sharing space among the weird and the wonderful was Beausoleil's Orkustra.

As a prime mover, Bobby shared freely in the Bacchanalian activity that was on offer. Indeed, the Orkustra kicked off the happening on the Friday evening, along with a troupe of nude belly dancers from the Sexual Freedom League. Also present somewhere in the throng was filmmaker, artist and master aficionado of the black art, Kenneth Anger. During the mid-1960s, Anger had carved himself a sizeable niche in indie film-making. With San Francisco piloting the ambitions of the New Age, Anger was in his element in this experimental melting pot.

At some point during 'The Invisible Circus', Anger caught sight of Beausoleil playing on stage with the Orkustra. Anger was entranced with Beausoleil's impish beauty and assertive movements. At the conclusion of the Orkustra's set, a captivated Anger rushed the stage, screaming, 'You are Lucifer!' (High praise indeed!) Afterwards, Anger cornered Bobby, saying that he wanted him for the lead in his next project, a cinematic projection of the second coming of Satan, entitled *Lucifer Rising*. Beausoleil agreed, with a proviso that he and his band would provide the music for the soundtrack. In awe of Anger's all-consuming enigma, Bobby dropped his band's Orkustra tag, and searched for something more 'occult'. For this, he rejigged the band into the Magick Powerhouse of Oz. Where the Orkustra had offered a dilettante approach to blending various styles of music, Beausoleil's new group mined the primeval influences that were closely allied to Anger's occultist interests. Anger was so intoxicated with his new acolyte that he underwrote all of the band's studio time.

For a while things jogged along fairly harmoniously between Anger and his young apprentice, the pair working together on *Lucifer Rising*. Gelling the relationship further, Bobby moved into Anger's quarters, a decrepit mansion block that had once been the Tsarist consulate in San Francisco's Fulton Street. Under Anger's tenure, the place was filled with all the trappings of a master magician. While the walls vibrated with purple and orange tones, the house was filled with Anger's expansive collection of mystical paraphernalia. Anger's own personal altar dominated the floor space, but previous house guests had also left their mark, from sacrificial totems and amulets to motorcycle parts discarded by visiting biker gangs. Since Anger's influences leaped out from every bookshelf and wall, Beausoleil began to acquaint himself with the labyrinthine environs of the occult. Anger was keen to school his young acolyte in the works of his mentor, Aleister Crowley, and even handed over a walking cane adorned with an entwined serpent's head that had once been part of Crowley's wardrobe. To get him around town, Anger bought his young charge a converted Studebaker truck that looked just like an earthbound spaceship.

Anger's infatuation with Beausoleil soon turned nasty following a disastrous autumn equinox party the pair had planned for 21 September 1967. Held at the city's Straight Theatre, 'The Equinox of the Gods' was marred by a malfunctioning sound system, and other props that failed to work. Tripping on LSD,

Anger flounced off the stage, blaming Beausoleil's ineptitude for the whole debacle. The party was over.

Anger placed an immediate curse on his former partner's soul, and undertook several cleansing rituals to fully rid himself of Bobby's presence. With Anger temporarily out of town, engaged in an attempt to exorcise the Pentagon during an anti-Vietnam rally, Bobby had plenty of time to move himself out of Anger's house. While gathering up his gear, Beausoleil noticed that Anger had dismantled parts of the truck he'd given him, and placed it on his satanic altar. Aware that the vehicle wouldn't function without these components, Beausoleil grabbed them off the altar and took off.

On his return from Washington, Anger claimed that Bobby had taken the negative of the film *Lucifer Rising* out of spite for his dramatic eviction. In months to come, Anger complained that Beausoliel had demanded a heavy ransom for the negative, before destroying it in the California Desert. Eventually (depending on whose story one believes), *Lucifer Rising* was either recut or reshot, leaving Beausoleil's music out. In the vanguard of the Rolling Stones, Anger would soon travel over to England to revel in the Satanism with which the group was flirting.

Somewhat scorched by the whole experience, Beausoleil headed south in the Studebaker to spend some time with his family in San Jose, before travelling to Malibu to try to kick-start his sidelined musical career. While Beausoleil claims that he never met Manson in San Francisco, their paths were fast converging.

Regardless of their own dabbling with the fringes of cult activities, Charlie and the girls were aware that, at street level, vibrations in San Francisco were starting to get heavy. Whilst the hippie elite fed from more intellectual fruit, on ground level things were starting to deteriorate badly. For those living and working on the front line of the scene, Scott Mackenzie's number one hit, 'San Francisco (Be Sure to Wear Flowers in Your Hair)', was delivering a wholly ironic message. While the amiable tune flew up the charts during the summer of 1967, the reality was much darker.

Manson's parole officer at the time, Roger Smith, explained the situation. 'By 1967, if you came to San Francisco, you needed to wear a .45 in your belt. It had changed that fast. The kids were still coming from all over the United States, for the same set of expectations, but the welcoming committee was very, very different. There was a brand of street theatre that was hard to imagine. It was a scene that if you grew your hair and talked the talk, you fit in.'

'No one prospectively sensed a fall,' recalls Dr David Smith of the Haight-Ashbury Free Medical Clinic. 'We could have sensed that by the type of patients we were seeing that were sicker and sicker. Also (retrospectively), any movement built on drugs is bound to turn sour. It was really quite a blow to me to see this idealistic movement die.'

Since the hippie lifestyle was largely fuelled by hallucinogenic chemicals, it was perhaps inevitable that gangland dealers would take control of the area. Given the passivity of many of the Haight's inhabitants, it was the perfect place for the dealers to take advantage. As is always the case, LSD and marijuana were soon followed by the arrival of amphetamines and other more strident chemical stimulants. While LSD demanded a fairly complex understanding of chemistry, amphetamines were relatively cheap and easy to produce. With the proliferation of speed, and its more virulent sisters PCP and crystal meth, paranoia crept in through the back door. Although the likes of the legendary chemist Stanley Owsley had provided much of the staple ingredients of the LSD diet, other chemists began to stir up the darker regions of the subconscious, often with devastating effects. STP, a heavily compressed potpourri of hallucinogens and amphetamines, was the most powerful of these hybrids; it hit the streets, with considerable fanfare, in mid-1967. While users with enough stamina and resilience raved about its startling properties, the potency of the drug – whose effects could last up to three days – would also bring about episodes of psychosis and other mental traumas that in some cases were irreversible. Soon hospitalisation and mental institution committals were occurring at a frightening rate.

Despite altruistic members of the community advising caution, more and more rugged and unscrupulous elements began to take control of what was fast becoming a turf war. Soon drug burns, rapes and protection rackets became prevalent in the district. With this once beautiful dream now rapidly sliding towards bitter nightmare, many of the original protagonists began a retreat towards the calmer realms of the California countryside.

Whereas the scene had grown out of a beatnik ideology of peaceably challenging authority, as seedier elements chipped away at the fragile manifesto, the necessity for change became nothing more than a reason to party. With no evident restrictions, the shadowy underbelly of humanity was starting to assert its influence over the gentle voices in the area. By the autumn of 1967, San Francisco's authorities had grown tired of seeing the entire youth of the city stoned. With rumours abounding that San Francisco's water supply was to be spiked with LSD, police engaged in a violent, knee-jerk reaction, clamping down on what was fast becoming a dark carnival.

Watching all of this from the sidelines was Charles Manson. His senses well honed to criminality, Charlie was aware that the so-called 'Summer of Love' was due to implode. Like many, Manson had done a bit of drug-peddling in his time, but the major players on the Haight's drug turf were bigger and far bolder than he could ever be. While Charlie thrived on the philosophical spin-offs from the hippie movement, organised criminality was of little interest to him. Mary and Lyn had also stumbled into a few distinctly dark scenarios in San Francisco that had scared them badly. Additionally, for the ex-con, the increase in police activity in the area was profoundly unsettling.

At the sharp end of the culture, Charlie had his own thoughts on its demise, duly captured in John Gilmore and Ron Kenner's *Garbage People*. 'I'd seen the bad things that were coming into the Haight,' recalled Manson. 'The wild problems and the people all around me, getting bugged and harassed in the doors of their own places. And there were all the problems on the streets. Wherever we gathered, the policemen were coming with their sticks and their guns and their badges, and they were running the kids up and down the streets like cattle being chased. It was chaos.'

It wasn't just the likes of Charlie that sensed an end to the era. *Time* magazine, which had been keen to rally the scene early on, was now there to ponder its demise. 'It might be the evening scene in any city slum. Unkempt youths clot the stoops of dilapidated tenements, talking over-boldly of drugs; drunks reel along gutters foul with garbage; young toughs from neighbouring turf methodically proposition every girl who passes by, while older strangers hunt homosexual action. The night air smells of decay and anger. For all its ugly familiarity, however, this is not just another ghetto. This is the scene in San Francisco's Haight-Ashbury district, once the citadel of hippiedom and symbol of flower-power love. Love has fled the Hashbury.'

Aware more than anyone else that the scene was self-destructing, the Diggers, Haight-Ashbury's heart and soul, prepared a cleansing ritual to get rid of the contaminants that were polluting the movement. With an edict to bring a conclusion to this once glorious experiment, many of the movement's elders, led by the Diggers and a mime troupe, paraded through the streets of Haight-Ashbury on 6 October 1967. Under the title, 'The Death of Hippie', these original flower children, complete with open coffin, urged all true believers to divest themselves of any of the paraphernalia that had become associated with the marketing of the 'hippie' dream. As requested, a plethora of beads, bells and other accoutrements were tossed unceremoniously in the wooden coffin. The march culminated in a mock funeral in Buena Vista Park, where the coffin and all its contents were summarily burned on a large pyre. Once all had passed into smoke, those present were able to leap over the dying flames and embers of a once beautiful dream.

While many would continue to identify with the hippie movement long after the parade, the detritus left behind resembled nothing more than a flea market of tacky souvenirs. Predictably, sections of the establishment that had looked down their noses at the idealistic kids were now cashing in on the act, with shops and stores offering 'hippie' wigs, plastic flowers and other tawdry products to unsuspecting punters. Somewhat predictably, the arse-end of Hollywood would belatedly train their lenses on the district to capture any tawdry behaviour for voyeuristic film buffs. Soon, pictures such as *Psyche Out*, and *Alice in Acidland* were beaming confused signals around the globe. Adding to the cynicism, a firm began running regular bus tours of the region. Known as the 'Hippie Hop', for a few dollars the curious could watch the antics of the counterculture, while listening to a commentary that wouldn't have been out of place on a safari. The few imaginative residents left behind would run alongside the bus holding up mirrors, so all the tourists could see was their own avid reflections.

With these and other dark omens closing in on Manson and the girls, there was a strong desire to relocate out of the city. Lyn was now keenest to go, finding the area claustrophobic. As soon as Mary was able to cash her last cheque and recover the deposit on her flat, they were ready. With Charlie's 1948 Chevrolet kitted out with an enormous collection of food and other supplies, the trio hit the road.

Seeking anonymity, Charlie, Mary and Lyn headed off north in the direction of Mendocino County, settling in the so-called 'ghost' town of Casper. The area was a much-needed salve for Charlie and the girls, with its Pacific beachfront location and surrounding arboretum of giant redwoods. Much to the locals' chagrin, it had become a popular retreat for the hippies, who were drawn by its organic, rustic charm. Charlie, Mary and Lyn soon chanced upon a log cabin on the fringes of the beach and, as had become the norm, attracted a legion of fellow travellers and soul-searchers wanting to share in their company.

While basking in the natural beauty of the area, Charlie and Lyn had their first physical encounter. As Lyn was dealing with a whole host of psychosexual issues that she'd harboured since adolescence, it was to be an emancipating, at times traumatic, experience. As Charlie assumed his roll as guide and liberator, Lyn felt as if she was finally throwing off her past, and the troublesome elements that had held her back.

Meanwhile Mary Brunner was finding Charlie's random sharing of affection hard to swallow. Sensing a split, Charlie laid down the law, stating that although they were all part of one entity, no one belonged exclusively to one another. As if to reinforce the point, Mary was encouraged to watch Charlie and Lyn's next sexual performance. Somewhat reluctantly she did, and then switched places with Lyn for a further romp with Charlie, ensuring that any barriers of propriety that had previously existed were all but dissolved.

As the weather in Casper had, at certain times of the year, a tendency to envelop everything in mist, Lyn suggested they head for brighter climes. A trip down towards the more reliable temperatures of Santa Barbara was planned; coincidentally, an old acquaintance from Charlie's prison days lived in an apartment on Manhattan Beach.

En route, Charlie was keen to make a return call on his evangelist friend, Reverend Deane Morehouse. Although Charlie was enjoying the company of his adoring duo of females, he couldn't get the thought of the preacher's daughter Ruth Ann out of his mind. Despite her young age, Charlie was eager to secure her affections, and equally to have another devout female under his wings.

Charlie and the girls were received warmly by Morehouse and, despite his wife's reservations, he allowed the trio to make themselves at home. As was customary, there were nightly communal singsongs around the piano. In fact when Charlie remarked on how much he enjoyed the subtle tones of the instrument, the Reverend immediately told Charlie he could have the piano as a gift.

While at the Morehouses', Manson had caught sight of a black Volkswagen minibus parked at a neighbouring property. Offering ample bed-space and sufficient room for additional travellers, it appeared perfect for Charlie and the girls' expanding needs. There was now a pressing need for a more agreeable sleeping pad; Mary Brunner had discovered she was pregnant with Manson's child.

Somehow, Manson managed to rustle up $35, and approached the owner of the bus with a view to trade. After some bartering a deal was struck, with Charlie putting Deane Morehouse's piano up as part-exchange. The Reverend kept to his word and, with the use of a tow-truck, his piano was shifted next door.

Ultimately, it was Deane's wife who called time on Charlie and the girls' stay at the house. Not only was her husband spending an inordinate amount of time with Manson, but Charlie was obviously still infatuated with their daughter Ruth. Manson and his women were a bad influence, and had to be removed from the household.

She was too late. Leaving Mary and Lyn in situ at the Morehouse home, Charlie snuck away with Ruth into the Mendocino countryside. It didn't take long for her parents to put two and two together and alert the police to their daughter's disappearance. The police duly caught up with Charlie and Ruth on 28 July 1967. The fifteen-year-old was sent back to her parents, while Charlie (masquerading as a minister) received a thirty-day suspended sentence for interfering with police investigations.

Undeterred, Charlie engineered a plan for the girl to run away and catch up with them all later on. With the Morehouses relieved to see the back of Charlie and the girls, the bus continued its carefree amble towards California's southern coast for a meet-up with Manson's old prison contact.

Once there, Charlie wasted no time in catching up with his old mates. The trio were quite taken with the region (and in any case it was home territory for Lyn), and took out a short lease on a property on the outskirts of the town, 705 Bath Street. One early autumn evening, the tribe called on Charlie's buddy in the neighbouring district of Manhattan Beach. Quite by chance, they arrived as a party was beginning to take shape and, as per usual, Charlie squatted down on the floor and started playing some of his songs. A late arrival at the gathering was eighteen-year-old Patricia Dianne Krenwinkel. She'd finished her day's work at a local bank, and on her sister's recommendation, was joining the party. By the time she arrived, the air was thick with marijuana smoke and shared banter. With Charlie's voice and guitar wafting in and out of the conversation, Patricia settled down to quietly engage in the collective vibe.

With Charlie's mojo fully primed, he was able to observe Patricia's shy demeanour. A quiet, reserved girl, Charlie could nevertheless already tell that she was wholly captivated by his presence.

Seeing that Patricia had to leave early, Charlie sent Lyn to escort her home. As they walked along the beach, Lyn was able to play up Charlie's positives. Sharing a knack for verse, the pair composed a short poem together that night. As they parted ways, Patricia scribbled down her contact details so that Charlie could come and find her later.

Patricia's life bore marked similarities to Lyn's. Born on 3 December 1947, she was the only child of an insurance agent, Joseph Krenwinkel and his wife Dorothy Huber. The Krenwinkel family made their home in Inglewood, a leafy and fairly affluent suburb of south-west Los Angeles. Although Krenwinkel already had a daughter, Charlene Ann, from his previous marriage, they were a close family unit, with mother and father doting equally over the two children. Just like Lyn, the young Patricia busied herself with a variety of after-school pursuits, joining the girl guides, playing with her pets and studying wildlife. With half-sister Charlene as her closest confidante, all appeared harmonious.

However, as she got older, Patricia had become aware that the thin veneer of family values shrouded her parents' deep desire to be accepted. Nothing controversial was ever discussed in the Krenwinkel home and, as a thoughtful and deeply sensitive child, much of Patricia's innermost needs were simply ignored in favour of more pressing social expectations.

Although a conscientious and hard-working student, socially Patricia was reserved. Not only was she slightly overweight, but she suffered from excessive body hair. Unsurprisingly, she spent her teen years feeling unattractive and unloved, and doctors prescribed a variety of pills to combat her depression and counteract her weight gain.

Things came to a head when her parents divorced when Patricia was seventeen years old. Evidently the strain of appearing as a happy, respectable unit had been too great. Choosing to stay with her father in Los Angeles, Patricia spent more and more time at church and began teaching at a local Catholic Sunday School. Such was the depth of her religious devotion that she was ready to hand herself over to God and become a nun. With this plan in mind, Patricia moved to Mobile, Alabama, where her mother now lived, and began studying at a Catholic college. Unfortunately things didn't work out there either, and within one semester she'd dropped out and gone back to LA to be with her father.

Depressed by the meaningless path she seemed to be treading, Patricia was urged by her father to take an office job while she decided what to do with her life. She found a position as a cashier clerk at the Insurance Company of North America, but the numbingly tedious work jarred heavily with her creative sensitivities. Meanwhile, her father was forever urging Patricia to strive for higher and better targets, and she was growing tired of his constant expectations. When the opportunity arose to move into her sister's apartment in the trendy El Porto district of Manhattan Beach, she leapt at the chance.

Within weeks of moving to Charlene's flat, she became depressed again, though, and began looking for ways to escape her angst. She later put these thoughts into a poetic form.

> I was dying,
> And each corner of my apartment
> My cage
> Was held together by a cheque
> Banked at a branch of America
> Giving me the convenience
> Of a new 'twinkie' added to my shelf
> Next to the beans and tortillas

Although the move to her sister's Manhattan Beach flat provided some semblance of independence, Patricia soon ran into yet another set of problems. Sister Charlene's boyfriend was heavily into narcotics, and had pulled Charlene with him into a heroin dependency. Compounding the problem, Charlene had become pregnant, and the boyfriend had turned his attentions elsewhere. Although Charlene gave birth to a baby boy, her all-consuming heroin addiction kept her preoccupied. With Patricia shouldering the bulk of the bills and spending her free time childminding, it was hardly the perfect living environment for any of them. Although Patricia had dabbled in a variety of substances since her early teens, she found it difficult to contain her sibling's addiction. While her day job offered a mundane distraction of sorts, she was deeply unhappy. Charlie's arrival that night was perfectly timed. As ever, Manson had an excellent 'nose' for girls like Patricia.

Following their beachside amble, Lyn duly passed on Patricia's note to Charlie, containing her thinly veiled hints on how to find her once he'd done with the party. Charlie followed these up a few hours later, needing little sweet-talking to gain entry to the sisters' flat. Following some perfunctory small talk, Charlie made his move. Thanks to his experiences with Mary and Lyn, Charlie now had a tried-and-tested formula for ensnaring these highly vulnerable girls, systematically tearing down Patricia's meagre defences. While for Patricia the sex with Charlie was liberating, it was the words that accompanied it that really changed things for her.

'That night we slept together,' recalled Krenwinkel in 1994, 'I felt really loved by him, almost immediately, mostly because I think at that point I was really desperate for someone to care. When we made love, all I remember is just crying and crying to this man because he said, "Oh, you're beautiful." I couldn't believe that, I just started crying.' Afterwards the couple talked together long into the night. With her head on his chest, Patricia vowed her immediate and unconditional alliance to Manson, now and forever.

With another girl successfully ensnared, Charlie was happy to hang around Patricia's apartment for the next few days. There he further reinforced his twisted sexual dominance by getting his convert to believe that he was assuming a fatherly role. Manson was more than aware that this played strongly in these young girls' minds, especially at an age where sexual identity was paramount. Adding to Patricia's dramatic rebirth, Charlie would soon christen her with a new name, a practice that was to become standard for all inductees to his fold. For Patricia he chose 'Katie', a bastardisation of her awkward surname, and much more in line with her innocent looks.

On 12 September 1967, 'Katie' left her cashier's job at the insurance company. As she noted in her poetry, it had become just another 'prison'. She, very quickly, abandoned everything to hit the road with Charlie and the girls. Indeed such was her haste to get on board, she neglected to cash her final two pay cheques. Her car too would meet an ignominious end, dumped in the parking lot of a service station. However, she happily handed over her personal fuel card, bankrolled by her father, to Charlie to cover their future petrol costs. In a letter dated 25 September 1967, she wrote to her father. The contents were brief and to the point: 'For the very first time in my life, I have found inner contentment and inner peace. I love you very much. Take good care of yourself.'

Lynette Fromme recognised the symptoms: 'She was looking, like all kids are, looking for something that was real; and the truth. She was looking for peace and someone to love her . . . She could see there was a way out of it, and we just left.'

Moulding Katie proved easy. Mixing and matching the action, Charlie upped the odds to include group and lesbian sex. Mary and Lyn had met these sex sessions with some initial resistance; Katie, high on the enormity of her rebirth, became a fierce and loyal supporter of anything suggested by Manson. He would later comment that Katie's conversion had been the most satisfying of his initial conquests, becoming his fastest and most 'complete reflection'. Katie's baptism included the stepping up of her LSD usage, and she'd embark on a heavy, almost continuous, acid trip for the next two years.

With time in Manhattan Beach coming to a close, the VW van was loaded up for yet another sojourn into the unknown. Regardless of the bus's limit on space, the quartet happily slept in a crisscross fashion at the rear of the vehicle. While they were outwardly free spirits, Charlie still had to touch base with his parole officer back in San Francisco, and so they headed back up north.

The tribe, short on cash, had to rely on the occasional piece of busking, street theatre or paid menial work, to sustain them en route, but despite the financial hardship, the atmosphere surrounding them was joyously happy, with Charlie always directing their moods. During their travels, they'd meet with a rogue's gallery of the great and the good, and while some would only be fleeting contacts, others were destined to become more permanent allies.

It was during this trip back to San Francisco that the Manson tribe made contact with Bruce McGregor Davis. He was older than the girls, and, at twenty-five, had led a very different life. Like most of his vintage, he'd retained all the elements of a hippie traveller, and yet he shared some startling similarities with Charlie. A native of Tennessee he, like Charlie, delivered his words in a distinctive drawl. His hair was long and flowing, and he liked to talk of Scientology and other mind-boggling philosophies. Intrigued by these similarities, contact details were shared, ensuring that Bruce would catch up with them later on their travels. He was to play a major role in the darkest days of the Manson Family.

With the VW camper's springs close to collapse under the weight of the gang's misuse, Manson was on the lookout for something a little more robust for their needs. Conveniently, he'd caught sight of an old yellow and black school bus that was up for sale. With a down payment and the VW taken in exchange, the school bus was duly signed over to Charlie, reportedly by a one-legged Dutchman. Yet another personality in awe of Manson, the Dutchman, along with his six children, helped refurbish the bus's ailing mechanics at no extra cost.

At the time old buses had a unique currency. Legendary author and *enfant terrible,* Ken Kesey and his band of Merry Pranksters had commandeered a similar school bus for their journey across the United States. Converting the vehicle into living quarters, the Pranksters embarked on a chemical odyssey that set out to douse America with LSD. Despite their dubious intentions, the vibe was wholly good natured and free of the lofty evangelising that had begun to envelop the acid culture. In particular, it was the Pranksters' rambling and unpredictable course that set a glorious template for other seekers of the era and beyond to follow, Manson and the women included.

While Charlie may well have acquired the bus for a handsome deal, mythology has told of a harrowing scenario relating to the vehicle's history. According to this enigmatic Dutchman, the school bus had once been involved in an incident where it had careered into a lake, drowning many of the children that were on board. Manson's irreverent sense of the demonic meant he'd embellish fantastical yarns to the girls about the children who haunted the bus's interior. Legend also has it that Charlie's women, their newly redrawn characters receptive to any form of possession, re-enacted the deceased children's personas during their travels. They even embarked on an exorcism to channel the tortured spirits out of the bus.

Once the rows of seats were jettisoned, the real business of interior design could take place. Like women possessed, the girls transformed the interior with a spray of peacock feathers, velvet pillows, tapestries, beanbags and other accoutrements. A hookah pipe was placed on a coffee table in the centre of the bus, adding to the atmosphere of a Bedouin tent on wheels. While the girls busied themselves on the inside, Charlie got to work constructing a large black box for their possessions to sit on top of the vehicle. This top-box would often come away from its securing, and slop around the roof, giving the impression of a large black hat, doffing itself at every bend.

Charlie and the girls continued their meander around the foothills of California towards San Francisco, with reports of them landing in places as far afield as Eureka, Oregon, Seattle, Nevada and Las Vegas. As they trundled through the small villages and towns, they were mostly afforded a generous welcome; the harem of women ensuring that they were never short of an enthusiastic reception.

'Every place we stopped, someone wanted to join us,' Charlie recalled in 1989. 'Countless people had experiences in that bus they will remember as long as they live. Freedom, love and music were our thing, and understanding – each willing to honour the feelings and thoughts of others – tightened our circle.'

Charlie eventually touched base with his parole officer, Roger Smith, in San Francisco. Although Charlie's swank assurance and adoring posse caused heads to turn, seasoned watchers such as Smith were starting to get concerned by the worrying amount of power Manson wielded over his charges. 'I saw him on a weekly basis,' Smith said. 'He would bring the girls into the office, it was a big occasion. I would go out to [their] home and see them ... I began to get increasing uncomfortable with the amount of control, and the way that he used them, and you could see his sense of power and control growing.'

With the bus in situ in the Haight, Manson reacquainted himself with the scene. Although reports are sketchy, it is at this point that he met some of the decidedly dark figures that were now operating out of San Francisco. Not surprisingly, with the district's innocence in sharp decline, operations such as the Process Church had been infiltrated by rogue elements of the satanic movement. Reportedly, Charlie mingled in these disparate circles, and gained some fame for his 'wizard'-like persona. Whether Charlie held any genuine satanic convictions has proved difficult to ascertain. However, it is abundantly clear that he could shimmy with any collective if there were pickings to be taken. It was through one of these channels that Manson bumped into Susan Denise Atkins.

Susan's history was a chequered one. Born on 7 May 1948, and now eighteen years old, she was the second of Edwin and Jeanette Atkins' three children, and grew up first in Millbrae, close to San Francisco, and then Cambrian Park, a pretty quarter of San Jose. Not exactly affluent, Susan's parents both worked to make ends meet: father Edwin was in construction, while mother Jeanette found occasional work in call centres.

If to some Susan appeared to enjoy her formative years, any happiness masked a deeper sadness. Both of her parents were alcoholics. She'd later reveal a distressing catalogue of molestation by her older brother and other family members. These disturbing experiences made her very detached from a young age and, although she appeared to enjoy school, her quiet, reserved manner alerted those around her that all was not as it should be.

To make things worse, when Susan was fourteen her mother was diagnosed with leukaemia. The following Christmas her mother's condition worsened, and a tearful Susan encouraged members of their church choir to sing carols underneath her mother's window.

The death of Susan's mother kicked the bottom layer out of the Atkins family house of cards, and ended her daughter's faith in

God. Despite relatives rallying round, the bills for the treatment and care of Susan's mother had amounted to a terrifying sum. Compounding their problems, her father became unemployed. As a result, this already fractured family fell apart under the financial strain. In a misguided attempt to provide support for herself and her family, Susan began shoplifting, and soon became proficient enough to earned the title of 'best shoplifter' among her peers.

Not wanting to live with her strict grandparents, Susan had opted into the care of an aunt. With school proving less and less of an interest, Susan began to broaden her experiences in other areas. In the wake of her family's disintegration, and in the absence of any parental guidance, she'd discovered boys in a big way. She even began an affair with one of her teachers. By the age of eighteen, with her grades plummeting, Susan abandoned her studies. Constantly craving attention, she began moving from house to flat, spending time with relations, friends, and anyone who'd have her. Eventually, a job came up as a telephone survey operator in San Francisco. With nothing left to detain her in San Jose, she took off, severing all family ties in the process.

Once in the city, Susan took up lodgings in a boarding house. With no apparent friends and scant social life, the loneliness was too much for her and she attempted suicide. Through the haze of an entire bottle of barbiturates, Susan managed to summon help before collapsing. When the emergency services arrived, she was found unconscious in her room, a photograph of her mother in one hand, and a copy of the Bible in the other; apparently her act had been inspired by a scene in the film, *The Slender Thread*. Susan was immediately committed into psychiatric care but discharged herself as soon as she regained consciousness.

Back on the streets of San Francisco, Atkins began pitching up at a variety of flats, funded by various stints in bars and other seedy establishments. As was becoming a pattern, she began to fall in with a multitude of bad pennies, starting many a fleeting, empty love affair. At one point during the summer of 1966, she embarked on a disastrous robbing spree with a couple of ex-convicts. Together, they pillaged gas stations and liquor stores, while relieving a multitude of owners of their cars. As word soon spread of their antics, the law mounted an extensive search for the trio. Eventually they were caught near Oregon, but due to Susan's age she only received a short custodial sentence. Shortly afterwards, she returned to her family base in San Jose but, bored by the docility of the suburb, she swiftly headed back to the streets of San Francisco. As she'd proved her prowess on the numerous dance floors around town, Susan easily found work; first as a cocktail waitress and then as a topless go-go dancer. There, she met with a range of weird and wonderful characters, all keen to exploit her 'no boundaries' persona. While the shadiness of the circles she moved in threw up an assortment of characters, none were quite as extraordinary as Howard Levey, a.k.a. Magus Anton Szandor LaVey, self-styled High Priest of the Church of Satan.

While his critics hysterically charted his enthusiastic alliance with the demonic, LaVey saw himself more as a performance artist, worshipping Satan as a literary metaphor, rather than a fallen deity. While this brought him into conflict with more fundamental Satanists, he garnered a labyrinthine index of celebrity contacts, many of whom were rooted in Hollywood. Over time, LaVey's church included the likes of James Dean, Jayne Mansfield, Dean Martin and Sammy Davis Junior. A spookier degree of separation reportedly led him to cross paths with Polish film director, Roman Polanski. Polanski was already in possession of a script entitled *Rosemary's Baby*, a story that mined the murky practices of modern day Satanism. With LaVey's name freely referenced in Hollywood as an authority on these and other black arts, it's long been suggested (but never confirmed) that LaVey helped out with the movie's pre-production.

As LaVey was continually on the lookout to bring many of his chosen practices to life, he booked a San Francisco nightclub called the 'Kandy Kat' to stage a Witch's Sabbat-cum-satanic revue. With LaVey featuring (naturally) as chief protagonist, some suitably attractive participants were required to augment the action. With Susan already plying a very successful trade in clubland, an offer was made to temporarily switch her talents over to LaVey's production.

Susan readily agreed, imagining that this performance could well be a ladder to greater exploits. Atkins, and a few other women, convened at LaVey's infamous 'Black House' on 6114 California Street, to rehearse for the show. The Victorian manor was like something out of *The Addams Family* TV show, and the interior matched the house's funky exterior beautifully. Among a menagerie of stuffed animals, was a shrunken head, and a reproduction of Tutankhamen's sarcophagus, while a real-life lion by the name of Togare strutted around in the backyard. Though Susan has since claimed that she fled the house of horrors, she did actually reappear later at the club to perform in LaVey's revue. Atkins might have been nervous at the prospect of what was about to occur that night, but events would transcend to another level, aided in no small way by a tab of acid, dropped earlier in the evening.

Tripping out on the satanic livery dotted around, Susan nervously awaited her moment where she would be encased in a casket for the torture scene. By Susan's accounts, her performance was something of a hit.

'I had shaken several people with the reality of my performance when I had risen from the casket and pointed a long, blood red fingernail at the audience and marked them as my next victims. Gasps, from both male and females, had sounded all around the club. But as I lay there, I fancied the idea of being dead and still hearing all the sounds around me.'

While Susan was enjoying the limelight, the accumulated backlog of her lifestyle had begun to take a considerable toll. The upshot of sleeping with anyone who'd taken a passing interest in her was that she was now riddled with venereal disease. Furthermore, her prodigious ingestion of drugs was systematically breaking down her psyche. Following her opening night at LaVey's Sabbat show, she was hospitalised.

When Susan recovered from her brief psychosis, she hot-footed it back to the Haight. Once there, she found accommodation at a property on the corner of Lyon Street and Oak Street. The house had a notorious reputation; its main purpose being as a clearing house for illegal substances. Later, the house would score further notoriety as the headquarters of an LSD-based religious cult. Coincidentally, her next door neighbour happened to be psychedelic chanteuse, Janis Joplin. Susan would often pop out to the porch at the rear of her house to listen in on one of Janis's numerous parties and occasional rehearsal sessions. Adding to the freakiness of the area, up the road lay the current headquarters of the Process Church.

It was early in November 1967 that Susan first met Charlie. He'd dropped in at the house one evening to score some drugs, and with his guitar coming along for the ride, he'd decided to try out a few of his tunes.

People quietened down as Charlie began to sing. Manson had the power to charm even the most stoned participant with his extraordinary presence, and a small circle of admirers formed around him. Despite being in the kitchen of the house, Susan couldn't fail to hear Charlie's unique music. Entranced, she wandered out to see who was responsible for the music. On witnessing this hobo-cum-siren delivering tunes from the lounge, Susan was instantly bowled over. 'Even before I saw him,' recalled Susan years later, 'his voice just hypnotised me, mesmerised me. Then, when I saw him, I fell in love with him ... '

Dressed in the familiar mode of a hippie chick, Susan had a good figure, with ample breasts and long black hair that bordered an impish smile. She moved well, impressively so. With marijuana smoke dominating the atmosphere, Manson's words began to take on a physical presence. Susan has recalled that the song he was playing was called, 'Sunshine of your Smile':

> The sunshine of your smile
> When you are gone,
> Will colour all my dreams
> And light the dawn.

Once Charlie had finished his song, his gaggle of new admirers congratulated him; none more so than Susan who, for reasons she couldn't explain, felt the need to bow down and kiss the musician's feet. While Manson's music was meant to be transcendental, it wasn't exactly something you could dance to. That didn't hinder Susan; she'd take any excuse to shake her stuff, lost most of the time in a soundtrack only she could hear.

When the party required raunchier sounds, the house's sound system was ignited, spilling forth tracks from the Doors' eponymous first album. Charlie rose from off the floor and whirled Susan around the room in a swirl of electric voodoo lounge. As the Doors began their trademark keyboard assents through 'Break on Through', the pair became locked in a frenzied dance, shocking some of the more comatose stoners with the way they slipped and slid across the floor. With Susan glued to his waist, the pair continued their primeval dance when everyone else had moved on.

'Suddenly, something happened that has no explanation,' Susan would later recall. 'I experienced a moment unlike any other. This stranger and I, dancing, passed through one another. It was as though my body moved closer and closer to him and actually passed through him.'

Although under normal circumstances, the action would have continued its way to a bedroom upstairs, Charlie, aware of the considerable power of the unexpected, held back and left. Susan, primed to expect the obvious, was simultaneously impressed and enchanted. 'It blew my mind because he was inside my head,' Susan recalled some years later. 'I knew at that time that he was something that I had been looking for.'

A couple of days later Charlie returned to the house and took Susan on a wander around the Haight. En route, he satisfied her newly smitten interest with tales of his extraordinary adventures. Widening her eyes further, he spoke of his putative success in the music world, and told Susan of his imminent relocation to Los Angeles to begin recording. Although the eighteen-year-old had already been through numerous suitors, no one had yet shown her any respect beyond the length of an orgasm. To Susan, Charlie's was a revelation. The pair soon repaired back to a nearby communal house. It was there that the inevitable finally occurred.

Unlike his previous conquests, Susan's feisty and insatiable demands dominated Charlie's not inconsiderable libido. Employing his now familiar coital routine, Charlie encouraged Susan to believe that she was making love to her father.

'I was eighteen,' Susan recalled in her memoir, 'but older inside. I was free. My father, brothers, and I were irreparably torn apart, it seemed. I had come close, but so far had found no substitute.

Charlie had instantly seemed more of a father to me than my own father.'

So swift was Susan's conversion, she immediately booked a place in Charlie's rambling caravan, by then getting ready to head south. Susan also roped in two friends, Ella Jo and Barbara, to come along for the ride. During that first week of November 1967, Susan met with her parole officer. She informed him that she was embarking on an evangelist tour with a preacher by the name of Charlie. For added effect, she mentioned that the caravan included a further six women and, potentially, a couple of males, and that their destination was Los Angeles. Her parole official was understandably sceptical about Susan's new plans, and an attempt to revoke her probation was completely stymied by her swift escape. In among the menagerie of lies she told the official, she had told the truth about one thing: Manson, his girls and his unborn child were off to Los Angeles, where Charlie was keen in call in an audition with Universal Studios. Buoyed up by his devoted harem, Manson felt ready for anything; even the bright lights of Hollywood.

chapter 4
Roll

'It's all in the eyes of a dreamer.
It's all in the eyes of a man.
All the things that we've done in life,
And all the things that we've planned.'

From 'Eyes Of A Dreamer' by Charles Manson

ITH the lights of San Francisco fading into the
distance, Manson's yellow and black bus made its way south.
While the vehicle was primarily following Charlie's stardust trail,
there were plenty of other distractions to keep everyone amused.
The trip doubled as a celebration of the group's newly defined
union and, passing through a patchwork of towns and villages,
the gang kept up their carousing. In amongst the throng of ready
bodies and impressionable minds, an easy, open-door policy was
maintained. Such was the fun they enjoyed en route; they didn't
arrive in Los Angeles until the end of November 1967.

'As we headed for LA,' recalled Charlie in 1986, 'the mansion
on wheels was getting smaller. Bodies and possessions were
everywhere, but there always seemed to be room for one more.'

A temporary base was soon established at San Jose, and, much
to Charlie's delight, Ruth Ann Morehouse managed to catch
them up. Following on from her earlier liaison with Manson,
she'd further enraged her parents by marrying a bus driver. It
later transpired that Charlie had told her that she needed to
get hitched to free herself from any legal parental restraints.
Following Manson's advice, Ruth Ann promptly dumped her new
man, and then headed off after Charlie and the girls. But word
of her reunion with Charlie soon reached the Morehouse family

home. Inflamed by Manson's duplicity the Reverend Morehouse went into a rage, vowing to retrieve his daughter, and at the same time, sort out Manson the cradle-snatcher.

Three days later, Morehouse managed to track Charlie down on the outskirts of Los Angeles. Incandescent with anger, the Reverend confronted both Manson and his daughter about their relationship. Charlie was prepared for this. He'd already played out his familiar father-sex mind-game, ensuring Ruth Ann's loyalty and her unconditional love. Raising her father's temperature considerably, Ruth Ann proclaimed: 'Daddy, I love Charlie. We made love together and I want to be with him.' At this, the Reverend flew into an apoplectic fit. Brandishing a gun, Morehouse called down fire and brimstone to punish Charlie for his treachery.

Using his peculiar brand of double-speak, Manson attempted to curtail the Reverend's anger. However, seeing there was little that he could do to stem Morehouse's evangelical tirade, Charlie sent one of the girls to fetch a couple of ice-cold sodas to cool the Reverend down. The show of hospitality worked; Morehouse put down his gun and took up Charlie's offer to talk things through. Charlie then suggested that the Reverend take one of his 'special' pills; remarking that it was good for reducing blood pressure. Morehouse obediently downed the tablet with a large gulp of soda. Soon, the Reverend began to slow down, becoming gradually more and more distracted.

Still unaware that the pill was a tab of LSD, Morehouse began to mellow further as the acid took hold. Charlie took the opportunity to fill in the Reverend about his own divinity, shared between the Devil and Jesus Christ. Under the spell of the drug, Morehouse became hugely receptive, and swiftly acknowledged that Manson was indeed the Second Coming. Pleased with his instant convert, Charlie suggested that Deane take some time out to contemplate on the enormity of what he had just been told. In his frazzled state, somewhere between Jerusalem and Los Angeles, Deane readily agreed and left.

However, within days Deane Morehouse was back. This time any thoughts of retrieving his errant daughter had been laid aside; what he wanted was more LSD, and more information about the gospel according to Charles Manson. Understandably,

Manson was delighted with the Reverend's chemical conversion. With Reverend Morehouse putty in his hand, Manson now had a psychedelic pastor to add to his collection of disparate souls.

Record producer Gary Stromberg was a prime mover in LA's entertainment industry, whose interests straddled both music and film. His connections in the rock world included such groups as the Doors, Three Dog Night and other Hollywood musical luminaries. It was through these dealings that Stromberg occasionally collided with Manson's old cell-mate Phil Kaufman, and it was through Phil that a connection with Charlie Manson was made. Stromberg maintained an office at Universal Studios in Hollywood, and he clearly remembers the day that Charlie arrived with his shambling caravan of admirers.

'I received a call one day from Charlie,' recalls Stromberg. 'He asked if there was anything I could do and, because he was a friend of Phil Kaufman, I invited him to come and see me at Universal Studios. And very shortly thereafter onto the [studio] lot arrived a yellow school bus containing Charlie and a handful of his young followers. Charlie came into my office, we talked for a bit. I was very much kind of in the same space as he was, in terms of my outlook and attitude to drugs and stuff. I understood this guy (I thought!). He started playing songs for me and the girls started dancing around, and getting high, and I was very enthused by this. He seemed to possess some talent.'

Although Stromberg was intrigued with Charlie, he alone couldn't make him a success. However, Gary knew that Universal had set up a new record label, Uni Records, its brief to exploit new and unusual talent. Stromberg called the head of the label, Russ Reagan, suggesting that Charlie might be suitable for their roster. Gary and Charlie then made the short trip over to Reagan's office for a swift audition, with Manson's girls naturally in tow. Charlie's entrance was highly idiosyncratic, sweeping Reagan's papers off his desk before leaping on top of it.

'Charlie was a combination of intimidating and ingratiating,' recalls Stromberg. 'He was wearing hippie regalia and he started teasing Russ, and he sat on Russ's desk, and started playing songs on his guitar, and Russ was looking at me like, "Who is this man?" Towards the end of this performance, he was improvising and making up songs as he went along ... At the end of this little charade, Russ said to me, "Well, I don't know what to say here, but if you want to go into a studio and do a demo, I'll pay for it."'

Stromberg timetabled a recording date for Charlie at the legendary Goldstar Studios in Hollywood that November. Even by 1967 standards, Goldstar had set an enormously high benchmark in record production, and was the preferred choice for heavyweights like Phil Spector and the Beach Boys.

Stromberg went in as producer for the session and, with a house engineer from Goldstar in the control booth, they were ready to commit Charlie to tape. Regardless of any recording studio etiquette, Manson turned up with his girls, who in preparation for the auspicious moment were heavily spiced on a variety of drugs.

Gary Stromberg: 'Charlie and the girls showed up and they were all very loaded, they were all taking drugs. They just went in there improvising. He had nothing planned. He started strumming and making up songs, and it was wild, and it was nuts. I was just listening in and laughing, I was having a good old time, listening to all this crazy stuff. But it was going on, and I had no concern about the time or how much this was costing. It went on for a while, and then into the studio Russ Reagan appears, and he peeks in and he sees this mayhem in the studio and he says, "What's going on here?" and I said, "I don't know, they're just doing what they're here to do."'

As financier of the session, Reagan was conscious that that someone should at least attempt to apply some sort of method to the madness, but, according to Stromberg, Charlie wasn't having any of it. He was in his stride, and was not going to allow anyone, least of all a record executive, to rein him in. Eventually, a time out was called, and Charlie and the girls were shepherded out of the studios while the engineer attempted to collate the fragments of songs into some semblance of order.

The tape was compiled overnight, and prepared for a preview with Russ Reagan and Garry Stromberg. Listening to this reel of songs and banter some forty-two years later, it offers a startling insight into the mind of Manson, offering a rare opportunity to hear the man before future events completely twisted his psyche into madness. Remarkably, the tapes are uninterrupted, allowing Charlie's nervous asides to be preserved intact. At one point, a clearly apprehensive Manson asks, 'Give me a little time. I'm not used to a lot of people.'

'And a lot of people aren't used to you,' retorts Stromberg with a chuckle.

'You should get a job making people nervous,' Charlie replies, self-consciously. At times, Stromberg is clearly trying to reassure the novice. 'Do whatever you feel like, man. Just groove and tell us when you want to start and we'll turn the machine on . . . You can check out what you want, and the rest you can chuck away.' During the first take of the session – the apocalyptic track 'Sick City' – Charlie breaks down, laughing, 'No, you want something happy.' He continues playing, again with his sharpened nerves punching holes in his vocals. 'If I can make myself nervous,' he says to one of the girls, 'I can make myself un-nervous!' With that, the assembled audience dissolves into a mass of guffaws.

From what can be gathered from the producer's instructions, Charlie was scheduled to deliver his material over a two-hour period. Below is the set list, gathered from the raw tapes from the session. While the titles are as fractured and disparate as Manson's persona, it is evident that he had a considerable catalogue of work ready to commit to tape:

> Sick City
> Devil Man
> The More You Love
> Two Pair of Shoes
> Maiden With Green Eyes (Remember Me)
> Swamp Girl
> Bet You Think I Care
> Look At Your Game Girl
> True Love You Will Find
> My World
> Invisible Tears
> This Is Night Life
> Run For Fun

The House of Tomorrow
Close To Me
She Done Turned Me In
Twilight Blues
Your Daddy's Home

While there is little that is overtly commercial, collectively the tracks present some interesting themes. Manson's singing is fairly competent throughout, but his guitar-playing transcends the predictable three- to four-chord sequences most singer-songwriters rely on. If there is one standout feature, it is the symbiotic rhythm that Manson simultaneously beats out on the strings, a furious percussion, born from years of busking.

Lyrically, the bulk of the songs show Manson's proclivity to revel in allegory and metaphor. However, one track offers an unambiguous and frank reflection of Charlie's inner psyche during 1967. It is listed as 'My World', and is a delicate, unusually self-deprecating portrait. Hard as it may seem to think of Manson as a sensitive soul, in the song he delivers a heartfelt summary of his suffering and remote positioning in society

My world is a sad world,
Often wondered if there's blame?
Such a fool in a mad, mad world.
With no pictures in my frame.

Everyone says crazy fool,
You're always gazing at the night.
With my arms around the tree,
Loving life with all my mind.

Crazy as I may seem,
Not knowing what to do.
Living with one crazy dream,
In a frank world of blue.

I awake every evening,
And somehow stumble through the night.
Such a fool in a mad world,
Loving life with all my mind.

My world is a sad world,
Often wondered if there's blame.
Such a fool in a mad, mad world.
With no pictures in my frame.

Loving you without a name.
With no love,
There's no one to blame.

While the tracks were delivered swiftly and with no over-dubs, the tape succeeds in capturing some of Manson's spirit. Between songs, the nervous wannabe pop star engages those present with his verbal repartee. Notably, there is a complete absence of any hostility and anger, lending an interesting counterweight to the myth of Manson as an untamed beast. While studio personnel later condemned Manson's unwillingness to abide by recording protocol, the preserved audio here offers little evidence that Charlie was playing any major mind-games. He sounds like a regular guy trying to break into the rock world.

The tape was delivered to Gary Stromberg at Universal Studios the following morning, then shuttled over to Russ Reagan's office for a preview. The notices were poor. 'We can't do anything with this,' Russ informed Gary, and in the cold light of day, Stromberg knew it too. Not eager to break the bad news to Charlie, Gary maintained a discreet distance. Not surprisingly, Manson was soon in touch. Gary deferred delivering a complete rejection, informing Charlie that if any suitable offers came along, he'd let him know.

Taking the producer's comments literally, Charlie maintained his shadowing of Stromberg at Universal, using any possible leverage to get him on board with his own adventures.

'Charlie tried to enlist me in his little merry band of psychos,' remembers Stromberg today. 'He came over to my house on a couple of occasions in Hollywood to see what I could do to help him. He also wanted me to hang out with him . . . '

With the possibility of any further recording in abeyance, and with Charlie hanging around, Stromberg was keen to divert Manson into other, less volatile creative avenues.

Aside from his musical endeavours, Stromberg's connection with Universal was as an aspiring film-maker. With the youth movie-market gathering considerable momentum during 1967, companies such as Universal, were keen to exploit the new genre, and had contracted young creative minds such as Stromberg to come up with any saleable ideas.

One project that was up for discussion was a modern-day adaptation of Christ's life – the story to be set in America's Deep South, and starring a black Jesus.

Gary Stromberg: 'Charlie somehow heard about this and he asked if he could be the consultant on this. He started sitting in with us while we talked over our story ideas. He assumed the role of Jesus, and with great authority told us how Jesus would have reacted to the circumstances and situations. I saw that he wasn't just thinking about this, he was really assuming the character and thinking that it was him. He was, in his own mind, Christ-like. I found it kind of fascinating, but at the same time, I found it kind of spooky.'

Charlie evidently milked the opportunities at Universal, and used his association with Stromberg to wangle other introductions. With the run of the studio lot, Manson ingratiated himself with a litany of Hollywood's best, many drawn in as much by Charlie as by his gaggle of attentive women. Not surprisingly, the party invitations began to mount up. With Manson believing he was on the cusp of a major recording deal, he easily fell in with the retinue of celebs, wannabes and star-fuckers. According to his own fragmented reflections, Charlie got it on with more than one household name he'd met at Universal, and for a while was paid to perform lewd acts with one of Hollywood's most famous couples. Additionally, he got a unique insight into the sordid machinations of certain quarters of Tinseltown, being privy to the S&M parties that were conducted behind many a locked gate.

It was during this time that Charlie began supplementing his income with, of all things, a job as a babysitter. Actor Al Lewis, most famous as 'Grandpa' in the popular TV series *The Munsters*, had three young boys. When he and his wife Marge went out they'd entrust Charlie with their children's care. 'He was a nice guy when I knew him,' Al Lewis recollects. 'He wanted to be in the music business. He needed money, and so I gave him a job babysitting my three kids. He didn't chop no heads off, he was very nice with me. I met him in front of the Whisky A Go Go on Sunset Boulevard. He sat for four or five hours, he amused the kids, he brought the guitar and he played, no big deal, no sweat.'

Still waiting for news of a recording deal, Charlie's parallel involvement in the movie business also fell on stony ground. He argued with Stromberg's production team over casting a black Christ character, something that clashed uncomfortably with Manson's strong views on race and religion. With no headway made in either music or film, Stromberg soon realised that Charlie had outstayed his welcome. Manson eventually confronted Stromberg and his wife at their Hollywood home over the failure of his recording dreams, and stormed out in a huff. Stromberg was only too happy to be free of Manson's sponging.

'Although he had a dynamic personality,' Stromberg remarked, 'Charlie was a street hustler, and he learned how to survive on the street, and he could play you. He could look in your eyes, and he could figure out where your weaknesses were. He could really play you.'

While Charlie felt aggrieved at Hollywood's rejection, the bus continued its merry meander around Los Angeles. With a dozen or so bodies crammed under its roof, the group decided that something a little more accommodating was required. Through a connection from Anton LaVey's Church of Satan, Charlie found a suitable pad in Malibu, The owner, known as 'Gina', had allegedly been a leading light in California's dark side, and had been courted by Charlie during one of his many recces around San Francisco. She apparently excelled in all varieties of hedonistic behaviour, and had been taken with Manson's grasp of many disciplines.

Aware that Charlie and girls were heading southwards, Gina invited Manson to use her property as a base. It was a timely offer, as the group were currently camped under a railway bridge near Malibu.

The property that Manson and the girls were to occupy looked as though it had slid off a movie set. Teetering perilously on the side of a small hill overlooking the Pacific Coast highway, the property had already moved several feet away from its original setting. Inside, it was a botanist's paradise, as wild flowers and other plants pushed their way through the foundations. As if to further qualify its organic provenance, a small stream ran through the ground floor of the house, bordered by sand and rocks. The interior's primary feature was a staircase that wound its way up through the middle of the house to the higher floors. One of Charlie's girls swiftly christened the place 'Spiral Staircase', a name that soon stuck with everyone.

Local authorities had wanted to condemn what remained of the house. In fact, it was only still standing because no one had been able to find Gina to serve her the demolition papers. Given its shambolic condition, Gina was happy for Charlie and the women to stay in the property rent-free. Her only condition was that they maintained an open-door policy at all times.

'I [didn't] know much about the history of the place,' Manson recalled in 1986. 'But long before we arrived there, it had become a meeting place, a party house, a freak-out pad and, for some, a hideout. Its isolated location served a lot of purposes for a lot of different people... Some far-out, spaced-out, weird people were frequent visitors.'

The property carried an exotic reputation as a halfway house between 'earth and the universe', and there were many that dropped by to check that the chaos was being actively maintained. With music, sex and drugs on offer, thrill-seekers of all kinds turned up to indulge. According to Charlie, in addition to the usual hedonists, several pillars of Hollywood society were often to be seen indulging in their preferred perversions. One reported visitor was Processian in Chief, Robert DeGrimston; while Charlie has never confirmed DeGrimston's presence in the Spiral Staircase property, Katie has since said that associates of a satanic cult once visited the house, led, as she recalls, by a 'blond-haired Englishman'.

Aside from the alleged sex orgies and drug parties, there were other, more bizarre activities that stretched even the Manson gang's broad consciousnesses. One well-dressed man, apparently a respectable businessman, had a particularly terrifying kink. His preferred thrill was to throw himself out of a top-floor window, land in the creek bed some twenty feet below, and then repeat the performance time and time again until he was too sore to continue.

Another visitor to the house was Bobby Beausoleil, who was now staying close to the Spiral Staircase, and couldn't have failed to have heard the electrical mayhem spilling out of it. One night Beausoleil dropped by to check out the action. In 1999 he spoke to journalist Michael Moynihan, recalling his initial impressions of meeting Manson at the house.

'I just wandered over there and it was Charlie Manson singing and playing guitar, and there were some other guys and some girls. I sat down, I listened for a while, and I picked up this thing called a melodica. It's designed on the same concept as a harmonica, except it has keys. There was one sitting on the table next to me, and I picked it up and started improvising some counterpoint melodies, which kind of blew everyone's mind – maybe they were all loaded on acid. I played along for a little while and checked out what was going on, then I left.'

The activities within the Spiral Staircase could easily upstage the maddest scene of the most avant-garde movie, and occasionally the action spilled out onto the beach. An eyewitness who wishes to remain anonymous, was privy to one of these alfresco fandangos and recalls an incident that highlights Charlie's remarkable ability to wrong-foot any possible negativity.

'Charlie was on the beach leading this sing-along with the girls and they're all dancing around. And some guy walked up to him and said, "You know what man, you're really full of shit. You're singing about all this love and not having all these possessions and all this, and look, you drive up in this big school bus. Y'know you're just a hypercritic [sic]." And Charlie said to him, "You want my bus?" and the guy looked at Charlie, and now everyone's looking at this guy, and he said, "Yeah, I want that bus." And Charlie said, "Here man, here's the bus," and he gave him the keys ... So the guy started walking towards the bus, and he turned around and came back and gave Charlie the keys. And he said, "I didn't want the bus man, I just wanted to see where you were at."'

As well as these amusing interludes, at night the beach hosted much darker activities. Manson has since recalled a shift within the group mindset after Charlie and the girls were exposed to some of their guests' more disturbing occult behaviour. It's apparent that Charlie's love of animals clashed sharply with some of the satanic sacrifices allegedly taking place, and after a while they decided it was becoming far too heavy.

Charles Manson: 'I think I can honestly say our philosophy – fun and games, love and sex, peaceful friendship for everyone – began changing into the madness that eventually engulfed us in that house.'

While the Spiral Staircase had offered a base of sorts, the freaky atmosphere ultimately spooked the tribe out of staying there on a permanent basis. Instead they returned to the school bus which, although cramped, could easily accommodate most of the gang. Manson also scored some parachutes and army tents to cater for any stray bodies not fortunate enough to get a place inside the bus.

The bus was frequently pulled over by the police and, tiring after a while of the constant intrusion, one of the tribe scrawled 'Fuck the Man' along the bus's side, provoking even more hassle from the police. To evade suspicions, Charlie decided on a less conspicuous colour scheme for the exterior. He had obtained a large consignment of black spray paint from a gang of bikers. With help from the girls and a few other freewheeling conspirators, the vehicle was transformed. Such was their zeal to make over the vehicle, the passenger windows also underwent a monochrome paint wash. The cheerful old bus had gone; in its place stood a sinister-looking dark van, with blacked-out windows.

Charlie had planned to write 'Hollywood Productions' on the side of the bus, to give them an appearance of a film crew en route to some location – a not unusual sight in California. A French girl who was hanging out with them offered to help. Although adept in lettering, her English was less confident, and she inscribed 'Holywood [sic] Productions' across the side of the bus. It was a highly ironic misspelling, especially given the amount of preaching and lecturing that was to accompany the van on its travels. The multi-talented Bobby Beausoleil also helped out on the redecoration, adorning the paintwork with a 'Goat of Mendes' design.

With few regrets about leaving the Spiral Staircase, the gang took off again on yet another protracted odyssey up to the north of California. As life on the road afforded plenty of opportunities for lounging, partying and little in the way of discipline, Charlie's following began to grow at a considerable rate. Many fellow travellers hung out with the caravan for a few weeks, while others stayed for just a few days before disappearing off.

With the bus traversing the fringes of Hollywood, they'd often collide with people connected with television or the big screen. One such was Deirdre, daughter of the famous actress Angela Lansbury. After chancing upon the bus on one of its numerous trawls of the district, Deirdre and her friend Nancy Pitman hopped on board.

While Deirdre saw the Manson episode as a fleeting adventure, Nancy viewed her induction as nothing less than a call to arms. She'd grown up in relative affluence in Malibu, one of three children born to socialite parents. The seventeen-year-old found life in the conventional family setting tiresome and predictable. She'd later remark: 'I had nothing to keep me there. It wasn't a family; we just occupied the same house.' Not surprisingly, she leapt aboard the Manson bus with considerable enthusiasm. And, like those who made up the hardcore of the group, she underwent a name change, becoming Brenda McCann – the new identity serving to distance her from her family life.

Like Brenda, Dianne Lake was another slender, pretty LA girl, with a mass of auburn hair. She was only fourteen when she first encountered Charlie and the girls, yet already she'd led a fairly hectic and unconventional life. Like a lot of the runaway flower children, Dianne was one who had developed quickly, as if hot-house grown. She had spent the early 1960s being dragged by her progressive parents from commune to commune in search of the good life. At one point in early 1968, Dianne went up to Haight-Ashbury with a boyfriend. Also on the road were Dianne's parents, who'd ended up in the Mojave Desert. During their retreat in Mojave, the couple had met up with Charlie and the girls, and, like many, were very taken with them. 'My mum was really impressed,' recalls Dianne. 'They had some sort of a psychic experience out in the desert, and they just thought that this was cool.' In between mystical moments, the couple proudly showed Charlie young Dianne's photograph, and Charlie asked if he could keep it. Smitten by her untamed beauty, Manson planned a mission to San Francisco in an attempt to try and find her.

Dianne's parents had a base of sorts at the Hog Farm commune, situated just outside Hollywood in the Verdugo Hills. During the desert trip, they'd invited Manson and the tribe over to the commune. Dominated by the larger-than-life 'Wavy Gravy' (a.k.a. Hugh Romany), the Hog Farm collective had established itself as a successful example of community living. Although the Hog Farmers enthusiastically embraced the acid culture of 1967, they were keen to transform psychedelic imagery into something more demonstrable. With a sizeable dose of humour mixed in with their ambitions (Gravy himself was a part-time clown), the extended 'family' of the Hog Farm created a lasting impression on all they met. As their altruistic aims came with the promise of much hilarity along the way, the commune was a much-needed antidote to the lofty pretensions spewing from some of the higher echelons of the counterculture.

Despite his cynicism about hippie culture, Manson could easily don a new guise, especially if it meant advancing his own celebrity. With Dianne Lake's parents' invite still rattling round his head, Manson took the bus out for a ride to touch base with the commune, and hopefully recruit some new converts. At the Hog Farm's rambling premises, Charlie mooched around with the girls, sharing songs and, apparently, attempting to persuade everyone (including Wavy's wife) to hop a ride with them later. 'He'd play the guitar, he had songs, he had a jail patois,' recalls Wavy today. 'A lot of people were taken with him.' At some point during the day, Manson and his tribe interrupted a group mantra session that Wavy Gravy and other Hog Farm members were holding.

Wavy Gravy remembers: 'We were all gathered in a circle chanting "Om" when Manson drove up with his "wives" in that black bus. Charlie leant out of the window and he started choking and holding his throat. His women were also leaning out of the bus and shouting, "Stop! Stop! Stop!" And so we stopped. Charlie then jumped out of the bus and went to the centre of our circle. There, he started putting our scene down in no uncertain terms. I don't know what happened, but something inside me made me bigger than I am, and I rose up and told him to get out! And he just walked off and left! He was the only person I really kicked off the Hog Farm. I'm happy he didn't take it personally!'

But unbeknownst to Wavy, Charlie got exactly what he wanted out of Hog Farm: a connection with Dianne Lake. After returning from San Francisco, she'd been living at Hog Farm off and on with a surrogate family, but wasn't too comfortable within the collective. With Charlie extending an invite to Dianne's guardians to come over to the tribe's current bolt hole in Topanga Canyon, he was confident that Dianne would come too.

Dianne Lake remembers her arrival there. 'When I walked in, all these girls were saying "Charlie Charlie, she's here, she's here." They made me feel like a princess, like a queen . . . I was just like in shock, like how did they know? And it turns out that he had met my parents, and my mother had given him a picture of me, and told him I was in San Francisco. They had actually gone to San Francisco looking for me! They made me feel I was a part of them and felt really, really special.'

Such was the spirit of the times that fourteen-year-old Dianne was able to join Charlie and the women with no interference from parents, surrogate or otherwise. She soon became a popular addition to the group, and was rechristened 'Snake'. The nickname was not, as has been repeatedly claimed over the years, on account of any viper-like movements she made during group sex sessions, but because of her particular way of moving and the simple fact that it rhymed with her surname.

Whilst Dianne Lake was a seasoned commune dweller, other Manson followers came from far more conventional settings. Sandra Good was twenty-four years old when she first met Manson. The youngest of three girls born into the socialite enclaves of North California, she had battled with serious health problems for most of her early years, before having to endure her parents' separation. While her father indulged his youngest daughter's every wish, Sandra's mother – busy with children from her new relationship – struggled to cope with her demanding daughter.

Bright and instinctive, Sandra attended the University of Oregon and graduated with a degree in English Literature. She then transferred over to San Francisco State College where she continued studying Spanish and then Marine Biology. Between studies, she lived with her sister and worked as a sales assistant at San Francisco's big Emporium department store, selling scarves and headbands. Like many of her generation, she'd involved herself with civil rights causes, and was an active voice for social change. She'd come across Manson and the girls during one of their trips to San Francisco in early 1968. Such was her fascination with the gang that she'd talked a friend into accompanying her down to Los Angeles to hitch up with them. The pair flew to LA in a private plane, and then hired a car to track down Manson.

Sandra's joy at her alliance with Charlie and the girls was such that she reportedly handed over $6,000 of her own savings into the collective coffers. Although her parents were confused by her disappearance, Sandra ensured that her $2,000 monthly trust-fund cheques from her father were transferred over to maintain the tribe's needs. Such was the power of her belief in Manson that she claimed that her health issues were instantaneously cured as soon as she met him.

Unlike most of the malleable souls in Charlie's circle, Sandra's confident, steely mindset – reflected by her cobalt eyes and fiery red hair – required careful steering. Although she was clearly infatuated with the scene, she still stuck rigidly to her own standards, sometimes infuriating Charlie in the process. Whilst Manson forbade his women to wear make-up, she continued to use it. When he discovered she was taking birth control pills – a considerable crime in his books – Manson swiped them and trampled them underfoot. When it came to her later pregnancy, Good would again assert her independence. Ignoring Manson's edict that 'doctors are only good for curing the clap', Good insisted on having her baby in hospital. Furthermore, she temporarily moved in with her father following the delivery, to receive medical aftercare. These defiant acts aside, 'Sandy', as she was best known, became Manson's most determined and sustained ally, whose loyalty was unswerving.

During these formative days with the group, Sandra maintained contact with her boyfriend – Joel Dean Pugh, a twenty-six-year-old physician's son from Minnesota. From what is known, Pugh remained firmly on the fringes of Manson's circle. However, tragic events in London in 1969 would cast a dark shadow over his brief association with Charlie's gang.

Sandy Good had found Charlie and the girls nesting in Topanga, where the bus had completely ground to a halt. Their extended travels had taken its toll on the vehicle, and it was seriously in need of repair. Not that it bothered Charlie; he felt at home in the deciduous environs of Topanga Canyon, its offbeat atmosphere wholly receptive to the musicians and drifters that gravitated there. By 1968 Topanga was well established as an organic retreat of some note. Neil Young, a later acolyte of Charlie's, was a local, as was singer Linda Rondstadt. In addition, the band Spirit (which Charlie would often look in on during rehearsals) and Canned Heat maintained a presence in the area. At the core of the music community was the 'Topanga Corral', a roadhouse bar and club, that hosted regular gigs attracting many rock luminaries.

Since his 'escape' from San Francisco, Bobby Beausoleil had become a popular resident in Topanga. Here, he and Manson began formulating plans for musical collaboration. In need of somewhere to service the bus, Manson approached Bobby for temporary living space in the grounds of his house at 19844 Horseshoe Lane. The property had previously been used as a base for a pornographic film company, and it maintained a sleazy ambience that was as rancid as the green slime that covered its unkempt swimming pool. With Beausoleil moving between the property and a basement belonging to his music-teacher friend Gary Hinman, he agreed to let Manson and his girls have free run of the place.

The atmosphere at Horseshoe Lane wasn't new to Bobby – by this point he'd already been intimately involved with the film-making process. His unique personality had already been vividly captured in the 1967 documentary, *Mondo Hollywood*, and he went on to take a more challenging role in a soft-porn film, charmingly entitled *The Ramrodder*. Quite by chance, sometime in early 1968, Beausoleil had been living in a tepee close to where the picture was to be shot. One of the production team had chanced upon Bobby's encampment while scouting for locations and, suitably impressed by Beausoleil's al fresco abilities, commissioned him to construct a few set-ups for *The Ramrodder's* exteriors. Given Bobby's boyish looks, it wasn't long before he was taken on in an acting capacity as an Indian chief. Shot on a minuscule budget with little in the way of a storyline, *The Ramrodder* relies heavily on the spectacle of a few randy cowboys making out with various scantily clad girls.

During the shoot, Beausoleil met Catherine Share, a pretty actress who'd been cast as 'Cochina', an innocent squaw caught up in the mayhem. Her most controversial scene in *The Ramrodder* found her being raped by some of the cowboys. As the atmosphere on the film became more chaotic, Catherine, Beausoleil, and his partner Gail would remove themselves from the set, and retreat to calmer territories. They in turn introduced her to Charlie.

Born in Paris in the midst of the Second World War, Catherine Share was immersed in drama from the very start of her life. Both her Hungarian father and her mother, who was of German extraction, were involved in the French Resistance movement; while they managed to elude capture by the Nazi occupiers, towards the end of war they killed themselves in an act of revolutionary suicide. Their daughter was passed from orphanage to orphanage until, at the age of eight, Catherine was fostered by an American psychologist and his wife, who took her over to California.

Despite her fractured start in life, Catherine excelled in her studies. Like her father, she became adept at playing the violin, lending credence to the Romany alter ego she adopted in later years. Sadly, history repeated itself during her teens, when Catherine's foster mother killed herself during the final stages of terminal cancer. Meanwhile her foster-father's failing sight meant that by now he required constant care. Despite the hardship, Catherine would pursue a course in music, but ended up dropping out a year into her degree.

Following her brief spell at university, Catherine married, but the relationship didn't last the distance and the couple soon split up. With few options available, she began accepting bit parts in movies, *The Ramrodder* being her biggest part to date. Disenchanted by her experiences in the porn industry, when fellow actor Beausoleil introduced her to Charlie, she felt as though she'd found a safe haven. On account of her swarthy skin, shock of black hair and fiddle-playing skills, Share soon became 'Gypsy', one of Manson's prime warriors.

While Manson had plenty of female acolytes, few males were drawn towards Charlie in the same way. One exception was eighteen-year-old Paul Watkins. The epitome of a roaming flower child, Watkins possessed great potential, and yet, like many of the acid generation, had found it difficult to assimilate himself into conventional society. Prior to his first life-changing meeting with the Manson tribe, Paul had witnessed the Family bus darting around Topanga Canyon, and he'd noted the funny black box that looked like a large hat wobbling around on the roof.

Watkins was yet another teenage soul in search of some meaning to his existence. His father had worked in the petrochemical industry, and Paul had grown up in the Middle East before the family settled in Southern California. Like many of those drawn to Manson, religion was an important part of his childhood. His parents were devout Methodists, and, like Manson before him, Paul enjoyed the singing that accompanied church services. He developed an active interest in music. Later, in his teens, he took his commitment to Christ several stages further, absorbing himself in evangelical worship and study. Gradually, an interest in drugs began to outweigh his Christian aspirations. Soon, he abandoned his studies and became, by his own admission, 'a fugitive flower child in search of enlightenment and truth.' Eschewing conventional work, Watkins ambled around the suburbs of California, playing songs and looking for something or someone to believe in.

Watkins first collided with his destiny on Monday 18 March 1968, when Paul hitched up to Topanga Canyon looking for an old friend. When he arrived at the house of his pal, it was Dianne Lake and Brenda who answered the door. Watkins was disappointed to find that his pal had moved on, but his nose easily detected the sickly sweet aroma of marijuana wafting out from inside. Paul was ushered in. Holding court in the centre of the room, Manson was playing his guitar, while Bruce Davis, newly arrived from his own odyssey of discovery, was the only other male among twelve young women. With a warm smile, Charlie invited Paul to stay and 'make music' with them.

Watkins needed little encouragement to stay the night, what with the copious amounts of flesh, music and drugs freely on offer. He left the following morning, seemingly unmoved by the experience. Yet on a subconscious level, something had registered deeply with him. Later he recalled, 'He was fascinating and I became addicted to him ... The fact that he controlled all these young women that I was fascinated with was fascinating! But then, how he was able to do that fascinated me. I was interested in how he was able to do that. I was also interested in the music. He was very talented and animated and he seemed shamelessly uninhibited. He was a trip!'

While Paul planned to continue his wanderings around Southern California, the siren call of Charlie and his women meant that he soon returned to join the group. Once fully under Manson's wing, Watkins became 'Little Paul', Charlie's prime sidekick, and sensory ear to the generation Manson most wanted to snare.

Paul Watkins acknowledges: 'I became his mirror, reflecting the emergence of the flower child in him, the emergence of his own long-stifled love.'

On 1 April 1968, Mary Brunner gave birth to Manson's child, conceived during their first flush of love the previous summer in San Francisco. Although Manson decreed that absolutely no medical care should be given at the birth, Mary was allowed to use marijuana to ease the pain.

For the delivery, Mary was suspended in the air, both legs akimbo. With little drama, the child dropped into the arms of Charlie and all the other members of the group. Such was their delight, they held a party in honour of their collective first offspring. Seeing as Charlie was still obsessed by Heinlein's *Stranger in a Strange Land*, the infant was christened, after the book's protagonist, Valentine Michael Smith. And so, on April Fool's day of 1968, Michael Valentine Manson became the group's first tangible product. The girls nicknamed the little mite 'Pooh Bear', in honour of their woodland environment.

With child-rearing duties now an essential daily part of their rituals, the group started referring to themselves as a 'Family', something they took to with consummate ease.

Unbeknownst to Charlie (but perhaps following the same cosmic thought-line), hippie extraordinaire Mel Lyman had also established a commune that called itself 'The Family'. Based on the East Coast of America, Lyman – a musician and self-styled, 'world saviour' – had collected together a group of adoring acolytes and was living in communal harmony. In fact Lyman's 'Family' shared much of Charlie's group's uniformity and devotion to its leader, Lyman also comparing himself to Christ and other deities. One major difference was Charlie's racial absolutism. Despite the free sharing of affections, Manson's one rule was that any lovemaking should not go across racial boundaries; something that had become a minor obsession with him.

During this happy, halcyon period, Charlie decided to reignite his musical career in earnest. With Beausoleil sharing in the Family's daily activities, there was plenty of time to jam and bullshit about future glories. One of these proposed projects culminated in the forming of the Milky Way, a grafting of the Manson/Beausoleil talent into one musical unit. With Charlie and Bobby rehearsing feverishly, other musicians arrived to augment their talents, and soon a six-piece band was established. Reportedly, one of these musicians was music teacher Gary Hinman, a native of Topanga. Eventually the Milky Way managed to secure a booking at the legendary Topanga Corral club. However, despite the support of all of Charlie's loving contingent, the spaced-out sonics of the band drove most of the regulars out of the club. They were not booked again.

As was becoming the norm, circumstances soon required this newly defined Family to move on. However it seemed that the beneficent forces around Charlie and his acolytes would always reward them with a new place to hang out. While they'd spent time in a ramshackle collection of squats and houses over the last few months, they were soon to be elevated into the highest echelons of celebrity living.

Despite Charlie's well-reported dictatorship, in reality the Family remained, at this point, an organic, easy-going entity. Several of the girls would occasionally trip off for the day, or even longer if the mood took them. While the bus was not normally available to anyone other than Charlie, the rest of the Family happily embraced their default mode of transport: hitching. On one sunny spring day in early April 1968, Katie and Ella Jo Bailey were enjoying an amble through Malibu. While standing at the kerbside with thumbs aloft, a gleaming red Ferrari pulled up. Inside was a suave young man, with cool blue eyes and wavy golden hair. With him was a member of his house staff; the pair were reportedly off to the mountains to enjoy an LSD trip. The girls eagerly climbed into his car. It was little surprise when their attractive new friend announced that he was a card-carrying rock and roller. His name was Dennis Wilson, one third of rock's first family of musicians, and drummer in the Beach Boys.

The middle of the three talented Wilson brothers, Dennis shared his siblings' ambitions to break into the music industry. While they went on to form one of pop's most famous fraternal bands, the Beach Boys were no overnight success. In fact the band's smiley image belied a childhood littered with upset. The boys' father and manager, Murry Wilson, was bitterly resentful of his own failings in the music industry, and reacted to his children's success with great anger and occasional bouts of violence – frequently directed at Dennis.

Ironically, Murry's jealous reaction only helped propel his sons towards stardom. Brian Wilson, the Beach Boys' principal songwriter, drew on his father's bitterness to imbue the group's sound with an underlying sadness. Brian's skilful mastering of agony and ecstasy added a qualitative dimension to their songs that few could emulate.

The Beach Boys' early music rode a wave of popularity around the globe, but by 1966, the band had abandoned their carefree tunes in favour of more spiritual and insightful lyrics. While the group had scored a critical hit with Brian Wilson's opus, *Pet Sounds*, their next album, entitled *Smile*, pushed Brian's fragile nervous system to the brink of a major collapse. Ultimately, Brian's attempt to remould the narrow pop formula would take nearly forty years to see daylight; all it did in 1967 was to drive an enormous wedge between the band members. While Dennis was wholly in tune with Brian's ideas, other sections of the Beach Boys were more muted in their response. Vocalist Mike Love believed that the pretensions of *Smile* would only alienate their core audience which, he believed, identified with their trademark sound. Under immense pressure, Brian gave up on *Smile*, and went off into a spiral of depression that would take more than two decades to shake off.

With *Smile* shelved indefinitely and two patchy recordings wholly slammed by the critics, in the spring of 1968 the group went back into the studio to lay down some demos for a new album, optimistically entitled *Friends*. These new tracks were a world away from the obtuse, fragmented sound bites that had muddied their previous two albums, and were milder and less ambitious. They had recently been introduced to transcendental meditation and this influenced their new sound. Dennis was the first Beach Boy to meet with the discipline's prime exponent, the Maharishi. The swami had instructed Dennis to 'Live your life to the fullest' – an edict Dennis followed with considerable gusto. Other members of The Beach Boys would in turn immerse themselves in meditation, singer Mike Love travelling to India to study the philosophy with the Beatles. As a result of this introspection, a gentle simplicity infused the group's music.

With Brian Wilson incapacitated by paranoia and drug abuse, each member of the group now had to contribute songs to fill the new album. Dennis's first forays into song-writing produced some remarkable tracks. His time, it seemed, had now come, and bolstered by the impressive results, his confidence was sky-high. Regardless of Brian Wilson's slow withdrawal, the sounds emanating from the group were compelling, with Dennis now a fellow innovator rather than just a pretty drummer boy.

While Dennis dug the new mood enveloping the group, he nonetheless maintained his partying and revelry around

Hollywood; running wild with likes of Terry Melcher, Doris Day's son. Terry had also tried his hand at performing, although in the end his skills found better use in production. During the mid-1960s, he'd produced several of the Byrds' early hits, before going on to produce acts such as the Mamas & the Papas and Paul Revere and the Raiders. Through his work he met Dennis Wilson, with whom he shared an insatiable interest in the opposite sex. Song-writing pal Gregg Jakobson was another one of Dennis's close retinue of friends. He later helped draw out Wilson's burgeoning songwriting skills, and would provide a reliable sounding board for many of his later projects.

To confirm their status as successful young Hollywood players, Wilson, Jakobson and Melcher formed a group called the Golden Penetrators, and revelled in their ability to charm a legion of beautiful women into partying with them.

Katie and Ella Jo were mightily impressed with Dennis, and were equally pleased when he agreed to drop them off at their destination, one of the girls leaving her purse behind in the back seat like a latter-day Cinderella. A few days later on Thursday 11 April, the girls were out hitching when their Prince Charming came across them again. This time Dennis took the excited girls back to his sumptuous manor in Beverly Hills, at 14400 Sunset Boulevard.

Parking the Ferrari in the driveway alongside his brown Rolls-Royce, Dennis took the girls on a tour of his manor. Set in over three acres of woodland, eucalyptus trees filled the air with their heavy aroma. The single-level property was styled like a rambling cowboy's ranch and fashioned in pine. In addition to its twenty rooms, the property also housed several separate servants' quarters. The centrepiece of the grounds was an enormous swimming pool, shaped like the state of California.

Inside, it was no less ostentatious, with gold discs and other awards from the Beach Boys' illustrious career displayed everywhere. Wilson's mirrored bedroom was equally flashy, with its huge sunken tub taking pride of place. The property was a fair measure of the man's success, but it had come at a price; Dennis maintained a steely resolve to prove himself as more than just the drummer of the band.

Inevitably, Dennis steered the girls into his bedroom for a marathon session between the sheets. In between the hanky-panky, the girls would constantly refer to Charlie, something that intrigued and then annoyed Dennis, his celebrity status challenged by such reverential references to another performer.

Later that day, Dennis got himself together in preparation for an evening recording with the rest of the Beach Boys, their first in a long while. Dennis magnanimously let the girls take their time sorting themselves out before they left. It was an unwritten rule in the groupie handbook of etiquette not to outstay your welcome, and most star-fuckers knew their place. Katie and Ella Jo made their way back to Charlie, bubbling with excitement. Over in Brian Wilson's studio, Dennis regaled the other Beach Boys with tales of his double conquest.

Charlie was impressed with the girls' exploits with the Beach Boy, but he has since recalled that he'd crossed paths with Dennis on at least two previous occasions. The first was at a seedy dope-house in San Francisco in late 1967, where he bumped into Wilson while both were scoring. After some perfunctory small talk, Dennis extended an invitation for Charlie to drop by if he happened to be in Los Angeles. More recently, Manson remembered meeting him at Elvis Presley's Bel Air mansion during a poker game. The claim that Manson hobnobbed with the King has never been substantiated, although with Charlie's sinuous movements around Hollywood, anything is possible.

Whatever the true genesis of the connection between Dennis and the Manson Family, it is evident that, following Katie and Ella Jo's afternoon romp with Dennis, the black bus rattled and coughed its way down the drive towards Sunset Boulevard. Without so much as a by-your-leave, Charlie and the girls entered the rock star's house, and made themselves fully at home. After living on the bus for so long, it was pure luxury to lounge about in Dennis's sumptuous home. With Wilson busy till the early hours of the morning, there was ample time for the Family to make themselves comfortable.

Wholly adept at spotting potential weaknesses, Manson knew that Dennis's prime desires were drugs and a regular supply of women – the wilder the better. Aware that Dennis was in the midst of a divorce from his wife, Carol, Charlie ensured that all the girls were in the most receptive state possible for Dennis's arrival. With a dozen or so of his women provocatively displayed, the welcoming party was designed to appeal to Dennis's primary needs. The air was thick with marijuana and incense; the sound system was pumping with the sounds of the Beatles. Charlie had naturally brought along his guitar - an audition with someone from the highest echelon of rock stardom was far too good an opportunity to miss. The stage was set for Dennis Wilson's return.

chapter 5
Home

'So burn all your bridges,
Leave your old life behind,
You can be what you want to be,
Just don't let your mamma find you.'

> From 'Your Home Is Where You're Happy'
> by Charles Manson

DENNIS Wilson finished the recording session at around 3 a.m. The night had been a fairly typical one, with twenty-seven takes of the jaunty song 'Busy Doin' Nothing' taped. As The Beach Boys left to go their separate ways, Dennis travelled the short distance from brother Brian's studio to his house on Sunset Boulevard. The absurdity of the of the black school bus parked in his driveway would have been impossible for Dennis to miss.

Once out of his car, Dennis was surprised to hear the Beatles blasting out of his own stereo system and the house's lights casting a tangle of shadows across the lawn. Bewildered, he wandered around to the rear of the property to see what was happening. It was at that minute that Charlie stepped out of the kitchen door. Despite his lanky frame dwarfing Manson by more than fifteen inches, Wilson was still apprehensive about the cocky apparition heading in his direction. As Charlie got within spitting distance, Dennis called out, 'Are you going to hurt me?' In response, the interloper just smiled his beatific grin, replying, 'Do I look as though I am going to hurt you?' With that, Manson dropped to his knees and began kissing Wilson's white canvas trainers. Of late, this had become Charlie's preferred way of greeting people he wanted to impress. There was method in his madness, as the reverential gesture short-circuited Dennis's adrenaline rush, and put his mind at ease.

Charlie led Dennis into the house to show him what he and the girls had prepared for his return. While the Beach Boy noted Katie and Ella Jo's presence, his eyes bulged further at the sight of all Charlie's other women sprawled around. They had evidently been busy helping themselves to his food and liquor. To divert his host's attention, Charlie took Dennis aside and set to work softening him up. With any animosity erased, the pair rapped and jammed together through the night.

If Dennis thought that Charlie and the girls were just 'passing through', he couldn't have been more wrong. Compared to their previous ramshackle abodes, life under the Wilson roof was infinity more appealing. In return, the girls provided a non-stop supply of drugs and sexual pleasures that easily endeared them to their host.

Initially, Dennis turned a blind eye as the girls ransacked his wardrobe of fancy clothes, cutting them into makeshift dresses and other billowy costumes for their own use. Soon other personal items began to disappear as the Family embedded themselves. Dennis would also become painfully aware of the more antisocial aspects of all this indiscriminate partying. Given the fevered use he'd made of Charlie's harem, it was difficult for him to deny the girls cash to cure their assortment of venereal diseases. When the bill came in from his Beverley Hills physician, Wilson mused that it was 'probably the largest gonorrhoea bill in history.' Soon, other medical bills started to roll in as the some of the women took the opportunity to have their teeth fixed up courtesy of Wilson's generosity.

Lost in Manson's kaleidoscopic world, Dennis's vision was becoming blurred. Charlie took the opportunity to lean on Dennis, enlisting his help to fulfil his long-held dream of becoming a rock star. With the girls acting as highly attractive collateral, Wilson was force-fed Charlie's sweet tunes and psychobabble lyrics. LSD acted as a very powerful catalyst, and Dennis became totally absorbed by Manson's music. Wilson soon started raving about Charlie to the other Beach Boys at brother Brian's studio. The group were used to Dennis's wild enthusiasms, but still they were keen to hear what all the fuss was about. Even Dennis's mother Audree popped over to Sunset Boulevard to check out the new incumbents. Like many in the Beach Boys' extended family, she found Manson a kindly, if slightly eccentric soul.

With Charlie's recording adventures at Universal ending prematurely, he would have been very aware that the Beach Boys had established their own label, Brother Records. In tandem with a growing desire for the group to assert some independence in their business affairs, there was a plan for Brother Records (like the Beatles' Apple venture) to scout out new talent. Intoxicated with Manson's presence, Dennis went public with his 'discovery' of Charlie in May 1968, during an interview with the hip magazine, *Rave*. Whilst the feature took a broad overview of life in the Beach Boys' camp that year, some of Dennis Wilson's remarks to reporter Keith Altham reveal how deeply he was sunk into Manson's world.

Keith Altham: 'You live your life in an apparently fearless manner, but is there anything that frightens you?'

Dennis Wilson: 'Fear is nothing but awareness. I was only frightened as a child because I did not understand fear – the dark, being lost, what was under the bed! It came from within ... Sometimes the Wizard frightens me – Charlie Manson, who is another friend of mine who says he is God and the devil! He sings, sings, plays and writes poetry and may be another artist for Brother Records.'

Keith Altham: 'Did you ever want to do anything else other than be a drummer?'

Dennis Wilson: 'I wanted to join the forest commission – have my own trees to look after, the peace of a piece of land. I wanted to be a gardener and skipper of a boat.'

Keith Altham: 'What would you say for you was the happiest time you spent with the Beach Boys?'

Dennis Wilson: 'Right now, because of the mere fact that I'm alive now. I live now – I can look back at the past and dig it, but there is more you can do about enjoying life now.'

With Dennis's expenses being taken care of by the Beach Boys' management, all seemed blissful for Charlie and the girls during the summer of 1968, and they heavily indulged in everything that

Wilson had to offer. In return, they intrigued their generous host. Having been pampered for the majority of his Beach Boys' years, Dennis revelled in the Family's vibrant stories about their trips around California, and how their survival instincts had sustained them en route. Such was Dennis's excitement at these tall tales, he'd beg to be included in some of their scams and pranks. To keep things sweet, Charlie arranged for the girls to cook and clean for the men between marathon sex sessions.

As Dennis was one of the prime movers on the LA music scene, like-minded celebs would regularly drop in to hang out with him. According to Charlie, Neil Diamond was one of these visitors, as were actress Jane Fonda and her husband Roger Vadim. In a 1991 interview, Charlie claimed that he'd also met actress Sharon Tate 'two or three times' at the property. Meanwhile, Dennis made excited overtures to John Phillips, singer with the Mamas & the Papas. 'This guy Charlie's here with all these great-looking chicks hanging out like servants,' Dennis enthused. 'You can come over and just fuck any of them you want. It's a great party.'

Alex Chilton, growly lead singer with the Box Tops, scored a few days' stay at Dennis's house during Charlie's tenure. He recounted this overwhelming experience to *Select* magazine's David Cavanagh in 1992. 'Occasionally, things got a little uncomfortable. One day I was going to the store and some of the girls heard about it and showed up with a long list of groceries for me to buy. So it's like, OK, I've got some money and, hey, this is California, I guess it's cool, I'll buy the groceries. And the girls meet me in the driveway and look through the bags and they go, "Oh, you forgot the milk." And they're like staring at me very intently. So I'm goin', "Gee, I'm sorry. Forgot the milk, uh?" Oh boy. So they go in the house and I'm kind of ambling my way round to the door and by the time I get there two of 'em are standing in the doorway blocking my way. And they say (really intense look), Charlie says "go get the milk" . . . Can you believe that? So I'm like, "Charlie, which one is he again? Oh yeah. Little guy. Plays guitar. Yeah, I got him. So he wants me to go get the milk? Uh-huh." And, well, what with one thing and another, I didn't go get the milk.'

Neil Young, then of the seminal folk-rock outfit, Buffalo Springfield, was another celebrity schmoozer who encountered

Manson at Wilson's pad. Like Dennis, Young was captivated by Charlie and his revolving carousal of female acolytes. He'd reportedly later give Charlie a motorcycle as a symbol of his appreciation. Young would detail his time spent with Manson for biographer Jimmy McDonough in 1989:

'We just hung out. He played some songs for me sitting in Will Rogers' old house, on Sunset Boulevard. Dennis had the house there and I visited Dennis a couple of times ... Charlie was always there... and all those girls ... They only paid attention to Charlie. Dennis and I felt like we weren't there, OK? Now that may seem unusual, but – it is. Because both Dennis and I were known, these girls couldn't see us. [He] made up songs as he went along, new stuff all the time, no two songs were the same. I remember playin' a little guitar while he was making up songs. Strong will that guy. I told Mo Ostin [president of Warner Brothers] about him, "this guy is unbelievable – he makes the song up as he goes along, and they're all good".'

In addition to mingling with stars on Sunset Strip, Charlie was also attempting to ingratiate himself in another funky district of Los Angeles, Laurel Canyon. Home to the likes of Joni Mitchell, Jim Morrison, Crosby, Stills and Nash, The Mamas & the Papas, and Frank Zappa, it was fast becoming rock's very own sovereign kingdom. In 1968 Jimi Hendrix arrived, still glowing with his new-found success. Manson had picked up on Hendrix's arrival, and had travelled over to Laurel Canyon to ingratiate himself with the guitarist.

Mick Cox, a musician with British band Eire Apparent, was staying with Jimi at the time, and he clearly recalls Charlie's advances. 'Manson was loosely a face around town. I remember his name coming up a few times, and I heard that he wanted to come to the house where we and Jimi were staying. I remember we bumped into him at one point at a general store in Laurel Canyon where the band was doing a bit of shopping. One of them said, "That's Charles Manson." He was very interested in getting in with the Hendrix gang which would have given him some considerable kudos ... He was someone you couldn't shut up once he got going, and he sort of built himself into this chemical-induced guru. He was a very intense kind of person. He was the sort of thing that in those days was a little bit impressive for a while, but you sort of got wise to it all. Noel [Redding] and Mitch [Mitchell] sussed him straight away, being East London boys. My own personal take on him was another weirdo just trying to push some sort of thing.'

At around this time Charlie also re-established contact with Phil Kaufman, his old prison cohort who'd been released during the spring of 1968. With Kaufman back in circulation, Charlie utilised his friend's numerous contacts around town. One of these was Harold True. He lived in the affluent Los Feliz district of LA with a bunch of party-loving students. Manson attended numerous parties at the house on Waverly Drive during 1968, making the most of True's open-door policy. At one LSD-charged gathering, someone taped Manson's jam session. Remarkably, the recording still exists. On it the heavily intoxicated Charlie finds it impossible to string together even a few bars of music without breaking into hysterical, high-pitched laughter. More disturbing is Charlie's acolytes' constant chorus of 'yeahs' as he talks. The dialogue is fairly typical for Manson in those heady early days of the Family.

'Everything is the way it is because that's the way love says so. When you tune in with love, you tune in with yourself. That's not really a philosophy, that's a fact and everyone who's got love in their hearts knows it.'

Back home at Dennis Wilson's house, Charlie met with the other Beach Boys and their associates. Whilst there are sketchy reports that some members of the group were taken with the Family, the reality was that Charlie was strictly Dennis's concern. Around that time Manson also met with celebrity record producer, Terry Melcher.

Since 1966, Melcher and his beautiful blond girlfriend, Candice Bergen, had rented an exclusive property in nearby Benedict Canyon, at 10050 Cielo Drive. Although Melcher had now put his Golden Penetrator antics aside, he still found time to go over to Dennis's pad to shoot the breeze and talk music business. With the Family in situ, Charlie was impatient to show Terry his roster of songs. Manson's estimation of Melcher rose exponentially when he discovered that he was loosely employed as a talent scout for the Beatles' Apple label. Having already produced Grapefruit, one of the Beatles' 'house' bands, his brief was to flush out any suitable West Coast talent for the label. A seasoned audiophile, Melcher was certainly intrigued by Manson's songs, and more so by Dennis's ravings. With the Beach Boy's fiery support, Charlie was promised recording sessions where they could properly evaluate his potential.

Word travelled fast about the Family's comfortable set-up on Sunset Strip, and other revellers and freeloaders began to gravitate to Wilson's house. Among them was Reverend Deane Morehouse. Since being turned on to LSD, Deane had enthusiastically begun spreading the gospel, dosing all and sundry with acid at every given opportunity. Convinced it was the sacrament that engendered the highest spiritual awakening, he'd begun delivering his message in tablet form, with the added tag that Charlie was the new messiah. Deane had even extended his activities to the school yard, where he was spotted handing out LSD to some youngsters. In addition to his playground antics, Morehouse had dosed his wife, leaving her in an extremely fragile state. Not welcome at home, and with a need to re-engage with Manson, Deane caught up with the Family at Dennis Wilson's house in June of 1968. Morehouse rushed to kiss Charlie's feet, before handing over to Charlie the truck he'd come down in, and all of his possessions.

In addition to his reunion with Charlie, Deane was able to check on the welfare of his errant daughter. While Ruth Ann was happy in the collective bosom of the Family, the acid-fried Reverend soon became a heavy embarrassment to Charlie and Dennis. To keep him out of harm's way, Dennis gave Morehouse free use of a caretaker's lodge on the grounds in exchange for carrying out some menial duties around the property.

En route to Los Angeles, the Reverend Morehouse had picked up nineteen-year-old Brooks Poston, a genial hippie-child from Borger, Texas. Brooks combined interests in music and spirituality, and had left high school to take off to California. With the Family full to bursting with adoring females, the sensitive and receptive Brooks was quickly pulled into Manson's world. Charlie systematically relieved Brooks of all his possessions, and then sent him off to join his ranks. As a rite of passage, Brooks underwent his first LSD trip while hanging around the Family. Under the influence, Charlie delivered what was fast becoming his standard question to all newcomers, 'Are you ready to die for me?' Brooks evidently was, and went into a trance-like coma for many hours. Confirming his powers to those present, Charlie brought Brooks out of his reverie and on to his feet.

Brooks Poston later recalled: 'To us, he was a Christ figure. I believed a hundred per cent he was Christ. I was on acid then but I saw him do things, like he would grant eternal life to people. He was miraculous.'

Despite his obvious devotion, Charlie was still uncertain about the sensitive Brooks. As a result, he challenged him to have sex with every female member of the group, whilst being watched by an audience. When Brooks admitted he wasn't up to the task, Charlie relegated the lad to 'the bottom man on the totem pole', and shunted him away into Reverend Morehouse's quarters.

Meanwhile, Dennis Wilson began to happily muck in with the Family's daily routines, and was content to share his possessions with them. Additionally, Dennis would let the Family use his cars for their frequent food and drug runs, even though both his Rolls-Royce and beloved red Ferrari would be damaged by their wayward driving. Without transport, the rock star was forced to engage in a spot of hitchhiking. The imposition didn't bother him; instead Wilson felt liberated by the freedom he felt on the road. These freewheeling experiences would be put to good use some years later, when he starred in the acclaimed road movie, *Two Lane Blacktop*, in 1971.

One particular evening, Dennis was camped out by the roadside on the Sunset Strip, thumb outstretched, golden hair shining in the fast-fading light. A 1935 Dodge pick-up truck pulled in and offered him a lift. It was driven by an athletic young man: Charles Watson. An ex-pat from Texas, Watson had moved over to California in search of new opportunities and good times. As he'd later recall, he was impressed by his passenger's celebrity tales. 'When he told me his name was Dennis Wilson it didn't mean anything to me, but when he said he was one of the Beach Boys I was impressed. I remembered all those surfing songs banging out of my brother's room back in Copeville [Texas] and grinned to myself, wondering what he would think if he could see me now – with Dennis Wilson taking a ride in my truck.'

Charles Denton Watson had been born in Dallas, Texas, on 2 December 1945. Religion played an enormous part in the Watson family's daily life. Watson's father ran a garage-cum-grocery store, whilst his mother played dutiful housewife, and ensured that her three children adhered to strict religious principles. Initially Charles, the youngest, was a compliant son, and lived up to the expectations within the Watson family, excelling at school and on the field, and breaking many sporting records for his home state.

Charles graduated from high school with flying colours – where ironically, his end-of-term paper was written on the perils of drug addiction – before enrolling at North Texas State College in September of 1964. However, fuelled by his recent discovery of drugs and a sudden contempt for the narrow perimeters of his religious upbringing, Watson lasted just one term before dropping out. For a while he bummed around, taking on any work that could fund his new habit. At one point, a college friend tipped him off about a vacant baggage-handler's job at Braniff Airways. Despite the tedious nature of the work, it did offer the lucrative perk of free travel. Already engaged in some dealing on the side, Watson took the opportunity to take holidays in Hawaii, and then California. The Golden State had an immediate effect on him, and he soon made plans to relocate there.

Watson enrolled in California State College on a business course, and in order to support his studies, he began working part-time for a toupee company. Such were his talents in sales, he abandoned his coursework to concentrate on the business full-time. For a while things looked promising, with Watson living in some of the funkiest areas of LA, such as Laurel Canyon and Wonderland Road, before finally settling in Malibu. With a pretty air-hostess girlfriend in tow, he'd become the epitome of the Los Angeles' cool: stylish, sleek and possessed with youthful exuberance.

Ever the entrepreneur, Watson and a friend from college established their own wig business. With the company christened Love Locs, premises on Hollywood's swanky La Cienega Boulevard were leased. However, the good life and constant distractions got in the way of business. With exorbitant rents absorbing profits, Watson and his partner decided to operate from their homes in Malibu.

With no office to go to, Watson soon fell into an itinerant lifestyle, and his wig business begun to fall by the wayside. To supplement Love Locs' gradually dwindling resources, Watson's drug-dealing enterprise was stepped up, and quickly overtook his legitimate work. With his conventional life slowly disappearing over the horizon, Watson was able to give himself fully to any new experiences that might come his way.

Having promised Dennis he would take him right back to his Sunset Boulevard home, Watson's truck wended its way slowly down the tree-lined driveway. Once inside, they found Deane Morehouse, his hair and beard now grown to messianic proportions, seated around a table with a few of Charlie's girls. Following a typically bizarre audience with Morehouse, Watson was led into the living room to meet Manson. Charlie was sitting on the floor playing guitar; looking up, he greeted Watson with a huge smile. Such was its warmth, it seemed to penetrate Watson's soul. It was an altogether mystical moment, so much so, that Watson felt compelled to kneel down. While to Watson, Deane Morehouse had initially appeared nothing more than a 'fat old man with a greasy beard, trying to look like a hippie', Charlie was something much more authentic.

'Here I was,' Watson later reflected, 'accepted in a world I'd never even dreamed about, mellow and at my ease. Charlie murmured in the background, something about love, finding love, letting yourself love. I suddenly realised that this was what I was looking for: love. Not that my parents and brother and sister hadn't loved me, but somehow, now, that didn't count. I wanted the kind of love they talked about in the songs – the kind of love that didn't ask you to be anything, didn't judge what you were, didn't set up any rules or regulations – the kind of love that just accepted you, let you be yourself, do your thing whatever it was

– the kind of love I seemed to be feeling right now, sitting around this coffee table getting zonked on some of the best hash I'd ever had, with a rock star and a fat old hippie and the little guy with the guitar who just kept singing softly, smiling to himself. It occurred to me that all the love in the room was coming from him, from his music.'

Although Watson left Wilson's house after a few hours, he returned the next day, and then the day after that, severing his remaining links with the outside world. As the final initiation into Family life, Reverend Morehouse gave Watson his first LSD trip.

Soon after Watson's arrival, and seemingly under intense pressure from his close associates, Dennis began making noises about moving out of the Sunset Boulevard property. Dennis's management later estimated that the true cost of hosting the tribe was close to $100,000 – around a million dollars in today's money. With Manson's recording contract paramount, Charlie reckoned that a swift relocation would preserve relations with Dennis. Nonetheless, in case of future emergencies, Manson relieved Wilson of a few of his Beach Boys' gold discs.

After a few weeks visiting several desert regions in the North of California, Charlie figured that enough time had passed and the black bus headed back to Sunset Boulevard to see if the heat had cooled at Dennis's. When they arrived, they found that Wilson had moved out, and a team of security guards were now patrolling the grounds. There was good reason for this. Despite the Family's eviction, word had hit the streets about Wilson's open-door policy, causing a stream of visitors to descend upon the house. Despite having a few weeks left on his lease, Dennis had moved into the cellar of friend Gregg Jakobson's house.

Wilson wasn't exactly left empty-handed by the Family. To augment the drugs and sexual favours that the Family had bestowed upon him, their host had been given Watson's truck, apparently in lieu of the damage they'd inflicted on his range of cars. Despite the Family's relocation, Wilson had been deeply affected by their tenure at the house, and was still spouting familiar Mansonisms when interviewed by Keith Altham.

Keith Altham: 'Is this story true that you are living in a cellar in California at present?'

Dennis Wilson: 'Yep – it's a little room about half the size of this hotel room. I look at it as my mind. There's a piano in there and a bed and that's all I need. People fill their lives and their rooms with so much stuff that they don't need – watches, furniture, cars – and they pour their life into keeping and acquiring these things. They spend all their time working to pay for that car, which they keep in a parking lot all day long.'

Keith Altham: 'Are those stories true about you giving your money away?'

Dennis Wilson 'Sure – I give everything I have away. What I am wearing and what's in that suitcase is it. I don't even have a car. I have a 1934 Dodge pick-up truck which someone gave me. I could have anything I want. I just have to go out and get it. If it's worth having, it's worth giving. The smile you send out will return to you!'

While contact with Dennis was still maintained, it seems that for Manson's tribe, the Sunset Boulevard gravy train had come to a halt. Charlie immediately decreed a comprehensive search to be carried out to find the Family somewhere to live.

It was Sandy Good, fast becoming Charlie's foremost emissary, who came through with news of a receptive space for the Family. She'd talked enthusiastically about a ramshackle collection of buildings that had once been a movie set to the north of Los Angeles. The fact that Sandra's informant was a mechanic was doubly fortuitous, seeing as the Family's legendary black bus was once again desperately in need of repair.

Early in August 1968, the Family bus made its way towards Chatsworth, some twenty miles from downtown LA. Charlie, unwilling to attract suspicion, decided to hold back from making a mass entrance and parked the bus in the hills overlooking the property. There, the Family planned their approach with military precision.

*   *   *

Chatsworth, as an area, had seen little action since warring Mexican factions inhabited the district back in the seventeenth century. With precious little in the way of natural resources, there was little to draw people to the region. However, during the early part of the twentieth century, the growth of Hollywood's film industry saw a small uplift in the region's fortunes. A rugged terrain of mountains and canyons, and not least, its close proximity to Hollywood, made it ideal for Los Angeles' movie moguls. Given that the demand for Westerns had become a global phenomenon, a plethora of purpose-built ranches sprung up around Chatsworth to catch the falling dollars from the movie industry.

One of the more modest of the many movie sets was to be found between the rocky landscapes of the Santa Susana Pass and Devil's and Box Canyons. The façade had been established by veteran silent-move star William S. Hart, to capitalise on the movie rush in the 1920s. As a result of Hart's celebrity, legends such as Roy Rogers, William Boyd and Tom Mix had played out many a celluloid yarn of goodies and baddies in front of this scenic backdrop.

Hart's death in 1946 left the ranch in limbo before the tenancy came up for renewal in 1948. Enter George Spahn, a fifty-seven-year-old former dairy farmer from Pennsylvania. He took the property on with expectations of securing his own slice of movie history. Prior to moving to California, he'd led a largely itinerant life as a dairy farmer, siring ten children who, legend suggests, he named after his favourite horses.

Given the residual reputation of the ranch, for a while the income was good. With television prompting a revival of the Western format, the likes of *Bonanza*, *The Lone Ranger* and *Gunsmoke* utilised the ranch's sets for the occasional episode, and for a few years the future appeared promising.

To keep things moving along smoothly, George Spahn employed a loose band of casual labourers, drawn mainly from the stuntmen and wannabe cowboys who frequented the area. However, by the mid-1960s, the genre was starting to run out of steam, leaving the likes of Spahn's ranch to explore other avenues or simply fold. In the mid-1960s, a couple of early porn films were shot in and around the ranch's boundaries, but this brief shift in genre was hardly indicative of a glorious future. By 1968, the bulk of the ranch's income came from day-trippers leasing horses for rides around the nearby hills

Now approaching his eighties, George Spahn's haphazard management style was starting to falter; his dwindling health, coupled with acute myopia, made even the most basic of tasks impossible. A variety of drifters had been hanging round the property, many engaging in shady activities. Additionally, to the rear of the ranch, a group of hippies had taken up something of a permanent residence in an old backhouse. Although they kept themselves pretty much to themselves, their slacker presence was anathema to the testosterone-charged workforce, who prided themselves on their ability to work twelve-hour shifts, six days a week.

George had a savvy cohort named Ruby Pearl, a redheaded circus-girl whom George had made manager in an attempt to keep some semblance of order. With Pearl taking on the bulk of Spahn's administrative duties, George was often to be found on the decks of one of the sets, sitting in a rocking chair as he batted the flies away from his face, a chihuahua perched on his lap.

Following Manson's instructions, a couple of the girls approached the ranch and made their way to George Spahn's quarters. One of the girls broke the ice by offering to make him lunch, while another set about helping with various menial tasks around his house. Spahn was impressed, both with their willingness to help, but more so with their polite approach. When the girls asked him if a few of their friends could come and stay for a while, Spahn readily acquiesced.

With their introduction rubber-stamped, Charlie drove the Family bus down Iverson Road and off onto Spahn Ranch's main strip. As he alighted from the bus, Charlie took a deep breath and surveyed the landscape. Here he was, standing in a virtual town, the remoteness of the area meaning there would be little or no interference from law-makers, government agencies or other prying eyes. Manson also noted the labyrinth of caves and fallen boulders at the ranch's base, which could easily hide Charlie's minions in times of trouble. In short, not even Manson's fevered imagination could have conjured up somewhere as perfect as Spahn Ranch, He'd later pen a tribute to his new locale:

> The pass where the Devil you can see
> Flying along in sight for all to see
> On the edge of infinity
> Santa Susana is the pass where you look to be
> Santa Susana is the pass where you look for me
> 12 in the night love or fight
> Any way is right
> If you come out in the night
> It's so out of sight in Devil's Canyon

The rest of the girls were pretty impressed too, and they scuttled off like excited children to explore the shacks and decaying movie sets. While small, the nameless clapboard town nonetheless housed most of the elements that would have been found in a thriving settlement, and came complete with a jailhouse, a hotel and an undertaker. With cinematic names such as 'Longhorn Saloon' and 'Rock City Café' still clinging to the rooftops, it made for an alluring backdrop. In contrast to the ramshackle collection of campsites and squats they'd were mostly used to, Spahn Ranch appeared to be a wonderland.

Manson wasted little time in collaring George Spahn for a spot of mutual bartering. Charlie spun the fragile seventy-year-old into circles of delight with promises of an army of attentive girls who'd take care of his every requirement. He also promised that he'd fix up some of Spahn's old cars and trucks, and arrange for him to be taken into town whenever he wanted. Manson also introduced George to the rest of his girls, and not surprisingly, the old boy agreed to the Family taking up immediate residence at the ranch.

Despite some dissension from the ranch hands, George thoroughly enjoyed the fresh breath of life the girls brought to the otherwise dusty, deathly boredom of the place. Charlie ensured that the girls' pampering presence was maintained at all hours. As designed, Spahn became fully dependent on the women, as they continued to cook, clean and even to dress him every day. George gave most of the girls pet names: Katie became 'Katydid',

Ruth Ann Morehouse became 'Ouisch' (pronounced 'Wish') and, most famously, Lyn Fromme would be christened 'Squeaky', on account of the high-pitched yelp she'd let out when he tweaked her thighs. It wasn't just the women that old George rechristened. He'd heard Charles Watson's heavy drawl and started calling him 'Tex', a name that would stick from that day on.

While it is not clear how far the girls went in pleasing George Spahn, their constant attention ensured that, as far he was concerned, the Family's presence at his ranch was never an issue.

Others were drawn to the dusty idyll. Just two weeks into their tenure at Spahn's, they were joined by Leslie Louise Van Houten. She'd arrived courtesy of Catherine 'Gypsy' Share, Bobby Beausoleil and his then partner, Gayle. On the surface, Leslie was a bright, all-American teenager, a product of middle-class values and aspirations. She was born on 23 August 1949 in Altadena, California, to Paul, a car auctioneer, and Jane, a teacher. The parents enjoyed and actively promoted family life. In addition to Leslie and her older brother, they'd adopted two children who'd been orphaned in Korea. For a while, all appeared good; the Van Houtens enjoying the spoils of the economic boom-time of California in the early 1960s.

At thirteen, Leslie began to deviate from this promising path when her parents separated. With her father relocating elsewhere, it meant that Leslie's mother was now raising four children as well as returning to work. Initially, Leslie seemed to weather this emotional storm, and was twice elected 'homecoming queen'. However, at seventeen, Leslie got pregnant after a fling with a classmate. The resulting abortion precipitated a slide into drug use, most notably LSD. Having graduated from high school, Leslie eschewed university, opting instead to train as a legal secretary. Moving in with her father, she attended business school to equip her with the necessary skills for the vocation.

Like Patricia Krenwinkel before her, Leslie briefly considered life as a nun with a Yoga-based organisation, which she cites as a reaction to the trauma caused by her abortion. However, by the age of eighteen, Leslie left conventionality behind her, and threw herself wholeheartedly into the interminable party scene that seemed to be enveloping the nation's youth. By the summer of

1968, Leslie was living in Haight-Ashbury. There she'd called her mother to say that she was exploring new avenues, and wouldn't be hearing from her for a while. On the West Coast hippie trail, she'd collided with Bobby Beausoleil, his wife Gayle, and Gypsy, who invited Leslie to return with them to Los Angeles. Feeling an immediate kinship with her new friends, Leslie left with the trio, and began a sexual relationship with Beausoleil. From here she would very soon tread the well-worn path to Charles Manson's door.

'I was absolutely intrigued and mesmerised by Manson,' recalls Van Houten. I believed that he was something very special and extraordinary . . . I think that perhaps he viewed me as a way to keep and lure Bobby to the ranch and be with him.'

Although Spahn's provided a rent-free home for the Family, they still had to attend to their basic needs. One of the Family's preferred means of sustenance were the frequent excursions to supermarket rubbish skips. To Charlie, this was a joyous metaphor for their 'leftover' status, and a savage indictment of the disposable society they so despised. Once or twice a week, several of the girls ventured into town to see what out-of-date and damaged provisions had been dumped into the skips at the rear of local supermarkets. Often, the pickings were rich.

Whereas other 'freegans' of the era undertook these garbage runs under the cover of darkness, the Family took great delight in slipping in and out of the waste skips during daylight hours, much to the astonishment of the staff and customers. Despite rumours that the stores sprinkled rat poison and other noxious substances over the food to discourage looting, the Family snaffled enough booty to feed up to twenty people a day. On the occasions when things got out of hand with the management, one of the girls would offer some personal 'services' to the store's boss to avert any potential action. If for whatever reason the skips were empty, the girls would scrounge food from churches and other charitable organisations.

Dennis Wilson was even enlisted to accompany some of the girls on many of their regular scavenges. It made for an incongruous sight, with Dennis chauffeuring the girls to the skips in his vintage Rolls-Royce. As the girls gleefully submerged themselves in the mass of rotting bread, fruit and vegetables, they would often sing lines from a song that Manson had written:

> When you're livin' on the road
> And you think sometimes you're starvin'
> Get on off that trip my friend
> Just get in them cans and start carvin'
> Oh garbage dump my garbage dump
> Why are you called my garbage dump?
> Garbage dump my garbage dump
> Why are you called my garbage dump?
> There's a Market Basket and an A & P
> I don't care if the box boys are staring at me
> I don't even care who wins the war
> I'll be in them cans behind my favourite store

As the Family cemented their presence at Spahn's, a daily timetable emerged. Contrary to received wisdom, Charlie's contingent didn't spend all their time making love or lying around wasted on drugs. Manson told the group that to make Spahn's a secure base they had to prove (at least initially) that they were integral to the greater good of the ranch. And that they did: they buckled down, worked hard, and gently assimilated themselves into their new environment without any fuss. Anything else would have aroused suspicions.

Most days, Charlie's contingent woke at around 7 a.m. After the horses had been fed and transferred to the paddocks, they'd eat a communal breakfast before returning to get the horses ready for the first riders of the day. While some cleaned out the paddocks and shovelled up dung, others acted as friendly guides for the more novice riders until work tailed off at sundown. Such was George Spahn's pleasure at the Family's dedication to these duties, he allowed them to upgrade their quarters from the rear of the paddock to the movie sets on the main boulevard. The male members took on a lot of the heavy duty tasks around the ranch, such as maintaining the ranch's vehicles and repairing the buildings. Tex Watson had also been enlisted to start work on building Manson a house on the property, dubbed by Manson the 'in-case place'.

Once the daily tasks had been completed, the real business of the Family could commence. These nightly group sessions were vitally important in establishing Charlie's position as leader and mentor of the Family. Most evenings, a mainly vegetarian meal of food from the bins would be prepared. Once ready, it was then transported down towards the creek-bed area at the ranch's base. There were no individual plates as such; large bowls would be passed around the members. Following dinner, the group would engage in some communal singing before Charlie delivered his evening sermon. More often than not, it was handed down from the top of a fallen boulder, with the Family members gathered reverently underneath.

These sermons were well structured and crafted, serving to inform and impress the neophytes, while reinforcing the message to the Family's hard core. Charlie's verbal diatribes would cover a multitude of subjects, normally relating to behaviour, conditioning, and how society was sliding into an abyss of its own making. This unique excerpt, recorded during late 1967, is representative of the type of oration he'd deliver to his flock.

'I was so smart when I was a kid that I learnt that I was dumb – fast. That's the way it is with everyone, not just me. You're taught that you can't. They even teach you the word. They give you the words. Take all the words away, and don't think in right and wrong, just think in truth. All the answers are there; the sound of one hand clapping is simply the sound of one hand clapping, no big answers. All the big colleges that we've been building are taking people the other way. The smartest people in the world are really the most cut-off. It's the common people man with the soul, it really moves ... Progress? There's no such thing as progress, there's only change. You dig a hole in the ground and you build up a city and you fight a war and you call it progress? You call it change. And it's a beautiful game and it's a perfect game, and whoever wants to continue playing general and go on killing themselves, well, my goodness. I wouldn't want to play that game myself, but if they want to play it, I love them for it ... But it boils [down] to just one thing. As long as there is hate in your heart, they'll be hate in the world. You cannot fight for peace and you cannot capture freedom.'

Manson made frequent references to the simmering tensions between black and white communities in LA, and how the failure of racial integration was leading to an inevitable apocalypse. Each session would be met with attentive silence, lest Manson's flow was interrupted. On the rare occasion that a mutter became audible, it was usually silenced by a bowl or some kitchen implement being hurled in that direction. However, these outbursts were few and far between, and Charlie basked happily in his role as leader, and the undivided appreciation from his devotees.

Charlie constantly made reference to the parallels between himself and Christ (or 'JC' as he referred to him). In case any further clarification was needed, he made sure that all of them knew that the name Manson was in truth, the 'son of man'; the misunderstood prophet who'd been beaten and ultimately crucified for being who he was. On these occasions he'd refer back to his well-thumbed copy of the Bible, and turn to Revelations 1:12–16, a section he quoted regularly. In time, other parts of the controversial last book of the New Testament informed the Family's idolatry of Manson.

'I turned round to see the voice that was speaking to me. And when I turned I saw seven golden lampstands, and among the lampstands was someone like a son of man ... His eyes were like blazing fire ... and his voice was like the sound of rushing waters. In his right hand he held seven stars, and out of his mouth came a sharp double-edged sword. His face was like the sun shining in all its brilliance.'

In tandem with his own self-deification, Charlie elevated his followers' fragile self-worth, proclaiming them disciples – beings who were blessed for acknowledging his existence. With most of the Family having suffered guilt-ridden adolescences, they lapped it all up, obediently replying 'Amen' after any statement that resonated with them. When he became particularly animated, Manson reaffirmed his belief that he'd absorbed both Christ and the Devil into his persona. To back up these claims, he'd use the old Process Church line that if love were indeed unconditional, then Christ would have forgiven the fallen angel and absorbed him into his soul. Equally, nothing could be criticised under this all-loving, all-embracing mantle. Therefore there was no wrong; to do whatever you wanted was no crime. Not surprisingly, the Family members lapped it all up.

And, of course Charlie was never afraid to employ a little bit of theatre to these proceedings. Leslie Van Houten remembers: 'Sometimes he would re-enact the crucifixion when we were on LSD. And it was very realistic, and then the questions would begin. "I have died for you. Will you die for me?"'

Following Charlie's lecture, the group would repair back to one of the buildings on the main strip to smoke a little weed and, by candlelight, sing along to some of Manson's songs. Once or twice a week, a bag of LSD made an appearance, and would be ceremoniously shared out amongst those present. In the early days of the Family, drug use was confined to marijuana and LSD. Occasionally, a stash of peyote or mescaline would pass through the group, but that was the sum total of the group's excursions into narcotics. Manson strictly forbade opiates and amphetamines of any kind, and with good reason. He'd watched the speed freaks and junkies of San Francisco replace the gentle bonhomie of the 'Summer of Love' with a harder, more selfish vibe. As a result, legions of communities were decimated, as speed-crazy psychotics destroyed the conviviality of shared living. Manson knew only too well the divisive properties of certain drugs, and was equally aware that they could destroy his carefully staged mind-games.

More than any other psychoactive tool that Manson had to hand, psychedelics were the main key for unlocking the minds of his followers. During these communal acid sessions, Charlie remained studiously in control, ensuring that all members of the group partook in the experience. To sustain his position as chief guide and guru, Manson would either take half a tab of the drug, or none at all. He was careful to be temperate; given the potency of LSD at the time (around ten times more powerful than it is today), a full-on dose would effectively lay the user redundant for the next ten to twelve hours. For the duration of the Family's collective trip, Charlie carefully watched over his charges, monitoring their individual strength of character; which under LSD was magnified enormously. He would duly note any weaknesses within the members' psyche, which he would return to at a later date to explore, challenge or exploit. By the time the acid had worn off, truth and fantasy had seamlessly merged. With Manson's potent suggestions embedded into the subconscious, even those with more resilient wills were twisted in his direction.

Paul Watkins said later, 'Basically, Charlie's trip was to programme us all to submit: to give up our egos, which, in a spiritual sense, is a lofty aspiration.'

Aside from LSD, the other communal interaction that the Family favoured was group sex. As the majority of the Family had come from middle-class backgrounds, it was imperative to Charlie that they were fully exorcised of any sexual inhibitions that might hold them back. Like LSD, sex was part and parcel of Manson's deprogramming kit, and was especially useful in determining the individual's propensity for personal fear. As chief initiator, Manson slept with all of the group's female members to see whether they held on to any previous hang-ups, or 'sex trips' as he put it. Homosexual acts with male members was not beyond his scope either, especially if it meant he could gauge their potential for 'letting go' and 'complete submission'. For those who held back on a particular sexual scenario, Charlie was on to them like a shot, gently or violently cajoling them into performing the act.

Given the Family's predilection for sexual adventure, and Charlie's strict ban on contraception, pregnancy was a regular occurrence. As Spahn Ranch was such a harmonious environment, many of the girls became pregnant within weeks of their arrival. Not surprisingly, most had little or no idea of who the father was although, when pushed, most claimed it was Manson. The arrival of new babies created a blissful ambience within the Family during the late summer of 1968. Regular garbage runs and occasional handouts from concerned relatives and other benefactors and the lack of desire for anything other than the basics, made life on the ranch a relatively simple affair. Nonetheless, new members were still encouraged to divest themselves of all their worldly possessions, and if that included credit cards, monthly allowances and bank accounts, then all the better. Charlie would also encourage his runaways to call their parents for an emergency cheque to fund the return trip home. As a result, several thousand dollars in aborted ticket fares made their way into the Family coffers.

In addition to this fundraising, Charlie had been on a secret mission to charm various wealthy females in the area. While work at Spahn's came first and foremost, Charlie was not above hiring out his obedient workforce to clean the swimming pools or sweep the driveways of their rich neighbours.

'There were ladies from Malibu who gave to [Manson],' Paul Watkins noted. 'Money just came in. We'd sometimes walk around with several thousand dollars in our pockets at any given time. It was hard to tell if we were doing anything wrong. We certainly were not living in poverty and were hardly sleeping in alleyways or gutters and walking around with our rags hanging off us.'

Susan Atkins recalled: 'As people would come, and people wanted to drop out of sight, they'd give us mostly everything they had and we'd usually give away . . . In other words, we never held on to anything, we always gave it away. In fact, we gave away more than we ever had.'

The days were long and arid during the summer of 1968, and yet the Family quietly and diligently set about their duties. On occasions, the girls would venture up to the hills overlooking the ranch, and sit for hours repairing clothes for the male workers, while singing nothing but Manson's songs. When the repairs were out of the way, the girls worked on an intricate ceremonial vest for Charlie. Taking hundreds of hours to complete, the waistcoat was a magnificent and fascinating piece of work. Through its intricate embroidery, the vest charted the evolution of the Family; from its formation, to their children and the adventures they'd shared along the way. Later, when circumstances dictated the ceremonious cutting of hair, the girls' locks were woven into the coat.

During their spare time, the girls would go down to a large waterfall at the base of the creek bed. There, they'd bathe naked and were often joined by the male members of the Family. They'd also play in and around the caves, rocks and gullies of the canyons, like a bunch of kids let out on school break. Occasionally, their skip-rummaging trips were rewarded with swathes of linen and material, which they'd then make into costumes.

Leslie Van Houten remembers that, 'At first, the *Magical Mystery Tour* was that we'd be cowboys or gypsies or pirates. A different world so we could get out of ourselves. Every day was Halloween.'

It appears that Charlie too, took an active part in these imaginary games. He looked back fondly on these amateur dramatics during an interview with Tom Snyder in 1981. 'We used to have games when we play on the movie set. We would take on different people. I'd be "Rif Raff Rackas", and Steve [Grogan – a late arriving Family member] would be "John Jones", who'd just come in from Minneapolis, driving a truck. And we'd just take other people and play-act other people. And then we lost track of who we were, and it went off into other dimensions and levels of thought and understanding and comprehensions that were beyond most people's minds . . . '

Keen to spread the Family message beyond Spahn Ranch, Charlie also seriously considered branching out into other parts of California. In June 1968, with an edict to infiltrate the woodland paradise in Mendocino, Manson sent Sadie, Katie and a few other females to Booneville, a rural industrial town that relied heavily on its timber industry. Along for the ride was Mary Brunner with her baby 'Pooh Bear'. The women occupied a small cabin around seven miles north of the town. Word soon spread among the predominantly male population that this group of women had recently moved into the outskirts of town. Soon, the girls were apparently sharing more than just the drugs they'd brought along to keep themselves occupied. Given their notoriety, they soon garnered the name, 'The Witches of Mendocino'. One night, a posse of older men arrived at the cabin to party; when they were turned away, they blabbed to the local police about the girls' narcotics stash. Unsurprisingly, a raid followed on the night of 22 June 1968. Charlie's women were arrested, along with some local teenagers. Whilst they were held at police headquarters, a group of disaffected older men went over and totally trashed the girls' quarters, writing, 'Get out of here or else' on the cabin wall. The girls were charged with possession of LSD, marijuana and other substances; fearing further trouble, they scuttled back to the relative safety of Spahn Ranch as soon as bail was granted.

Music was always an integral part of these adventures, serving as it did as a soundtrack to their lives. Not surprisingly, Beatles music featured heavily in the Family's playlist. Although Charlie's love affair with the Fab Four had remained constant, it was the group's *Magical Mystery Tour* album that sparked his more fanatical appreciation of the quartet. The album's release in the States was a slightly muted affair, especially following the tumultuous success of *Sgt Pepper's Lonely Hearts Club Band*. While the Beatles had the stamina and talent to exist long after the 'Summer of Love', *Magical Mystery Tour* saw the Beatles' psychedelic carousing head off in a more whimsical direction.

Owing a lot to the ambience of mid-1960s America, *Magical Mystery Tour* emanated from an experience Paul McCartney had while visiting Los Angeles in the spring of 1967. Like many with their ears to the ground, McCartney had heard tell of Ken Kesey's Merry Pranksters careering around the States in an old bus, dosing all and sundry with LSD. As the Beatles were on the lookout for a new cinematic vehicle, McCartney referenced the Pranksters' antics as a possible inspiration for their next filmic adventure. Despite the death of their manager Brian Epstein in August 1967, a disjointed and fragmentary movie was cobbled together and released to savage reviews in December of 1967. The film's release also spawned a soundtrack of six new songs. While fans in the UK were presented with a modest seven-inch package containing two EPs and a small booklet, American punters got something much more spectacular for their dollars and a lavish LP and book were compiled exclusively for the US market.

Charlie and the Family lapped up *Magical Mystery Tour*. For them, it was a joyous confirmation that the Beatles were following the same path. The imagery contained within the album was proof enough in itself. Their poking of fun at the 'Beautiful People' on the album's track 'Baby You're a Rich Man' spookily echoed Manson's scepticism regarding the hippie phenomena. To Manson, it was evident that although the Beatles may well have adopted the attendant paraphernalia of the counterculture, they were first and foremost four Liverpool lads in search of money, sex and universal fame. These connections formed the basis of many a fireside rap and after-dinner conference.

Manson wasn't alone in his idolatry of the Fab Four. Timothy Leary, the mischievous LSD guru and establishment iconoclast, was equally in awe of the band. In typical outlandish and ostentatious style, Leary declared that the Beatles were 'prototypes of evolutionary agents sent by God with a mysterious power to create a new species – a young race of laughing freemen. They are the wisest, holiest, most effective avatars the human race has ever produced.'

Although Manson's and the Beatles' music were the principle soundtracks for the ranch, Charlie also allowed the occasional album from the Moody Blues, the English group, who like the Beatles, had fallen head first into psychedelia. Their 1967 album, *Days of Future Passed*, trod a similar trail to *Magical Mystery Tour*.

In amongst this musical extravaganza, the Family was further delighted when, on 7 October 1968, the garrulous Sadie gave birth to her first child – a boy. The birth was again a Family affair, witnessed and aided by the collective. Just who the father was has been open to speculation over the years, although it mattered little at the time of the birth – it was a Family baby, and it belonged to them all.

Paul Watkins describes the birth. 'She'd been out riding a horse, and she said "I'm going to have my baby now." The contractions got very close, and so everyone picked her up and suspended her in the air. Charlie got more and more nervous and he took a razor blade and slit a little hole, so that they'd be a bigger hole for him to come out of. On one of the contractions, he just plopped out, and when he came out Snake [Dianne Lake] bit off the umbilical cord, and then Charlie took a guitar string and tied it up so it didn't bleed everywhere.'

Sadie's offspring was dubbed Zezozose Zadfrack Glutz. With yet another addition to the Family's growing ranks, Charlie was keen for the children to remain untarnished by society. He'd elucidate on this during a conversation with Sadie. '[Babies] are the kings of the world – completely uninhibited and free from all the garbage of society. We can let them grow up free – free from the plastic world. They won't even have to go to school. They'll learn in their own freedom – even how to talk.'

Back in the 'plastic world', even though the so-called 'Summer of Love' had, for all intents and purposes, been little more than a media invention, 'dropping out' was still a popular life-choice. By 1968, the thousands who had beaten a path to join in with the counterculture often found themselves without any reputable information or guidance. As a result, commune living seemed the only real alternative for a sustainable lifestyle. Despite Charlie's declaration that the Family was a solitary thorn in the side of the American dream, there were many others who continued to see themselves as warriors on the cultural front line.

While the establishment took a dim view of the various youth revolutions, it was left to the few agencies that monitored the culture to try and give it some sort of direction. Attempting to disseminate this research dispassionately was the *Journal of Psychedelic Drugs,* published under the auspices of Haight-Ashbury's unique Free Medical Clinic. The clinic had been formed in June 1967 by Dr David Smith, and its motto, 'Health care is a right, not a privilege' ensured a large swathe of the counterculture sought out gratis treatment at its Clayton Street headquarters.

Charlie and the girls frequented the clinic on numerous occasions. As VD and drug-related freak-outs were occupational hazards, the centre became a familiar drop-in point. Despite Manson's enormous charisma and expanding caravan of girls, he was just one part of a multitude of disparate personalities appealing for health care. Al Rose was the clinic's outreach worker and had delivered healthcare to many of the communes in California. Given their minor celebrity around Haight-Ashbury, Charlie's Family appeared to be a fascinating blueprint for collective dwelling, and worthy of further investigation. With a research project commissioned, Al Rose travelled down to the ranch for a closer look at the Family's unique structure and behaviour.

Entitled, 'A Case Study of the Charles Manson Group Marriage Commune' the 2,700-word document undertook a comprehensive sweep of the Family ethos, underpinned by their daily activities at the ranch. The selected excerpts below pay testament to Smith and Rose's dispassionate attempt to understand Charlie and the Family's culture:

Structure of the Group Marriage Commune

Most group marriage communes that survive for a long period of time have a 'father figure' as the spiritual leader of the group. The group marriage commune under study had a 'father figure' (Charles Manson), a 35-year-old white male with a past history of involvement with the law.

Although there were three people with some college education, including one person having a Master's degree, members disapproved of the whole process of formal institutional education in America. They believed that education was a means of conditioning or 'brain washing' a young person with the values and mores of the dominant culture. Manson felt that a person should be 'open to change' and willing to accept new values, but insisted that once someone has been indoctrinated by society, his value system became rigid.

Approximately 20 members of this commune referred to themselves as a 'family', but we have chosen the term 'group marriage commune' because of the polygamous sexual relations, but affairs outside the 'family' were rarely endorsed. In cases of sexual conflict, Manson made the final judgement as to what constituted acceptable behaviour. Manson was thirty-five years of age, and had no college education. He was an extroverted, persuasive individual who served as absolute ruler of the group marriage commune. What he sanctioned was approved by the rest of the group, but what he disapproved was forbidden.

Tales of Manson's sexual prowess were related to all new members ... One popular story often told was that Manson would get up in the morning, make love, eat breakfast, make love, and go back to sleep. He would wake later, and make love, have lunch, make love, and go back to sleep. Waking up later, he would make love, eat dinner, make love, and go back to sleep – only to wake up in the middle of the night wanting to have intercourse again.

Given what has been written since, Smith and Rose's observations do little to uphold the party line that Charlie and his coterie of admirers were law-breaking, anarchic entities. Moreover, to such seasoned eyes as Smith and Rose, they were nothing more than a freewheeling band of young men and woman, searching for some semblance of identity in a disenfranchised world. However, what was made abundantly clear in the report was that Manson's mercurial personality had the potential to turn in many different directions.

Charlie had a persuasive mystical philosophy placing great emphasis on the belief that people did not die and that infant consciousness was the ultimate state. However, Charlie's mysticism often became delusional and he on occasion referred to himself as 'God' or 'God and the Devil'. Charlie could probably be diagnosed as an ambulatory schizophrenic.

Still on the lookout for areas to expand into, Charlie became aware of a nearby community based in Box Canyon, home to a religious order that went by the name of the Fountain of the World. The community had been established by one 'Krishna Venta' in the late 1940s. Born Francis Herman Pencovic in 1911, he shared some startling similarities with Charlie. In his early years, Pencovic had been incarcerated for a series of minor crimes, including burglary, fraud and larceny. Additionally, he'd spent time in a psychiatric hospital suffering from delusional behaviour. His conversion to 'Krishna Venta' occurred in 1951, whereupon, he claimed, he'd originally been born on the planet Neophrates, was actually over 240,000 years old, had travelled to Earth in a rocket, landed in Turkey, and had spent time in the Garden of Eden.

Krishna had a small circle of predominately female devotees collected around him, and had given each a colour which collectively formed a 'rainbow' of worshippers. Despite Venta's bizarre personality, life at the commune prospered, with the tribe endearing themselves to the locals with a series of philanthropic and charitable acts. However, as time passed, rumours of group sex and financial irregularities started to sully the air. Things turned decidedly nasty when two disillusioned male associates detonated twenty sticks of high-powered dynamite inside the group's headquarters. As a result of the explosion, Venta and nine of his followers were killed.

Those who survived the blast continued their devotion to Venta, while maintaining a presence in the remote Santa Susana mountain range. Manson had been monitoring the retreat with considerable interest, taking note of Venta's past activities, and his heavy alliance with Christ. In an attempt to infiltrate the order, Charlie ordered some of the girls, including Mary Brunner and Sadie, to stay at the community and spread his word.

As photographs and eyewitness testimony confirms, Venta often performed mock crucifixion re-enactments at the Fountain of the World. These acts took place close to their headquarters, atop some unusual, skull shaped rocks. All of this was hugely appealing to Manson, who in turn wrote these performances into his own presentations.

Venta's cross had been left close to the Fountain of the World premises in honour of their charismatic leader. At one point, Charlie decreed that young Paul Watkins needed to consider killing himself, claiming, 'If you're willing to die, then you don't have to die.' To test his obedience, Manson ordered Watkins towards the Fountain of the World, ordering him 'to get up on that cross and be crucified'. Sensing a challenge, Watkins recalls how had to appear compliant with the request. 'I wasn't sure how I would get up on that cross. But I was hip to what was going on. I knew if I was willing to hang up on that cross I wouldn't have to. But I had to be truly willing because Charlie could sense that. He was keen.'

In the end Watkins wasn't crucified, and Charlie's bid to be Venta's successor failed

However, among his own Family members, Manson ruled supreme. In fact, that heady, playful summer of 1968 turned out to be the peak of the Family's happiness; the calm before the terrible storm that blew all the remnants of peace, love and understanding away.

'People say I'm no good.
But they never never do they say,
Why their world is so mixed up
Or how it got that way.
They all look at me and they frown,
Do I really look so strange?
If they really dug themselves,
I know they'd want to change'

> From the song 'People Say I'm No Good'
> by Charles Manson

A S the 'Summer of Love' descended into the twentieth century's most prolonged hangover, there were plenty of disillusioned minds heading towards Spahn's Ranch. By the first half of 1968, somewhere between eighty and a hundred people had come and gone through the Family circle since its loose inception. Although the core group consisted of around twenty followers, there were other, more peripatetic voyagers, or 'sympathetic cousins', as Charlie like to refer to them. Tripping in and out, these rolling tumbleweeds wanted nothing more than a smoke, and maybe some no-strings sex, if it was available. Manson was always keen to welcome new male members to the fold. However, as joining the Family meant divesting oneself of autonomy as well as material possessions, there were few who were prepared to live up to the demands. As a result, in the core group females always outweighed males by at least three to one.

As the Family became the dominant presence around Spahn's, the few hippies that occupied the back house began to drift away. At seventeen, Steven Grogan was one such traveller who'd grown tired of their passivity, and was looking for a raunchier manifesto. He'd been hanging around the ranch off and on for the last year, and spent some of his time assisting with the horses. Despite his hippie appearance, Grogan had proved himself to be a highly complex personality. Grogan's crazy, drug-fuelled behaviour was also out of kilter with his respectable, middle-class background. His propensity for extremism came from his curiosity about anything that offered a greater meaning than his staid family life. He expanded on this during a parole hearing in 1981.

'What was happening with me was that there was a point in my life where I was being real romantic about my life . . . where I was a real philosopher, philosophised a lot about my life, and its meaning, deep meaning . . . When I viewed my parents, I viewed it as a regular, boring, drab everyday life; everyday run of the mill. I thought it was plastic. It was just, go to work, you die, you're buried; that was it.'

Charlie saw a lot of himself in the young tearaway, and with his acid-fried consciousness receptive to any new philosophy, Grogan was absorbed into the commune with ease. Such was Manson's fondness for his protégé, he called him 'Clem Tufts' or 'Scramblehead'; which, given the young man's propensity for chaos and confusion, was more than apt. Although the irony was no doubt lost on Clem, the teenager's fucked-up mindset was a much easier one to unpick than many of the more buttoned-up girls. Such was the speed and ferocity of Grogan's whirlwind conversion that he began to mirror Charlie's behaviour, right down to his dress and speech patterns.

In spite of his years and colliding thought patterns, Grogan was able to sum up the peripatetic attraction of life at Spahn's: 'There was a small number of people that would come and go, but it was more like people that were drifting in and out of the area and knew about the place, they could stay for a day. But the strong, the people that were in the group generally stayed there. There wasn't that much leaving and going. If they did it, it was maybe for a couple of weeks and they'd come back and when they come back, they feel all guilty and stuff. It was like they had to go through some penance to get over their own guilt feelings.'

While the routines at Spahn Ranch occupied the bulk of the Family's day, there was still the business of Charlie's recording dreams to attend to. Despite Dennis Wilson's hasty retreat from his Sunset Boulevard manor, there was absolutely no way that Manson would cut off his main conduit to rock stardom. Forever on his coat-tails, Charlie pursued Dennis relentlessly; first to Gregg Jakobson's flat in Beverly Glenn, and then to a beachfront apartment on Santa Monica's Pacific Palisades. In spite of the enormous debts that the Family had racked up for him, Dennis still maintained social contact with Manson and Co., frequently visiting Spahn's to party. Although Charlie's long-promised recording deal was often hinted at, Dennis was able to bullshit his way out of any concrete promises.

On more than one occasion, Dennis was given a sharp reminder of the destructive nature of some of the Family's behaviour. One particularly crazy day, Dennis unwisely let Paul Watkins and *enfant terrible* Clem take the wheel of his brand-new red Mercedes. During a frazzled spin, Clem managed to completely wreck the vehicle on a bend close to Spahn's. Whether high on drugs or his own speed, the fact that the car was uninsured was evidently lost on Clem, who laughed his way out of the incident with trademark goofy inanity.

Leaving the wreckage – both emotional and otherwise – behind, Dennis was soon out of the country, occupied with an extensive Beach Boys' tour of Europe. The group was determined to regain ground lost through their disastrous flirtation with psychedelia the previous year. Despite their sound being temporarily out of favour in America, fans on the Continent royally welcomed the band, especially in Czechoslovakia, where they became the first Western band to play behind the Iron Curtain. With Dennis absent abroad, Charlie maintained contact with Wilson's close confidant, Gregg Jakobson. Impressed with Manson's acid-edged talent, Gregg allowed Charlie and his associates to commit a selection of his catalogue to tape.

Sound City on Cabrito Road in Van Nuys was the venue chosen to capture Manson's current sounds, in early August 1968. Whereas Charlie's first recording effort was a solo affair, the session in Van Nuys saw Charlie joined by Bobby Beausoleil,

Paul Watkins and some (if not all) of the Manson girls. In between Charlie's guitar and raspy vocals, other instruments would blend into the mix, including French horn, sitar, bongos and violin.

Delighted to reacquaint themselves with the studio interior, Charlie and the Family dressed up in a variety of colourful costumes in honour of the occasion. With incense and marijuana billowing out from all corners of the studio, Charlie delivered his tunes, while the woman breastfed their children, smoked grass and sang along with their leader's songs.

Compared to Manson's previous offering, there is more than a dash of spit and polish evident on these fourteen tracks. While the Universal demo had been rough and ready, this second recording session seems to have been a more determined attempt to get something approaching a finished product.

The most commercial track to emerge from the date was 'Look At Your Game, Girl', one of Manson's older tunes. Weaving in and out of a rotating chord pattern, the swirling mantra of the song came together as a likeable and accessible two minutes of pop. Despite the sugar-coating, the lyrics were familiar Manson territory.

> There's a time for a living
> Time keeps on flying
> Think you're loving baby
> But all you're doing is crying
> Can you feel?
> Are those feelings real?
> Look at your game, girl.

After this sweet opener, things descended into more predictable realms with the next two tracks, 'Ego' and 'Mechanical Man'. While 'Ego' sounds like a mishmash of Charlie's ravings put to sound, 'Mechanical Man' is a free-form rap drawn from deep within the Family's psyche. While the kaleidoscope of sounds and words is largely impossible to penetrate, it does offer an aural snapshot of the Family's collective mindset. The lyrics, if indeed they were ever written prior to the take, show off the verbose patois that formed the Family's lingo. One thing that leaps out from the song is Charlie's use of the word 'Family' to

his describe his group; something he'd later claim was purely a
media invention.

> I am a mechanical man,
> A mechanical man.
> And I do the best I can
> Because I have my Family.
> I am a mechanical boy,
> I am my mother's toy,
> And I play in the backyard sometimes
> I am a mechanical boy.
> Sometimes, it's an illusion
> Postulated, mocked up
> Through confusion.
> Confusion, it's an illusion
> Utter confusion
> Live on in your illusion

While the lyrics might have sounded unique to acid-tripped
ears, it was hardly material that would appeal to the wider
public. There were other tracks recorded, some new, some, by this
time, old favourites from the Manson jukebox such as 'Garbage
Dump' and 'Sick City'. At one point during the session, the girls
sans Charlie were brought up to the microphone to deliver 'I'll
Never Say Never to Always'. This song of Manson's had, of late,
become the accepted national anthem of the Family, and would
accompany them as they went about their daily activities.

> Always is always forever
> As one is one is one
> Inside yourself for your father
> All is none all is none all is none.
> So bring all the young perfection
> For there us shall surely be
> No clothing, tears, or hunger
> You can see you can see you can be

The session wrapped and, as before, the waiting game
commenced. With no one brave enough to come to any decision,
the tape ended up being shelved. While Manson waited in vain

for some encouraging news, the Beach Boys' tour of Europe was an unqualified success, and a much-needed boost to their own fortunes.

Shortly after the Sound City taping, Charlie was given another shot in the studio; this time purportedly under the auspices of the Beach Boys: Brian, Dennis and Carl Wilson. It's likely that Terry Melcher and Gregg Jakobson were also there or, at least, given an early preview of the tape. Some details have escaped over the years, despite a cloak of utmost secrecy. What is alleged is that Charlie recorded an album's worth of material at Brian Wilson's home-studio during late 1968. While some of the rumours emanating from the session have elevated it to mythical status, it is known that Steve Desper, the Beach Boys' house engineer, was present for the recordings.

'I got a call from the Beach Boys' manager. He wanted me to stay real late and record a friend of Dennis's. Of course nobody knew anything about Charles Manson at that time, except that he was more or less a street musician, and there certainly were a lot of those. So I stayed late one night, and I recorded Charles . . . He brought nothing, except a half dozen girls, and they stayed in the studio with him and smoked dope. I guess I got on Charlie's good side, because the first thing that happened was he pulled out a cigarette and didn't have a match, so I went to the kitchen and got a match for him. He was very impressed that someone would go to the trouble just for him. He made a big deal about that . . . What struck me as odd was the stare he gave you. It was scary.'

Bobby Beausoleil was also present at one of these tapings and recalled the airborne craziness. 'The session was, like most things Charlie was involved in, a disorganised mess. He insisted on trying to do the session in exactly the same way he played music with the group at the commune, with the girls singing along and jingling things, etc. This made it a nightmare for the studio engineer whose job it was to get a good balance between sound elements, with mic positioning, while keeping the focus on Charlie's voice and guitar. No one in the group understood much about the recording process, least of all Charlie, who was impatient with the engineer's efforts to isolate sound elements somewhat. Limited time was allotted for the session, and everyone left feeling frustrated, with not much accomplished by way of recordings.'

Manson also enlivened events in his own way by resorting to some of his familiar tactics. One night, with events not exactly going his way, Charlie dug up his trusty knife to test Steve Desper's mettle. '[Charlie] pulled a knife on me, just for no reason really, just pulled the knife out and would flash it around while he was talking. I called [Nick] Grillo [the Beach Boys' manager] and said, "Look, this guy is psychotic . . . The guy is too weird for me. I don't know if I'm going to say something that's going to tick him off and he's going to pull a switchblade on me."'

Gaining access to the tapes themselves has proved impossible. Adding further to the enigma, the Beach Boys' manager Nick Grillo stated in a later *Rolling Stone* interview, that they cut 'close to a hundred hours of Charlie's music' at Brian's studio. Mike Love, a familiar presence at his cousin Brian's house claimed in 1971 that, 'We've got several eight-track tapes of Charlie and the girls that Dennis cut . . . chanting, fucking, sucking, barking.' Engineer Steve Desper has recalled that, on more than one occasion, the session descended into a full-blown orgy, with bisexual activity mixed into the action. While it has been impossible to ascertain exactly what took place, one clearly heard sensual sound-bite made it on to one of Dennis Wilson's Beach Boys' tracks; 'All I Wanna Do'. The song ends in a wild, orgasmic frenzy, although who exactly was getting it on has never been fully determined.

Despite the shenanigans, one of Manson's songs, 'Cease To Exist' made a considerable impression on Dennis Wilson. Dark in tone, the song holds back from making any profound message, preferring to wallow in metaphor and allegory. The lyrics, indulging in the mind game of submission, seem partially borrowed from Manson's Process/Scientology fascination.

> Pretty girl, pretty, pretty girl
> Cease to Exist
> Just come and say you love me
> Give up your world
> C'mon you can see

I'm your kind, I'm your kind
You can see
Walk on, walk on
I love you pretty girl
My life is yours and
You can have my world
Never had a lesson
I ever learned
But I know we all get our turn
I love you
Submission is a gift
Go on, give it to your brother
Love and understanding is for one another
I'm your kind, I'm your kind
I'm your mind
I'm your brother
I never had a lesson I ever learned
But I know we all get our turn
And I love you
Never learned not to love you
I never learned

With their spirits high after their successful European jaunt, the Beach Boys had scheduled a romp through the Ersel Hickey standard, 'Bluebirds Over The Mountain' for their next single. Needing a B-side, Dennis chose a reworked version of Manson's 'Cease To Exist' for the flip side. To prepare the song for release, the bulk of Manson's lyrics were rewritten, muting Charlie's abstract semantics. Also jettisoned was the title, in favour of 'Never Learn Not To Love'. Perhaps under pressure from his bandmates, Dennis transposed the lyric 'Cease To Exist', into the more palatable 'Cease To Resist'. While the Beach Boys' version manages to transfer much of Manson's darkness on to vinyl, Dennis's mournful vocal does little in the way to inspire, and more than anything the track harks back to the group's lacklustre *Smile* era. One original feature that survived the cull was the song's finale; this six-note descendent chant was one of Charlie's meditation mantras, which had been used as an accompanied to numerous Family births.

The single endured a long incubation period before its eventual release at the beginning of December 1968. With a picture sleeve replete with a sketch of the Beach Boys, it did little to ignite the public's interest, charting at a high of number sixty-one in the US. Fans in the UK, still intoxicated by the group's recent visit, took it to a slightly more respectable number thirty-three; but still it was hardly a glorious success. Some months later, 'Never Learn Not to Love' was played live on the top-rated *Mike Douglas Show*. With Dennis temporarily relived from drumming duties, he took centre stage to deliver a competent rendition of Manson's song.

With this modicum of reflective glory, Charlie pressed again for his own talents to be acknowledged in the form of a much-coveted record deal. Terry Melcher might have been the most likely candidate to produce Manson's tracks, but he was not over-eager to let the undisciplined cult leader loose in his studios. Citing other more pressing work, Melcher made it clear that Charlie was low on his priority list. Manson's recording hopes had once again crashed and burned.

As 1968 began to draw to a close, Manson decided the Family needed to regroup and plot their next direction. Additionally, Charlie knew the importance of keeping moving to divert any suspicious minds. The move afforded Manson some time to think on where he was heading with the Family. Despite his meagre advances in the music industry, the influence he'd held over his ever-expanding retinue had been much more successful. In little over a year, Manson had collected a remarkable unit of souls, all obedient to his will. However, to further manifest his vision of total unity, Charlie hankered for an environment in which these dreams of 'oneness' could develop.

During early 1968, the Family had made a brief stopover in the Mojave Desert. While there, Charlie felt truly at one with the total anonymity and evident lawlessness of the environment. While Spahn Ranch was rural, its close proximity to LA made it impossible to assimilate totally with Mother Nature. By contrast the desert was a real wilderness – the ideal backdrop for the Family's final, sinister transformation.

It was around this time that Catherine Gillies fell into the Family ranks. The eighteen-year-old had been hanging out with the band Buffalo Springfield before a chance encounter with the Family led to her induction during the summer of 1968. Pretty and affable, she'd earned the nickname 'Capistrano' from old George Spahn. In time, the Family further chipped away at her moniker, and she became 'Cappy' or just plain 'Cap'. With Charlie talking continuously about relocating to desert climes, Gillies had mentioned that her grandparents, James and Arlene Barker, had some property in Death Valley, situated near Independence, Inyo County. In fact, they owned two ranches – Barker and Myers – lying within a quarter of a mile of each other. While Gilles' grandmother occasionally occupied Myers Ranch, the other, more expansive property lay vacant, used mainly by visiting gold prospectors as an overnight retreat from the harsh elements. Ironically, Barker Ranch was built in 1940 by a retired Los Angeles Police Detective named Bluch Thomason, who'd hoped to mine gold to supplement his pension. In 1956, the ranches were sold to Gillies' grandparents.

Barker Ranch appeared tailor-made for the Family, with ample living quarters, a kitchen, bathroom, toilet – and even a small reservoir that doubled as a swimming pool at its rear. Additionally, both ranches nestled at the bottom of the desert floor, creating numerous places to hide if things turned nasty. Hemmed in by the expanse of the Panamint mountain range, the location made for a gloriously isolated setting.

Even the name Death Valley was enough to energise Charlie into action. The region's celebrated notoriety came from its status as the hottest, driest patch of land in the United States. The heat generated within its 3,000 square miles, most of it below sea level, afforded it a reputation as one of the most unforgiving environments in the world. Few dared venture into its expanse without some elementary knowledge of the power the valley's microclimate wielded. While the heat could easily kill an unprepared traveller by day, at night freezing temperatures posed the very real threat of hypothermia.

In the autumn of 1968, Charlie made the first of many trips over to the desert to assess its potential, finding the expanse and solitude of Death Valley a powerful magnet. One of Manson's pet sayings was, 'no sense makes sense', and the phrase found

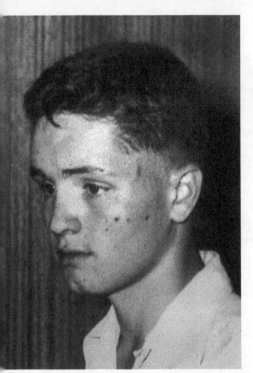

Charles Milles Manson; pictured here at age around 14. Despite his tender years, Manson's infractions with authority were already starting to accumulate.

All smiles as Charlie signs into Indianapolis' famous Boys Town reformatory, March, 1949. Manson would abscond from the institution only four days later.

Spahn's Movie Ranch. A run-down film set on the fringes of Los Angeles. The tiny hamlet of faux houses would host the majority of the Manson Family antics. From here, two nights of indescribable horror would be planned.

80-year-old ranch owner George Spahn.

A rare view inside one of the interiors at Spahn's Ranch during the Manson Family's tenure. While the cinematic facades and livery were preserved on the outside, Manson and his tribe would make the interiors their own.

Despite legend telling of a feral existence, the Manson Family was fairly domesticated, and had constructed a kitchen within the ranch to cater for their meals.

Susan Denise Atkins AKA Sadie Mae Glutz, seen here larking around Spahn's Ranch in early 1969.

Charles Tex Watson, caught in happier times at Spahn's during 1969. The once athletic, all-American youth, would become the most brutal of Charlie's many followers.

Manson had always compared the Family's retreat into the desert with Rommel's North Africa campaign. This police surveillance photo sees Sadie, flanked by Sandy and Brenda, prepare for their escape to Death Valley aboard a converted Volkswagen Beetle.

Oh Garbage Dump! In among the rotting vegetables and out-of-date bread, Squeaky encourages Sandy, Ruth Ann Morehouse and Mary Brunner during one of their supermarket sorties. These trips were the family's weekly food shop.

Members of the Family at play deep in the woods behind Spahn's Ranch.

Mary Brunner, Sadie, Gypsy and other members of Manson's Family enjoy quality time among the hay at Spahn's Ranch.

Gary Hinman: Tibetan Buddhist, music teacher, and drug dealer. Hinman made the mistake of crossing the Manson Family, and would pay heavily for his error.

Jay Sebring: hairdresser to the stars, seen here with actor Paul Newman. Despite his split from Sharon, Sebring would remain close friends with his former lover.

Voyteck Frykowski: childhood friend of film director Roman Polanski. Finding little reward in Hollywood's movie world, Frykowski would find the nefarious world of Los Angeles drug dealing far more lucrative.

Abigail Folger: partner of Voyteck Frykowski and heir to the enormous Folger coffee empire. Despite her socialite connections, Folger was a kindly altruist; working in some of Los Angeles' most deprived areas.

Leno and Rosemary LaBianca: a wealthy, middle-aged couple from the Loz Feliz district of Los Angeles. While Leno was a director of Gateway supermarkets, his wife Rosemary was a business woman of considerable zeal.

Sharon Tate: her fragile beauty epitomised the gentle innocence of the 1960's.

no better example than the natural unreality of Death Valley. Attractive to Manson, too, was the complex infrastructure of animals and plants that thrived in the harsh region. 'We found a whole world out in the desert,' he said. 'Then I got to see that the animals are smarter than the people. You know, like I've never been around many animals. In jail there are hardly any animals around. Then I got to looking at the coyotes, and I got to looking at dogs and snakes and rabbits and cats and goats and mules. And we walked around for weeks, following the animals for weeks and just saw what they do. And there is a lot of love there. That's where most of the love is, in the young people and in the animals. And that's where my love is.'

It is around this time that the fabled Family bus finally came to the end of the road, finished off by the demanding trips to the desert. A new bus, with municipal green livery running down the sides, was acquired with the 600 dollars that Sandy wangled out of her father.

The first Family trip in the new bus occurred during the late autumn of 1968. While their ultimate location was totally remote, there were a few outposts on the way into the desert. The nearest of these was Ballarat. Lying at the base of the Panamint Mountains, Ballarat had become home to a motley collection of gold prospectors and other desert rats. As the canyons and mines had been comprehensively stripped over the years, Ballarat's heyday as a vibrant mining town had long since past. The derelict buildings and decommissioned businesses of the once thriving settlement now resembled a ghost town. Nonetheless, for the few who hung on, a small store was still operating, selling essential supplies, which was handy for anyone travelling towards the desert.

With Ballarat some twelve miles behind them, the imposing spectre of Golar Wash soon came into view. Before you could reach the desert proper this tract of mountains had to be negotiated. While these days a track of sorts has been established, in 1968 it was nothing more than an uneven, rubble-strewn gradient leading into a mountainous unknown. Although Manson's driving was quite skilful, even he knew that attempting to take the bus through the spiral of rocks and holes would seriously challenge the new vehicle's limits. As a result, the bus was pitched at the wash's base, and the advance party continued on foot.

Once freed from Golar Wash and safely inside the natural amphitheatre of the desert, the landscape was like a living hallucination. Now the others could see the substance behind Manson's fevered descriptions of the area. Underneath the desert plains lay a myriad of rivers and streams that fed numerous exotic plants that burst through the dry desert floor. With his imagination running riot, Manson thrived on the area's folklore that suggested that a vast underworld existed beneath the arid surface. Charlie embellished these fables, conjuring up a hidden hinterland of streams and river that defied science, and ran uphill and upside down.

Alongside his biblical interpretations, Charlie often referenced Shoshone Indian legend that spoke of an entrance to the underworld. Giving considerable credence to this theory, an entry point was situated at the north of Death Valley, around ninety miles from Las Vegas. From its modest opening, Devil's Hole, as it is known, leads into water-filled caverns, estimated to be over 300 feet deep. While geologists claim that the caves were naturally created over 500,000 years ago, no one knows exactly what lies in the furthermost regions. Manson, fired by biblical tracts detailing a 'bottomless pit', was immediately drawn to the Devil's Hole. Riffing off these fables, Charlie sold his followers a tale of a subterranean city that was waiting for the Family to retreat into. This neverland, where chocolate fountains endlessly spewed honey and milk and trees bore a different fruit for each day of the week was, he claimed, going to be theirs for the taking. The Family, at times struggling to recognise reality over their own acid-driven imaginations, were ecstatic at the prospect of reaching this heaven on earth. High on these possibilities, Manson had sent a couple of Family members down inside the hole to check out its furthermost reaches. As the waters underneath were indeed deep and expansive, Charlie's explorers couldn't advance any further without diving equipment. With plans to delve even further, Manson added aqualung apparatus to his inventory.

Manson's initial audience with Cathy Gillies' grandmother was cordial and productive. As bankable collateral, Charlie handed Cathy's grandma one of Dennis Wilson's Beach Boys' gold discs, proclaiming that he too was on the verge of imminent success. Transaction completed, Manson begun the task of subtly introducing the Family into Death Valley. To achieve this, Manson hung around the town of Ballarat, Barker Ranch's nearest settlement. For the few die-hard residents of the little town, Charlie was courtesy exemplified, and he ingratiated himself to all with his effusive charm. Manson had good reason for this active canvassing. Despite the remoteness of the ranch, news of an influx of thirty to forty people would easily make its way back to the residents of the little town, their senses highly attuned to any newcomers. In turn, these reports could make their way to the park rangers who policed the desert.

Manson certainly impressed a few diehards in the area. Geologist Emmett Harder was one. He came across Manson and the Family numerous times: 'I found Charlie Manson to be a dedicated person,' the miner recalled to local press in 1969. '[Manson was] dedicated to taking care of the people camping with him.' Charlie had evidently done his homework: a photo from this time taken of him with local miner, Carlo Ruona, presents a reserved Manson, replete with ten-gallon hat and cheesecloth shirt; every bit the weathered desert hand.

With everything rosy in the desert, Manson returned back to Los Angeles, full of hope for the next chapter of Family life. If Death Valley manifested Charlie's beliefs into a visual reality, another, more aural, experience was about to take his apocalyptic visions even further.

With Manson still firmly fixed on his dreams of stardom, he made sure he kept an eye on the activities of those he had adopted as his transatlantic brothers, the Beatles. While Charlie's recording career was on shaky ground, in 1968 the Fab Four were continuing their remarkable ascendancy. Following the enormous global success of their anthemic single, 'Hey Jude', they'd been beavering away at a collection of less commercial songs for their next album. Entitled simply, *The Beatles,* the album was a seismic shift from their previous incarnation as *Sgt Pepper's Lonely Hearts Club Band.* With a plainer sensibility, and an abrasive edge to many of the compositions, the album was a revelation to both fans and press.

Ironically, the Beatles' interlude with the Maharishi had served to slam the lid shut on their so-called 'Love' period. The group's trip to India in early 1968 to study meditation with the mystical swami had ultimately ended in disappointment. Ringo left after only ten days, fed up with the spicy food and the flies. Paul fared a little longer, but he too left after six weeks. George and John attempted to last the distance, but rumours regarding the allegedly less than holy behaviour of the Maharishi caused them to leave abruptly. By the end of April, all four Beatles were back in England and ready to start recording again. If their experiences in India had proved mixed, the visit nonetheless produced a huge amount of material, which the group was keen to immediately transfer to tape.

The Beatles had booked EMI's Abbey Road studios for an indefinite period starting in May 1968. Ultimately, they'd end up spending over four months in the white, stuccoed building laying down the tracks. There's no mistaking that the bulk of these songs turned out to be remarkable creations – even for minds less warped than Manson's.

With over two discs worth of material, and half a dozen tracks discarded at the last minute, the album was scheduled for release on 22 November 1968. Three days later, it surfaced in the US. Tired of hunting around for a suitable name, the group decided on an eponymous title for the album. The album's design was as basic as its title, with a monochrome sleeve housing the two discs. With buyers unsure what to call the album, a more descriptive moniker, the 'White Album', rose from the streets and became part of global consciousness.

The world that the 'White Album' emerged into at the end of 1968 was a schizophrenic melee. While there were still plenty who were still touting the hackneyed 'Summer of Love' idealism, it now looked decidedly out of place against the harsher realities emanating from the streets. With anti-war riots and a plethora of student and youth disorders breaking out across America, there was a distinct odour of dissatisfaction in the air. Adding to the discontent, Republican Richard Nixon's elevation to power on 5 November only served to inflame sensibilities further.

The 'White Album' became the fastest-selling Beatles album to date, shifting a million units in America alone during the first week of release. Where US Beatles' albums prior to *Sgt Pepper* often had their own idiosyncratic sequencing, on the implicit instruction of the group, American copies of the *White Album* were presented as the Beatles intended. In all, twenty-nine tracks were spread over four sides of two vinyl platters, each displaying the group's new Apple label. As an added treat for the fans, initial copies of the album were franked with a unique individual number. Inside, four colour photos of the Beatles were printed alongside a large collage of disparate images of the group throughout their career. On the reverse of the poster, and much to the chagrin of their music publisher, the group had reprinted the entire lyrics of the album.

If the Beatles' previous Stateside offering, the fractured but optimistic *Magical Mystery Tour* had acted as an amusing aural backdrop to the Family's meandering, the 'White Album' tore through any existing structure that held their world together. Previously, Charlie had noted the similarities between his and the Beatles' lyrics, evidenced by the playful imagery on many of the *Magical Mystery Tour* songs. Manson also noted John Lennon's biblical appropriation in 'I Am The Walrus'. Taken from John 14:20, the passage 'I am in He, and you in me, and I in you,' joyously confirmed the Family's one-mind-and-body status.

Charlie first heard the 'White Album' in early December 1968 He'd stopped off at a friend's house, en route from one of his numerous trips from Death Valley to Los Angeles, and someone had put the record on. After that, Manson wasted little time in scoring a copy of the album for himself.

While it's true that the Family had enjoyed the Beatles' back catalogue, no one was prepared for the group's latest concoction. As of late, Manson's proclamations to his followers of an impending apocalypse had been gaining momentum. Although the Family lapped up Charlie's words with due deference, Manson knew that, aside from the Bible's text, he had little in the way of evidence to support his ravings on an imminent Judgement Day. Now dropping in, as if by magic, the Beatles' 'White Album' went an enormous way towards endorsing every word of his frenzied discourses. To Charlie, a two-way thought-line had been established between him and the Beatles. Heightened by acid, the discovery of Death Valley and his own idolatry, it seemed patently obvious. While more erudite critics saw the 'White Album' redrawing the narrow perimeters of pop music; for Charles Manson it was nothing less than a call to arms.

After spending time processing the album, Charlie revealed his seismic findings at a party in Death Valley on New Year's Eve 1968. In honour of this unbelievable synchronicity of like minds, Charlie had purchased a battery-operated record player to take with them to the desert. Susan Atkins, at that point acquiescent to Charlie's ever-changing moods, recalled the night Manson made the announcement of his link to the Beatles' thought-line. 'It had a tremendous impact on our lives, especially Charlie's. One night, when many of us were playing records and listening to the album, Charlie said, "They're speaking to me." He was convinced that he had some sort of apocalyptic connection with the Beatles. I never fully understood it, but Charlie, our unchallenged leader, was deeply affected. And I and most of the others believed that, in some way, "Helter Skelter", the end of the world, was "coming down fast."'

To attempt to understand this enigma, one has to look at where the Beatles' heads were at this point, and equally, how their ambivalence could draw in people like Manson. Many of the tracks were composed in India during their meditation stint with the Maharishi in early 1968. With little outside influence, the lyrics drew heavily on the Beatles' inner psyche. Obviously, Manson at that time had no inkling about the derivation of any of the songs. Charlie's own translation relied on nothing more than the reflections of his own thought process. Regardless of the sheer craziness of the connections, it is said that Manson pinpointed thirteen tracks off the album that correlated to his views on an impending apocalypse.

While the intricate detail concerning Manson's interpretations came out during the trials (much of it from disaffected cohorts of Manson), the connections are worthy of investigation, as they give a sense of the charged atmosphere around Manson. Indeed, if Charlie truly believed what he had deciphered in the recordings, then the album unwittingly offers a vivid prelude to the eventual carnival of terror.

To the uninitiated, 'I Will' was a fairly innocuous love song that Paul McCartney had written in India. To Charlie though, the song was a clarion call, asking Manson to pitch his voice 'loud' so the Beatles could hear him in the UK. Another McCartney track, the skittish, 'Why Don't We Do It In The Road?' was seen by Manson as the Beatles' acknowledgement of the violence on the streets of America. Mind you, Charlie also claimed the rise in arson was caused by fans inflamed by the Doors' single, 'Light My Fire', so his signal-reading was evidently in overdrive.

Even McCartney's weaker offering on the album, the pithy, music-hall homage 'Honey Pie' didn't escape Manson's receptive ears. With references to 'Hollywood', 'magic' and all other sorts of whimsy ephemera, Charlie believed that McCartney was talking directly to him. Later in the song, Manson detected what he believed was a direct invitation for him to 'sail' over to England, where he evidently belonged. The song also describes an infatuation that the protagonist is too 'lazy' to follow up on. As a group, the Beatles had abandoned touring for over two years, and so they, according to Charlie, were keen for him to make the trip over the Atlantic.

Ringo Starr only contributed four tracks to the entire Beatles oeuvre, but he did put forward 'Don't Pass Me By' for the 'White Album'. The song is elementary, and Manson inferred far more from it than Ringo could ever have intended. As it talked about listening for approaching 'footsteps', Charlie believed that the Fab Four were anticipating his own advance towards them.

George Harrison's contribution included the track 'Piggies', a swipe at the rich and ruling classes, which at one point suggests that they need a right royal 'whacking'. In America, the term 'Piggies' held further connotations, especially within the revolutionary Black Panther movement, who used 'pig' as a derisory term for the white establishment. Black Panther Party leader Bobby Seale frequently peppered his speeches with diatribes against the 'pigs', handing Manson an association on a plate.

Bobby Seale: 'The only way that the world is ever going to be free is when the youth of this country moves with every principle of human respect and with every soft spot we have in our hearts for human life, in a fashion that lets the "pig" power structure know that when people are racistly [sic] and fascistically attacked, the youth will put a foot in their butts and make their blood chill.'

Whereas the Panthers used the word 'pig' for police and lawmakers, for Manson, the term of abuse could be aimed at the rich and famous; especially those who were denying him a shot at a recording contract. In 1980, Harrison would take a rare opportunity to play down any bold inferences fans like Manson may have drawn from the track.

George Harrison revealed: '"Piggies" is a social comment. I was stuck for one line in the middle until my mother came up with the lyric, "What they need is a damn good whacking", which is a nice simple way of saying they need a good hiding. It needed to rhyme with "backing", "lacking", and had absolutely nothing to do with American policemen or Californian shagnasties!'

There were several other tracks that correlated with Manson's beliefs on the album, and others that just appeared hugely coincidental – not least the licentious track, 'Sexy Sadie'. As far as the Beatles were concerned, John Lennon's oblique paean to a shunned lover was heavily coded. Written in a fit of pique, Lennon hoped that signals from the song would travel towards the Maharishi in India, with whom he'd fallen out after a raft of unsubstantiated sexual allegations surfaced during their stay in India.

Months before the release of the 'White Album', Manson had christened the sex- and drug-crazed Susan Atkins Sadie. However, no one in the Family was prepared for the Beatles uncanny vinyl reference. This apparent synchronicity helped validate Charlie's observations, especially as the frazzled Sadie was adept at turning on all and sundry while breaking all the known rules. Not surprisingly, Sadie was cock-a-hoop about 'her song'.

From 'Rocky Racoon', Paul McCartney's vaudeville about the Wild West, Manson drew a racial inference, having extracted the syllable 'coon'. Additionally, references in the song to gun battles over Bibles were further confirmation to him of an impending black uprising. During a *Rolling Stone* magazine interview in 1970, Charlie explained his 'Rocky Racoon' theory: '"Coon". You know that's a word they use for black people ... "Revival" ... re-vival. It means coming back to life. The black man is going to come into power again. "Gideon checks out" means that it's all written out there in the New Testament, in the Book of Revelations.'

John Lennon's quasi-junkie song, the fractured, 'Happiness Is A Warm Gun', was said by Manson to further signify the impending black uprising. Lennon's gung-ho lyrics, originally inspired by a hunter he'd come across in India, were seen by Manson to be encouraging blacks to take up arms in their struggle.

Less coded was 'Blackbird'; Paul McCartney's poignant metaphor for the civil rights struggle in America. Within the bare acoustic delivery, the thinly veiled lyrics needed little in the way of embellishment to be interpreted as a call for an uprising. It was a rare political statement from McCartney, who'd enjoyed sitting on the fence up until that point. Significantly, Manson cited the song's challenge to 'arise' as the clarion call for the blacks to begin to seize power.

If the lyrics on the 'White Album' gave credence to Manson's apocalyptic logic, then the sonic vibrations on 'Revolution 9' formed the soundtrack to it. With gunfire, screaming, mob chanting and other jarring sounds charging in and out, it's like an audio depiction of Armageddon. Manson's subconscious and LSD-addled reality were blurred into one.

While mono versions of the original pressing would lose all of the sequencing from channel to channel, the repetition of the phrase 'all right', (itself clipped from the vocal track from 'Revolution 1') was easily perceptible to the ears. Manson, erroneously concluded that Lennon was shouting 'Rise', which provided an echo for him back to 'Blackbird', and a further indication that the Beatles were predicting the black community's forthcoming insurrection.

Save for a few passages of nonsensical gibberish, most of the words spoken in 'Revolution 9' are totally indecipherable. During the trial, when the mass of this information was presented, it was claimed that Manson had heard the words 'Charlie, Charlie, send us a telegram' during the track. Although George Harrison does indeed mutter the word 'telegram', it's difficult to ascertain whether 'Charlie' is mentioned at any point. The prosecutor would also claim that the Family heard the phrase, 'lots of stab wounds', although there is not even a hint of the words in its muddy soundtrack. Even more bizarre were claims that embedded in the track were the Beatles chanting, 'Charlie, can you hear us? Charlie can you hear us? Call us in London. Call us in London.'

Squeaky (and possibly Charlie too) certainly bombarded the group's Apple offices in London with telegrams, letters and phone calls alerting the Fab Four to their presence. Apple Records had to endure a daily litany of freaks attempting to contact the group for the strangest of reasons, and the Family's efforts, like those of all the others, were studiously ignored. Undeterred, Charlie would later send an emissary over to try to meet the Beatles to discuss matters further.

While there were snippets of other tracks that were significant to Charlie, 'Helter Skelter' became the strongest sign of the impending apocalypse. In late 1967, McCartney had read an interview with the Who's Pete Townshend, about the band's latest single, 'I Can See for Miles'. During the feature, Townshend described the song as the 'the loudest, nastiest, sweatiest rock number' that the Who had ever put to tape. The quote stuck with McCartney and, never one to be outdone by his peers, he set about creating his own ruckus.

Paul McCartney: 'Just reading those lines [of the Townshend interview] fired my imagination. I thought, Right, they've done what they think was the loudest and dirtiest; we'll do what we think. I went into the studio and told the guys, "Look, I've got this song but Pete said this and I want to do it even dirtier." It was a great brief for the engineers, for everyone – just as fuzzy and as dirty and as loud and as filthy as you can get it is where I want to go. I was happy to have Pete's quote to get me there.'

The completed version of 'Helter Skelter' made its way on to side three of the album, wedged in between John Lennon's 'Sexy Sadie' and George Harrison's highly under-rated, 'Long, Long, Long'. Without doubt, 'Helter Skelter' is the most ruthless track in the Beatles oeuvre, and a template for punk bands to emulate some eight years later. While McCartney has always been at pains to step back from the track's revolutionary implications, the electric frisson of chaos and confusion speaks for itself. No one, least of all the Beatles, was prepared for Charlie's appropriation.

John Lennon: 'We used to have a laugh about this, that or the other, in a light-hearted way, and some intellectual would read us, some symbolic youth generation wants to see something in it. We also took seriously some parts of the role, but I don't know what "Helter Skelter" has to do with knifing someone. I've never listened to it properly, it was just a noise.'

With the 'White Album' crammed with innovative sounds, 'Helter Skelter' was largely passed over by both critics and fans on its release. For Charlie, however, it was the band's fiercest stake; the strongest lyrical conduit between them and the biblical apocalypse he'd begun referring to with an alarming regularity. Within the scatterburst of lyrics on 'Helter Skelter', the repetitive chant of 'coming down fast' was, to Manson, the signal that the end was nigh. He is clearly in defensive mode when he talks about the track to *Rolling Stone* in 1970.

'Helter Skelter means confusion. Literally. It doesn't mean any war with anyone. It doesn't mean that those people are going to kill other people. It only means what it means. Helter Skelter is confusion. Confusion is coming down fast. If you don't see the confusion coming down fast, you can call it what you wish. It's not my conspiracy. It is not my music. I hear what it relates. It says, "Rise!" It says "Kill!" Why blame it on me? I didn't write the music. I am not the person who projected it into your social consciousness.'

For Charlie the track's 'confusion' was wholly in line with his own interpretations of the book of Revelation, the final book of New Testament. Manson's fascination with the Bible went back to the Sundays spent sitting in the pews of McMechen, West Virginia, with his grandmother, aunt and uncle. Despite being on the sharp end of their Christian admonishments, he'd revisited the texts in jail, and had his own deep-held convictions about what Revelation signified, particularly chapter nine.

Charles Manson: 'What do you think it means? It's the battle of Armageddon. It's the end of the world. It was the Beatles' "Revolution 9" that turned me on to it. It predicts the overthrow of the establishment. The pit will be opened, and that's when it will all come down. A third of mankind will die. The only people who will escape will be those who have the seal of God on their foreheads.'

For Manson, the Beatles' album and Revelation – the only book in the Bible to openly cite apocalyptic themes – were part of the same terrifying vision of the future. In chapter nine, verse one of Revelation, it states, 'And the fifth angel sounded, and I saw a star from heaven fallen unto the earth: and there was given to him the key of the pit of the abyss.' Manson was convinced that the Beatles were heavenly deities and, as he allied himself so closely with the group, he saw himself as the 'Fifth Beatle'. The 'key of the abyss' related directly to the bottomless pit, and with Charlie was clearly the one with the key. According to his warped reading of Revelation 9, Charlie believed that, with the Family safely ensconced in the desert underworld, or 'pit of the abyss', they would sit out the bloodbath in the city, waiting until their numbers reached 144,000, a figure he'd derived from Revelation 7, which talked of twelve tribes of 12,000. With the blacks assuming power in what Charlie assumed would be an inept and haphazard fashion, the Family (now swollen in number) would re-emerge to clean up the mess, and ultimately take over.

Paul Watkins remembers: 'Blackie then would come to Charlie and say, you know, "I did my thing, I killed them all and, you know, I am tired of killing now. It is all over." And Charlie would scratch his fuzzy head and kick him in the butt and tell him to go pick the cotton and go be a good nigger, and he would live happily ever after.'

In Revelation 9:3 it says, 'And out of the smoke came forth locusts upon the earth; and power was given them as the scorpions of the earth have power.' Naturally, Manson figured that these bugs were kin with The Beatles. Moreover, Manson's birth sign was Scorpio. It all had a certain mad logic.

However, it was Revelation 9, verses 7–9 that were most significant to Manson: 'The locusts looked like horses prepared for battle. On their heads they wore something like crowns of gold, and their faces resembled human faces. Their hair was like women's hair, and their teeth were like lions' teeth. They had breastplates like breastplates of iron, and the sound of their wings was like the thundering of many horses and chariots rushing into battle.'

Manson had reportedly deduced that the 'locusts' were in fact the Beatles, and that their 'crowns of gold' signified their dominance of world leaders of the pop world. 'Their hair was like women's hair' was true of the Fab Four at the time. The 'breastplates like breastplates of iron', was meant to signify the Beatles' electric guitars, strapped to their chests. And one only had to listen to 'Revolution 9' to hear that 'the sound of their wings was like the thundering of many horses and chariots rushing into battle.'

In verse fifteen, the passage that claimed 'the four angels' would be prepared for the killing of 'a third part of men' was, to Charlie, a direct reference to the black community overthrowing civilisation and culling a third of mankind in its wake. Given that Revelation's chapter nine was explicit in its timeline of 'five months', Manson worked out that this uprising would take place in the summer of 1969.

As crazy as it all might seem, it wasn't just Manson who was out to decode subliminal messages in the Beatles' songs. There were many who were convinced that the Beatles had impregnated copies of *Sgt Pepper* with LSD, while others believed that if they smoked the album covers they could get high. Upon the release of the 'White Album', fans across the world were scouring the album in search of clues – especially as strange rumours began circulating about the death of Paul McCartney. Not surprisingly, the nebulous mutterings of 'Revolution 9' came in for the most scrutiny, apparently offering a host of significant clues to the manner of McCartney's death. It was said that if the 'number nine' mantra was played backwards it revealed the words, 'Turn me on, dead man.' To stem the tide of a growing belief that he had indeed passed away, McCartney finally had to speak out: 'If I was dead, I'm sure I'd be the last to know', he quipped through gritted teeth.

While McCartney and the other Beatles enjoyed the success of the 'White Album', Charlie used the so-called revelations encoded on the album to take the Family to a much darker place. The album was played almost continuously, Manson's nightly ravings bending the Beatles' lyrics into believable equations for his receptive followers. Naturally, Charlie summed it up succinctly for them. For Paul Watkins, and the other Family members, it was vindication of everything Manson had been pointing to for months.

Watkins articulated the Family's sense of uncanny realisation following Charlie's exposure to the 'White Album'. 'Things were never the same ... At that point Charlie's credibility seemed indisputable. For weeks he had been talking of revolution, prophesying it. We had listened to him rap; we were geared for it – making music to program the young love. Then, from across the Atlantic, the hottest music group in the world substantiates Charlie with an album that is almost blood-curdling in its depiction of violence. It was uncanny.'

'Helter Skelter' was coined into the Family's lexicon as the prime metaphor for confusion, and by broad extension, the impending racial apocalypse. From the night of the Family's joint exposure to the 'White Album', events took a sharp left turn and headed off into the unknown. Similarly, the otherworldly landscape of Death Valley was working a transformation on Manson and the Family, subtly darkening their daily existence. Not surprisingly, Charlie was inspired to write many new songs on the strength of these experiences, the lyrics inspired by the isolation and barren landscape. Overall, it seems Charlie was keen to realise the vibrations and inferences the 'White Album' had merely hinted at. Manson's projections were anything but modest; he predicted that his new music would draw all the 'young love' from areas such like Haight-Ashbury, and have them riding with the Family. He talked this over with Paul Watkins. 'Are you hep to what the Beatles are saying?' he asked Paul. 'Dig it, they're telling it like it is. They know what's happening in the city; blackie is getting ready. They put the revolution to music ... it's "Helter Skelter". Helter Skelter is coming down. Hey, their album is getting the young love ready, man, building up steam. Our album is going to pop the cork right out of the bottle.'

Despite all Charlie's hot air, he'd underestimated Death Valley's mercurial climate. The nights were unbearably cold, and the rickety ranches offered little in the way of protection from the elements. As they huddled together on their motley collection of old mattresses and sleeping bags, Manson decreed a move back to Los Angeles to begin preparations for the impending Helter Skelter. Nonetheless, he ensured that a presence was maintained at both the desert ranches and at Spahn's, to ensure the Family could retreat there when things got too heavy.

Back in Los Angeles, temporary accommodation was found in a two-storey property at 20910 Gresham Street, close to the San Fernando Valley. The area was fast gathering a sleazy reputation as a centre for California's pornography industry. For the likes of Charlie, it was the ideal location to slip into without too much bother. Since the house's frontage was painted a shocking, garish yellow, they started calling it 'Yellow Submarine'. Inside, with many rolling bodies and minds squeezed into every nook and cranny, the Yellow Submarine took on a life of its own.

Paul Watkins recalls: 'He called the Gresham Street house the "Yellow Submarine" from the Beatles' movie. It was like a submarine in that when you were in it you weren't allowed to go out; you could only peek out of the windows.'

Manson acquired use of the building from Bill Vance, an ex-con, who knew lots of shady characters, all eager to join in the revelry. Whilst Charlie kept them on the boundaries of his inner circle, he enjoyed their steely presence. In time they became important in helping acquire and maintain vehicles bound for the desert. Around the back of the house, work began on the construction of numerous Dune Buggies for the desert retreat. All manner of duplicitous transactions occurred in the race to have them ready. One scam to raise cash was to flog stolen vehicle parts back to legitimate dealers. This caught up with them on 9 April 1969, when they tried to sell the parts of a Volkswagen back to the dealer they'd originally stolen it from.

Keen to ingratiate himself in the area, and raise some much-needed finance, Charlie visited various seedy clubs with some of his new retinue. With his pimp credentials to the fore, Charlie attempted to get the girls work as dancers in topless bars. When some were denied work because of their small breasts, Manson even considered getting them silicon injections to bolster their assets.

As a result of Manson's murky schmoozing, a seedy rogue's gallery began to fill up every crevice of the Gresham Street house. Manson described the 'Yellow Submarine' as a 'concert hall for musicians, a porno studio for kinky producers, a dope pad, a thieves' lair, a place to dismantle stolen cars, and just about everything else.' Some of the retinue passing through the revolving door were members of Los Angeles' notorious biker gangs, charmed out of the clubs and bars of the district. Manson enjoyed their presence, as well as their survivalist nature. Soon, they'd be sharing in Charlie's numerous mind and body games.

Manson's new beliefs armed those of the Family with a harder, more resolute direction. With Armageddon fast approaching, Manson tugged hard for another spot at recording. Initially, Charlie had difficulty in locating Terry Melcher, whose previously ambivalent responses only served to inflame his determination. Manson left copious messages for Melcher to come over and hear some of his new songs at the Family's Gresham Street property. Somewhere along the way word got back to Charlie that Melcher might just drop by after work one night to hear these new tunes. Ignited by the prospect, Charlie and the girls cleared up the property, baked cakes, and even prepared a few joints in case Melcher needed to relax further. With the clock ticking and Melcher nowhere to be seen, no one, least of all Charlie, was prepared to admit that Terry was probably only paying lip service. Eventually, time was called on Melcher's hollow promise, and Manson was reportedly left livid at the slight.

Tex Watson, darting back and forth from the Family, recalled the scenario in his memoir, and the deep imprint it made on Charlie's sensitive psyche: 'Once again, Terry Melcher had failed Charlie. More than ever, Terry Melcher, in his house at the top of Cielo Drive, with his power and his money – was the focus for the bitterness and sense of betrayal that the Family felt for all those phony Hollywood hippies who kept silencing the truth Charlie had to share. These "beautiful people", Terry and all the others, were really no different from the rich piggies in their white shirts and ties and suits. And just like them, they too deserved a "damn good whacking".'

While Manson and Co. were spilling bile at Terry Melcher's apparent snub, it appears that the producer had far more pressing details to attend to than the likes of Charlie Manson. Over Christmas 1968, Terry's stepfather Martin Melcher had died, leaving a heap of financial irregularities to be sorted out. With his mother, Doris Day, still in shock after losing her third husband, Terry decided to move in with her at her beachside address in Malibu, allowing him time to sort out the mess. As a result of this, the lease on Melcher's Cielo Drive property was terminated early.

The house at the end of Cielo Drive wasn't exactly virgin territory for members of the Family, and it had featured occasionally in their interminable jaunts around town.

Shortly after Terry Melcher's relocation, the Reverend Deane Morehouse, an embarrassment to both Charlie and Dennis Wilson, needed to be sent well out of everyone's reach. With the landlord's consent, the sparkly reverend was installed in the guest-house at Cielo Drive. Once ensconced at the property, Morehouse invited various Family members to party around the grounds, and skinny-dip in the swimming pool. These included Tex Watson and Susan Atkins, who were soon to return to the property with a far more sinister purpose. Indeed, Tex had also driven Dennis Wilson up to the house in his truck during Melcher's residency, and even hung out in the lounge. Charlie too, had apparently visited the property 'five or six' times. Wilson and Melcher's friend, Gregg Jakobson later testified that Charlie 'would come by, swim, visit'. In more recent times, Manson has revealed, in typically obtuse style, that he used to consort with 'several homosexuals' who stayed at Cielo Drive. Despite much fevered debate, no one has ever figured out to whom Manson was referring. Aside from these speculations, it's clear that Manson was familiar with the house and its layout – knowledge that he'd use to terrible effect in a few short months.

Like the residents who passed through its doors, 10050 Cielo Drive had its own idiosyncratic charm. A distinct anomaly in the district, the design of the building owed more to Provence than to the glitz of Bel Air. Commissioned by French actress Michèle Morgan and designed by noted architect Robert Byrd in 1944, the house had a distinctly rustic appearance, with its low-slung, plunging roof and chintz decor. The three-acre site also housed a small coterie of outbuildings, a swimming pool and a one-bedroom chalet for the caretaker. The garden hosted a mini-arboretum of pine trees, cherry blossoms, avocado bushes, and other sweet-smelling plants. At the edge of the garden, over-looking Los Angeles, was a split rail fence where roses were intertwined with the wood. Melcher's partner, the actress Candice Bergen, was totally enamoured with the house's slightly surreal, gingerbread atmosphere. 'I felt at home,' Bergen would recall later, 'Surrounded by tall, thick pine trees and cherry blossoms, with rose-covered rail fences and a cool mountain pool grown over with flowers, it snuggled up against the hillside ... It was a fairy-tale place, that house on the hill, a never-never land far away from the real world, where nothing could go wrong.'

Like a lot of Hollywood's jet set, some effort had been made to secure the property from the voyeuristic gaze of curious passers-by. At the front of the house a ramshackle metal gate, roughly measuring six by eighteen feet, had been erected. To dissuade anyone from attempting to breach its defences, some barbed wire had been loosely tacked to its top. Despite the absence of an intercom, a secreted button operated the electric gate from the outside. The nearest neighbours were over a hundred metres away. The house had a definite celebrity feel to it and, over the years, the likes of Cary Grant, Henry Fonda, and members of Paul Revere and the Raiders had all hung out there.

News that Terry Melcher and Candice Bergen were vacating the beautiful property swiftly passed through the district. Coincidently early in 1969, thirty-two-year-old Polish director Roman Polanski was looking for somewhere secluded, yet close to Hollywood, where he and his wife, the actress Sharon Tate, could settle. Tate was newly pregnant with the couple's first child, and with the house situated high on Benedict Canyon, it was a perfect escape from the balmy temperatures in the city. With the $3,000 monthly rental no obstacle, the Polanskis arranged to move in during February of 1969.

The celebrity convergence of Tate and Polanski was nothing less than a Hollywood fairy tale. At twenty-six, Sharon Tate was on the cusp of major international stardom, her extraordinary beauty coupled with a rare innocence that during the 1960s was hugely marketable. Her swift ascendancy through the ranks of the film world had seen her career expand well beyond the confines of Hollywood, and she'd been accepting work in Europe to bolster her extensive American television resume.

It was during one trip to London in 1966 that Sharon had met Roman Polanski. A survivor of the Warsaw ghettos, Polanksi had overcome his numerous disadvantages to study film in his native Poland. His obvious talents were rewarded with a string of well-received films, critics noting his subtle understanding of dark and unsettling psychology.

With Britain basking in a cinematic renaissance during the 1960s, Polanski immersed himself in the country's celluloid scene. After winning critical success with *Repulsion* and *Cul-De-Sac*, Polanski took a brief hiatus from 'serious' film-making for his next venture; a witless pastiche entitled, *The Fearless Vampire Killers*, a.k.a, *Dance of the Vampires*. Sharon Tate's theatrical agent offered to produce the picture, but with the tag that his client should be considered for the role of licentious vampire 'Sarah Shagal'. Although Polanski was at first ambivalent over Tate's inclusion in the picture, it was felt she'd prove useful for the Anglo-American market.

Sharon first collided with Roman in one of London's swinging nightclubs. Reportedly, the attraction wasn't immediate, and yet their close proximity on set soon changed all that. By the end of the filming of *Vampire Killers*, Sharon had moved into Polanski's London flat and terminated her relationship with long-term boyfriend, the celebrity hairdresser Jay Sebring.

Despite their growing infatuation with each other, the couple both had heavy workloads which often necessitated them being away from each other for long periods. In early 1967, Roman began preparing his next work, *Rosemary's Baby*, while Tate found critical acclaim in the proto-*Hollywood Wives'* exposé, *Valley of the Dolls*. With rumours flooding the gossip pages about the couple's relationship, Sharon and Roman were finally married on 20 January 1968 in Chelsea, London, under the glare of the world's press.

Regardless of the marital bond, the couple continued their independent, hectic schedules, Roman maintaining his roving eye and active casting couch. Things came to a temporary halt when, in late 1968, Tate discovered she was expecting the couple's first child. With a peaceful base required for the final stages of her pregnancy, Cielo Drive's vacancy appeared a blessing. Sharon, in particular, was heavily enamoured with the property's cosy ambience, labelling it her 'love house'. In stages, the Polanskis begun to move their possessions into the house during the tail end of February 1969.

The Polanskis were very much the toast of Hollywood, and their dual celebrity had garnered an enormous roster of society contacts. As a result, it wasn't unusual to find the likes of Warren Beatty, Steve McQueen, Peter Sellers, Mia Farrow and Peter and Jane Fonda relaxing in their company. Sharon particularly enjoyed the company of musicians, and aside from being ecstatic at meeting the Beatles in London during 1968, some of LA's finest groups like the Doors, the Mamas & the Papas and the Byrds became frequent house-guests.

While there were few physical traces of Terry Melcher's tenancy around the property, there were other pieces of detritus that would unexpectedly pop up; one of them being Charlie Manson.

Such was Manson's desperation to make contact with Terry Melcher, on the afternoon of 3 March 1969, Charlie made a proactive attempt at catching up with him face to face. With security systems nothing more than a laughable formality for Charlie, he managed to breach Cielo Drive's feeble defences and gain entry to the grounds. Manson went to the main house and rang the bell. Iranian photographer, Shahrokh Hatami, answered the door. A close friend of both Sharon and Roman, Hatami was there to take some photographs of Sharon before she left for Europe the next day to begin work on the film *The Thirteen Chairs*. The sight of bedraggled, unkempt Manson startled Hatami, and he loudly informed Manson that he wasn't aware of anyone by the name of Melcher living at the house. Since Charlie didn't appear entirely satisfied with the answer, Hatami suggested he try the guest house next to the swimming pool. Hatami's tone served to arouse the others' curiosity, and they all came to the door to check out what was happening. For a brief moment Sharon Tate, and her house-guests, Voytek Frykowski, Abigail Folger and Jay

Sebring glimpsed the man that in less than a year's time would link their name and souls for eternity.

Manson duly headed over to the caretaker's chalet and rang the bell, to no avail. Undeterred, he returned later in the evening and made for the guest house yet again. There he encountered Cielo Drive's landlord Rudi Altobelli, who was preparing to leave for Europe with Sharon Tate the following day. Rudi clearly remembered Manson as an unwelcome face from the past. He had shown some scant, perfunctory interest in Charlie's music at Dennis Wilson's house some time earlier, and since then Charlie had been keen to make new inroads if the opportunity arose. As he'd just come out of the shower, Altobelli didn't bother opening the door, and conducted his conversation with Charlie through the fly-screen. He described the meeting to John Parker for his biography, *Polanski.* 'When I saw him standing there I was surprised. He said he was looking for Melcher, and skilfully turned the conversation around to his tapes. I told him Melcher had moved, and I had no time to discuss it, because I was leaving for Europe.'

Altobelli told Charlie that he would be away in Europe for the best part of a year, and wouldn't welcome any advances concerning his music. When Altobelli queried Manson's presence at the guest house, Manson claimed that residents in the main house had directed him there. Altobelli admonished Charlie for disturbing the house guests earlier, and asked him in no uncertain terms not to trouble them again. With the agent's harsh words ringing in his ears, Charlie disappeared up the stone path and into the darkness.

The next day as Altobelli and Tate shared the long journey over to Rome, she asked about 'that creepy-looking guy' who'd gone over to the guest house the previous day. Altobelli told her that Manson was one of the freaks attached to Dennis Wilson's caravan, and the conversation was left at that. Sadly, Tate was to find out first hand just how freaky Manson and the Family could get.

chapter 7
Bad

'Don't do anything illegal
Beware of the eagle
That's right in the middle of your back
Don't be the eagle
Got you in the back
They got you in a sack
And they keep you lookin' back'

From 'Don't Do Anything Illegal' by Charles Manson

I T wasn't long before the Yellow Submarine house began to implode under the weight of too many frazzled minds and wayward bodies. Keen to maintain their fluidity, Charlie suggested yet another move. For a short while, the Family squatted in a run-down property in Malibu Canyon that had previously been leased by the rock band Iron Butterfly. The property was large enough for their growing needs, and the fact that it overlooked the sea was highly symbolic for Manson, by then high on the prophesies from the book of Revelation. Manson was recalling chapter ten verse two, where the 'mighty angel' stands with 'his right foot upon the sea, and his left foot on the earth'.

It was in this squat that plans to produce the physical apparatus for Helter Skelter began to take shape. Manson's knowledge of history, coupled with his interest in Nazism, had led him to recall Rommel's desert campaign in North Africa. Since dune buggies were the closest you could get to Panzer tanks in California, Charlie decreed a comprehensive sweep for any rear-engined vehicles that could be easily stripped down and converted. With Volkswagen Beetles then heavily in vogue, many found their way over to the Family's reconstruction quarters to be blitzed and reformed as dune buggies of the apocalypse.

Just two weeks into their stay in the cliffside squat, time was called and they were forced to move on. Following a few uncomfortable nights camping on top of a hill, a return to Spahn's was mooted. While there had never been any love lost between the Family and the ranch's workforce, Charlie had ensured that George Spahn had been kept sweet. With Squeaky and a couple of the other girls left behind as sensual retainers, he felt there should be little problem about the Family retreating back to their Wild Western hideout.

The move back to the ranch would provide more space to prepare for Helter Skelter, and for Charlie to continue with his songwriting. With the Family's cash flow restricted to dealing, cadging and occasional thievery, a large influx of money in the form of a record advance would be very useful.

With Terry Melcher otherwise engaged, Manson began to lean heavily on Dennis Wilson, but – the initial novelty long past – Charlie had started to become a thorn in Wilson's side. When Manson made the trip over to Dennis's flat on Pacific Palisades, he'd help himself to food, clothing and anything else that took his fancy. Once Charlie even took off in Gregg Jakobson's Jeep, planning to convert it for the Family's desert campaign. Still at the root of all this freeloading was the prickly subject of the song Manson had given to the Beach Boys. While Manson claimed that he didn't receive any formal payment from the royalties, the issue was useful collateral, allowing Charlie to call in what he wanted, when he wanted.

With Manson still badgering his old host about his recording career, Dennis conferred with Melcher and Gregg Jakobson on the viability of his musical future. Since Dennis was still a little too close to Manson to be properly objective, Gregg Jakobson offered to give an unbiased opinion. He arranged yet another recording session for Charlie in March 1969, this time without the girls, leaving just Bobby Beausoleil to back him on guitar.

Bobby Beausoleil remembered: 'I did one session with Charlie, just he and I, at a small studio in Santa Monica in the spring of '69. The studio time was arranged with the help of Gregg Jakobson. This was the best one of them all – just Charlie and his acoustic, with me accompanying him on electric guitar.'

The master tape to the session again went missing shortly after the recording, but evidently did little to promote Manson's career. Still, Gregg Jakobson was prepared to look for other ways to market Charlie's strange charisma, and the startling presence that he believed Manson's music could only hint at.

Jakobson thought back to a night when Charlie and the girls were still living with Dennis, when they all headed to Hollywood's legendary club, Whisky A Go Go. Within walking distance of Dennis's Sunset Boulevard house, the venue had garnered an great reputation for showcasing class acts who enjoyed the close proximity to their audience. While bands such as the Who, Jimi Hendrix, the Doors and Cream made significant appearances during the late 1960s, Jakobson would remember the somewhat more idiosyncratic magic that Charlie and his wayward band brought to the dance floor that evening.

Jakobson, with his keen visual sense, was captivated by the performance. 'Charlie started dancing,' Gregg would recount in Steven Gaines' *Heroes and Villains*, 'I swear to God, within a matter of minutes the dance floor would be empty and Charlie would be dancing by himself. It was almost as if sparks were flying off the guy. [He] was like fire, a raw explosion, a mechanical toy that suddenly went crazy.'

Propelled by Charlie's transformation into a psychedelic Tasmanian devil, Gregg Jakobson cajoled Terry Melcher into taking a trip out to Spahn Ranch to witness Manson in his own environment. Jakobson's theory was that, while Charlie's musical oeuvre was interesting, once nailed down on to tape, a large swathe of atmosphere was lost in translation. Undoubtedly, Charlie had bundles of presence, and never more so when his loving, captive audience were around him. Trying to recreate the smoky ambience in the stuffy confines of a recording studio was a non-starter, despite the Family's vain attempts. Equally, if the public were going to warm to Charlie's songs of isolation, impending apocalypse and prison life, they needed the benefit of some visually pleasing backdrops. As Manson's lyrics could be obtuse in the extreme, they required some validation. As far as Jakobson was concerned, Charlie truly came into his own amidst the smoke and burning embers of the campfire setting.

Jakobson's argument seemed plausible enough, and Bobby Beausoleil agreed with him, saying: 'Back in the day, Charlie's unique musical presentation was occasionally (as in not always) interesting, socially relevant for the times, original, and engaging within appropriate circumstances, or context. The problem was that it did not translate well to environments outside of the communal living space, in a circle of friends and intimates.'

Ever the opportunist, Jakobson felt that the Charlie and Family could benefit from a multimedia approach. 'The guy should be captured on film, not just on record,' Jakobson enthused to Melcher. 'It'd be like having footage of Castro while he was still in the mountains.'

Thanks to Jakobson's championing, Melcher made time to pop over to Spahn's to see Charlie play on 18 April 1969. When Melcher and Jakobson arrived that night, Charlie was there to greet them. They were then led towards the top of the creek-bed, where in the distance a small hillock towered over the stream below. Waiting expectantly around a fire were the Family, full of smiles and other delights. Although it appeared totally inaccessible, a rope was thrown over to Charlie, who swung himself over to the isolated mount, then passed the rope back over for Melcher and Jakobson to do the same

Once safely transported over to Family Island, Terry and Gregg quickly surveyed the scene. The girls had prepared themselves in accordance with Charlie's orders, and most were nakedly lolling around, furnished with a variety of musical instruments; some conventional, others clearly carved from the local wood. Although Melcher knew about commune dwelling, the set-up Charlie had engineered for his arrival that night nonetheless intrigued him.

In his only media interview concerning Manson (given to the BBC in 1994), Melcher recalled the scene. 'I arrived and then a bunch of people sat down, and they played a dozen songs around a big campfire. Manson played the guitar, and all the girls sung parts and harmonies and background stuff, and it was quite an interesting thing. And they talked about how they all shared this and that, and it was one big family, and that these were people who were basically disenfranchised by their biological families, who didn't understand them and didn't want to listen to them, and had cast them adrift, and that he had picked these poor wandering homeless. And I thought, all right, this is what is going on today.'

It turned into a happy, joyous jamboree, and outside the restricting walls of the recording studio, the gospel according to Manson seamlessly blended with the surroundings. While Terry was impressed, he realised the logistics of capturing all of this would to be difficult. Still as the night progressed, there was a positive vibe that something could be achieved, although Melcher held back on rubber-stamping a deal. When Melcher and Jakobson made their exits, they promised to regroup in due course and chew over the possibilities. As he left, Terry handed over the contents of his wallet, $50, a generous gesture that meant Manson could buy everyone some food.

When Terry and Gregg later conferred, both were convinced that Charlie would only have marketable value if people could see him. Therefore, the pair began concocting a rough storyboard for a film that would present Manson and the Family as a typical example of commune dwelling; with Charlie's music as the mescaline icing on the cake. This proposal was taken seriously enough for Jakobson to shoot a show-reel of the Family at work and play, as well as taking numerous photographs of them in their natural habitat.

Gregg Jakobson recalled: 'The picture that I had, that I thought at the time would be nice for the film, in other words, what my eyes took in as I stood there on the field out in the back of the ranch with the motorcycles and the girls and the guys and the horses and the trucks and the brown grass and the green trees and the blue sky and the stream, would have made a very nice picture for other people to see as well as myself in the context of a film.'

To check on the logistics of recording the Family at large, Melcher revisited Spahn's on 6 June 1969, with Michael Deasy, one of LA's most respected session musicians. Fittingly, Deasy had the benefit of a mobile recording unit, and was in a good position to gauge the possibility of capturing the Family's sound. While Deasy enjoyed partying with Manson and some of the women, he was thrown seriously off beam when Charlie slipped him some LSD by way of a sweetener. The experience was not one that Deasy appreciated; claiming that Manson had attempted to 'suck his brains' out while under the drug's influence.

Melcher experienced vibes of a more earthly variety on his next trip to the ranch with Gregg Jakobson. As Terry's presence at Spahn's was tantamount to a state visit, Charlie was enraged when one of the old ranch hands waved a gun in his direction in a fit of bravado. Incensed, Charlie screamed, 'Don't draw on me, motherfucker', before beating the old boy senseless in front of a startled Melcher. Adding to the dismal atmosphere, two policemen arrived to quiz Charlie over the alleged rape of a young girl at the ranch a few days previous. Melcher was further spooked when they began to discuss the proposed documentary. As Charlie openly despised the counterculture, the idea of the Family being used for a hippie travelogue was wholly repellent to him. Instead, Charlie revealed his own storyline.

Charlie implored Melcher and Jakobson to embrace his newly defined Helter Skelter vision as the template for the film. With proposed footage of the Family's retreat to the desert, intercut with assorted cutaways of war, carnage and other social strife (naturally, all set to Charlie's music), Manson felt it would make for one spectacular movie. In his enthusiasm Charlie proudly showed Melcher his dune buggy production line. Naturally, Charlie's proposed ideas were a million miles from what Melcher and Jakobson had envisaged and, although they didn't say so at the time, all plans regarding Manson were quietly shelved.

With Charlie's long-awaited musical career in limbo, Manson made some tentative plans with Bobby Beausoleil to kick-start events from ground level. With the Beatles' song 'Helter Skelter' still ringing in his ears, Charlie decided to capitalise on the buzz and inaugurate an eponymous club in its honour. Buzzing with excitement, Charlie and the girls converted the interior of one of the ranch houses into a small nightclub. Painted out in black with a parachute suspended from the ceiling, the scant light came from Beatles lyrics painted on the walls in luminous paint. Every night the Beatles dominated the sound system, until Charlie took to the stage with Beausoleil, under the banner of 'The Family

Jams'. In amongst Charlie's familiar cannon of work was a new song, whose chorus urged, 'You better get your dune buggy ready ... you better get your dune buggy ready'.

With a glass jar at the entrance vainly asking for 'donations', the club succeeded in collecting the more ragtag locals. While Charlie's music was an acquired taste, the environment of the club nonetheless provided an excellent backdrop for other, more nefarious activities. However George Spahn and his workforce weren't impressed by all the after-hours activity. As usual, Charlie had failed to ask permission to redecorate the property, let alone use it as a nightclub. With people darting in and out of Spahn Ranch at all hours, the police were soon bearing down on the owner, serving George with a fine for allowing the club venture to take place. Under enormous pressure, George Spahn started dropping thinly veiled hints that the Family's activities were causing him considerable strife. When Manson heard this, the club idea was abandoned. Manson had good reasons for the retreat. He'd been leaning on George's favourite girl, Squeaky, to see if the old boy would change his will and sign the ranch over for the Family to inherit when he died.

Despite the Helter Skelter club's closure, Spahn's reputation for illicit entertainment continued unabated. During their brief time at the Gresham Street property, Charlie had collected a retinue of dodgy characters looking for action. Some, like Manson, had a lengthy prison record, and they warmed to Manson's philosophy of sensual and mental absolution. With the addition of copious sex and drugs, they swiftly became fervent devotees of the Family ethos; and when Manson left the 'Yellow Submarine' property, they followed in his slipstream. Among them were members of some of LA's notorious biker gangs, The Straight Satans, Satan Slaves and the Jokers Out of Hell. Charlie enjoyed the edge these bikers brought to the docile ranks of the Family, and he offered the services of some of his more attractive females in return for any favours he might need. Pimping, it seemed, had never left Charlie Manson's blood.

Patricia Krenwinkle ('Katie') said: 'When men would come and he wanted power over them, he would offer them whatever women he had. He had certain women that he always put out front, which he called his "Front Street Girls". They were the ones who he thought were the most beautiful, the ones he thought would be the most enticing and that's what he would do. I mean he was an excellent pimp.'

One of these visitors was a chap called Danny DeCarlo. As he was more approachable than the other bikers, he was soon absorbed into the Family. Manson had good reason for allowing DeCarlo associate Family membership: his muscle and connections were good insurance against any attack. DeCarlo was well liked by the girls, earning himself the flattering nickname 'Donkey Dick Dan'. His sharp sense of survival meant that he could withstand most of Manson's mind games, while still appearing generally compliant with the Family ethos. This would prove vital in the future, when he'd have to prove his mettle. Between the years 1961 and 1965, DeCarlo had been trained by the coastguard as a weapons' instructor, and had put the knowledge to good use. Within the unregulated boundaries of Spahn's, DeCarlo took charge of Spahn's small arsenal of weaponry, which included rifles, shotguns and even submachine guns.

This seedy element ensured that the police kept a close eye on the comings and goings at the ranch, and thought of the Spahn Ranch first when any crimes were committed in the area. One of their major investigations was following the death of Mark Walts, a sixteen-year-old who'd been known to hang out at the ranch. He was found on the morning of 18 July with multiple blows to the face and head and three bullets in his chest. In the end, police were unable to link the crowd at Spahn's with the boy's death. Walts' brother, however, called Manson up and accused him directly: 'I know you done my brother in, and I'm going to kill you.' Despite his brother's chilling conviction, no one was ever charged over Mark's murder.

Added to the dubious reputation the Family was building up, for the regular employees at Spahn Ranch there was a simmering uneasiness at the Family's unsettling presence. To the uninitiated, these youngsters looked like wayward, undisciplined hippies, and yet they were prepared to integrate themselves fully into the day-to-day operations. Adding to the confusion, Charlie's angels were unfailingly polite and charming, and had won over George Spahn and even ranch manager Ruby Pearl. This led to considerable debate about what the Family's real motives were for being on the ranch.

Donald 'Shorty' Shea was one such sceptic. Like some of the other ranch hands at Spahn's, he'd been forced to abandon his dreams of being an actor and stuntman and take up menial tasks around the paddocks. Like most of the male workforce, Shea was taken with Charlie's girls, and yet disappointed that they weren't more keen to share their affections with him. In a vain attempt to woo some of the women his way, he'd try to break their loyalty to Manson. 'Charlie's bad news,' he'd bark, usually though a mist of alcohol. 'If you stick with him, you're going to end up in jail for long terms. Get away from him.' All too quickly, Shea's comments made their way back to Charlie.

Manson already had cause to dislike Shorty Shea. Shea had married a black dancer from Las Vegas, breaking Manson's strict taboo on racial integration. Much to Charlie's annoyance, Shorty had also taken great pleasure in showing his wife's relatives around the ranch. Guilty of backtalking and miscegenation, Shea was now top of Manson's hit-list.

Like Manson and the Family, Shorty was keen to maintain his presence at Spahn's Ranch well beyond old George's lifetime. Given Spahn's perilous health and finances, the property could be sold at any moment. At that point Shea was living in his car, so any possibility of a share of the ranch interested him keenly. Raising Charlie's hackles considerably, Squeaky had overheard George Spahn negotiating with neighbour Frank Retz about a possible sale. Retz had become something of a Family nemesis after repeatedly cautioning them for incursions onto his property. He'd already purchased a swathe of Spahn's ranch in 1967, and was keen to take on the rest of the property when it became available. Squeaky had overheard Retz saying that on completion of the proposed sale, he'd employ a bunch of 'Nazis' and kick the Family off the property. Apprehensive about the Manson clan's reactions, George Spahn suggested that Shorty Shea could act as Retz's bodyguard while negotiations took place. Retz tentatively agreed to the idea, and suggested a weekly retainer amounting to $75 and provisions.

Pre-empting any 'official' eviction notice, Shorty had already sensed a major victory over Manson and the Family. 'It's all over for you,' Shea gleefully told Charlie. 'They've already told me they don't want you and that gang to be here.' Charlie made a few characteristically obtuse retorts in the cowboy's direction, but Shea wasn't in the slightest bit rattled. 'You might tell some of those kids what to do, but not me,' Shea declared. 'I know how to handle you.' It was a threat he'd later come to regret.

There was a sense of increasing paranoia around Spahn's, most of it emanating from Manson. He began taking his frustration out on the women, and a newer, more aggressive attitude began to be the norm.

Patricia Krenwinkle recalls: 'He began to do things like grab me by the hip. I remember when I laughed at him once and he jerked me by the hair and said, "You won't ever laugh at me again." And then I started watching him beat Mary Brunner, who was with us, and to do that to anyone who ever had a problem with him . . . At times when we were out in the woods there was this thing of trust that we had, that he wanted us to develop. [He'd] stand us up against a tree and he threw knives above our head; he'd throw hatchets over my head into a tree.'

With Charlie's paranoia increasing daily, old George Spahn's severe myopia was even called into question. One night, with suspicion heavy in the air, Manson forced Spahn to sit on a chair for three hours while he lit matches and threw punches within a hair's distance from his face. At one point, Spahn heard the door open and shut. Terrified, he waited and then put his hands out, touching Charlie's shoulder. 'That's right, George,' offered Manson, 'I'm still here.'

As usual, the campfire was the preferred forum for Manson's discourses. However, unlike the genial, happy-go-lucky scene of only a few months back, these fireside gatherings were fast becoming fanatical rages against outside forces; Manson's ever-increasing predilection for bloody imagery gaining heavy momentum. With the Beatles' 'White Album' imagery melding with the rise of black militancy, Charlie wove the dark strands of his thought process into horrific scenarios.

Paul Watkins remembered: 'There would be some atrocious murders; that some of the spades from Watts would come up into the Bel Air and Beverly Hills district and just really wipe some people out, just cut bodies up and smear blood and write things on the wall in blood, and cut little boys up and make parents watch. So, in retaliation – this would scare; in other words, all the other white people would be afraid that this would happen to them, so out of their fear they would go into the ghetto and just start shooting black people like crazy. But all they would shoot would be the garbage man and Uncle Toms, and all the ones that were with Whitey in the first place. And underneath it all, the Black Muslims would know that it was coming down.'

As a result of Charlie's mania, activities around the ranch became much more regimented – far removed from the carefree, halcyon days of former times. It is something that Patricia Krenwinkel remembers: 'We started to have a lot more guns at the ranch, and knives. And people were on lookouts. We were pretty much all running on definite fear.'

In tandem with the defensive atmosphere, the Family were trained in how to deal with any approaching attack. Charlie inaugurated self-defence classes, and even pulled in a martial arts expert to demonstrate how best to deter a physical advance. Additionally, Charlie instructed Tex to show everyone how to use a knife when stabbing someone.

Barbara Hoyt recollects that '[Tex] demonstrated how to stab a person. He told us, "Don't just stick the knife in and out," he said. "Bring it up, when you cut someone, so that you cut up more stuff," and he made us practise.'

The heightened levels of fear didn't stop the Family continuing to dabble with a host of psychedelics. One notable discovery was belladonna, a plant that for centuries had been associated with witchcraft and the supernatural. Better known as 'deadly nightshade', it has some beneficial effects when used in microscopic doses; however, an increased measure can lead to a nightmare trip of unimaginable horror. One tumbleweed traveller attached to the Family at the time was known as 'Indian' Joe; he alerted the girls to some wild belladonna growing freely near the waterfall at the top of the creek bed. With a few instructions on how to prepare a safe dose suitable for tripping, young Brenda McCann set about making a drinkable version, commonly known as Telaachte tea. While she carefully measured the ingredients, Tex stumbled in and quizzed her about it. Hearing that the potion held unique and stupefying properties, Tex picked up an entire plant, gobbled it whole, and shambled off.

This wasn't unfamiliar behaviour from Tex. Veering from one drug-fuelled bender to the next, he'd excelled in pushing his consciousness to the extreme. Nonetheless, since just a few shreds of the belladonna plant would provide a lengthy, challenging trip, Tex's consumption of the entire plant ensured he was in for one hell of a rough ride.

Plant ingested, Tex wandered off happily enough to catch a bus into town. En route he passed Charlie, and was composed enough to shout 'see you later' before heading towards the nearby bus stop. Charlie made his own way towards the kitchen, only to find Brenda collapsed on the front porch, eyes swimming in her head, having ingested some of the belladonna fumes from the kitchen pot. While Charlie rallied some support for the young girl, he soon discovered the truth about Tex's earlier massive ingestion of the plant.

Tex evidently made it into town, but once there, life under belladonna became severely twisted. 'It ended up with me slithering across a sidewalk,' he later said, 'on my hands and knees through a crowd of schoolchildren, unable to walk, unable to make any noise except little mechanical sounds, over and over: "Beep, beep . . . beep, beep, beep." Before it was over, ten days later, I would have seen space people beeping back at me, landing and taking off from circles of light; I would have seen the wind itself.'

It was little surprise that Tex was apprehended by police and charged with being under the influence of drugs, fingerprinted and photographed. The resulting photos offer a memorable image of the stoned and giggly Watson looking unkempt and dangerously demented.

Tex sweated out the belladonna for three days before being released from police custody. On arrival back at Spahn Ranch, his mindset, already pretty scrambled prior to the belladonna experience, now appeared to have shifted several notches. As chief monitor of the Family's consciousness, Charlie was shocked by Tex's turnaround, noting that, from the belladonna incident onwards, he 'never seemed the same again'.

Although Tex's escapade ultimately proved pivotal in the downfall of the Family, other members were keen to use the substance for a variety of reasons. Sadie and at least one other member of the Family had successfully relieved a lorry driver of his goods after spiking his coffee. Charlie, in awe of the plant's stupefying properties, allegedly made plans to dose the entire population of LA with the drug. With a plot to lace the city's water system with belladonna, the idea was that the mass spiking would easily precipitate Helter Skelter, and allow the Family ample time to retreat to the desert.

Tex remembers: 'His tactics of fear was a plan to poison the Los Angeles water supply with belladonna plants, which contain strychnine. These poisonous plants grew abundantly in the hills around the city. [The Family] was to harvest thousands of these plants, chop them up, boil them to remove their poison and use the poison to pollute the city water system. The city water tanks could be seen in the distance. He spoke of polluting lakes and aqueducts. His plans did not seem foolish or impossible to us.'

Plans for Helter Skelter were now gathering pace, and the cost of the desert relocation was swiftly draining the Family's already meagre coffers. Somewhere along the line, a large set of topographical maps of California was purchased. Laid out on the dusty track at Spahn's, Charlie drew a line between the ranch and Death Valley. At suitable points along the way, Manson earmarked sites for the essential supplies of gasoline and food to be secreted.

With car parts essential to equip the growing army of desert dune buggies, a fresh influx of motor parts became a priority, and a raft of vehicles was stolen to meet the increasing demand. Much to the delight of Charlie, the sweet and angelic Mary Brunner excelled herself by driving into the ranch one day in a sparkling Volkswagen she'd taken for a test-drive and never returned. Within hours, the car was filleted, before being ditched out of sight.

In addition to the more traditional sources of procurement, the Family's new regime now involved the 'Creepy Crawl'. This involved breaking into a house at the dead of night, somewhere in a wealthy district of LA. Initially, these break-ins began as a prank to bolster the Family's feeling of impregnability; but they certainly made the most of the expert tutelage provided by the Family's growing criminal element.

Dressed in black, Charlie and his fellow Family members would slip into various residences, and then hover around the living quarters, while the occupants slumbered above undisturbed. Although they'd happily squirrel away anything they found useful, they also enjoyed rearranging furniture in the weirdest of fashions. Once away from the house, these 'crawlers' would gleefully anticipate the residents' surprise the following morning at finding their homes all topsy-turvy.

As Manson revelled in anything that showed off his no-boundaries approach to life, he enjoyed the pure theatre of the 'Creepy Crawl' and eagerly encouraged it. Not only did it challenge internal fear, but the fact that they never got caught was welcome confirmation of the Family's divine powers.

'The fear and thrill was exhilarating,' reports Susan Atkins. 'I had always liked danger, although it kept me close to hysteria and panic. Furthermore, I felt we were perfectly justified in what we were doing. We were in "the thought" ... "in the now" ... "free from thought" ... escaping from a doomed society.'

In addition to the anonymous Hollywood homes, they'd occasionally hit more familiar targets. Dennis Wilson, by now in fearful exile, had his property 'rearranged' in his absence. Terry Melcher underwent a comprehensive sweep of his Malibu property, the Family taking a telescope of his for their own use. Relatives of the Family members certainly weren't safe either. Leslie Van Houten's father's house was Creepy Crawled and relieved of anything considered useful to the campaign. Additionally, crooner Jack Jones had his house in Sherman Oaks broken into. In addition to several credit cards taken, the Family were thrilled to find a white felt western hat of the singer's, which they duly lifted.

* * *

It wasn't these Creepy Crawls, however, which were garnering the Family unwelcome attention. With so much car theft occurring around the Chatsworth area, it wasn't surprising that the police were routinely checking out the ranch. They'd been keeping a tacit eye on the Family's activities following complaints over the Helter Skelter nightclub. Owner George Spahn was well aware of the behaviour of his itinerant tenants, and he had threatened an immediate eviction if Charlie and the Family didn't curtail their excesses. Still harbouring a hope that the ranch could be turned over to the Family, Manson stepped up the care roster for George, ensuring that his favourite attendant, Squeaky, was taking care of his needs at all hours.

With Charlie's race for the desert on red alert, it has since been claimed that Manson hit on the idea of extorting some dollars out of the local drug mafia. Although Tex and Sadie have since validated this story, the scheme seems cockeyed and hugely dangerous even by Manson's rapidly twisting standards.

There were certainly rich pickings to be made that balmy summer. Although the LSD supply was easily maintained, the demand for marijuana in Los Angeles was at an all-time high, as there had been a significant drop in the amount of pot on the market. This had lead to a scurry to ferret out new suppliers and dealers with good connections. Tex Watson was well placed to pick up any soundings from the local drug patch. Given this palpable fever to score, Tex (or Manson, depending who you believe) decided that there was some quick cash to be made from 'burning' or ripping off a dealer, and a scam was concocted.

Through a contact in Hollywood, Tex had arranged a bulk-buy from a group with Mafia connections, with the intention of trickling it down through the network of small-time pushers. With a cartel of local dealers apparently in on the bulk buy, Tex worked out that he would be able to collect a huge sum of money from either one or all these prospective buyers and then disappear. Despite the very real danger of the operation, to Tex's fried sense of reality it all seemed relatively easy.

As well as freely dipping into Charlie's girls, Watson had an on/off girlfriend by the name of Rosina Kroner. Rosina rented a flat in Hollywood, a world away from the dust and rocks of the Spahn

Ranch. Indeed, this flat at 6933 Franklin Avenue was a veritable paradise, situated in the middle of a leafy arboretum and close to the famous Chinese Theater. With Tex needing somewhere more salubrious than a street corner to do his business, Rosina's flat was employed as a negotiating base. To encourage business, it is said that Watson briefly smartened up his act, and had his hair fashionably styled. The call was put out on the drug network to come share in the bulk buy, and interest was such that a meeting with a dealer by the name of Bernard Crowe was convened.

Crowe's reputation within the drug community of Los Angeles was defined by his dude-presence rather than his criminal pedigree. Known variously as 'the Crowe Man' or 'Lotsapoppa', the Afro-American appeared seasoned to any scams, especially when dealing with itinerants like Tex. Given the spider's web that connected the drug community, Lotsapoppa had reportedly crossed paths with members of the Manson family on their various trawls for narcotics. Whereas many have been keen to paint the dealer as peripheral to the Family, research has revealed he was more intimately involved with them than first thought. Dianne Lake even referred to him as 'the Negro member of the Family.' Crowe was a neighbour of Cass Elliot, and had many entertainment contacts.

Tex's idea was that Lotsapoppa would hand over the cash, and then wait for him to return with the gear. However, despite the shortage of dope in the neighbourhood, there was no way that he was going to hand over ready cash to some random hippie in the vain hope the drugs would materialise. With the dealer's two henchmen in reserve, a compromise of sorts was struck, and they all drove out to the property Tex purported was the supply point for their deal. Once there, a lot of bluffing back and forward ensued, as Tex insisted that only he could go inside, claiming the imposing sight of Lotsapoppa and his two henchmen could easily scupper the deal. Eventually, Crowe and his sidekicks agreed that Tex could take the money and go in alone. But they needed insurance, so decided to hold Rosina as guarantor until he returned with the dope. If Tex did indeed attempt a 'burn', Rosina would pay the consequences for his escape.

Tex reassured them with a cheeky grin that of course he'd return, claiming that the safety of his girlfriend was much more important to him than a few grands' worth of weed. As planned, Tex went in through the front door of the property to his appointed deal. What Lotsapoppa and his minders didn't know was that Tex had chosen an empty house with easy access out back. To aid his escape, Tex had employed the genial services of peripheral Family member, Thomas John Wallerman. TJ, as he was known to all and sundry, was a likeable bear of a man, whose passivity and willingness to help made him a popular character around Spahn's. He claimed no prior knowledge of Tex's scam, and was apparently only acting as driver for the day. Once out of the property and in TJ's truck, they wasted no time speeding off back to the Spahn Ranch where Tex was eager to boast about the ease of the operation.

Back at the ranch, Tex gleefully shuffled wads of cash in front of Manson. It apparently mattered little to Tex that Rosina was now in the hands of some very irate hoods, whose anger at being burnt on the deal could well manifest itself in horrific violence against her. As expected, the solitary payphone at the Spahn Ranch soon started ringing. For effect, Lotsapoppa got a terrified Rosina to make the call. She initially asked for 'Charles' – meaning Charles 'Tex' Watson – but in the confusion it was Charles Manson who took the call. Through her tears, Rosina told Charlie that Lotsapoppa and two of his cronies were intending to cut off her head if their money wasn't immediately returned.

The phone was then passed to Lotsapoppa. Charlie, using his legendary skill for wheedling and double-speak, embarked on a labyrinth of diversions to thwart the angered dealer. With a deceptive chuckle, Manson claimed that Tex had left the Family some time back, and that his current whereabouts weren't known. Lotsapoppa wasn't convinced by Charlie's rap, and from information he'd gathered from Rosina, he surmised that Tex was probably back at Spahn's, enjoying the fruits of his scam. Without prolonging the dialogue, Crowe informed Manson that if his money wasn't returned, he'd be over at the ranch at the drop of a joint, with a posse of the nastiest hoods he could muster. He explained that when they'd finished tearing the male contingent to pieces, they'd start on the Family's women.

Lotsapoppa's fevered threats were peppered with ghetto patois, prompting Charlie to believe there might be a connection with the Black Panthers. With this dark scenario colliding with his Helter Skelter imagery, Charlie felt obligated to sort the situation out, and promised to meet immediately with Crowe. In the interim, Manson vainly attempted to rally a few of the bikers around the ranch, but when the Black Power angle was presented to them, they passed. Gathering what little muscle he could around Spahn's, Charlie got TJ to race him back to Hollywood to sort matters out.

In anticipation of a violent standoff, TJ brought along a .22 Longhorn revolver, which belonged to a ranch employee by the name of Randy Starr. Randy was an old rodeo performer who'd had some minor cinematic celebrity over the years as a stuntman. Legend had it that Ronald Reagan once used the Buntline revolver on one of his B-flicks in the 1950s. In the future, the weapon was to attain a bloodstained celebrity of its own.

Manson and TJ soon arrived to confront Lotsapoppa at Rosina's flat. The area had some past resonance for Charlie, as it faced the apartment where he'd ran his bogus 3-Star Enterprises talent 'agency', back in the late 1950s. But with the prospect of dealing with an irate dope hood, nostalgia was the last thing on Charlie's mind.

Despite his presence and girth, gentle giant TJ was not naturally predisposed to violence. Knowing this, Charlie took the Longhorn revolver and hid it in the rear of his trousers; reasoning that TJ's threatening presence alone might be enough to scare the hoods.

Over the years, Manson has frequently reiterated that reconciliation was the primary objective of the visit, and that taking the gun was nothing more than a precaution. This too was confirmed by TJ on numerous occasions before his death in 1994. However, whatever their intentions, the situation ended up spinning out of all control.

On arrival, Charlie knocked on the door, and after a quick confirmation by one of the dealer's associates, they were led in. Soon, they saw Rosina, gagged and bound on the bed, her face crumpled with fear. Despite the presence of two well-proportioned minders, Manson casually sauntered over to the bed, and began to untie the frightened girl. The dealer's henchmen were totally wrong-footed by Manson's cool and collected presence, and did nothing but watch. With Charlie's charm in full swing, the girl was safely untied and despatched to make some coffee while Manson went about clearing a small table in preparation. Again this act of domesticity from the five-foot two-inch Manson did nothing but confuse the minders, who frantically debated their boss's instructions. With no evident fear, Charlie and TJ helped themselves to some coffee, and awaited the arrival of dealer-man Crowe.

Eventually, the door opened and in stepped Lotsapoppa, his enormous frame supporting some 300 pounds of flesh. Seeing Charlie and TJ enjoying their coffees, Lotsapoppa berated his henchmen: 'What's that broad doing up walking around? I told you guys to keep her tied!' He then turned on Manson. 'And you, you smart little bastard, where's my money, and that other bastard?'

In trademark stalling mode, Charlie cheerily asked for some time to collect the money. Despite Manson's charm, Crowe became more and more het-up – with good reason: a burn was the lowest scam anyone could pull in the underworld, and to be duped enormously undermined a player's standing. With Charlie the most visible connection to this scam, Lotsapoppa was keen to enact revenge, however remote the link.

Sensing he was making little headway, the dealer turned his attentions back to Rosina, reiterating his threat to kill her. Aware that he sounded serious, Charlie stepped in. Turning the big man's violent theatrics into a reverse, Manson got down on both knees and took the Longhorn revolver out of his trousers. Handing it over to Lotsapoppa, Manson proclaimed, 'You can't take my friend's life, you must take my life!' This stunned dealer was momentarily silenced, which bought Charlie enough time to turn the tables, grab the gun back and point it straight at Lotsapoppa.

'All right you motherfucker,' Charlie laughed in the direction of Lotsapoppa and his two henchmen. 'I'm taking the girl out of here, and you can say goodbye to her, me and your dollars.'

In spite of the gun, Lotsapoppa wasn't intimidated by Manson's stance. Sniggering, he informed Charlie that even if they escaped now, he'd soon be up to the ranch to enact a horrific revenge against the Family. Charlie kept composed, but the dealer started to advance towards him, calling his bluff. The sight of the portly dude certainly had an effect, and aware that he might be overwhelmed, Manson pulled the trigger on the revolver. There was nothing more than a quiet click. Lotsapoppa and his minders laughed openly at the sound. Charlie too giggled, 'See, how could I kill you with an empty gun?' Not missing a beat, the dealer wrapped his hands around Manson's throat and picked him off the floor and pushed him hard against the wall.

Gasping for air, Charlie managed to bring the revolver up to his assailant's waist and pull the trigger a second time. Still there was no response. Charlie tried the gun again. This time a deep thud permeated the air, and Lotsapoppa began to slide towards the floor. A moment's silence was punctuated by the renewed moans of Rosina. As Manson would later recall, 'I looked down at the body and, though there wasn't any blood showing, I knew he was dead.'

Charlie looked around and began sizing up his next move. With the unarmed minders in shock, it was easy for Charlie and TJ to coolly make their way out. Before he left, Manson took a fancy to a leather-fringed buckskin jacket shirt that one of Lotsapoppa's guardians was wearing. Charlie got the henchman to remove the shirt, which he then took with him. Manson regularly wore the jerkin, right up to his arrest a few months later. The fancy piece of apparel came at a price, though, as it turned out that its former owner was a friend of Gregg Jakobson's. Naturally, news of this incident would swiftly wing its way over to Terry Melcher and Dennis Wilson.

With TJ in tow, Charlie quickly left the apartment, although Rosina, ostensibly the main reason for their trip, was left behind. Although loyally subservient to the Family, TJ was freaked by what he'd seen Charlie do. Belonging strictly in the peace and love camp, he could barely bring himself to talk to Manson, other than saying 'Geez Charlie, did you have to kill him?' Manson retorted that he was acting in self-defence, and reminded TJ that he'd originally brought the gun. The pair maintained a tight-lipped silence for the remainder of the thirty-minute ride back to Spahn's. Once there and with the clock nudging dawn, Charlie headed off to bed. Despite the night's unplanned shooting, he was happy about one thing: as Manson had extricated Watson from his impossible situation, the Texan now owed Charlie 'big time'.

While Manson slept late into the morning, Brenda and TJ listened to the morning's news on the radio. In amongst the broadcast, they heard a report that a member of the Black Panthers had been shot the night before, and his body had been dumped at the entrance of a local hospital. TJ quickly ran over to Charlie's quarters to tell him of the news. With his nightmare coming to life, Manson went into a frenzied spiral and shook Tex from his sleeping bag to confront him with the bloody mess he'd created. Tex, somewhere in a void between reality and fantasy, just handed Charlie a large wad of cash with a cheesy grin. Knowing that extracting an apology from Tex would be a waste of breath, Charlie took the money and hurried away to prepare defensive tactics.

While Manson believed he had killed Lotsapoppa, the reality was markedly different. While the dealer had indeed been shot, he had survived Manson's bullet. Co-incidentally, there had been a shooting of a Black Panther on the same night, which was duly reported in the media. Predictably, this news sent Manson into a spiral of panic, pulling everyone in.

On the militant front line of black resistance, the Black Panthers' predilection for civil unrest was underpinned by a heavy connection to criminality. With the distinct probability that Lotsapoppa was linked in some way to the Panthers' shadowy world, Charlie envisaged word being fed back to the group's elders, who would undoubtedly seek revenge.

With these scenarios playing out in his brain, Manson gathered everyone together to announce the urgent need to prepare for Helter Skelter. Charlie was more explicit than ever before, his words boring a deep crevice into the group's fragile consciousness and awakening any sleepers. 'We are going to have to change the way we have been living around here,' he barked. 'We have to be more observant. More than just the police, the blacks are rising up ... You all know they're all after us, and they'll be cracking down harder and harder.'

Previously, similar speeches had dissolved into the midnight air, but now they were louder, brighter and more urgent than ever before. There was other circumstantial evidence that fuelled Charlie's paranoia, which had been bubbling beneath the surface well before Lotsapoppa's apparent murder.

Tex Watson: 'Charlie got even more nervous when almost immediately it seemed that all kinds of blacks started showing up, renting horses. He was convinced they were Panther spies and he started posting armed guards at night and having us sleep scattered back in the hills. If we'd needed any more proof that Helter Skelter was coming down very soon, this was it, blackie was trying to get at the chosen ones.'

With the Family now on high alert, awaiting an impending attack, Charlie began to seriously rejig the group's activities around the ranch. Whereas life at Spahn's had been akin to an adult playground, it was soon to resemble a secure war zone. Under Manson's explicit instructions, the Family began to construct lookout points in the hills overlooking the ranch and set up a constant watch over the dilapidated buildings. To encourage vigilance, it's been reported that Manson was handing out 'bennies' (benzedrine) to the watchmen. This was a fair measure of his desperation, as Manson generally despised chemical propellants.

Around 1 a.m. on the night of 28 July, local police discovered Manson and some of his tribe hiding out in woods behind the Spahn Ranch. Talking from a badly camouflaged dune buggy, Charlie informed police that they were out 'watching for the Black Panthers'. With candour he told police that they'd got 'into a hassle with the Panthers and put one of them in the hospital, and they said they'd get us for that.' On being asked the reasons for the spat, Charlie mentioned it was because they'd made advances to one of the Family's women. Manson pointed to the hills, telling officers that many of his tribe were holed up in the mountains with guns, and could easily wipe them out. Whether they believed him or not, the police left, but reported Manson's words on their return to base.

Charlie might have been bluffing about his infantry in the mountains, but arming the thirty or so members of the Family came at a price. Initially, the Family required little more than the occasional handout to sustain their chilled-out life at Spahn's. Now, with Manson's martial plans taking priority over every aspect of their life, more adventurous and suspect ways were employed to ensure that the coffers were kept topped up. The women found it easy to go into bars, supermarkets and restaurants, and relieve the customers of their wallets and purses. Aside from ready cash, credit and fuel cards were also highly desirable items. With no immediate trace system available in 1969, they could be used liberally before anyone noticed that they were stolen.

In many ways the Family's fall from grace stands as a striking metaphor for the wider disillusionment in the counterculture. With the hippie explosion of 1967 reduced to a rumble, there were still many thrill-seekers looking to consolidate the expectations of the movement. As some of the era's major players had abandoned trendy frugality for more material delights, scepticism was slowly undermining unconditional trust. Of course, Manson took great delight in pointing out these failings; they proved he'd been right about the hippie movement all along.

One free spirit still searching for salvation was eighteen-year-old Linda Kasabian. Born Linda Darlene Drouin on 21 June 1949 in Biddeford, Maine, her CV was fairly typical for the era. She'd dropped out of high school, and then fled home in defiance of a dictatorial stepfather. Like many, Linda headed west, confident that all of the answers lay in Haight-Ashbury. There she'd fallen easily into the generic hippie lifestyle, moving from crash pad to commune floor, using LSD and venturing into the occult. Indeed, such was her interest in the dark arts, her friends started calling her 'Yana the Witch'. She'd married twice, and had a daughter named Tanya with her second husband, the charismatic Robert Kasabian. With that marriage now under strain, Linda and baby moved back in with her mother in New Hampshire to escape the scene. However, Robert soon pined for his pretty wife, and began sending signals that he was after a reunion. When he mooted plans for a sailing trip to South America, Linda headed back out west to be with her husband.

For a while, things seemed good. The couple hung out at various communes in and around California's Topanga Canyon district, building up a wide group of friends. Their shared joy was short-lived, though, and as Robert's wanderlust returned, he became distant with Linda. With the trip to South America scuppered and her relationship ending, Linda felt that her destiny lay elsewhere.

It was Robert Kasabian's marine cohort, a bearded guy by the name of Melton, who introduced Linda to Catherine 'Gypsy' Share. As a card-carrying member of the Family, Gypsy had little trouble in selling the paradise at Spahn Ranch to Linda. In an emotional vortex, Linda absorbed the fantastical tales of Charlie's all-encompassing love, which made for a welcome diversion from her domestic strife. 'I felt like I was a blind little girl in a forest,' she'd later recall of her first trip to Spahn Ranch. 'I took the first path.'

Linda got a textbook induction into the Family ranks. From the moment she wandered down Spahn's main drag, Family members emerged to greet her in their characteristically tactile fashion. Although Gypsy had bragged to Linda about Charlie's 'no rules' approach to living, some technicalities had to be satisfied before she could fully assimilate herself. Ostensibly for the greater good, Squeaky Fromme, the Family's 'bursar', took Linda's money, credit cards and driving licence into the collective coffers. Even her baby Tanya was taken away to be kept with the other children in a separate area of the ranch.

Despite her nervousness about being separated from her baby, the outwardly positive vibrations at the ranch reassured Linda that all would be okay. There was still the meeting with enigmatic Charlie to look forward to, and Linda had been intrigued by Gypsy's animated descriptions of how he was going to lead them to a sparkling wonderland, deep beneath the desert. That first night she slept with Tex Watson, which turned out to be 'totally different' to any sexual experience she'd ever had. The following morning, Gypsy and Mary Brunner accompanied her back to her husband to inform him of her new direction. Whilst there, Linda felt little compunction in relieving his friend Robert Melton of $5,000 which she'd found in his camper truck.

Linda's initial meeting with Manson on 5 July coincided with a group LSD session, and, as the Family passed around the acid, Charlie honed in on Linda, separating her out from the rest of group. She was impressed with Charlie, and his buckskin shirt, which she noted gave him a Christ-like veneer.

With acid acting as a powerful mental and emotional tool, Manson systematically unravelled Linda's mind, taking control of Linda's by now fragile and malleable psyche, and proceeded to make love to her. By the time it was all over and the acid began to subside, Linda was convinced that Charlie was exactly what she had always been missing from her life.

Linda Kasabian: '[Charlie] was a God Man . . . A second Jesus Christ. . .What he said seemed to be pure truth. This is what I had been looking for.'

The realisation was so overwhelming that she handed over the $5,000 she'd stolen from Robert Melton the day before. Melton was hugely aggrieved at the betrayal, and traced Linda back to the ranch. There he was met by Charlie. '[He] showed me this big knife,' recalled Melton. 'He said, "Maybe I should kill you just to show you there's no such thing as dying", and I felt fear and split.'

Despite Charlie's continued ability to capture receptive minds and souls, outside of his comfort zone he was having no luck in pursuing his musical dreams. With precious little room for manoeuvre, Charlie attempted to exploit the minimal contribution he'd made to the Beach Boys' songbook. Since his solitary offering 'Never Learn Not To Love', had been relegated to the flip side of the single 'Bluebirds Over The Mountain', he'd felt seriously let down. So far Manson had been mollified with vague promises of a recording contract, but now the evident lack of interest from Wilson and Co. only served to ramp up his own resentment; especially after he discovered that his song had been included on the Beach Boys' compilation album, 20/20.

This pallid collection of *Smile* album out-takes and B-sides could barely compete with their critically acclaimed *Pet Sounds*, yet royalties nonetheless rolled in to the Wilson brothers' bank accounts. Whereas 'Never Learn Not To Love' had initially been credited to C. Manson on the single release, for the 20/20 album, it was now solely attributed to Dennis Wilson. Naturally, the American branch of the PRS directed all proceeds from sales and airplay over to Manson's former friend.

As Manson was closely monitoring the Beach Boys, it's likely he would have been aware of a landmark settlement the group won in a lawsuit against Capitol Records. With Helter Skelter looming and finances of the utmost importance, Charlie made a beeline to the Beach Boys' management office in Hollywood to see if there were any royalties due to him. Although hippies were a common sight on the streets in 1969, Charlie's dusty, unkempt appearance was deeply alarming for the suits at the agency. Not surprisingly, the accountant's secretary asked the bedraggled Charlie to wait while she talked to her boss over the phone. A polite but firm message was relayed: there was no money owing to Charles Manson. End of story.

Not in the slightest bit fazed, Charlie burst into the manager's office and exploded with anger and resentment. 'You know what, man, you owe me the money,' he later recalled saying. 'Just pay up or I'm going to have to do something to make you regret it.' Used to Hollywood's hangers-on and peripheral crazies, the manager didn't scare easily, retorting: 'You know what, Manson? You're a flaky little nothing. You haven't got a contract or any kind of agreement, we owe you nothing.' Spitting with rage, Manson vowed to burn the man's house to the ground.

With rejection ringing in his ears, Manson managed to track down Terry Melcher to see if he could offer any help with his stalled recording career. In reality, Melcher had long since rejected the idea of taking Manson on. Although the demos they'd recorded were passable, Charlie's increasingly dark character meant that he just didn't want to work with him. Dennis Wilson was now deeply in retreat, and Melcher wasn't going to pander to Charlie's needs. With his work for the Byrds and Paul Revere and the Raiders, and his scouting duties for the Beatles' Apple label, Melcher had no desire to champion an unbalanced unknown like Charlie.

Face to face with Charlie, Terry was upfront: Manson's wild and unpredictable reputation now preceded him, and overshadowed his musical abilities. There was, however, another reason for Melcher's cooling interest. He'd heard, through the grapevine, about Manson's shooting of dealer Bernard Crowe, and with his experience at Spahn's still vivid in his mind, he didn't want to get involved. Although Melcher was cordial in his dismissal, Manson left harbouring a bitter resentment.

Charlie wasn't giving up until he'd explored every last avenue that might lead to a rock-and-roll stardom. Dennis Wilson was his next stop. The Beach Boy had been incredibly helpful in the past – now he might be Charlie's last shot at a musical career. Manson raced down to Wilson's Pacific Palisades beach house to confront the drummer, and see what they could salvage.

Dennis had already had a call from the Beach Boys' management offices on Hollywood Boulevard, warning him of Charlie's manic mission. Charlie burst into Wilson's quarters and immediately demanded money from Dennis, ignoring Wilson's tales about living the simple life. As he'd done time and time again, Charlie emptied Wilson's fridge and wardrobe of their contents and stormed off back to Spahn Ranch.

Such was Manson's anger at this point, it's been reported that he seriously considered eliminating Melcher and Wilson permanently. A freewheeling character at Spahn's by the name of Edward 'Sunshine' Pierce was considered a likely candidate for the job. Despite allegedly being offered a $5,000 payment plus a motorcycle to carry out the hit, Pierce fled the ranch soon after the suggestion was made to him. It was a lucky break for his old pals Dennis and Terry. Others wouldn't be so fortunate.

Back at Spahn's, the Family atmosphere was getting edgier and more chaotic. Not surprisingly, the ranch's increasingly murky reputation had spread like wildfire among LA's biker fraternity, including the legendary Hell's Angels. The gangs dug Charlie and the girls, and with the ranch offering a cornucopia of sensual treats, bikers were soon riding in and out of Spahn Ranch at all hours of the day and night. One member of The Straight Satans even gave Charlie a ceremonial sword, which Manson took to parading around the ranch, claiming it was 'magical'. He was so taken with it, that he had a scabbard welded on to the side of a dune buggy to transport it. This vehicle was looking more and more fantastical. Fur skins kitted out the interior and Charlie had ordered a winch to be attached to the front of the vehicle, so that he could pull up trees if the advancing forces had them trapped.

Given that the biker gangs required a steady supply of chemicals and wild women to propel their hectic lifestyle, the ranch soon became a clearing house for all manner of substances. Although traditionally the bikers were drinkers rather than drug-takers, they were becoming more experimental. Psychedelic ambassador Ken Kesey had recently helped publicise this cross-fertilisation of biker sensibility and mind-expansion. Always on the look-out for new ways to promote acid's chilled-out properties, they'd arranged a hallucinogenic day out for one chapter of the Hell's Angels. The idea was that the drug might sideline some of their more extreme tendencies; but, although it made for an interesting experiment, once the effects of the drug wore off, the bikers swiftly fell back into their alcohol and speed-dependent lifestyles.

Two years on from the 'Summer of Love', young America's appetite for drugs still appeared insatiable, not least in sunny California. LSD still held a special place in the counterculture's tripped out hearts and minds. After it was criminalised in 1966, a legion of underground chemists began to make up the shortfall from legitimate outlets, which were now denied a licence. Most took their lead from the legendary Augustus Owsley Stanley III, who had become the most successful mass-producer of LSD. It has been claimed that during these first, halcyon days of the drug's popularity, Owsley manufactured over five million tabs of LSD. Despite considerable efforts to circumvent his activities, Owsley avoided capture until late 1967, when he was finally caught and sentenced to three years in jail.

Adding his own little contribution to this widespread turn-on was thirty-four-year-old Gary Hinman. Hinman lived in the green and pleasant surrounds of the Family's old stomping ground, Topanga Canyon, and fitted in easily with the artistic community. Gary had the use of a pretty and secluded property at 964 Old Topanga Canyon Road. Fashioned from pine, the house had a unique and idiosyncratic charm. Because the house was on a steep incline, the living room and kitchen quarters were effectively on the second floor. Underneath lay a couple of bedrooms, which given Gary's generosity, had become something of a communal crash pad.

Hinman was a thoughtful and mellow character, whose six-foot two-inch muscular frame belied a chilled-out personality that endeared him to all he met. Something of an intellectual, Hinman had left UCLA in 1964 with a degree in Chemistry, and a postgraduate diploma in Political Science. Not exactly career-orientated, he directed his attentions to music and soul-searching. When not working at a local music store, he was happy to pass on his instrumental skills to a host of disciples.

Hinman had become loosely allied to the Family, principally through Bobby Beausoleil. As both were in awe of the power of sonic vibrations, they'd quickly become friends. Once Bobby began to fraternise with Charlie and the Family, Gary was naturally introduced to the circle. Although Hinman was a genuinely altruistic guy, there may have been reason for his special interest in the Family. Hinman was gay and, allegedly, strongly attracted to both Charlie and Bobby.

As befitted his genial spirit, Gary had been happy to help the Family when things got tough. When social services had attempted to take Mary and Charlie's son, Pooh Bear, into protective custody, Gary had stepped in and vouched for the safety of their child. After this, Gary became a minor celebrity among Family ranks for his gentle kindness.

Like many of the psychedelic new breed, Hinman's belief system lay well outside conventional religion. As a keen cosmic voyager, he'd explored the esoteric doctrines of the Buddhist world, and was a member of a local Buddhist society. Eschewing its more familiar tenets, he'd recently opted for the more cult ambitions of Nichiren Shoshu Buddhism. Followers claimed that through the incessant chanting of the mantra 'Nam Myoho Renge Kyo', believers could not only attain a blissful state, but also be granted anything they desired. Such was the depth of his immersion into Buddha's world that Gary was planning a pilgrimage to Japan. Perversely, he combined his spirituality with rather more worldly adventures: narcotics trafficking. Using his degree in Chemistry, Hinman had constructed a fairly lucrative laboratory that specialised in synthetic mescaline, a drug delivering a less intense ride than its LSD cousin. Although Hinman operated under a vague shroud of anonymity, word of Hinman's antics soon spread. When Spahn Ranch became the local drug hub, Hinman started dealing to members of the Family and their extended circle.

Towards the end of July 1969, members of The Straight Satans biker club were looking to replenish their chemical supply, and so went over to the ranch to see what was available. Since the group were organising a major party, and wanted something different to their usual beer and amphetamine binges, the bikers grilled Bobby Beausoleil on the possibility of acquiring some hallucinogenics. The gathering was going to see a major convergence of rival biker gangs, so they wanted to keep the mood mellow. Eager to ingratiate himself, Beausoleil mentioned Gary Hinman, confident that with his lab he'd be able to easily meet the bulk order. With Beausoleil acting as agent, $1,000 was put up against the promised return of a thousand tabs of the drug. With Bobby hoping for a successful introduction to the bikers' ranks as a result of the deal, he dashed over to Hinman's house and struck the order.

It turned out that Hinman had a stockpile of mescaline so, with the quickest of turnarounds, Bobby ferried the drugs over to Danny DeCarlo, who in turn, transported them over to the expectant bikers back at Spahn's. Although pleased with the speed of the delivery, they weren't interested in inviting Beausoleil to join in the fun. Deal done, a somewhat deflated Bobby went over to party in the more familiar surroundings of the Family quarters.

Any lingering hopes that Beausoleil might still have had of getting in with the bikers were soon dashed for good. Late in the afternoon of Friday 25 July 1969, some of the bikers turned up at Spahn's and angrily demanded their money back. The story goes that on imbibing Hinman's mescaline, some of the revellers promptly keeled over, while others had an intensely bad time on it. When Bobby asked for the remains of the rogue batch to be returned to have it checked out, he was told that it had been 'dumped'. To show they meant business, one of the bikers held a knife to Beausoleil's throat. Although Bobby vainly argued Hinman's corner, the bikers weren't interested in negotiating. Charlie later claimed that he witnessed the confrontation, and sweet-talked them out of taking action against Bobby. 'We'll see our man,' Charlie reportedly said. 'If he thinks the shit could have been bad, he'll make it good for you. Give us time to talk to him.' With that the bikers left the ranch, vowing to return later for their cash.

The fact that neither Beausoleil or Manson had tried Hinman's mescaline meant that they had no choice but to take the bikers at their word. Frightened, but still harbouring ambitions of joining the bikers' ranks, Bobby set off to confront Gary over the deal gone sour.

Charlie maintains that he called Hinman to sort things out. Hinman asked to see the mescaline, but was told that it had been discarded; he plainly told Manson that he wasn't interested in repaying the money or supplying a new batch. After this officious response, Sadie heard Charlie raging around the ranch shouting, 'I oughta kill the motherfucker.' Manson has since claimed that he was joking. But it turned out to be no joke for Hinman.

Beausoleil, under pressure from all sides, had no other option but to retrieve the $1,000 or face a severe beating at the hands of the aggrieved bikers. Given his friendship with Gary, Beausoleil figured that the situation could be resolved without too much bother, and without anyone getting hurt. He was wrong.

In the increasingly paranoid world of the Family, violence was never far beneath the surface. That day, Danny DeCarlo handed Beausoleil a 9-mm Radom pistol to take with him. Danny, as the main link between the bikers and Manson, had a vested interest in the transaction being quickly reversed and the money returned. He apparently told Bobby that the gun was merely to improve their bargaining position, but if things did deteriorate he was to 'hit him over the head' with the pistol. Like most of the Family at that moment, Bobby and the girls wore a sheath knife, but his beatnik instincts balked at the presence of the gun. But with time being of the essence, he took the weapon and headed off to arrange transport over to Gary's house, hoping that the gun's presence would be enough of a persuasion.

A gang of Family members soon congregated to drive over with Bobby to sort things out with Hinman. With Bruce Davis (a friend of Hinman's) roped in as chauffeur, the posse's numbers were further bolstered by Sadie and Mary Brunner, who came along for the ride. Despite the current friction, members of the Family had previously enjoyed the mellow vibes over at Hinman's, so any excuse to go over to his house was usually a good one.

Bruce dropped them all off at Gary's Topanga Boulevard house and returned to Spahn's. The remaining trio made their way up the steep incline of steps to Gary's front door. Hinman had been busy that afternoon, finalising the paperwork for his upcoming trip to Japan, and preparing himself for a bagpipe music festival on the Sunday. As was customary, Gary welcomed them in. While the girls made themselves at home in the spacious library, Gary and Bobby sat themselves around the kitchen table to talk business. Within seconds, Beausoleil came to the reason for his visit

'Look, Gary,' Beausoleil implored, 'you sold me bunk and I've got to get the money back. There's no two ways about it, it's really a bad scene.' Bobby told him about the atmosphere with the bikers back at the ranch, and how the dodgy mescaline had put him in an impossible situation, with little room for manoeuvre. Hinman was surprised. He'd had no previous complaints about his wares and reiterated his demand to inspect some of the rogue mescaline to see what had gone wrong. With Beausoleil unable to produce any of the capsules, Hinman simply refused to provide a refund.

Feeling the heat of the bikers' breath running down his neck, Bobby began to freak out. On reflection, he has said: 'I suppose that if I had given myself time to cool down I could have come up with a number of ways that I could have dealt with the problem without resorting to violence. I probably could have gotten out of town. That would have been one option, and there have been many, many times when I've wished that was the option that I'd taken.'

Practically, there was no way that Beausoleil could opt for a life on the run, especially with the likes of the Hell's Angels on his tail. If Hinman didn't change his mind, it was Bobby who was going to have the thousand dollars beaten out of him. It was obvious to Bobby that Gary was resolute in his decision not to refund the money. In any case, Gary informed Bobby that the money had already been spent on his trip abroad. As if to confirm this, he showed Bobby his cheque book, bank statements, and a leather wallet containing a solitary $20.

Increasingly desperate, Bobby felt he only had one option left. Recalling Danny DeCarlo's words, Bobby took out the gun, and hit Hinman around the head two or three times, chipping a tooth in the process. Hinman, a totally peaceful and non-violent soul, was shocked by Bobby's actions, imploring him to stop and explaining that he didn't have the money.

Bobby Beausoleil later said: 'I'm not really a violent person. I'd never done anything like that . . . I did hit him a couple of times and I tried to emphasise to him that I was desperate. I needed to get the money back for the bike club.'

Events turned even nastier when Bobby handed the gun over to Sadie, telling her to train it on Gary, while he ransacked the house to find any of the money. As Beausoleil began his search, a cry came out from the kitchen. In Bobby's absence, Hinman had got the gun from Sadie, and was now training it on her. Sadie began screaming, 'Bobby! Bobby! He's got the gun!' and Beausoleil ran back into the kitchen. Not intimidated by the sight of a Buddhist with a gun, Bobby leapt at Gary, and the pair fell to the floor. In the ensuing struggle, the pistol went off; the bullet tearing into the sink. At the sound of the gunshot, Hinman froze, allowing Bobby to retrieve the pistol, and regain a fragile control of the situation.

Since Hinman wasn't stumping up the money, Beausoleil began desperately casting around for alternatives. The only apparent item of value in the house was a baby grand piano. Aware that the bikers would have little use for that, Bobby turned his attentions to Hinman's two vehicles – a small Fiat car and a VW camper van. Although both were old and beaten-up, it was possible that together they might collectively add up to the $1,000 necessary to pay off the bikers. In fact, as Gary had paid $800 for the shabby Volkswagen, it seemed a fair exchange. With Hinman sensing Beausoleil's uncompromising stance, he reluctantly signed off the pink slips transferring ownership into Bobby's hands. Things might well have ended there had someone not pre-empted events and called for assistance.

While Bobby and Gary had been wrestling on the kitchen floor, one of the girls, probably Mary Brunner, had managed to sidle away and find Hinman's telephone. Evidently in fear for all their lives, she'd rung Spahn Ranch for assistance. Perhaps not wanting to inflame the situation, she didn't tell Beausoleil about the call. Word soon got to Manson that Hinman had a gun and was threatening them. Despite the fact that Hinman had already signed over his cars, a misguided cavalry in the form of Bruce Davis and Manson were soon on their way to Topanga Canyon to sort out matters. Given Mary's desperate phone call, Charlie came armed with the sword he'd acquired from The Straight Satans biker.

With the fraught negotiations at Hinman's house now approaching some semblance of closure, Beausoleil and the girls began their retreat. At that moment, Manson knocked at the front door. Hinman figured the situation was now under control, so he automatically went to turn the latch and see who was outside. There he was confronted by a ramped-up Charlie, with the sinister figure of Bruce Davis bringing up the rear. Hinman could barely utter a greeting before Manson slashed him across the face with his blade, tearing off most of his left ear in the process.

As Hinman fell to the ground, Manson screamed at him, 'That's how you be a man.' Pushing past him, Charlie ran through the house in an attempt to take control of what he believed to be a highly charged situation. What he soon gathered was that the issue had already been settled, and that his spectacularly violent attack was wholly superfluous. Embarrassed and immensely irritated, Manson swiftly left in one of Hinman's cars, leaving Bruce Davis to drive their own vehicle away. For reasons of his own, Charlie also took with him a set of Hinman's bagpipes.

What had started out as a tricky situation had now been transformed into a horrendous mess. With Hinman bleeding profusely from Charlie's bayonet wound, he was desperately in need of urgent medical attention. If his injuries were left untreated, he could well bleed to death. Once more, Bobby was placed in a horrible situation. Knowing only too well that doctors would immediately call in the police on seeing Hinman's bloody state, there were few ways to turn.

In his panic, Bobby called Sadie and Mary over in a vain attempt to repair Hinman as best they could. Sadie grabbed an old sweatshirt to mop up the blood, but the gash was bleeding so profusely, she had to use a sheet from Hinman's bed to try to stop it. With Gary's face still haemorrhaging badly, a more desperate attempt was made to patch it up. Beausoleil had once stitched up his pet dog, Snowfox, when it limped home after a fight, and in his panicked state he assumed that the same logic could be applied to Hinman's butchered face. With this in mind, Sadie was dispatched to the local shops to buy some peroxide and dental floss to crudely stitch him up. While she was gone, Mary prepared Gary a Buddhist-friendly concoction of rice and vegetables. Seeing he was in no fit state to eat, she fed it to him with a spoon.

Sadie soon returned with the basic medical kit, and either Bobby or Sadie (or both) began the painful process of sewing Hinman's ear and cheek back together. Despite this crude needlework, Gary told them over and over that he still required hospital treatment. Fearful that he'd alert the emergency services, the trio decided to stick with him until he'd calmed down.

It was late into this first night that Bobby, Mary and Sadie decided to get some sleep. With Hinman already passed out, the others felt secure enough to grab a few hours themselves. While they crashed, Gary awoke and made a perfunctory bid for freedom. His movements awoke Bobby, who dragged him to the sofa and back under his watchful eye. To stymie any further breach, the trio decided to sleep in shifts. Their watch details at the ranch had prepared them for just this sort of military vigilance. From trying to help Hinman, they had slipped into the role of enemy jailors.

Things were no better the next morning. Although still traumatised, Hinman levelled his emotions through the incessant chanting of his Buddhist mantra. To help focus him on his meditative state, he asked for his prayer beads. At times he appeared to have come to terms with the horror, and yet at other moments, he was intent on seeking professional attention. This wavering continued through Saturday and well into Sunday night. Compounding issues, a phone call from one of Gary's friends was put through to the house on the Sunday evening. Hinman had been scheduled to appear as part of a bagpipe parade in Santa Monica during the afternoon, and his mate was worried when he failed to appear. Perhaps expecting Manson, one of the women picked up the receiver. Speaking in an English accent, she told the caller that Gary had gone back to Colorado as his parents had been involved in a car accident.

The call and the standoff with Hinman freaked Beausoleil out so much, he rung back to Spahn's Ranch to confer with Charlie on how best to extricate themselves from this mess. As it was Manson's violent act that had caused the situation to spiral out of control, Beausoleil was keen to throw the ball back into Charlie's court. But Manson was in no mood to debate the merits of staying or leaving. Couched in typically ambivalent terms, Charlie muttered darkly, 'Well, you know what to do as well as I do'. With that, Manson put the phone down.

Beausoleil looked over at Gary and weighed up the scene. Hinman had now fallen off the sofa, and was lying in a foetal position on the floor. He was still chanting softly, with just a tangle of dental floss holding his face together. Looking at the pitiful sight he'd help create, Bobby felt that he had backed himself into an impossible corner. 'I didn't give myself a chance to think. When it became clear that I wasn't going to be able to turn him around, and he was going to go to the cops, I believed there was nothing else I could do.'

With all options seemingly lost, Bobby went over and stabbed him in the chest. As Gary screamed 'No Bobby! No Bobby!' Mary Brunner ran into the lounge from the kitchen to see Bobby knife him a second time. That was enough – he'd finished what Manson started.

With their friend in the final throes of life, Bobby instructed the girls to ensure that the house was clear of any trace of their presence. To make the killing look as though it had been the work of some radical black element, Bobby dipped a gloved hand into some of the blood pouring from Hinman's wounds, and wrote the words 'Political Piggy' over the wall of his lounge. To give it some extra credibility, he finished it off with a symbolic paw-print.

There was some logic behind Beausoleil's bloody scrawls. As Hinman liked to keep company with some of the more revolutionary elements at UCLA, his death might appear to be the result of politicking with the wrong elements. To lend some verisimilitude to these hints of radical involvement, Beausoleil also burnt some of Hinman's Marxist literature on the floor of his house.

With Hinman's body still warm, the trio left the house, locking the door from the inside and climbing out through a small side window. All were consumed with varying degrees of guilt, sadness and disappointment at what had happened, and yet they agreed that there was little else they could have done under the circumstances.

As they turned to go down the winding steps, they heard sounds apparently coming from Hinman inside the house. Apprehensive that Gary was making what amounted to a miraculous recovery, Bobby panicked. With the door now locked, Bobby (some claim all three participants) climbed through a small window, and was missing for a few minutes. When he returned, he told them that to ensure Gary was dead, he'd smothered him with a pillow. As they left, Beausoleil told the girls, 'It's all over.' But he was wrong. In many ways it was only the beginning.

Beausoleil hot-wired Gary's white Fiat and the trio sped off towards a nearby restaurant called Topanga Kitchen. There, they visited the restrooms to check their clothes for any traces of Gary's blood. Casually strolling back into the restaurant they coolly ordered coffee and cherry pie, paid for with the $20 they'd took from Gary's wallet. Under the surface, though, tensions were high, and Beausoleil was freaking out. Looking over at his companions he hissed, 'I should have killed you as well, Sadie, for letting him get the gun.'

When they arrived back at the ranch, Charlie was eager to find out what had happened with Hinman. In their absence, the bikers had called demanding their cash. According to Manson, Bobby came up to him and said 'Gary's dead.' Manson flipped, swiftly backtracking from any dark ambiguity his words might have contained. Although he has referred to the scenario many times since, his most voluble response concerning Hinman's fate was captured during an interview in 1989.

'I know when I've done something and when I didn't do something. [Beausoleil] comes to me and says "I got a problem", and I said "What is it?" And they said, "Will you help me?" I said "Sure I'll help you." He said, "Well, can I be your brother?" I said "Sure I'm your brother. I'll help you do anything when it's a problem." He said guy owes me some money, and I said "Well, you're big enough, go get it. If you ain't, sit down and keep your mouth shut."

'He [Beausoleil] said, "Well, what would you do?" I said, "Fuck it man, it's only money. I wouldn't put my life up for no fucking money." He said "Well, I'm going to get my money", and I said, "Well that's up to you. It's got nothing to do with me." The guy went over and fucked the guy up and took his money, and he came back and said "I killed the dude." I said, "What the fuck you tell me for? You making me a conspiracy to something?"'

During Beausoleil's later prosecution, there were strong claims that Manson had ordered the trip to Hinman's to force him into handing over a considerable sum of money he was due to inherit. Allegedly, it was pitched somewhere in the region of $21,000, and Charlie had been eager to absorb both the money (and Hinman for that matter) into the planned relocation to Death Valley. Whether avarice or fear really prompted the murder, the result was the same: Hinman was dead.

According to legend, back at the ranch any guilt that those involved might have felt was shrugged aside as they performed a bloody re-enactment of Hinman's death around the campfire. However if any such pantomime of death did take place, it was evident that Beausoleil was not a part of it. Later court testimony from several members of the Family suggests that Beausoleil went back to Hinman's house in an attempt to wipe the 'Political

Piggy' motif off the wall. While there, it was said that he witnessed Hinman's rapidly decomposing corpse, with an infestation of maggots eating away at his body.

While these gruesome reports easily fit into the whole 'Carnival of Terror' surrounding the darker side of the Family, it appears that elements of the Grand Guignol scenarios were heavily embellished in line with the upcoming horrors. From the most reliable evidence presented since, there appears to have been a real sense of sadness following Hinman's killing.

Whatever the emotional state around the ranch, Manson was livid with the outcome. With two murders which could be ascribed to the Family, and the bikers bearing down on them, he sensed that his best move was to escape – and fast. Nonetheless, in a crude attempt to raise some cash before he split, Manson attempted to hike off Hinman's vehicles to a loose Family associate.

With Charlie gone, Beausoleil had to sort out the mess with the bikers single-handedly. True to form, they soon returned to the ranch, taking with them Hinman's VW van in exchange for the bad drugs. However, once they gathered that Hinman had been killed in pursuance of the debt, they kept their distance from the Family.

The bikers had now been effectively paid off, but Beausoleil considered that the ranch's atmosphere was too hot to be around; like Manson, he took off. Taking charge of Hinman's clapped-out Fiat, he drove off to gather his thoughts. As he had the use of a flat in Hollywood, it made sense to retreat to there for a while. However, such was his popularity, news of Bobby's presence in the district soon spread and visitors started turning up at his door. Unable to face his friends, he headed off for the relative seclusion of the California coastline.

Driving Hinman's car around the Californian coastline, Beausoleil's mind, addled by the horror of what he'd done, could barely come to terms with the bloody details. Although strong enough to withstand Manson's mind-warping manoeuvres, he'd nonetheless fallen into an impossible situation, largely of his own making. In his fractured consciousness, he'd left behind a trail of easily identifiable clues at the house. Moreover, he was driving Hinman's vehicle, and carrying the knife he'd stabbed him with.

Hinman's car was in a bad mechanical state, and Bobby had to pull into a lay-by in San Luis Obispo to attend to a leaking fluid pipe. The Highway Patrol – at this point eager to shunt on any hippie travellers who were using the highway as a cheap motel – pulled over to inspect the Fiat and its occupant. Inside, they found a dishevelled and possibly stoned Beausoleil asleep at the wheel.

When they stood him up against the side of car, the police couldn't fail to notice the bloodstains on his trousers and promptly instigated a thorough search of the vehicle. In the tyre well they found his sheaf knife, still with traces of Hinman's blood on it. While Bobby claimed he was en route to San Francisco, the ID he flashed turned out to be bogus. After a further check on the vehicle's provenance, Beausoleil was taken into police custody. As Bobby hadn't had time to fully process the pink slips on the car, the vehicle was still registered as Hinman's. With news of Gary's death already logged at police headquarters, and with blood from the knife sent off for identification, it wasn't long before the police matched the clues together.

On 6 August 1969, Beausoleil was charged on suspicion of Hinman's murder. While it was all over for Bobby, for the rest of the Family the Carnival of Terror was just beginning.

chapter 8
Time

'Now is forever lasting constant in the mind
Illusions with memories scheming at my end of the mind
All the time.'

From 'I Once Knew A Man' by Charles Manson

ANSON wasn't aware of Bobby's arrest, since he'd split from Spahn's soon after news broke of Gary Hinman's death. On Sunday 3 August 1969, Manson took off along the Californian coastline.

'We were living in a state of fear,' Charlie recounted in 1989. 'Fights were more common than lovemaking, and kids were drifting away. It was a situation that would have to be remedied once I got back, but for now I was on the highway heading away from all those problems.'

Manson's retreat wasn't just to escape the heat caused by Hinman's death. He also planned to drop in on some old comrades en route, and to score a shed-load of drugs to curry favour with everyone back at the ranch. To defer any suspicions of abandonment, Charlie left word at Spahn's that he was off to recruit new members for the Family fold.

With his eye for unique vehicles, Charlie had acquired from Danny DeCarlo the services of a 1952 cream-coloured bakery truck, complete with 'Hostess Twinkie' painted on its side. Like the 'Holywood Productions' bus, the van's commercial appearance was designed to evade suspicion. Charlie got a lucky break en route; while filling up with gas late into his first night away, he chanced upon Stephanie Schram, a blond seventeen-year-old from San Diego. Despite being with her boyfriend, Charlie easily charmed the teenager, and whisked her off to a nearby beach. Once there, Charlie laid on a heavily compressed version of his acid and sex initiation, and they cavorted into the small hours. By dawn's early light, young Stephanie was his latest convert. Despite Stephanie's fairly modest attractions, Manson was captivated by her Aryan qualities and Teutonic lineage, claiming she was 'the product of two thousand years of high-quality racial production.'

With Stephanie on board, Charlie headed north along the coastal route towards Big Sur on the Monterey peninsula. This breathtaking piece of Pacific coastline housed the Esalen Institute, a centre famous for attracting luminaries from many alternative spheres. As a Haight veteran, Charlie would have been well aware of Esalen. With its stunning remote location, the alternative institute had become a cosmic think-tank for the more altruistic sections of the counterculture.

Founded in 1962, Esalen enjoyed the patronage of an impressive range of psychologists, thinkers and philosophers. In addition to its plethora of mind-expanding courses, Esalen offered retreat space for those wanting to revive mind and body. Following the 'Summer of Love', a new, younger breed descended on the institute, looking for solace and meaning. These attendees ironically included many who would later cross Manson's darkening path, including actress Sharon Tate and her friend, coffee heiress Abigail Folger. Reports also suggested that Processian-in-chief, Robert DeGrimston, had also lectured at the institute at some point. With its unashamedly hippie pretensions, Charlie had labelled Esalen 'a sensitivity camp', where rich hippies went 'to play at being enlightened'. Despite his cynicism, Charlie was nonetheless upbeat about what the institute could offer him. Keen to spend some restorative time at Esalen, Charlie was also hoping to share his music with the soul-seekers at the Institute.

During his time at Esalen, Charlie relaxed in the resort's famous baths, and spent quality time rapping and philosophising with fellow attendees. For once he needed no clucking acolytes around him and, despite his infatuation with young Stephanie, he exiled her to the truck. As planned, Charlie found time to play his songs to a small coterie of the institute's top people. Faced with his revolutionary compositions, the Esalen's highbrows rejected Charlie's music as 'too heavy', while others, in Manson's words, 'just got up and walked out.' With yet another rejection to shoulder, Charlie stormed off to spend the night alone. The next morning, he returned to his van and, in a fit of anger, reportedly hit Stephanie. Deflated, the pair left the area. Nursing his bruised ego, Manson was eager to get back to Spahn Ranch to see if any more earthly action was being realised there.

Despite the friendly welcome that Stephanie got at Spahn's, she was aghast at the free love Manson enjoyed within the Family. The jealous teenager presented Charlie with a challenge: to remain faithful to her for two weeks. This caused some angst among the Family women, as monogamy had always been a dirty word for Manson. For possibly the only time in his life, the headstrong chauvinist was forced to concede to his new lady's wishes.

With a fair degree of tension in the air, Charlie and Stephanie decided to move away from the ranch and spend the night together somewhere less fraught. Charlie accompanied Stephanie over to her sister's flat in San Diego to collect a few of her possessions, but en route he was booked by police for not having a valid driving licence. At Stephanie's sister's house, those present witnessed an electrified Charlie madly raging about the impending black uprising and Helter Skelter. After spending the night in the van, they began a miserable traipse back to Spahn Ranch. Unbeknownst to Charlie, while they were away, news had filtered through to Spahn's about Bobby Beausoleil's arrest on suspicion of Gary Hinman's murder.

The night Charlie arrived back at the ranch saw the city of Los Angeles in the grip of a prolonged heat wave that made even the most basic of tasks unbearable. Those unforgiving, ninety-plus-degree temperatures did little to ease the tense relationship between police and black militants, particularly in run-down suburbs like Watts. This predominately black enclave of Los Angeles had barely recovered from a major riot in August 1965, which had turned the area into a virtual battle zone.

The disturbances had claimed thirty-five lives and caused forty million dollars' worth of damage; there was still considerable resentment at the fact that the underlying issues of unemployment, inadequate housing and poor schooling had yet to be addressed.

The death of Martin Luther King on 4 April 1968 had taken with it a multitude of hopes for the future. The assassination of the black community's most prominent role model prompted a huge backlash in many quarters of America, notably on Chicago's West Side, where more than 20,000 police and troops were deployed to quell rioting and looting.

Meanwhile, across the Atlantic, at around 10 a.m. on Friday 8 August, the Beatles stepped onto a zebra crossing in North London, their movements captured in an iconic series of photographs. Eventually whittled down to one shot, the approved image became the cover for the group's final album, *Abbey Road*. Like the *White Album* before it, the *Abbey Road* album would soon make its way into Charlie and the Family's possession and be filleted for any underlying messages.

If Stephanie Schram's conversion had offered a brief glimmer of light in Charlie's increasingly dark world, the news of Bobby's arrest only served to turn things completely black. With drug-dealer Bernard Crowe's death hanging over him, and his own involvement in Gary Hinman's death now under possible scrutiny, Charlie was gripped with the fear that either one of the murders could lead back to him.

According to Manson, during his trip to Big Sur, the women had concocted a plot that they hoped would defer any investigation into Bobby's role in Gary Hinman's death. Their fertile minds surmised that if another murder bearing the hallmarks of Hinman's death was committed while Bobby was in custody, it would throw police investigators off the trail and divert attention away from Beausoleil. With the bloody paw-mark already left at Hinman's property, a similar sign left after another murder might add credence to the theory that these were Black Panther 'hits'. Although Manson admired their loyalty to 'love of brother', he was not impressed with their harebrained plan. 'I'm getting my shit together right now, loading it in my truck and getting the fuck out of here,' he allegedly told them on hearing the idea. 'I'm not going back to prison because a bunch of kids can't handle their own problems.'

The girls were dismayed at Charlie's lack of enthusiasm. Most vocal was Squeaky, who implored Manson to stay, reiterating the Family credo of oneness and brotherly love. Sensing a contradiction that could easily undermine his own manifesto, Manson agreed to hang on.

That afternoon, Manson skulked around the ranch, deliberating on his troubling situation. In an attempt to revive their deflated sprits, Charlie dispatched Mary Brunner and Sandy Good in his bakery truck to gather provisions for a special dinner. Whilst the garbage bins were their usual source of food, on this day the girls entered the supermarket by the front door, armed with a stolen credit card that Charlie had passed on to them.

However, when they'd failed to return by early evening, paranoia began to bloom. In lieu of the feast that Manson had promised, Linda Kasabian was forced to prepare some leftover food on a camping stove. By sundown, Mary and Sandra were still missing, and everyone was getting anxious. At 10 p.m., the solitary phone at the ranch began to ring. Squeaky apprehensively answered the call. It was Sandy Good, calling from the jailhouse reception of Sybil Branch Institute for Woman. Sandy informed Squeaky that she and Mary had been arrested in connection with the credit card that Charlie had given them – the card had been checked against a missing list at the local store and identified as stolen. Not wishing to debate their innocence, the pair had tried to split in Charlie's van. A chase had ensued, with the police pursuing the pair around the winding roads of the San Fernando Valley. Following a collision, the girls were apprehended and summarily charged. When the police did a cursory search of the girls' truck, they, found the traffic violation notice Charlie had received while travelling back from Big Sur.

As Squeaky relayed the news to Charlie, it seemed that the final piece in this nightmare scenario had fallen into place. Incandescent with anger, fear and betrayal, Manson took himself off towards the creek bed. Once there, he repeatedly pounded his fists against a tree as his despair unfolded and his hopes and dreams caved in on him. 'Every abuse, every rejection in my entire life flashed before my eyes,' he'd recall later. 'All I could focus on was "What the fuck is happening here?" One by one this fucked-up society is stripping my loves from me. I'll show them! They made animals out of us; well, I'll unleash those animals! I'll give them so much fucking fear the people will be afraid to come out of their houses.'

Although Charlie has always remained characteristically vague about exactly what instigated the events that were to ensue that weekend, what is indisputable is that in the space of a few weeks, Manson's entire world had collapsed. The botched shooting of Lotsapoppa, Gary Hinman's death, Bobby Beausoleil's arrest, the rejection from Esalen, and now Sandy and Mary being held; there was now little left to go wrong. Underpinning all of this, was Terry Melcher giving the final blow to his musical career.

Utterly rejected, and with Helter Skelter the only weapon left in his armoury, he had little option but to bring it to pass. Whereas earlier, the girls' cockeyed scheme to free Beausoleil seemed ludicrous, it now made much more sense. Additionally, it fitted into the apocalyptical time-frame that the Beatles and the Bible had predicted.

Charlie stalked back to the campfire where most of the Family were sitting after dinner. In an uncompromising mood, Manson made a bold statement that electrified the air. Charlie had been monitoring reports of black militancy in LA, and his rant was dominated by the inability of the Negro community to organise a revolution because of their ineptitude and poor organisation. Although it was a familiar diatribe, this time the tone that accompanied it was overwhelmingly intense. 'If they can't do it,' Manson spat, 'well, someone's gonna have to do it for them!' With all eyes trained on him, Manson loudly declared: 'Now is the time for Helter Skelter.'

With his apocalypse set in motion, Manson instructed the younger and more marginal members of the group to make themselves scarce and not return until the next morning. He then pointed Sadie in the direction of the living quarters, telling her to find a knife, and a dark set of clothing. As she set off, Manson reportedly told her, 'Do whatever Tex tells you to do.'

Earlier, Charlie had spied Tex lounging on the boulders that bordered the creek bed, tripping on belladona. Like most of the Family that night, Tex had also partaken in some low-grade acid, handed out by Squeaky. Despite the fog of hallucinogens, Tex knew full well that, since the drug-burn incident, he owed Manson an enormous debt, and, he'd been waiting for it to be called in. Charlie took Tex around to the side of the Rock City Café, and leant against one of the cars that were dumped there. In no uncertain terms, Manson laid it on the line – because of his part in the Lotsapoppa debacle, he'd set off the cascade of shit that was now engulfing the Family.

To give his plan credibility, Manson told Tex that Mary and Sandra could easily be released on bail, but for that they needed money, fast, and the Family's coffers had all but run dry. Furthermore, they desperately needed cash for their preparations for the imminent Helter Skelter. Additionally, he reiterated the girls' scheme to clear Bobby of suspicion over Gary Hinman's murder.

According to Tex, Charlie's instructions were totally explicit at this point. 'I want you to go to that house where Melcher used to live,' recalled Watson. 'I want you to take a couple of the girls I'll send with you, and go down there and totally destroy everyone in that house, as gruesome as you can. Make it a real nice murder, just as bad as you've ever seen. And get all their money.'

As far as Tex was concerned, Manson didn't know who was currently living in the house since Melcher's relocation, or how many people would be present when they arrived. Although Charlie's prior reconnaissance mission to find Terry had included a fleeting meeting with Sharon Tate, Manson had little interest in any of the residents' celebrity status; muttering dismissively that the property currently housed 'some movie stars'. According to Tex, he did, however, give very clear instructions on how he wanted them slaughtered.

His plan was to round up a few of the girls, get them all to dress in black, and ensure that they had a change of clothes with them. They should then collect some knives, a length of rope and a pair of bolt cutters. As Manson was familiar with the layout of Melcher's Cielo Drive property, he warned them that an alarm system would almost certainly be in place. He instructed Tex to sever any telephone wires, before using their best 'Creepy Crawly' tactics to gain entry to the property.

Manson also reportedly told Tex that, once they'd finished with the Melcher house, they were to work their way through the neighbouring properties, inflicting similar brutality, before returning home. With that order delivered, Charlie left to round up Watson's partners for the night.

Sadie was his first choice. She had proved her unswerving subservience to Manson since their first meeting, and had already been involved with the Hinman killing. Katie was also ideally suited to the task, as her quiet exterior belied a steely determination to obey orders. She had been the Family's most consistent foot-soldier; the one to revive collective spirits when situations looked lost. Surprisingly, Squeaky, his closest and most loyal supporter, was passed over for the evening's work. Knowing her proclivity to lose herself in fantasy, he wasn't sure she had the necessary mettle to commit murder, even for his sake.

That afternoon, Katie had been enjoying an LSD trip. By late evening, she was coming down from the drug in the trailer where the Family children were housed.

Patricia Krenwinkel recalls: 'Charlie came and woke me up and he said, "Get up, I want you to go somewhere," and so I did. I was following Charlie's orders.'

Last to be chosen by Manson was Linda Kasabian. Although the extent of her commitment to Helter Skelter had yet to be proven, her swift induction into the Family meant she was considered capable of handling the duties. More pertinently, with Mary now incarcerated, Linda was the only Family member with a valid driving licence, which Charlie insisted she take with her on the trip.

While Katie, Sadie and Linda busied themselves, Tex took himself off to one of the ranch's cabins to fortify himself for this night of nights. In this corner of the ranch, the Texan had secreted a jar of the potent amphetamine, crystal meth, which he'd mixed with cocaine. News of Tex's jar would have enraged Charlie, as his dislike of amphetamines was well known. Tex had a willing co-conspirator in the form of Sadie, who had snuck off with him for a cheeky sniff from the magic jar earlier in the day. For Tex, the superhuman properties of crystal meth gave him a much-needed charge. This was especially useful to him as he was still coming down off his LSD trip. Grasping the magnitude of his bloody mission, Tex figured that a sizeable hit of methamphetamine would blitz any doubts about what lay ahead. With the chemical propellant running through his veins, Tex could see that Charlie's vivid descriptions of impending Helter Skelter were now to be realised. 'We'd practised so many times,' he said, 'in our heads, sitting around projecting scenes much like the one Charlie had just described on some imaginary piggie, and if the world was ending at any moment and if death was only a figment of the mind and if … and if … Despite all we'd been taught, I was spinning inside, trembling. I took a couple of deep snorts of speed and went to get the clothes and rope and bolt cutters as Charlie had ordered.'

It was just after eleven o'clock when the unit gathered on one of the ranch's boardwalks. Kitted out as instructed, they presented a rare example of monochromatic unity: Sadie swathed in blue denim, Katie in a blue skirt, Linda in black T-shirt and jeans, and Tex sporting Levi jeans and a polo-neck that chafed against his unkempt beard. Other than Tex, who wore cowboy boots, the girls were, as usual, barefoot. Furthermore Sadie was battling with a virulent strain of venereal disease that had begun to rupture out through her feet, making the wearing of shoes impossible.

For weaponry, the squad had four knives between them: three 'Buck' hunting knives and a kitchen blade, the handle of which was held together with adhesive tape. Manson slipped Watson the .22 calibre 'Longhorn' revolver he'd used at the Lotsapoppa incident, although Charlie was allegedly explicit that the knives were to be the principal instruments of death that night. Watson also had with him a pair of red bolt cutters and forty-three feet of white nylon rope that he slung over his shoulder. Tex then went over to George Spahn's house, where horse-wrangler Johnny Swartz was staying. Swartz had allowed the Family to use his clapped-out black and yellow Ford for their numerous garbage runs, and had not made a fuss when they'd removed the back seats to accommodate their booty. Since the vehicle seemed the most unobtrusive that they could muster for the mission, Tex asked Swartz if they could borrow it for a trip into town to hear some music. Permission granted, Tex and the women piled into Swartz's Ford, and took their positions for the fifteen-mile drive up into the Hollywood hills.

Although Linda had retrieved her driving licence from Squeaky's safekeeping, it appears it was Tex who took control of the wheel. While Linda acted as co-driver, Katie and Sadie squatted down in the rear of the car, trying desperately to appear normal, despite the discomfort of the seatless vehicle. As the car made its way up the drive towards the junction with Iverson Road, Manson flagged it down for one last instruction, concocted as his mind raced into overdrive at the potential carnage that lay ahead. 'Leave a sign to let them know you've been.' His voice was devoid of emotion as he leant in through the driver's window. 'You girls know what to do. Something witchy, and do it well.'

There is no confirmed record of how Manson spent the hours whilst his emissaries were en route to Cielo Drive. No one present at Spahn's has revealed his movements during that terrible night. Charlie's recollections of the evening are nebulous in the extreme, although a brief passage in his memoir offers what appears to be some skewed regret at his part in the events. 'For one short moment, I had an urge to overtake the car and bring them back . . . I thought how wrong it all was. Yet I had let the kids run with their scheme and, just minutes before, I had put the clincher on it by saying "It's time to go." I had shared in their madness. I had a moment of regret, but for the most part, bitterness and contempt for a world that I didn't give a shit about, allowed me to go along with anything that might come out of the night's activities.'

As the car left Spahn Ranch, Barbara Hoyt, one of the Family's youngest members, came out onto the boardwalk with a set of dark clothes that Sadie had requested earlier. Manson angrily admonished the eighteen-year-old for breaching his instructions to stay inside. When Hoyt innocently explained that Sadie had asked her to fetch a spare set of clothing, Manson just looked at her blankly and said, 'Well, they've already left.'

Inside the Ford, the ambience was an uneven mixture of expectancy and fear of what lay ahead for them that night. While Katie maintained her customary self-control, Sadie was excited. Although she'd been there for the killing of Gary Hinman, tonight's plans held greater significance, as it was the Family's first overt engagement with Helter Skelter. While Linda sat quietly in the front seat, Tex handed her the revolver and told her to place it in the glove compartment, with instructions to throw it out of the window at the first sign of potential trouble. Along the way, Tex filled the girls in on the details of Cielo Drive, and how they were to breach its feeble defences.

No one has ever confirmed whether Tex told the girls that murder was their principal objective that night. Katie has later claimed that they were under the impression it was a 'Creepy Crawl' to collect money for Mary and Sandra's bail. However, there is little doubt that some confrontation was expected, especially as they were armed to the teeth. Although Manson had allegedly ordered Tex to continue cutting a murderous swathe throughout the district, Watson apparently dropped no hint about an extension to the night's itinerary. All their minds were focused on Cielo Drive and its occupants.

The car made its way through Los Angeles' labyrinthine canyons and grid of streets. Despite Watson being familiar with the area during daylight, they ended up getting lost – perhaps because of Tex's chemically messed-up state, and the excitable energy in the car. Eventually, after much shouting, they rerouted themselves, passing through Santa Monica, West Hollywood, Beverly Hills, Sunset Boulevard and Benedict Canyon before turning into Cielo Drive. Then, at a hairpin junction, they travelled up a single-track, unmade drive that led to a dead end.

For the residents of 10050 Cielo Drive, Friday 8 August had been just a regular day. Following Terry Melcher and Candice Bergen's departure from Cielo Drive in February 1969, Sharon Tate and her husband Roman Polanski had gradually made their mark on the property. While both were keen to cement their tenancy at the pretty house, the couple's work commitments saw them often away on film shoots. With Roman away in Europe, Sharon's advancing pregnancy meant she was winding down her busy diary. By the first week of August 1969, she was eight and a half months pregnant.

At around 8 a.m. on Friday 8 August, the Polanskis' housekeeper,

Winifred Chapman, arrived at the house to start work. A favourite with the couple, Chapman had followed Sharon and Roman from house to house around LA until they'd settled at Cielo Drive. She was used to finding a mess from the prior evening's partying in the kitchen and lounge, which she'd always dutifully clear up before tackling the main bulk of her work. Outside, some labourers were doing some maintenance to the property, while, later, an interior decorator was expected to begin work on decorating a room the Polanskis had earmarked as a nursery.

At around 9 a.m., Sharon Tate began to stir. She'd attended a film premiere the night before, and was allowing herself a little lie-in. In these final stages of pregnancy, Sharon was keeping her activities to the absolute minimum. That morning, she took a dip in the horseshoe-shaped pool that lay just outside the kitchen. Lounging in a large inner tube in the shade, Sharon waited for Roman to call.

Polanski's protracted stay in Europe had become a major bone of contention for Sharon. He had been working on a script entitled *Day of the Dolphins*, but had met with several problems and was required to extend his stay in London. Extremely peeved, she'd reiterated the need for him to return as soon as possible. As well as the impending birth of their first child, Sharon had also arranged a party at Cielo Drive for her husband's thirty-fifth birthday on 18 August. However, on the 8th, after a strained conversation with his wife, Polanksi had decided to return home to finish the script back in Los Angeles. Being late on a Friday afternoon, his plans to leave were thwarted – the London American Embassy was closed for visa applications until the following Monday.

At around noon, Sharon welcomed two close friends, Barbara Lewis and British actress Joanna Pettit. Later they lunched together by the pool, and Sharon confided her disappointment at her husband's delay in returning from London. Not only was Roman's work increasingly keeping him away from her, but she'd heard worrying rumours of a string of casual affairs. Sharon had been devastated by the revelation that, while in London, Roman had had a brief fling with the Mamas & the Papas star, Michelle Phillips. Although Sharon had confronted Roman over this and other dalliances, he was evasive and told her he needed to retain his freedom. Sharon's pregnancy, which she'd hoped would have forged a deeper partnership, seemed only to put a further strain on the marriage.

That afternoon, Tate's younger sister Debra had phoned, looking to come over with her sister Patti. Sharon's two teenage siblings were visibly excited at the prospect of becoming aunts and, as they were both on summer vacation, were keen to pop over to see Sharon as much as possible. In the nicest possible way, Sharon told her sister that she was too tired for socialising, and promptly headed to her bedroom for a nap. Several others have since claimed that they called on 10050 Cielo Drive that day. Brian Wilson collaborator Van Dyke Parks visited during the afternoon looking for Terry Melcher, only to be told of his relocation to Malibu. The Mamas & the Papas members Cass Elliot, John Phillips and Denny Doherty were also due to arrive later that day, but ended up changing their plans. Close friend of Roman and Sharon, author Jerzy Kosinski, had also planned to arrive that night. Writer Jacqueline Susann had apparently been called over to the house by Sharon, but she was out with another friend. Aware that housekeeper Winifred Chapman was due to start early the next morning, Sharon had offered Chapman a room for the night. Despite the kind offer, Chapman declined. That decision ended up saving her life.

Also hovering around the house that day were the Polanski's permanent house-guests, Voyteck Frykowski and his partner Abigail Folger. They'd been renting a modest property over in Laurel Canyon since August 1968 but, not surprisingly, loved the house on Cielo Drive. With Sharon and Roman out of the country for most of spring and the early summer of 1969, their friends had been allowed a free run of the place. Additionally, Roman felt that, in his absence, Frykowski would be best placed to keep a protective eye on Sharon during her final weeks of pregnancy.

Frykowski and Folger had become a familiar presence in Hollywood circles. Twenty-four-year-old Abigail (or plain 'Gibby' to her friends) was no stranger to life in the limelight. As heir to the vast Folger coffee empire, she'd spent her teenage years on the debutante circuit around northern California. Following her graduation from Harvard in 1964, she threw herself into charity work around San Francisco. On her relocation to Los Angeles in 1968, Abigail concentrated her efforts on working with disadvantage people in troubled areas, such as Pacoima and Watts. Despite now being based in LA, she'd maintained contact with the Free Medical Clinic back in San Franciso, and hosted many fund-raisers for the centre – ironically raising funds to treat the likes of Charlie and the Family. Although she benefited from the wealth of her family, Abigail was modest about her affluence, a quality that endeared her to everyone who met her. She'd been an active campaigner for Robert Kennedy but, following his assassination, she'd grown disillusioned with politics.

During a visit to New York in 1968, Folger had met Voyteck Frykowski, an aspiring writer and actor who hailed from Poland. Although Frykowski's work wasn't well known, he had a likeable charm and an ability fit into any social situation. He'd been married twice, and had a son called Bartek with his first wife, Eva. One of Frykowski's peers was Roman Polanski. The pair shared a long history, growing up together in Poland, and Frykowski shadowed his more famous friend in the hope of basking in his reflected glory. In 1962, Voyteck came into some money, and helped finance a short film of Polanski's entitled *Ssaki*. After this, Voyteck concentrated on film-making. With Polanski in the ascendancy, Frykowski began to shine too, and at this point he came across Abigail Folger at a gathering in New York.

Despite their obvious cultural differences, the pair hit it off, and soon became an item. While the attraction to Folger was genuine enough, Frykowski had the added bonus of sharing the heiress's generous expense account, and he soon moved into her *pied-à-terre*. After some time in New York, the pair moved over to Los Angeles, where Folger was keen to continue her social work and Voyteck planned to direct his writing talents towards Hollywood. On arrival in LA, Frykowski renewed his friendship with Roman Polanski, and was introduced to Sharon Tate. Folger and Frykowski soon became a permanent fixture at the sparkling celebrity gatherings that the Polanskis held.

However, all that glittered was evidently not gold. Voyteck, and to a lesser extent Abigail, had one foot in Hollywood and one foot in the seedy world of drugs. While narcotic use was acceptable practice for the 'Beautiful People', there were many indications that Frykowski was expanding his interests into supply, perhaps prompted by his lack of success in the movie world. Of late, the only work he had been able to get had been some set construction for one of the studios down in Hollywood. Regardless of the list of contacts Polanski had provided, it was apparent that his foray into dealing was proving much more lucrative than his writing. Nonetheless, the pair were evidently a popular item around town, although somewhat known for their penchant for hard partying.

Another of the Cielo Drive regulars, Sharon's ex-boyfriend Jay Sebring, was also to play a tragic role that sweltering August Friday. The epitome of Hollywood cool, Sebring was the toast of the A-list and a stylish celebrity. Born Thomas John Kummer in Detroit, Michigan on 10 October 1933, Sebring fell into a career in hairdressing, a trade he'd picked up as a sideline during his time in Korea with the army. With his radical approach to cutting, Jay rapidly collected a glittering client list that included the likes of Kirk Douglas, Paul Newman and Steve McQueen. The Doors front man, Jim Morrison, had his tousled locks cut by Jay, as did Dennis and Brian Wilson of the Beach Boys. Warren Beatty was another celebrity who'd regularly frequent Jay's saloon – he'd later revive Sebring's charismatic presence for the 1975 film, *Shampoo*.

During the autumn of 1964, Jay had met Sharon Tate at the LA's renowned Whisky A Go Go club. Immediately captivated by the actress's awesome beauty, Sebring pursued her relentlessly around town. Sharon soon succumbed to his advances, and although their relationship gathered considerable pace, she continually refused Jay's demands for a formal engagement. Despite their evident fondness for each other, fate had something else in mind. During the filming of *The Fearless Vampire Killers* in London during 1966, Sharon began to fall for director Roman Polanski's charms. When their relationship began to develop off set, Sharon terminated her relationship with Sebring, and moved into Polanski's London apartment. Devastated by the news, Jay flew over to England to see what could be salvaged. He was too late: the new couple were obviously besotted with one another.

Nonetheless, Sebring managed to maintain a friendship with both Sharon and Roman, although it was obvious to everyone that he still held a torch for his ex.

Despite the rejection, Sebring poured his energies into establishing a chain of hairdressing saloons around LA, and a line of hairstyling products. Outside of his franchising interests, Jay's unique cutting talents were in heavy demand in the movie world. After styling Kirk Douglas for the film *Spartacus*, Jay soon found other work within Hollywood's studios. He even made it in front of the camera – once for an episode of the cult TV show *Batman*, and then again in *Mondo Hollywood*, a socio-cultural documentary profiling some of the extraordinary characters that lived in Los Angeles during 1967. Ironically, the film also featured another charismatic individual, the Family's Bobby Beausoleil. Adding to his multifaceted CV, Jay was also instrumental in promoting the career of martial arts exponent extraordinaire, Bruce Lee.

Being continually in the slipstream of the Polanskis, Sebring soon came across Folger and Frykowski. In time, he'd forge a loose business alliance with Abigail, and together they were looking to invest in business plans to expand his hairdressing interests. These legitimate deals hid a less savoury alliance that Sebring had with Frykowski. Together the pair began to indulge heavily their passion for chemical thrills. These adventures brought them into contact with a sleazy contingent of Los Angeles' drug lords and dealers. With Hollywood's insatiable appetite for exotic substances, there were rich pickings to be made, although procurement could come at a heavy price.

The month before, Frykowski, looking to consolidate a large patch of the drug scene, had made a deal with a well-known drugs baron to secure control of MDA, a prototype version of today's Ecstasy. Although cocaine was fast becoming the drug of choice for the Hollywood fast-lane set, MDA was a reliable stimulant that could level off the anxiety that came from heavy coke use. It soon gained the title, 'the love drug'. The dealer had returned from Canada with a large quantity of the drug, and begun negotiations with Frykowski to distribute it across Los Angeles.

During this first week of August 1969, events took a dark turn. On the end of a $2,000 cocaine burn, Frykowski and (allegedly) Sebring cornered one of their drug-dealing coterie at singer Mama Cass Elliot's house. There, in front of a crowd, the pair allegedly whipped and sodomised the dealer, reportedly capturing the action on videotape. This elaborate and vicious revenge became the stuff of urban legend. Actor Dennis Hopper, a man with his ear to the ground, recalled that he'd heard tell of a party of 'twenty-five people' who'd been witness to a video-beating-cum-buggery of a 'Sunset Strip' dealer.

During Roman and Sharon's absence, Abigail and Voyteck took advantage of having the run of 10050 Cielo Drive to host many parties, with narcotics an important part of the fun and games. When Jay Sebring tried hosting a party at the house, things again turned nasty when two drunken, uninvited guests gate-crashed the event, and became abusive when confronted. Although Frykowski and a few others evicted the pair, they threatened to return and 'kill' the Pole.

On another occasion, Voyteck had to sort out an incident at Abigail Folger's Laurel Canyon house. The spat involved Witold Kaczanowski, an artist friend of Frykowski and Polanski's, and Harrison 'Pic' Dawson, one of Mama Cass Elliot's loose entourage of hangers-on. During Folger and Frykowski's relocation to Cielo Drive, the couple had allowed Dawson to stay in their vacant property for a modest rent. When Dawson left temporarily in May 1969, Kaczanowski took up residence. At some point in the summer, Dawson returned and ended up sharing the house with the artist. Dawson was a notable, if somewhat dodgy, cog in the LA rock scene machine; his reputation earned from allegedly scoring narcotics for insatiable musicians. Reportedly, on this evening, Dawson had engaged in a heavy argument with Witold, the artist, and waved a gun at him. When Frykowski arrived, he threw Dawson out. In amongst the verbal sparring, Dawson had threatened to 'kill them all and Voyteck will be the first'. While scant attention was given to it at the time, events later that summer would mean the threat came back to haunt Dawson.

It appears Dawson had quite a reputation, having also been thrown out during a housewarming event that the Polanski's had staged at Cielo Drive earlier that year. That night, Dawson had arrived, uninvited, with three of his friends: Billy Doyle, Tom Harrigan and Ben Carruthers. A scuffle soon broke out between Doyle and Polanski's business manager, William Tennant. That night, the diminutive host succeeded in throwing them out, but the shouting and threats that accompanied the eviction served only to leave an atmosphere of heavy resentment.

Dawson, Doyle and Harrigan would feature in much of the speculation concerning the fate of Sharon and her house-guests on the night of 8 August 1969. Despite in-depth police investigations, nothing was ever substantiated concerning their involvement. What was ascertained, however, was that Frykowski's immersion into the drug world was considerable.

When the heavily pregnant Sharon returned from filming in Europe, she was disturbed at the new edgy vibe at the house. This was compounded by her friends' descent into heavy drug use, and at their tendency to bring all sorts of dubious people back to the house to party at all hours. Additionally, rumours had reached Sharon that Voyteck had been using the property to shoot pornographic photos around the pool. Although Sharon herself had experimented with marijuana and LSD, it worried her that Frykowski and Folger were using drugs continually. Sharon saw little threat in the genial and affable 'Gibby', but it was clear her partner was a toxic influence. Sharon was comforted to hear that Folger had started talking to her therapist on a daily basis, and was considering breaking up with Frykowski. Nonetheless, during her phone conversation with Roman that final morning, Sharon had strongly reiterated her desire for the couple to leave the house as soon as possible.

During the afternoon of 8 August, Jay Sebring paid a call on Sharon at Cielo Drive. Although he'd take any opportunity to see his former flame, Sebring had other reasons for dropping by. During the late afternoon, Voyteck and Jay were due to entertain a well-known narcotics dealer by the name of Joel Rostau. Later to be the target of a gangland execution, Rostau had reportedly brought with him a small amount of cocaine, and a consignment of MDA.

Meanwhile Abigail Folger was packing for a visit to her mother in San Francisco. She'd been into town to buy a bicycle, and had also found time to visit her counsellor, reiterating her need to start distancing herself from Frykowski.

By early evening, Sharon Tate had risen from her nap and joined Sebring, Folger and Frykowski in the living room. The friends were lounging around, playing music, drinking and chatting among themselves. Sharon had a prior arrangement to stay the night with Sheliah Wells, an old acting friend who'd invited her over to her house. However, she'd cancelled, favouring a relaxing evening close to home. Usually on a Friday night the house would be buzzing, yet on 8 August it was strangely quiet.

By early evening, Jay, Sharon, Abigail and Voyteck were in a mellow mood. At around 8 p.m., the group decided to travel down to the Mexican-themed El Coyote restaurant on Beverly Boulevard to eat. The party shared a few drinks around the bar, before being shown to their table. At 10.30 p.m., they repaired back to Cielo Drive. Abigail Folger made a late-night call to her mother in San Francisco to finalise plans for the trip there the following day, while Frykowski took up residence on the living-room couch. He'd dropped some of the MDA he'd scored earlier, and was watching the world go by in a blissed-out stupor. Abigail came down to the lounge in her white nightgown, joined Voyteck in a dose of the drug then tripped happily back to bed to read. Jay had followed Sharon back to her bedroom, and they were still chatting to each other as the clock nudged its way towards midnight.

The only other person on the property that night was nineteen-year-old William Eston Garretson. Born 24 August 1949, the native of Lancaster, Ohio had been employed by the property's landlord, Rudi Altobelli, to oversee caretaking duties while he himself was on a business trip to Europe. For this, Garretson was paid $35 a week, with the additional promise of the plane-fare home if he served out his term of employment. The residents had grown quite used to him being around, though Garretson still thought of Voyteck Frykowski as Roman Polanski's 'younger brother'. Garretson had also become all too familiar with the incessant partying within the house, and was aware of Frykowski's drug use. Despite the close proximity of his living quarters, the caretaker had only been inside the house on a couple of occasions.

With Altobelli abroad, Garretson had an easy lifestyle, rising late and performing the few tasks that required his attention. One of his main duties at Cielo Drive was to take care of the house's three dogs: two poodles and a Weimaraner belonging to the landlord. Garretson also had to care for Terry Melcher and Candice Bergen's cats. In their rush to leave the property that February, the couple had left behind a large menagerie of felines, twenty-six in total, which all needed tending to.

Friday 8 August started blearily for Garretson. He'd woken late and hung-over. The previous night he'd entertained one of the property's gardeners and his female friend. Garretson occasionally let them use the guest house for clandestine meetings, since the gardener was married. In an attempt at being sociable, the couple had brought some alcohol with them to share. At one point during the evening, Garretson's visitors headed off to the bedroom to make love. After they departed at 1 a.m., Garretson continued his own festivities: more alcohol, two marijuana joints, and a dexedrine tablet. Not surprisingly, Garretson was in no fit state to wake early the next day.

Late into the afternoon of 8 August, Garretson left the property in search of a takeaway meal and some cigarettes to sustain him though the evening. As most shops were a fair distance away, he relied on his thumb to catch a lift into downtown Beverly Hills. A lift soon appeared in the shape of a camper van, and Garretson gladly hoped aboard. Strangely, the young, hippie inhabitants of the vehicle were inquisitive about his movements that evening. Perturbed at their nosiness, Garretson revealed little, other than that he'd come from the property at the end of Cielo Drive. Eventually, the camper van pulled in close to Garretson's destination, and it was here that they shared an enigmatic exchange. William Garretson later recollected: 'I said you can let me out right here, because I'm going to be going straight (ahead). I believe it was the guy that was driving said, "If I were you, I wouldn't be going back up there ... where you came from." And that spooked me.'

Not aware of any reason not to return to the house, Garretson dismissed the warning and bade them farewell. He took a short stroll up Sunset Strip to collect his dinner, some cigarettes and Coke, before hitching back to Cielo Drive. Arriving back at the house, Garretson tethered Sharon Tate's two poodles in the 'dog room'. However, either for company or security, he took Christopher, Rudi Altobelli's silver-grey Weimaraner back to his chalet. Once inside his quarters, Garretson settled down for a quiet evening, listening to his stereo system and eating his take-out. At 10 p.m., he turned on the television, in the hope that a good movie might be on. A screening of *The Devils' Vampire* would start at 12.30 a.m.

At some point during the evening, Garretson took a call from Steven Parent, a guy he'd met hitching a few weeks before. Garretson often made friends with the drivers who picked him up at the roadside – in fact, he'd got this job after getting a lift with Rudi Altobelli. This hitching pal, Parent, was something of a loner. He'd spent time in a youth correctional facility following a series of minor thefts; there his probation report described him as having 'sadistic' and 'homosexual' tendencies. As a substitute for human interaction, Parent had immersed himself in the field of electronics. While preparing for university, he'd also taken on an evening job in a hi-fi store. Parent had picked Garretson up a fortnight previously, and the two had engaged in some friendly banter. Parent was evidently taken by Garretson's celebrity contacts, and he went out of his way to drop his passenger at the end of Cielo Drive. Garretson was grateful for the lift, and invited Parent to drop in next time he came that way.

That night Parent planned to head over to Cielo Drive once he'd finished his late shift at work, which on Fridays dragged on towards midnight. When he rang, he mentioned that he was at a loose end, and Garretson was only too happy to let Parent know how to negotiate the security gate once he arrived. The caretaker was a little short of distractions, and loved inviting people back to Altobelli's mansion.

Steven Parent approached Cielo Drive at around 11.45 p.m., and parked his white Ambassador car alongside the other vehicles in the drive. Wandering around the snaking path that led past the living room and twin bedrooms, Parent couldn't fail to notice the silhouettes of the house's occupants: in particular, those of Abigail Folger and Sharon Tate. Locating Garretson's chalet by the swimming pool, he knocked and was invited in. Parent had brought with him an electronic clock radio that he thought Garretson might be interested in buying. The caretaker listened politely as Parent offered a demonstration of the clock's abilities, but he wasn't interested. Instead they talked about the residents of the main house.

After drinking some cans of beer and listening to the new Doors album, Parent decided to leave. He'd asked Garretson to use his phone to call a friend of his, Jerry Friedman. He bragged to Friedman that he was 'excited and impressed' at being in the property of a famous movie star, and wanted to come over to his place to chat. Despite the late hour, Friedman agreed, expecting him around 12.30 a.m., so Parent said his farewells to Garretson and prepared to leave.

As he opened the door, Christopher, the Weimaraner dog, began to bark like crazy. A little scared by the animal's ferocity, Parent was reassured that it was just the dog's response to anyone coming on to the property. With that, Parent wished Garretson goodnight, and wandered back to his car. Garretson shut his chalet door and sat back down on his sofa, his thumping stereo masking the chilling noises outside.

It was approaching 12.30 a.m. when the yellow and black Ford containing Tex and the girls arrived at the front gate of 10050 Cielo Drive. Tex turned the vehicle around so that it faced down the hill. Getting out of the car, he retrieved the bolt cutters he'd loaded in earlier. Evidently knowing that telephone wires were accessible from outside the property, he began an eighteen-foot ascent up a telegraph pole to the right of the main gate. There were four lines that led from the head of the pole and, regardless of whether or not they might hold a power cable, Tex severed them all; the cables flopping down across the top of the gate. There were no sparks – Tex had obviously done his homework.

At that moment, William Garretson attempted to put a call through to his mother, and was surprised to find the line was dead.

Back in the car, Watson depressed the handbrake and let

the car silently drift down the hill towards the hairpin where the cul-de-sac joined the main bulk of Cielo Drive. Taking advantage of the foliage that surrounded the junction, the car was parked fairly inconspicuously. With the revolver retrieved from the glove compartment and the length of rope wound across Tex's shoulder, the party got out and ascended the hill on foot. As the quartet reached the property's entrance, their way was barred by the metal and mesh gate, with the cables that Tex had cut moments earlier hanging limply over the top. Mindful that the gate might be electrified, Watson ordered the party to make for the incline that ran up along the gate on the right.

Sadie was ordered to climb over first. She clasped the blade in her mouth and launched the bundle of clothes over the gate. Whilst her supple body easily made its way over the fence, her trousers snagged on the barbed wire. After some tugging, Sadie made it over. Next Tex raced up the steep embankment but, misreading the gradient, he reeled back on to the tarmac. The second time he fared better, and the rest of the tribe followed.

Aware that they were treading on private property, the quartet transformed themselves into the 'Creepy Crawlers'. Furtively surveying the property, they edged along the fence, and headed down the drive towards the house. They were momentarily startled as lights cut through the darkness, followed by the engine-roar of Steven Parent's white Rambler car, as it was leaving. Tex ordered the girls to back away out of the beam and to lie down in the bushes at the side of the drive. As the vehicle approached, Tex leapt forward with the revolver outstretched and cried, 'Halt!'

Parent slammed on the brakes, but kept the engine running. Given the arid temperatures, both the passenger and driver's windows were open. Tex bounded around the car and pointed the gun directly at Parent's head. Startled and confused, Parent tried to reverse his car out of Watson's gun-line, hit the white fence that bordered the property, and jolted to a halt. Tex was soon on him, and thrust the revolver through the driver's window.

Terrified, the boy cried out, loud enough for everyone to hear. 'Please don't hurt me, I won't say anything.' It mattered little to Tex. With Parent paralysed in fear, Tex took his revolver and pumped four gunshots into his body. One pierced his cheek, another slammed through his left arm, while two others tore through his chest. Within seconds, Parent was slumped over the wheel, his red and blue patterned shirt and denim jeans spattered with an unseemly collage of blood and bone fragments. But Tex wasn't finished with what he'd later refer to as the 'impersonal blob'. He lurched at Steven with his knife, mutilating his already wilting body. One of these blows slashed through Parent's wristwatch and flung it into the far reaches of the car. To Parent's side lay the clock that he'd try to interest Garretson in moments earlier, its time frozen at 12.15 a.m. Whilst Sadie and Katie were nonchalant about the shooting, Linda was distinctly spooked. The other girls had the benefit of over two years of Manson-induced detachment, but Linda was still a newcomer. 'It was like, not real,' was her initial thought. 'Y'know, did this really happen? It just didn't seem real, but it was real.'

Given the acoustics in Benedict Canyon, it would have been difficult to tell where Tex's gunshots were coming from. Evidently the residents of 10050 didn't hear the shots – or, if they did, had no idea how close they were. However, caretaker William Garretson heard something, but completely misread the noise. 'It seemed like firecrackers. And I thought maybe it was his [Parent's] car backfiring ... I had no idea. It didn't alarm me ... it just made me angry because I thought he was throwing firecrackers out and I thought, "If he comes back up here again, I'll give him hell" ... because I thought he was waking up the people next door or something.'

Neighbouring residents remember hearing gunshots and screams, although late on a sweltering Friday night in LA, perhaps the sounds didn't seem that out of the ordinary. In any case, no one reported them. Perhaps it wouldn't have made any difference if they had. Robert Bullington, of the private security firm Bel Air Patrol, heard three gunshots during his surveillance of the area that night. He reported the call to his headquarters, which in turn relayed the information to the LA police – who spectacularly failed to act upon it. The Manson soldiers had made their first kill, and none of the other residents of Cielo Drive were any the wiser.

Pushing Parent's limp body away from the wheel, Tex turned the ignition and lights off. With the women's help, he shunted the car towards the side of the drive. They then continued past the car, and walked around the two-storey garage area, following a winding stone path that snaked around to the porch. The entrance was locked, and Tex instructed Linda to do a quick reconnaissance for any doors or windows that might be open. Still in shock at the cold-blooded murder of young Steven Parent, Linda could only perform a half-hearted search of the property, and missed the two open windows to the newly decorated nursery. On being informed that every possible entry point was locked, Tex took his sharpened Buck knife, and began cutting the fly screen that covered the dining room to the right of the door. Once split, he was able to prise open one of the windows and gain entry.

Tex, now inside the house, carefully made his way through the hall and towards the front door, opening it and ushering the girls inside. Noticing Linda's apparent nervousness, Tex instructed her to go back to the gate and act as a lookout.

Tex, Katie and Sadie now made their way through the house and into the lounge. Dominated by an enormous stone fireplace, the room was criss-crossed by exposed loft beams. The light was minimal: a bulb from the hall offered some vague illumination, whilst a lamp on a side table only revealed some of the room's detail. Elsewhere, an incense candle burnt away.

The house stereo was still on, and at such a level that it would have easily masked any extraneous noise. The air was thick with a mixture of incense, tobacco and paint residue that had wafted in from the newly decorated nursery. The living room's decor was a mix of modern and vintage, bearing the hallmarks of Sharon and Roman's eclectic tastes in furnishing. Draped across the sofa was an American flag, left there a few weeks previously by Frykowski and Folger as a joke. Voyteck Frykowski lay dozing on the sofa. He'd dressed for the evening in striped, flared trousers and a black waistcoat. Tex ventured closer and nudged him with the revolver. Frykowski awoke and stretched his arms, disorientated.

'What time is it?' Frykowski asked, still not recognising the man in front of him. In addition to Tex, he would have also taken in Sadie and Katie, now standing in his line of vision.

Tex wandered around to face him straight on, and pointed the revolver at him. 'Be quiet. Don't move or you are dead.' To reiterate the point, Tex kicked Voyteck in the head.

Swiftly brought out of his reverie, Voyteck demanded to know who the Texan was and what he was doing there in the house.

Tex grinned and delivered an introduction that left little to the imagination. It would become one of the most iniquitous quotes in the annals of crime. Adding to the terror, it was delivered in a deep, rasping tone. 'I'm the devil, and I'm here to do the devil's business. Now, where is your money?'

Frykowski pointed over to the desk at the side of room, muttering that his wallet was somewhere in there. Watson then ordered Sadie over to the bureau. Rifling through the desk, Sadie failed to find a wallet. Watson scanned the hallway leading from the lounge. 'Go and see if there is anyone else in the house,' he barked to Sadie, who left without question. With Sadie engaged on her recce of the house, Katie became conscious of the fact that she was without a knife. Aware that a bloody scenario could well ensue, she ran back to Linda at the main gate to take hers. Like Tex had done before her, Katie told Linda to be alert for any sights and sounds that might spell danger.

Sadie wandered down the hallway. First she saw Abigail Folger, propped up reading a book in the bed she shared with Frykowski. Folger was enjoying the initial effects of the MDA she'd dropped earlier, and so Sadie's presence wasn't that much of a surprise. Indeed, given the house's late-night comings and goings, a hippie child floating down the hallway at midnight was nothing too out of the ordinary. Folger looked up, smiled and waved as Sadie passed by. Not wishing to provoke any undue suspicions, Sadie returned the smile and the gesture. Moving down the corridor, Sadie approached the next room where, through a slight gap in the door, she saw Sharon Tate lying in bed, a white negligee pulled over her bikini. Sitting attentively at her side was Jay Sebring. The couple was far too engaged in conversation to be disturbed by Sadie's stealthy reconnaissance. Quietly walking away, Sadie wandered back towards the living room, again passing Folger's bedroom. Once again, Abigail smiled.

With her exploration complete, Sadie went back to the lounge to inform Tex of her findings. She was then ordered to tie Frykowski's hands together with the end of the nylon rope Tex had brought. Sadie attempted to bind them in a cross-cross fashion, but it was obvious she was an amateur. Getting into his stride, Tex sent Sadie back down the hallway corridor to bring the three occupants, and all of their money, to the lounge. Sadie went first to Abigail's room. Raising her knife, she ordered Folger out, shouting, 'Get up and go into the living room and don't ask any questions.'

Walking backwards, Sadie took Abigail down the hall where she was greeted by Katie, knife outstretched. With Folger in custody, Sadie went back up the hall to retrieve Jay and Sharon. Blissfully unaware of the commotion, the couple were still engaged in their bedside chat when Sadie entered. Knife to the fore, Sadie ordered the startled pair down towards the lounge, hissing, 'Don't say a word or you're dead.'

Sadie led the couple out towards where Katie was standing guard over Abigail. The prisoners were then shepherded into the lounge where Tex was watching over Frykowski. Sharon gasped on seeing Voyteck bound on the sofa, and momentarily halted. Jay, too, was shocked, asking, 'What are you doing here?' Sensing a break in the choreography, Tex snapped at Jay to 'shut up'. Tex then leapt towards Sharon, pulling her roughly towards the centre of the room. As he did this, he flipped off the switch to the hallway light with his elbow, ensuring that the darkening scene would now be lit by the light of the solitary table lamp.

In the murky gloom, Tex ordered Jay, Sharon and Abigail to lie down in front of the fireplace. Sebring, incensed at Watson's handling of Tate, protested loudly. Tex firmly told Sebring what he'd told Voyteck earlier: that unless he kept quiet, they would all be killed; from the sofa Frykowski warned Jay that he meant it. Next Tex ordered Abigail and Sharon to lie face down on the floor. Out of her mind with horror, Sharon began crying hysterically.

The sight of the tearful, heavily pregnant Sharon vainly trying to kneel down was too much for Jay, and he leapt up, shouting at Watson. 'Can't you see she's pregnant?!' Tex was impassive, telling Sebring that 'one more word and you're dead'. Ignoring the warning, Jay stepped in front of Sharon to shield her. Unmoved by his brave attempt at protecting the pregnant woman, Tex pointed his revolver and shot Jay through the chest at point-blank range. Jay collapsed onto the Zebra-skin carpet, moaning as blood began to pour from him. To reinforce the act of savagery, Tex leapt over and booted him in the face.

With the women screaming, Tex calmly took the remainder of the rope from his shoulder. After throwing it over one of the loft beams, he wrapped a section around Sebring's hands. He then secured the coil tightly around the dying man's head. Tex then turned his attentions to Sharon Tate and Abigail Folger. Frozen with fear and horror, Tex wound the rope around their necks and hands and then pulled it tight.

With a noose round her neck, Sharon began again to scream. Folger, desperately trying to calm everyone down, quietly asked if there was something she could do to resolve matters without anyone else getting hurt.

'We want all the money you've got here,' Tex barked at her.

Folger mentioned that she had some money in her bedroom, and Tex untied her from the rope. Sadie then led Abigail back into her bedroom where she emptied the cash from her wallet. She also offered up her credit cards, but was told they were of little interest. When Sadie presented the $72 to Tex on their return, he screamed incredulously at Folger, 'You mean that's all you've got?'

'Well, how much do you want?' Frykowski asked from the sofa.

'We want thousands!' Tex shouted back.

Sharon stammered through her tears that, although there wasn't any more money in the house, she could get hold of some more if they were given more time. Tex just glared at her and sniggered, 'You know, I'm not kidding.' Given what had just happened to Jay, Sharon replied she knew that he wasn't. Tex then took the end of the nylon rope over to Abigail, where he retied her hands behind her back, looped the rope around her neck, before going over to the badly wounded Sebring, and adding a few extra loops around his head. Tex then pulled the rope tight, so that both Sharon and Abigail had to stand on their toes to avoid strangulation. Seemingly at this point, burglary was coming a poor second to butchery. The killers had chosen to ignore the expensive Cartier watch on Jay Sebring's arm; additionally, a wallet in his suit jacket contained $80 in cash. If they'd bothered to look elsewhere, they'd have found $18 on a night-stand, and other, small amounts of cash dotted around the house.

Aware of Sadie's poor rope job, Tex ordered her to find some other way of restraining Frykowski. Sadie returned with a white towel from Abigail's bedroom. Either through excitement or plain ineptitude, she made a poor job of it again. 'I was shaking so bad I couldn't tie his hands. But I got the towel around, even though I couldn't pull it tight.'

At this point Jay Sebring somehow managed to crawl across the floor, before Tex leapt at him, stabbing him, and kicking him in the head once again for good measure.

'What are you going to do with us?' Abigail managed to choke out, needing to know where this horrendous nightmare was heading.

'You're all going to die!' Tex answered.

Both Sharon and Abigail began to tearfully beg for their lives. While their emotional pleas fell on deaf ears, they diverted attention from Frykowski, who was beginning to loosen the towel around his wrist. With adrenaline quickly pumping any trace of MDA out of his system, Voyteck began jerking at the towel that bound his hands together. With his focus trained on the women, Tex ordered Sadie to go over and stab Frykowski. Sadie ran over to the sofa, knife outstretched. But Voyteck, now free, pulled her down onto the floor and grappled with her from behind. Flailing at him with her knife, Sadie managed stab him several times in the legs.

'Somehow, he got behind me,' she recalled, 'and I had the knife in my right hand and I was . . . I don't know where I was, but I was just swinging with the knife and I remember hitting something four, five times repeatedly behind me. I didn't see what it was I was stabbing.'

Such was the tension in his muscles that the blows of the knife glanced off Voytek's legs; one blow sent the knife flying from Sadie's hand where it buried itself deep into the cushions of the sofa. In full survival mode, Frykowski pulled Sadie's hair, while pushing her down towards the floor. At one point Frykowski ran towards the open door, with Sadie clawing at his feet. In the panic, Tex momentarily debated whether to try and shoot Frykowski, but with the pair so close together and in poor light, he figured he could easily miss and hit Sadie. As they lurched into the entrance hall, Tex finally made his move, and fired twice in

Frykowski's direction. Both shots hitting him, one in the back, the other in his left thigh.

Frykowski's continued to make his way down towards the open door. Tex aimed for a third time, but the gun failed him. Leaping over towards Voyteck, Tex begun beating Frykowski over the head with the butt of the revolver. The blows were so ferocious that Tex shattered the gun's wooden grip in the melee. Grabbing his knife, Tex began a fevered stabbing spree, splattering blood all over the walls of the room. Voyteck's willpower was so strong that he managed to make his way out in the direction of the garden. As the trio rolled outside the door, Voyteck began screaming, 'Help me! Oh God, help me!'

Still keeping sentry watch, Linda Kasabian heard Frykowski's pleas and made her way to the front of the house to see what was happening. What greeted her was a vision of total horror. 'There was a man just coming out of the door and he had blood all over his face and he was standing by a post, and we looked into each other's eyes for a minute, and I said, "Oh, God, I am so sorry. Please make it stop." And then he just fell to the ground into the bushes. And then Sadie came running out of the house, and I said, "Sadie, please make it stop" . . . And she said, "It is too late."'

In a vain attempt to curtail the nightmare, Linda shouted, 'There's someone coming!' But this bluff did little to ease the assault on Frykowski. With Tex now in control, he was set on finishing off his victim. Tex now weighed into him with knife-blow after knife-blow, while continually bludgeoning him over the head with the smashed butt of the gun.

Back inside the house, Abigail seized her chance to escape. Managing to free herself from the rope tether, she ran towards the hallway. Katie ran after her, and shouted to the others for help. Tex heard the commotion, and momentarily left Frykowski to run back inside the house. What he witnessed there was Folger pulling Katie's hair as she tried vainly to escape her clutches. On seeing this, Tex raised his knife. Folger cried out, 'I give up. Take me!' Tex then stabbed her in the stomach, the knife-blow knocking her to the floor.

Remarkably, Frykowski had managed to rise to his feet and begin a final break for freedom across the lawn. Such were his injuries, he could only move a few feet before falling to the ground. But even then he continued screaming, 'Help me! Oh God! Help Me!'

Tex heard Frykowski's screams from inside the house, and ran back out and easily caught up with him a few feet from the door. Tex then tore into his body with his knife, and when he was sure that Voyteck was finished, he got up from the ground and kicked him in the head.

Despite her adominal stab wound, Abigail Folger got up off the hall floor, and walked out through the back door of the house. Katie, her attentions now fixed on Sharon Tate, caught sight of Folger and set off after her. Although Folger had by now managed to get out into the garden, Katie, easily caught up with her, a few feet from the swimming pool. 'We went out through the back door, out onto the lawn, ' recalled Krenwinkel. 'And I ran her down and started stabbing her. I remember her saying, "Stop, I'm already dead."'

Inside the caretaker's house, William Garretson was still annoyed about Parent 'larking around with firecrackers', and now he could hear strange noises emanating from the garden. However, given the spirited gatherings that had occurred at the property during the summer, these sounds weren't entirely unusual. Intrigued, Garretson peeked around his curtain to see what was happening outside. 'I heard a scream,' he'd later recall, 'And it sounded as though someone was being ready to be thrown into the pool. I looked through the window and it seemed to me that here was a girl chasing a girl. I wondered, "What's going on?"'

Garretson's then heard Abigail's pleas for mercy, but couldn't make out their context:

'It didn't make sense. I mean, how can somebody be saying, "Stop, I'm already dead"? How would they be talking if they were already dead? It just [didn't] make sense?'

Meanwhile, Katie was flailing at Folger's body time and time again with her blade. Watson, who'd heard Folger's screams, went over to see what was happening. On seeing Katie stabbing Folger, he joined in.

The pair continued to stab Abigail until her body couldn't fight any more. Rising up from the grass after inflicting twenty-eight stab wounds on her, Tex and Katie looked down on the body, lying on her back, arms outstretched. Abigail's white night robe was so bloodstained that it was now almost completely red.

Tex's alert senses were now drawn towards the guest house. According to Garretson, the interior lights and sound system in his quarters were still on, clearly betraying his presence. Tex ordered Katie over to check it out and kill anyone she found inside. Dutifully, Katie walked up the stone path, past the kidney-shaped swimming pool, and towards Garretson's quarters. Luckily for the caretaker, fate intervened before Katie could carry out a full sweep of his quarters.

'It seemed like the handle was moved, like someone wanted to come in,' Garretson recalled. 'It seemed like a few seconds, and all of a sudden I heard someone running the direction of the main house.'

Despite having inflicted an horrific attack on Abigail Folger, Katie claims something inside held her back from entering the guest house. Her momentary qualms saved Garretson from joining the other mutilated corpses that were piling up that night in Cielo Drive.

'When I looked around,' Katie later admitted, 'I knew this [was] wrong. It was a like an echo from way back that said, "Wait a minute, this has finally gone into total madness."'

Back inside the lounge, an eerie silence prevailed. Hands held behind her back by Sadie, Sharon Tate was begging to sit down. Around her neck was the noose of the nylon rope that led over to her ex, Jay Sebring, now dead. Eventually, Sadie acquiesced to Sharon's requests to be seated and took her over to the sofa. It would be the sole act of mercy that Sharon Tate was shown that night.

Once on the sofa, Sharon begged for her life, sobbing, 'Please don't kill me! Please don't kill me! I don't want to die. I want to live. I want to have my baby!' Impervious to Tate's words, Sadie just looked at her straight on, and replied with a smirk, 'Look bitch. I don't care if you're going to have a baby. You had better be ready. You're going to die, and I don't feel anything about it.'

Sadie took great pride in her unemotional attitude to Sharon's desperate request to be spared. 'I didn't relate to Sharon Tate

245

to be anything but a store mannequin,' she'd recall later. 'She sounded like an IBM machine – words kept coming out of her mouth . . . Begging and pleading, begging and pleading. I got sick of listening to her.'

Following their massacres outside, Tex and Katie returned to the lounge. Having witnessed most of what had happened to her friends, Sharon knew exactly what was to come. Vainly, she pleaded with the trio to let her have her baby first. Tex just told her to shut up. In utter desperation, Sharon asked them to cut the baby from her womb before killing her. With the three Family members looking on impassively, she descended into a further bout of hysterical sobbing.

Watson, aware now that the clock was ticking, ordered Atkins to kill Tate. Despite Sadie's brutal words, something in her prevented her from striking the first blow. 'No Tex, I can't do it,' she reportedly replied. 'Katie? No, Tex you do it.'

Krenwinkel, taciturn for most of the evening, delivered a chilling overview of the situation: 'If you're going to kill her, then do it for God's sake. I mean, we've already killed everyone else here. What's the point? We either do it, or let her go, or just bring her with us and let her have her fucking baby.'

They didn't bother debating the options that Katie had coldly laid out. Instead, Tex embarked on a frenzied attack on Tate. Firstly, he sliced through her cheek with his blade, and then followed it with numerous cuts to her torso. Despite her earlier reticence, it appears that at some point Sadie, too, joined in with Tex's atrocities. The weight of these combined knife blows saw Sharon fall from the sofa to the floor. Lying motionless, Sharon could only murmur 'mother, mother' as the pair drove their knives into her body. When they had finished, Sharon had taken sixteen stab wounds, eight of which were considered to be of a fatal nature. If there was any doubt of her involvement, Sadie was soon boasting of her participation in the killing. 'It felt so good, the first time I stabbed her,' Sadie blabbed just weeks after the attack. She'd later claim that she'd even tasted Sharon's blood following the killing, and that the experience had been akin to an orgasm. 'To taste death and yet give life, wow, what a trip.'

With Sharon now unconscious and dying on the floor, Tex

revisited each body, checking for signs of life by violently kicking each of the victims, before dealing out some extra knife wounds for good measure. Satisfied, he then rounded the others up to leave.

Walking up the path towards the gate, Tex suddenly, it seems, remembered Charlie's instruction to leave a chilling message to the world. Ordering Sadie back into the house, Tex told her to leave something suitably creepy. Among the debris, Sadie saw the towel that had bound Frykowski's hands prior to his escape attempt. Taking it over to Sharon's body, she squatted down and dipped the towel in the blood that surrounded her. For a second, she claims, she was fascinated by the sounds emanating from Sharon's stomach, and if her initial testimony is to be believed, they brought forth a darker desire within her. 'I heard sounds,' she'd reveal later. 'Gurgling sounds, like blood flowing into the body out of the heart. I saw that she was pregnant. And I knew that there was a living being inside of that body, and I wanted to ... but I didn't have the courage to go ahead and take it.'

Noticing the pale front door, Sadie wandered over, towel sodden with Sharon's blood in her hand. Kneeling down, she daubed the words 'PIG' over the bottom panel of its white-varnished wood, echoing the message scrawled on the wall next to Gary Hinman's corpse. Job done, Sadie threw the bloody towel back into the lounge where it fell over Jay Sebring's face. She then hurried off to catch up with Tex and Katie, unwittingly leaving a bloody footprint on the path as she went.

Inside the lounge, Jay and Sharon lay a few feet away from each other, connected in death by a few feet of nylon rope. Sharon lay prostrate on the carpet, one arm across her belly and the other over her head. In the garden, Abigail lay on her back, a few inches away from a drainage grill. Voyteck's body was where he last fell alongside the stone porch, his left hand outstretched in a clenched fist, as if in a last gesture of defiance. The horror of this scene of utter desecration and carnage can only really be summed up in the cold facts of the statistics of the killing. Collectively, the victims had endured 102 stab wounds, six gunshots, many, many gun and fist blows to the head and body, and a final act of desecration that lay beyond anyone's comprehension.

chapter 9
Sick

'Restless as wind,
This town is killing me.
Gotta put an end to this
Restless misery.
And I'm just one of those restless people
That can never be satisfied with living.'

From 'Sick City' by Charles Manson

BY the time Katie, Sadie and Tex caught up with Linda she had retreated down the hill, and was sitting in the car with the engine running. Charged up by the slaughter, Tex had brazenly opened the front gate to the property using the electronic button; leaving a fingerprint trace on the switch. Suspecting that Linda had been preparing for her own escape, Tex was livid. 'What the fuck d'you think you're doing?' he screamed, getting into the vehicle and disabling the engine. Sadie and Katie entered through the rear doors, and assumed their positions squatting on the floor. Checking that the coast was clear, Tex began a slow descent down the hill with the lights turned off. Despite the magnitude of what had just occurred, Tex recalled Charlie's explicit instructions to carry their bloody attentions throughout the district. 'I suddenly remembered that Charlie had told us to go on to other houses until we had $600. But we were already heading out and I felt as though I didn't have the strength to do anything but drive back to the ranch.'

Tex got Linda to take over the wheel, while he peeled off his blood-sodden top in the passenger seat. Katie and Sadie did the same and all three put on some fresh clothes. Tex was angry to hear that Sadie had lost her knife at the house. Sadie moaned that

Frykowski had pulled her hair during their struggle, and then reportedly boasted of how she'd helped in the killing of Sharon Tate. The normally quiet Katie offered up that her hand hurt, due to the fact that her knife had kept on striking Folger's bones and glancing off. Linda sat with her head down, staring at the gun in her hands. At one point, she asked Tex why the handle was broken. He replied that the grip had shattered after he'd smashed it down on Frykowski's head. After that she didn't ask any more questions.

Although now in clean clothing, the killers still had plenty of blood and gore on their skin and in their hair. Driving into a residential area at Portola Drive, Pasadena, the group pulled up alongside a house where they spied a hosepipe. Imagining that the residents were either asleep or elsewhere, the gang wandered up the lawn, and turned on the water supply. Taking turns, they washed their hands, hair and faces, and took a few gulps of water.

Although it was now nearing 2 a.m., the owner of the property, Rudolf Weber, was a light sleeper. He heard the sound of running water coming from outside. Fearing a leaking water pipe, he had gone to check, closely followed by his wife, Myra. Once outside, Weber spotted the foursome busily cleaning themselves, and asked what they were doing on his property. Sensing possible trouble, Tex declared that they had been out walking, become thirsty, and had stopped for some refreshment. In accommodating tones, he added that they were truly sorry for the intrusion. As Tex further attempted to defuse the situation, the girls began to wander off in the direction of the car. Given the late hour, Weber wasn't convinced with their story, and he trailed the group down the path with his torch.

On spotting the tatty vehicle, Weber shouted out, asking whether the vehicle was theirs. Tex said it wasn't and reiterated their walking story. Instantly contradicting his words, the girls loaded themselves into the car, followed quickly by Tex. In the panic to get away, Tex flooded the car's engine, stalling the vehicle in the process. Weber ran over to the car and attempted to grab the keys out of the ignition, but Tex managed to hold off the man's clasp until the motor finally roared into action and pulled away, nearly tearing Weber's arm off in the process.

Undeterred, Weber made a note of the car's registration plate – GYY 435.

Now, suddenly in a panic, the quartet speed home through the deserted streets. Linda was told to take charge of all the soiled clothing, which she tied into a loose, bloody bundle. Tex also instructed everyone to hand their knives over to Linda so that they could be wiped clean of any blood and fingerprints. Tex's gun also received the same treatment. Approaching a sharp bend on Benedict Canyon that was bordered by a sheer drop, Tex ordered Linda to throw the incriminating clothes out of the window. Later, amid the winding roads and ravines of Mulholland, the knives were also jettisoned out of the car window one by one. Some distance further, the Buntline revolver met a similar fate. Presumably to distract any potential witnesses, Tex also threw a piece of white cloth out of the window in a bizarre attempt to divert attention away from the weapons.

Now on the home stretch, Tex stopped by a petrol station on Sunset Boulevard to load up with gas. Whilst Watson filed up, the girls took turns to visit the bathroom to carefully inspect themselves for any stray blood that might still be clinging to them. Inspection complete and car refuelled (paid for out of Abigail Folger's $72) the car and its occupants made their way back to Spahn Ranch and the inevitable audience with Charlie.

As the car pulled off Iverson Road and down towards the ranch, Manson could be seen cavorting naked with Brenda on one of the boardwalks. Surprised to see them back already, Charlie's first words were, 'What are you doing home so early?' Excited by her achievements, Sadie leapt out of the car, and threw her arms around him declaring, 'Oh Charlie, we did it . . . I took my life for you!' Manson pulled Tex aside and asked for a detailed report of what had occurred. Eager to confirm that they had done their duty as per instructions, Tex rattled out a vivid description of what had occurred. 'Boy it sure was Helter Skelter,' he blabbed, saying that it had all happened very fast and that, although there had been a lot of panic, it had all been 'perfect'. He'd later claim that it had been 'fun tearing up the Tate house', and watching 'people running around like chickens with their heads cut off'.

Manson was not impressed, either with the description of the killings, or the small amount of money they'd collected. Furthermore, he was displeased that the tribe had concentrated their attentions solely on one property, ignoring the other houses in the district. 'I told you to go to every house on that street,' he screamed at Tex. 'Now we'll have to go back!' Walking away, Manson went over to the girls, asking each of them in turn, 'Do you have any remorse for what you've done?' The girls, even Linda, who'd evidently been really shocked by events, reportedly said 'no', although both Katie and Linda were compelled to tell Charlie that the victims looked 'so young'. Unmoved, Manson was most concerned with whether they'd inadvertently left any physical evidence at the scene of the crime. As Sadie thought she'd seen a bloody imprint on the tribe's car, Manson got the girls to thoroughly wash the vehicle. Charlie then told them to go back to their quarters to sleep, and keep their evening's work strictly to themselves. Sadie, still in extended party mode, leapt into bed with one of the Family males, although such was her blurred, heightened state, she wasn't sure exactly who it was.

It appears that later that night Charlie made a snap decision to go back to Cielo Drive to see for himself what his agents had done in the name of Helter Skelter. Since he'd failed to enact Manson's orders to the letter, Tex might well have been press-ganged into accompanying him. It's also possible that another member of the Family made the trip back to the scene of carnage with Manson – the names Bruce Davis, Steve Grogan and Brenda have been bandied about over the years. What's certain is that Manson wanted to see the slaughter with his own eyes.

Author Ed Sanders, in his exhaustive tome, *The Family*, quotes from a conversation Charlie had with his legal team during his trial, where he admitted that he'd gone back to the house to 'see what my children had done'. If he had previously harboured any regrets at the brutality meted out on the innocents of Cielo Drive, this had evidently evaporated by the time he reached the house. 'I did not feel any pity or compassion for the victims,' he'd recall some years later. 'My only concern was whether it resembled the Hinman killing.'

However Manson's presence that night may well have betrayed a darker desire. Of late, Charlie's Helter Skelter ravings had become rich with bloody detail, and he'd become visibly animated talking about how hilarious it would be to have men, women and children gouged of their eyes and other body parts, and then have them smeared against the walls of their home. He'd later confirm that his trip back to Cielo Drive was to realise 'thoughts of creating a scene more in keeping with a black against white revolution'.

What has been determined by forensic evidence is that both Sharon Tate and Jay Sebring's bodies were transported from the lounge, and taken towards the front door; then, for whatever reasons, taken back again. In addition, a towel was now wrapped around Jay Sebring's head. In a likely attempt to divert suspicions elsewhere, someone had dropped a pair of glasses on the floor. Although it is possible that any number of innocent visitors to the house might have mislaid the spectacles, no owner was ever confirmed.

Adding further credence to this theory of a return, there was a conspicuous absence of fingerprints inside the house, indicating that a Family member might have engaged in a mopping-up operation. Given the indiscriminate fashion in which the killers went about their brutality, some semblance of an imprint among the debris would surely have been apparent. These returnees evidently did a thorough job in confusing the first forensic sweep of the house, although several prints were later discovered. A bloody heel print outside the front door that was clearly logged both on police reports and photographs was later claimed to be from one of the detectives attached to the investigation.

Fourteen-year-old Carlos Gill was up late writing letters in his bedroom at 9955 Beverly Grove Drive on the morning of 9 August. Despite the valley in between him and Cielo Drive, Gill's window offered him a clear view of the Polanski residence, while the acoustics in the canyon amplified even the quietest of sounds. At around 4 a.m., Gill heard something that 'so frightened him', he rushed towards his bed and hid under the covers. Under later investigation, Gill claimed that he had heard the sound of two or three people arguing across the valley in the vicinity of Cielo

Drive. By Gill's accounts, the tone of this argument increased in intensity before coming to an abrupt halt.

As the sun began to rise over Spahn Ranch on 9 August 1969, over at 10050 Cielo Drive, the first of a succession of people had begun to come by the house. The newspaper boy dropped off Polanski's *LA Times* at around 5 a.m.; then, as daylight broke, several of the neighbours emerged from their nearby houses. Some noted the severed cable over the gate, and the fact that the nightlight was still on, although neither warranted anything more than a glance at that point.

Housekeeper Winifred Chapman was the first scheduled visitor to arrive at the property. She had caught her usual bus to the end of Benedict Canyon and, being a little late for her 8 a.m. shift, she considered taking a cab to the door of the house. She was in luck, though, as someone who recognised her gave her a lift to the front gate. Although not unduly perturbed by the outside light being on, she was spooked by the severed communication cables strewn over the gate.

Once inside, Chapman walked down towards the house, picking up the morning newspaper from the mailbox as she went. With Steven Parent's car parked next to the other vehicles in the drive, she walked straight past it. As Chapman always entered via the rear of the house, she missed the carnage in the front garden. Entering via the kitchen, the housekeeper put her belongings down, and wandered through to the hall, where she tried to make a quick phone call, only to find there was no dial tone. With half a mind to report the fault, she headed towards the dining room. There she stopped in her tracks; a trail of sprayed blood led towards the open front door. Outside, she saw Frykowski's body lying prostrate on the lawn just beyond the porch.

Hysterical, Chapman ran out of the back of the house, screaming, 'Blood! Bodies! Murder!' Sprinting down Cielo Drive, she cried out desperately for help. She eventually found Jim Asin, a fifteen-year-old neighbour. Asin, a Boy Scout schooled in how to respond to emergencies, went back inside his house to call for immediate police assistance. Once connected to the emergency switchboard, the boy's message was duly noted as, 'Code 2, possible homicides, 10050 Cielo Drive', and was then directed over to West Los Angeles Police Station. As Chapman continued to cry uncontrollably on the stoop of the neighbour's house, the first of what was to become a constant stream of police cars drove up Cielo Drive.

At 9.15 a.m., police officer Jerry DeRosa arrived. He instantly ascertained from Chapman that something serious was afoot, and radioed for immediate backup. Chapman named some of the house's residents, but was too upset to be much help to the officer. With time of the essence, DeRosa cajoled a hysterical Chapman into taking him up to the house to point out where the body lay. As a precaution, DeRosa took a rifle from his car. Although initially reluctant, Chapman eventually relented and took the officer as far as the front gate, and showed him how to let himself through. Once inside, DeRosa cautiously surveyed the scene. He later recalled that it was 'very quiet . . . the only thing that I can recall hearing were the sounds of the flies that were on the bodies.'

A cursory glance inside the parked cars soon revealed Steven Parent's body. Radioing back for ambulance assistance, DeRosa was soon joined by police officers Robert Burbidge and Thomas Whisenhunt. Noting the bullet and stab wounds inflicted upon Parent, they began a thorough reconnaissance, revolvers primed in anticipation. It wasn't long before they caught sight of Frykowski's and Folger's battered bodies on the lawn. The officers then carried on towards the house. Avoiding the open front door in case the killers were still there, Burbidge and Whisenhunt entered the house through a window at the rear of the property while Officer DeRosa kept watch from the lawn. Within minutes, they happened upon the grisly spectacle of Tate and Sebring in the lounge.

Thomas Whisenhunt remembers: 'Obviously both of these people were dead. One was a female. She had blood all over her, and also had that kind of varnished mannequin look that was unrealistic when you looked at it, it did not look like a human.'

Moving away from the murder scene, they carefully checked out the remainder of the house for anything suspicious. With the killers evidently now departed from the house, the officers began a systematic search of the rest of the grounds and lodgings – including William Garretson's chalet.

The weird events of the night before had unnerved the caretaker. The few, disparate sounds he'd heard had been so unsettling that he'd found it impossible to get to sleep. When he tried to make a call and found the line was dead, he'd assumed the phone was faulty and brought out another telephone, only to find that one didn't work either. At some point, he let the dog out to do its business, and yet he himself didn't venture any further than the front door. Made apprehensive by his inability to interpret the night's events, he waited until daybreak before attempting to go to sleep. Even then, dozing off on the couch, he kept his trousers on in case he needed to escape quickly.

With the police scouring the area, Christopher, the dog Garretson had with him in the chalet for the night, began to bark. Still half asleep, Garretson shouted at the dog to quieten down. The dog continued to bark so, assuming someone must be on the property, Garretson looked out through his window. The police saw the caretaker through the glass door, and fearing that he was the assassin, burst through the door, guns primed.

A startled Garretson was wrestled to the ground and roughly handcuffed. The dog went for one of the officers and had to be restrained. Stunned at the ferocity of the entrance, Garretson pleaded, 'What's wrong? What's wrong?' unaware of the scope of the horror the police had witnessed moments earlier. Police told him, 'Shut up, we'll show you', and then handcuffed him and took him towards the main house.

Believing they had apprehended the culprit, the officers took Garretson on a tour of the victims' bodies. He could barely look at Folger's beaten body, and with the corpse now mostly unidentifiable, Garretson believed that one of them was Winifred, the Afro-American housekeeper. Shunted around, still handcuffed, he was then taken over to view Frykowski's body, which he identified as Roman Polanski's 'younger brother'. On their way out towards one of their squad cars, the officers took Garretson over to Steven Parent's body, slumped on the seat of his white rambler. Again, the stunned caretaker was too shocked to ascertain who it was. On leaving the property, Officer DeRosa, without thinking, pressed the electronic gate with his finger, wiping out Tex Watson's print in the process.

Outside of the house, Garretson was reunited with Winifred Chapman. It was with a mixture of relief and shock that he realised his mistake about the body he'd seen earlier, although this did little to control the housekeeper's own hysteria. With Chapman requiring sedation, the pair were driven to downtown Los Angeles – Chapman to the UCLA Medical Centre, and Garretson to West LA police headquarters to be booked on suspicion of murder.

With police believing they had apprehended the killer, the caravan that accompanies homicide was rolled out towards the Polanski residence. The trickle of personnel was now turning into a flood, the small cul-de-sac of Cielo Drive had become a congested circus of white and black municipal vehicles and flashing blue lights.

Given that local media monitored police radio logs religiously, it took only a little over an hour for news teams to begin congregating at the house. The media's presence on the ground was soon bolstered by a legion of helicopters, with cameramen broadcasting live images of the white sheets covering the bodies on the lawn. Soon, the reports of a possible series of murders began to be flashed up on radio and TV news. To counter the occasional leaks from the police teams now leaving the property, a spokesman was soon dispatched to confirm what had occurred inside the house.

'We have a weird homicide,' relayed a police press officer to reporters. 'Two bodies inside and two bodies outside.' Like greased lightning, the quote made its way over to the news desks and editing suites of Los Angeles. Under intense questioning, the media spokesman revealed little, although when pressed he let slip that the scene inside the house was 'like a battlefield'. Later, a policeman told waiting reporters that the murders appeared 'kind of ritualistic'. These words turned out to be the most telling descriptions of the day and, ended up causing immeasurable damage and delay to the ensuing trial.

While the residents of Cielo Drive kept a watchful eye on the mass of comings and goings, others further afield were also drawn to this hive of activity. Although police activity was a regular occurrence in Los Angeles, the swarm of helicopters flying back and forth over Benedict Canyon suggested that this was something more out of the ordinary. Mick Cox, a guitarist staying with Jimi Hendrix on Mulholland, recalls going out of the house with Jimi and other musicians that morning to see what was going on. Evidently, this was something big. 'We were literally up the road when it all came on. You could hear the noise of the police sirens from where we were. And we all went out into the garden to see all these helicopters darting over Benedict Canyon.'

With the identities of the dead still to be determined, the first of many concerned friends and associates began to arrive at the house. William Tennant, Roman Polanski's business manager, and a close friend of the couple, had been out playing tennis when his wife contacted him after hearing the news of a major incident at Cielo Drive. Still in tennis gear, Tennant was taken through press and police lines to identify the bodies. Like Garretson before him, he failed to identify Folger, so battered was her body and face. Taken inside the house, the butchered corpses so upset him that he ran outside and vomited. Through the shock, he was able to ascertain that the bodies were that of Sharon Tate and Jay Sebring.

While the police officers began to assemble the basic data, forensics scientists arrived. Among a mass of duties to be undertaken, a police photographer took numerous shots of the dead corpses from every conceivable angle. While the absence of any fingerprints initially flummoxed the investigators, the spectacles that had probably been dropped by Manson and Co. earlier were easily found. Additionally, they would have had little difficulty in retrieving the broken gun handle that had splintered off Frykowski's head, had one of the detectives not inadvertently kicked it away from the crime scene.

When autopsy staff arrived, led by noted coroner Dr Thomas Noguchi, they too were devastated at the condition of the bodies. Wholly seasoned to the sight of death, Noguchi (who'd ministered to the bodies of Marilyn Monroe and Robert Kennedy) was outspoken about what he'd witnessed. 'In all my experience,' he'd later recall on seeing Frykowski's bludgeoned body, 'I had never seen such savagery applied to one person.'

With police now forming a barrier against the mass of reporters lined up against the gates, the task of transporting the bodies from the house to the morgue began. It made for a sorry procession, as body-bags and gurneys exited, wheeled by soberly dressed mortuary staff. The feeble mesh at the gate easily allowed the press's lenses to capture this morbid spectacle. Celebrity watchers were then able to put names to the victims. Soon, communication wires across the world were buzzing with the news of the slaughter. Although Folger, Sebring, Frykowski and Tate had by now been identified, Steven Parent's origin remained a mystery.

When the bodies arrived at the city morgue, they were photographed on mortuary slabs, each victim given a serial number. After taking the perfunctory details, the laborious task of ascertaining the exact cause of death begun. Although it would be the source of many gruesome tales for years to come, the child Sharon was carrying was not stabbed during the frenzy, nor was any attempt made to excise it from her womb. However, Coroner Noguchi noted that the child probably lived for fifteen to twenty minutes following Sharon's death. To all intents and purposes, the Polanski baby was the Family's sixth and final victim of the night.

Given the celebrities involved, it was a priority for police to act quickly to prevent the media from broadcasting details before the victims' families had been informed. In some cases they were too late. Sharon Tate's mother, Doris, got a call from a friend who told her that a murder on Cielo Drive was being reported on the news. Doris called Sharon's number but, like other concerned parties that day, could not get through. Worried, she called Polanski's manager William Tennant, but he was already on his way to the house. After what seemed like an eternity, Doris Tate received the news she'd feared most from daughter Debra's boyfriend, Wayne. Reeling, she stumbled into her children's den where they were watching cartoons on TV. Distraught, she cried out, 'My daughter's dead', before collapsing. Sharon's father, Paul Tate, made his way over to the house at some point during the day, and witnessed the sickening results of the massacre first hand.

Roman Polanski was working in London and received the call from William Tennant in the early evening. Polanski recalled hearing the news and going into an immediate spasm of despair. 'I began walking around in small circles, my hands clenched tightly behind my back,' he later recalled. 'I kept moaning, "no, no" and punching the walls, then banging my head against them.'

With a coterie of close friends and business associates watching over him, plans for Polanski to return home immediately were rushed through. The US Embassy provided an emergency visa, and Roman boarded the first available plane back to LA, accompanied by his business manager, Gene Gutowski, and London Playboy club owner, Victor Lownes.

While relatives of Sebring, Frykowski and Folger were told the news by police, the media beat them to Steven Parent's family. Evidently doing their own detective work, reporters determined his home address from a TV newsflash that captured the boy's number plate. Later, two journalists managed to talk their way into Parent's family home. Callously posing as police, they snapped pictures of Parent from the mantelpiece, and then left without a word. Startled by the intrusion, and equally at a loss to understand why their son had not returned home the previous night, the Parents made a few tentative enquires. Later, a policeman arrived with the telephone number of the Los Angeles morgue and no explanation. It was only in the early evening, while watching the television news, that they saw Parent's car, and his body being transferred into an ambulance.

By nightfall, news of the murders had spread across the world. The gory and often erroneous details that had leaked their way out of the murder scene grew with frightening rapidity. The policeman's stray remark that 'it seemed kind of ritualistic' was instantly seized on by reporters eager to secure the most shocking story. As if five dead bodies in Hollywood weren't a strong enough headline, the added angle of a ritualistic blood bath was far too tempting for editors to ignore. The Los Angeles Times late edition of 9 August led the charge, declaring 'RITUALISTIC SLAYING, SHARON TATE, FOUR OTHERS MURDERED'. This headline was instantly disseminated around the world's news-desks. In England, the notoriously downmarket tabloid, the News of the

World, ran the story as their front page the next day, with the headline, 'FILM STAR DIES IN RITUAL MASSACRE'.

News of the Cielo Drive slayings enveloped Los Angeles. Respected writer and social commentator, Joan Didion, tasted the paranoia in the air. 'I recall a time when the dogs barked every night and the moon was always full. On 9 August 1969, I was sitting in the shallow end of my sister-in-law's swimming pool in Beverly Hills when she received a telephone call from a friend who had just heard about the murders at Sharon Tate Polanski's house on Cielo Drive ... I remember all of the day's misinformation very clearly, and I also remember this, and I wish I did not: I remember that no one was surprised.' Didion would later liken the killings to the slamming shut of the sarcophagus lid of the 1960s. 'Many people I know in Los Angeles believe that the Sixties ended abruptly on 9 August 1969, ended at the exact moment when word of the murders on Cielo Drive travelled like brushfire through the community, and in a sense this is true. The tension broke that day. The paranoia was fulfilled.'

Over at the Spahn Ranch, Saturday 9 August was pretty much business as usual, with a contingent of children and holidaymakers saddling up to ride around the hills. Sadie was up early, buzzing around the ranch. She was reportedly delighted to hear reports of the killings on the radio. When Charlie rose at midday, Sadie was keen to inform him that their activities had made the prime spot on the news. According to Manson, even Linda wanted to register her delight at this fact, despite her apparent reservations about the bloodshed. As Charlie listened in on reports, he claims he was surprised by the celebrity of the victims, and as a result even more irate that they had come away with such a paltry amount of cash.

Television wasn't much of an attraction at Spahn's, mainly because Charlie didn't approve of it. However, ideology was put aside as the murder squad descended on the solitary TV set at Spahns, situated in a stuntman's trailer to catch the early evening news. Charlie brought along his young protégé Clem, who was curious to catch the report. 'As I watched the TV reporters,' Sadie recalled later, 'I even laughed as they described the details of horror.' Assassin-in-chief Tex Watson was also in attendance, chuckling proudly as the it all unfolded.

Teenager Barbara Hoyt was also present in the trailer, and realised by their reaction that some of the Family were way involved in the carnage. As they left the trailer, biker Danny DeCarlo wandered over to ask Clem what the deal was. He replied. 'We got five piggies last night.'

In custody for the botched credit card fraud that might well have kick-started events, Mary Brunner and Sandy Good caught sight of a newspaper on 9 August. With the details of the murders leaping off the front page, they were in no doubt as to who had committed the crime. In the 1971 film, *Manson*, Sandy Good recalled that:'Mary [Brunner] and I were in jail the night of the murders, and we picked up the paper and Mary said, "Right on", and I said, "Wow, they finally did it."'

As evening fell, at Spahn's, it became clear that Charlie was readying himself in preparation for another mission. Sadie, with her new found relish for bloodshed, was again called up for duty. Katie too was commandeered, and with news of the previous night's activities fresh in everyone's mind, there were other takers eager to join the mission. Charlie didn't object to Clem going, and the teenager was keen to prove himself. Charlie's young protégé had been going badly off the rails in the past few weeks. In June 1969, he'd been arrested for exposing himself to schoolchildren. He was ordered to serve a ninety-day observational period at Camarillo State Mental Hospital, but had escaped and returned to Spahn Ranch after serving just two days of his referral.

There were others, too, who wanted to be part of it, but the transport limitations meant that only those chosen by Manson could ride along. Leslie Van Houten was keen to earn her stripes. Now mostly known as 'Lulu', the pretty nineteen-year-old was eager to display her full allegiance to Helter Skelter. This night she got her opportunity: 'He [Manson] asked me, "Do you believe enough in what I say to know that it is something that has to be done?" or something to that effect. And I said, "Yes, I do." I didn't walk right up and say, "May I go?" But I think everything on my face said that.'

Charlie told them all that he was disappointed with the sloppiness of the previous night's work, and that this time he was going with them to show them how it should be done. Furthermore, he told them he was keen to extend the action to more than one property – with two separate murder parties. To further sell the mission, he revived the girls' ploy that a further blood and guts rampage would work wonders in aiding Bobby Beausoleil's release. For extra effect, he threw in a sizeable dose of Helter Skelter, with a direct order to 'make it appear as though a full-scale war was being waged against the whites'.

Any amphetamine comedown that Tex was labouring under was blown away by a couple more snorts from his secret jar of coke and crystal meth. As with the previous night, Sadie was there to share with Tex. Fully charged, the Texan was happy to rap with Manson about the poor quality of the knives they had used at Cielo Drive, and how they needed to be better equipped for any further bloody tasks. With the Buntline revolver discarded the night before, Charlie handed Tex a compact .45 revolver. For his own use, Charlie availed himself of the chrome-plated bayonet he'd previously used in slicing Gary Hinman's face.

Following the routine of the night before, Manson ordered his select band to seek out a change of clothes, and to assemble by the boardwalk of the ranch. Johnny Swartz's yellow and black vechicle was again to be used.

In the rear sat Katie, Sadie and Clem. Katie, the thoughtful Sunday school teacher turned mass murderer, was hopelessly lost in a macabre dream. She was enchanted by life, and had held a deep regard for nature and living creatures, and yet she'd committed an indescribably brutal crime. Now she was out to do the same thing again. 'Charlie definitely had me go the second night,' she said. 'At that point I felt so dead inside it really didn't matter.'

Linda Kasabian was also recalled for the evening's work. Either through some semblance of blind loyalty, or more likely through sheer terror, she'd said yes to Charlie's demand that she should attend. Although it was evident that she had been the most affected by the horror of the previous night, her status as solitary licence holder overrode any emotional vulnerability she might have displayed.

Although Sadie, Katie and Linda have variously claimed they were unaware what lay ahead, various witnesses recall Sadie laughing and joking as they made their way to the car. Juan Flynn, a Panamanian ranch hand who'd become friendly with the Family, clearly remembers Sadie screaming, 'We're gonna get some fucking piggies' as the yellow and black Ford began its journey from the ranch.

Although Manson had been specific about the target for the previous night's atrocity, he appeared to be on an entirely random tour that night. As they careered aimlessly around LA, Manson quizzed Sadie and Katie about what occurred at Cielo Drive, and whether they'd left any other incriminating evidence that might catch up with them. Linda Kasabian was still heavily spooked by the turn of events. Noticing this, Manson directed a large amount of his agitation towards her during the ride.

After a while spent weaving in and out of various neighbourhoods, Manson directed the car towards a residential area of Pasadena. As they pulled in, Charlie had spotted a couple walking up the driveway to their relatively affluent abode, and he thought they were perfect candidates for the first targets of the evening. Getting out of the car with Tex, Manson ordered Linda to drive around the block and return in a few minutes. By all accounts, Charlie and Tex trailed the couple unseen up to the door of their house. However, on looking through the windows, they turned and walked back to wait for the car to return.

Linda Kasabian recalled that, 'Charlie told us that when he had walked up to the house and looked into the window that he saw pictures of children on the wall. He said he couldn't do it, he couldn't go in, but later on said that we shouldn't let children stop us for the sake of the children of the future.'

With this family spared, the car drove out of Pasadena and headed off to a more affluent area. Once there, Charlie pointed out a large mansion atop a hill that he thought would be perfect to target. On closer inspection, though, he went cold on the idea, as he felt that the neighbouring houses might hear the screams. With two aborted missions, Charlie then decided it would be a cool idea to garrotte a vicar. As the car passed a random church, Charlie leapt out and set off, bayonet in hand, to hunt down any stray clergy. Thankfully for the inhabitant, Charlie returned, claiming that no one had answered the door. Whether this was true, or just an element of Manson's careful stage-management, they drove off again.

Some moments later, while driving through Sunset Boulevard, they pulled up alongside a swanky white sports car. Taking an instant dislike to the driver of the vehicle, Manson ordered Linda to shadow the car to the next set of traffic lights. As they pulled up to the junction, Charlie informed everyone that he was going to kill the driver. As if on cue, as Charlie left the car, the traffic light turned to green and the driver shot away.

With four failed attempts behind him, Charlie was eager to realise some genuine action, whether with him at the helm or not. Although Manson's brief, as per Helter Skelter, was to hit random locations and individuals, he now appeared to know the direction they were taking. Directing Linda towards the residential hinterlands of Los Angeles, the car slowed as they entered the Los Feliz district. At just after 1 a.m., the Ford drew to a halt at the base of a Spanish-themed house at 3301 Waverly Drive.

Although it was virgin territory for some, even in the dark, the house opposite 3301 Waverly was familiar to Linda Kasabian. Over a year before her Family induction, Linda and her husband Robert had fallen in with a group of hippies who had taken them to the house for a party. The property had gained quite a reputation for all manner of chemical and sexual shenanigans, and they'd partied hard into the night. During one of these gatherings, Linda had made the acquaintance of one of the residents, Harold True. What Linda didn't know was that Charlie, Sadie and some of the Family had also visited the house on numerous occasions. For Tex, the area was doubly familiar, as he'd previously rented an apartment a stone's throw away from the house. According to True, Charlie even tried to move his gang into the house at some point, using the girls as bait. However, True stood his ground, and the Family had to look elsewhere for somewhere to live.

Although Harold True is usually referred to as the property's sole tenant, the house was actually rented by a number of students, who enjoyed a hedonistic lifestyle for the duration of their tenancy. Their presence enraged the residents of this otherwise sleepy district, and complaints were numerous, not least from next-door neighbour Leno LaBianca, who'd been to the house many times to object to the noise from their all-hours parties.

Allegedly, LaBianca blew his fuse several times, and – if one believes the reports – he once ended up taking out his frustrations on Charlie. In a note written to a friend in 1968, Leno articulated his despair at these noisy intruders, and also at nearby Griffith Park becoming a popular hippie hang-out.

'LA is getting to be a pretty scary place,' Leno wrote. 'There are a group of hippies that have taken over Griffith Park, and two pot parties have been broken up by the police just next door. That's a little too close for comfort.'

One frequent visitor to the house was Charlie's old prison cohort, Phil Kaufman. One of Harold True's close friends, Kaufman had reacquainted himself with Charlie on his release from jail in March 1968. Predictably, the thorny subject of Manson's faltering musical career was never far away, and Kaufman later claimed that Charlie had him in his sights since the breakdown of his recording dreams. However, if Charlie was intending to settle scores, he was way off target. Harold True, Kaufman and their associates had moved out of the property during September of 1968, nearly a year before Manson decided to return on the night of 9 August.

Sadie awoke with a start as the car pulled up and stopped. She recognised the Harold True house immediately, but decided to keep quiet. Linda was more vocal, asking in a worried tone if they were going to enter the familiar house at 3267. 'No,' she recalled Charlie saying assertively, 'I'm going next door.'

Next door was a white, Mediterranean-style bungalow that was set back some fifty metres from the road on a fairly steep gradient. It had once belonged to cartoonist Walt Disney, and was named Oak Terrace.

Despite what he'd told Linda, Manson walked straight up the drive to the True residence. However, on finding the house empty, he decided to return his attentions to the neighbouring property, where asleep on the couch in his pyjamas lay Leno LaBianca, a wealthy, middle-aged supermarket director. On a coffee table nearby were the weekend sports pages of the *Los Angeles Times*. Leno had taken a few swigs of beer, and conked out due to the late hour and the long day that had preceded it. In an adjacent bedroom, Leno's wife, Rosemary, was getting ready for bed. With eight years of marriage behind them, Rosemary and Leno had found considerable happiness after failed marriages on both sides. Leno had been a director in his family's Gateway supermarket chain, but was now in the process of stepping back to indulge his passion for racehorse breeding, collecting rare coins and the occasional spot of yachting. He was a familiar presence at local race meetings, maintaining an almost daily attendance at the tracks.

Leno had taken something of a hit in recent months. According to reports that have recently surfaced, LaBianca had a chronic gambling habit, which police pitched at over $500 a day. Independent reports also suggest that Leno had been borrowing heavily from his supermarket resources, much to the chagrin of his family and colleagues. Since 1964, he'd misappropriated over $200,000 from the company coffers. In mid-1969, he'd been asked to resign from the board of directors by his mother and other shareholders. Adding to the litany of debt, their house was heavily mortgaged, and Leno was also $30,000 in debt to various lenders. The most considerable security the couple could draw on was their Waverly Drive property. Oak Terrace had been in the ownership of the LaBianca family since the 1940s and, in 1968, Leno had purchased it from his mother.

Despite her husband's shaky fortunes, Rosemary had been a businesswoman of considerable success over the years. She'd opened a couple of fashion boutiques around Los Angeles, and was now making major investments in the share market. However, as police noted in a later report, despite Rosemary's successes, she was known around town 'as an alcoholic and heavy gambler'. To add to these issues, relations with Rosemary's daughter Suzan had recently taken a knock. Her fiancé, Joe Dorgan, was a biker who allegedly hung out with many shady LA characters, including (reportedly) Charles Manson and members of the Family.

It had been a typical Saturday for Rosemary and Leno. They'd been out for most of the day around Lake Isabella, Kern County, a popular and picturesque boating spot for weekend mariners like the LaBiancas. Evidently trying to patch up relations, they'd taken Rosemary's daughter Suzan along with them for the trip. In addition to a spot of sailing, they planned to pick up Rosemary's fifteen-year-old son Frank, who'd been holidaying with friends at the resort. He was due to come home with his parents that night, but was enjoying himself so much that the couple decided to let him stay on for another night. At around 9 p.m., Rosemary, Leno and Suzan had begun the 150-mile trip home; their boat trailing on the back of their green Thunderbird car. They'd dropped Suzan at her nearby flat and then pulled in at a newsstand to pick up an early Sunday edition of the *Los Angeles Times*. This had become something of a ritual for the couple, since Leno was always keen to see the racing results. This day, however, the couple couldn't fail to miss the news of the Tate massacre that was dominating the front pages. Rosemary was deeply moved by reports of the slaying, and began crying in the car on the way home.

Like most of residential Los Angeles, the couple were shocked by the events that had unfolded at Cielo Drive the night before. The LaBiancas, however, had additional reason to be apprehensive. Some inexplicable events had occurred in their house over the past few months, which had unsettled them. On one occasion the dogs, which were normally left inside the house overnight, had been let out. On another night, items of furniture had been moved around, while others were now missing. All of this was redolent of someone trying to spook them, but the couple were at a loss to know why it had been happening and who was doing it.

Charlie returned to the car from his recce and pulled Tex out. Using their best Creepy-Crawl techniques, they slipped their way back up the drive to the True house, and then made their way to the LaBianca bungalow over a small wall that divided the two properties. The duo entered Oak Terrace via an open door at the rear of the house; Charlie calming the couple's two dogs who had come over to greet them. The pair then crept into the L-shaped lounge. Quietly, Charlie approached the couch and nudged Leno out of his sleep.

Leno woke up, looked at Manson and offered a bemused, 'Hi.' Smiling, Charlie returned the greeting. Seeing Leno was spread-eagled on the sofa in his blue pyjamas, Manson chuckled, 'You look like Sophie Loren out there.' Pleasantries out of the way, Leno turned serious: 'Who are you? What do you want?' Charlie calmly stated that they were there to collect any money that happened to be around. Charlie reassured Leno, 'I'm not here to hurt you, just be calm. Just sit down and be still.' With that Charlie took a leather thong that was looped around his neck, and got Tex to tie Leno's hands behind his back. Leno secured, Charlie checked out the other rooms in the house. It wasn't long before Charlie discovered Mrs LaBianca as she was preparing to bed down for the night.

Coolly, Charlie asked her to come into the lounge to join her husband. Maintaining a collected exterior, he ensured that Rosemary had plenty of time to don some more clothing to cover her nightdress. He then led her to the lounge, sat her down alongside her shackled husband and tied her hands together. The LaBiancas were obviously frightened, but Charlie's easy confidence demanded obedience.

With his prisoners shackled, Charlie asked Leno where he could find their money, and sent Tex on a mission to recover it. With Tex on reconnaissance duties, Charlie reportedly asked Leno about the location of a 'black book' that he allegedly had in his possession. Manson's revelation to chat-show host Geraldo Rivera, in 1989, that he'd asked for such a book, has raised suspicions that LaBianca had serious connections with organised crime. Evidently, no book was handed over to Charlie that night, although an address book was found a few days later. Tracing through the labyrinth of contacts, police later discovered that LaBianca might have had dealings with the underworld while a director of the Hollywood National Bank. The organisation was said to have been bankrolled by 'hoodlum' money, which had led to some of its personnel being convicted for nefarious dealings. Despite police investigations that stretched over many departments, nothing was ever found to link Leno to any criminal deals.

Tex returned with Rosemary's wallet, a purse and various other sums of cash that lay around the house. It hardly made for a considerable sum, although Leno offered that he had more in the safe at one of his supermarkets. Charlie told him he wasn't interested in travelling elsewhere to collect more money. In other parts of the house were many items of value, not least a one-carat diamond ring belonging to Leno, and several items of expensive jewellery. Despite Charlie's claims about it being a straightforward robbery, the Family left this valuable booty untouched.

Leaving Rosemary and Leno shackled on the sofa, Charlie and Tex then quietly left the house, and headed down the drive towards the car.

During Charlie and Tex's absence, the tribe inside the car sat motionless, smoking cigarettes and saying little. In Sadie's fractured state, blurred by acid, speed and exhaustion, she claims she visualised Charlie tying the LaBiancas up. Breaking the quiet reverie, Charlie and Tex opened the car door. Manson did one last scan of his associates before deciding who would be commissioned into duty. Although Leslie was a newcomer, she was keen to earn her stripes. Katie was consistent, loyal and proven, and was unlikely to screw up. Sadie's wired behaviour led Charlie to believe she was a possible liability, and he passed on picking her. Linda did everything other than look at Charlie, and so she was out, although he would press her to bloody her hands later. Clem was also perhaps too wayward for a task Charlie that wanted to be deliberately ruthless and cold-blooded.

His selection made, Charlie ordered Leslie and Katie out of the car and lined them up alongside Tex. He then explained how he wanted the bloody deeds to be enacted. By his own admission, he told the killers to, 'Be nice to them. Don't cause them to panic. The last time you blew it, you panicked the people. Don't panic the people this time. Let them think it's going to be OK, so they'll go in peace.' Others have since claimed that Charlie's instructions became far more explicit, claiming he demanded they 'paint a picture more gruesome than anyone had ever seen . . . Make sure it's done so the pigs will put it together with Hinman and that pad last night.'

Charlie then had one last instruction for Tex. 'Make sure the girls get to do some of it,' Manson demanded. 'Both of them.'

Orders given, Charlie watched Tex, Linda and Katie make their way towards the house. As they dissolved into the darkness, Charlie drove away in the Ford with Sadie, Linda and Clem, ostensibly to perform more horror at some other location.

Tex, Katie and Leslie inched up the driveway. As Waverly Drive was a more densely populated area, Charlie had taken back possession of the solitary gun, lest trigger-happy Tex decided to let a few bullets off and wake up the neighbourhood. All three had knives, but it appears that, despite Charlie's instructions, a decision was taken for the girls not to use them.

The trio negotiated the slight incline to the house, feeling their way past the LaBiancas' car, trailer and boat, and went into the house through the now unlocked front door. On entering the house, they found Leno and Rosemary tied up on the sofa. Following Charlie's orders, they were polite to the couple, although this did little to reassure them, especially now that all their money had been taken. Tex then ordered that Rosemary be taken back to her room. The women, with Tex taking up the rear, dragged the terrified woman to the bedroom. Once there, they stripped the pillowcases from the couple's bed, and placed one of them over Rosemary's head. Tex wrapped the cord from the bedside-table lamp over the pillowcase. With Rosemary secured, the trio went back into the lounge and did the same to Leno. Like his wife, the pillowcase around Leno's head was also secured with the cord from a table lamp. Bound and blinded, the couple could do nothing but await their fate.

Katie, Tex and Leslie then went into the kitchen and began riffling through the drawers looking for implements with which to kill. Hearing this, Leno LaBianca guessed what they were planning, and began shouting, 'You're going to kill us, aren't you!' To silence him, Tex went over and threw Leno back on to the sofa, telling him to keep quiet. Despite Leno obeying him instantly, Tex started to stab him over and over with the bayonet.

In the bedroom, Rosemary heard her husband's cries for mercy, went into a blind panic and started screaming. Hearing this, Tex ordered the women back into the bedroom, while he continued to stab Leno. What Leslie and Katie witnessed was a truly pathetic sight. In absolute fear, Rosemary LaBianca had begun thrashing around the room, lamp and electric coil jerking in the slipstream of her terror. Katie struck the terrified woman's head, but with Rosemary flailing in all directions she missed, striking her on the collarbone, where the blade glanced off. The women were unable to contain Rosemary, and they called out to Tex for help. Hearing the commotion, Tex momentarily left off stabbing his dying victim, and ran into the bedroom. Seeing Rosemary engaged in a vain attempt to preserve her own life, Tex went over and stabbed her with his bayonet. The wound sent Rosemary to the ground. Once floored, Tex and Katie applied more fevered knife-blows to Rosemary's back, whilst Leslie retreated back into the hall. As Tex prepared to leave the room, he sensed that Leslie had held back, so instructed her to go back in and get involved in the murder.

Leslie Van Houten recollected: 'Tex turned me around and handed me the knife and said, "Do something", because Manson had told him to make sure that all of us got our hands dirty. And, I stabbed Mrs LaBianca in the lower back about sixteen times.'

By the time Leslie had finished applying her blows, Rosemary LaBianca had been stabbed a total of forty-one times. As was later noted in police reports, the poor woman had crawled some two feet following the frenzied stabbing spree. This vain bid for freedom had inadvertently pulled the electric cable even more tightly around her neck.

Although Leno was barely conscious by the time Tex returned from the bedroom, the head of the assassins continued to stab the forty-four-year-old into total submission. Such was the ferocity of his attack that Tex managed to break off the blade of a steak knife that he'd implanted in his victim's throat. On a high from stabbing Rosemary, Katie soon joined in. Revelling in her work and plunging a carving fork deep into Leno's stomach, Katie was mesmerised by the way the fork was so firmly stuck it vibrated when she pulled it back. Fascinated, she plucked at it like a child enchanted with a new toy. In a final act of bloody desecration, Katie scored the word 'WAR' into Leno's stomach with a knife.

She'd later attempt to rationalise the gruesome act to Family members, stating, 'This is one man who won't be able to send his son to war.' Adding their own sense of closure, someone placed a cushion from the couch over Leno's head.

Recalling Charlie's edict to keep a bloody continuity with the graffiti of the previous night, Katie collected some of Leno's blood onto some kitchen paper, and daubed the words 'Rise' and 'Death to Pigs' over the cream expanse of the living-room walls. She later reported that, whilst writing on the wall, she'd seen photos of the LaBiancas' children dotted around the house, and guessed that they'd probably all be coming over the following day for a Sunday gathering. Continuing the scheme into the kitchen, Katie scrawled the phrase 'Healter [sic] Skelter' on the door of the refrigerator; the blood barely sticking to its glossy aluminium.

Murder and bloody artwork completed, the trio settled down for a spot of domesticity, chillingly detached from the horror they had just inflicted. As they petted the LaBiancas' dogs which were roaming around, they ate some cheese and drank some chocolate milk they'd found in the refrigerator. As evidenced by some spent melon rinds in the sink, they'd also snacked on some fruit. They shared their food with the LaBiancas' dogs, who happily licked the killers' fingers. To rid themselves of any evidence of their horrific deeds, each in turn took a quick shower. Tex, his clothes filthy with blood, made use of some of Leslie's spare clothing. Confusing detectives later assigned to the case, other than the contents of Rosemary's wallet and some of Leno's coins (which Leslie apparently bagged), none of the LaBiancas' valuables were taken, and even their stock of rifles, shotguns and handguns were left untouched.

The three exited via a side door. In their seemingly detached state, little attempt was made to either close or secure the doors. Their bloody clothes were deposited in a waste bin a few blocks away. In an exhausted daze the killers wandered around the streets nearby for hours. At one point they walked through the hippie hang-out, Griffith Park. Eventually, they came across a waste treatment centre. Here Tex discarded the silver bayonet, launching it into a reservoir, never to be seen again. After resting under a tree until first light, the group attempted to hitch a lift back to Spahn's. Oddly enough, they caught a ride with a hippie character who was familiar with the ranch. He dropped them off near the entrance to Spahn's. In fact, so captivated was he with Leslie's charms that he arrived at the ranch the following day looking for her.

It's evident that Charlie had decided to split long before Tex and girls had even entered the LaBianca house. Pulling out of Waverly Drive, he'd emptied Rosemary LaBianca's wallet of its cash, and then given it to Linda to wipe clean of fingerprints. With the anticipation of Helter Skelter now uppermost in his mind, Manson informed those present they were to drive over to a black neighbourhood, and leave the wallet somewhere obvious. His hope was that some chancer would find it and use the credit cards, giving further credence to Bobby Beausoleil's claims that he was innocent of the Hinman murder.

With this on their minds, the clan pulled into a Standard all-night petrol station in the Los Angeles district of Sylmar – not exactly what one would call a black neighbourhood. The mistakes didn't end there. Linda was ordered to slip into the toilets and leave the wallet, but inexplicably she hid it in the cistern at the rear of the bathroom. Meanwhile, Charlie bought everyone milk shakes at a Denny's restaurant next door to the garage, and waited for Linda's return.

Back from the toilets, Linda told Manson where she'd left the wallet. Not surprisingly, he went ballistic, imagining (correctly) that no one would look in the cistern any time soon. In fact the wallet lay there for four months undisturbed. As going back would have drawn too much attention to the group, they took off in the direction of Venice Beach. On the way, Sadie, Charlie and Clem brainstormed about further targets to eliminate. Although Manson evidently had no intention of getting his hands dirty that night, he pushed for another strike on a 'piggy'. Once again, Charlie noticed Linda's reluctance to contribute anything to the discussion. Just south of Venice, he pulled the car in by a beach and took her for a short walk to separate her from the others.

The walk was eventful. At one point, they stopped to chat

with a friendly policeman, who engaged them in some affable banter. Law-enforcer out of the way, Charlie began digging for any shred of a potential target Linda might have in her mind. Sensing her unwillingness to highlight anyone suitable, Charlie recalled a story Linda and Sandy had told him about a fleeting liaison they'd had once while out hitching. It transpired that the pair had been picked up a suave young Egyptian film actor by the name of Saladin Nadar. Captivated by the feral beauty of Linda and Sandy, he'd invited them back to his apartment, overlooking Venice Beach, for a threesome. Although Linda engaged in a brisk romp with Nadar, Sandy had cried off, taking the opportunity to have a snooze elsewhere in the actor's swanky pad. As far as Charlie was concerned, Saladin Nadar's behaviour was worthy of the 'piggy' tag, and was therefore a perfect target.

Back in the car, a decision was taken to end the actor's life, all in the pursuit of Helter Skelter. Ignited by the prospect of further blood-letting, Charlie drove the trio down Venice Beach's promenade to retrace Linda's footsteps and locate the actor's residence. This they did quite quickly, and soon came across a mass of apartments at 1101 Ocean Front Walk.

Charlie and Linda got out of the car first, leaving Sadie and Clem behind while they checked out the complex of flats. Believing that Manson was going to personally shepherd her to her first killing, she decided to lead Charlie to a different apartment, hoping upon hope that the occupant would be out. With Linda leading the way, they walked up the stairs to the fourth floor, one level short of where Linda and Sandy had visited the actor.

As was becoming the pattern for the evening, Charlie clearly wasn't planning to be involved with any actual killing. Instead he was content to check out the layout and make mental notes. Preliminary work done, he and Linda walked back down the stairs and towards the car. Linda was to knock on the door, while Clem and Sadie would hide in reserve. Manson figured that the actor would gladly welcome Linda back into his quarters, especially after the liaison they'd previously enjoyed. Linda was then to slash the man's throat with a knife, and on a given signal, Clem and Sadie would pile into his flat. To finish the actor off permanently, Clem would then pump a few bullets into Nadar's body.

Handing out the weaponry, Charlie gave Clem the .45 pistol he'd taken back from Tex that night. For Linda, he brought out a small pocket-knife he'd hidden in his trousers. Linda, terrified at the prospect of having to follow Manson's orders, finally snapped at the prospect, 'Charlie, I am not you,' she bleated. 'I cannot kill anybody.' Charlie ignored her plea and demanded that she took the blade. Aware that this was not the most reliable of murder squads, he warned that if anything did go wrong, they were to leave immediately. With that, Charlie took over the wheel of the car, and headed off back in the direction of Spahn Ranch.

Linda trailed back into the apartment block, followed by Clem and Sadie. As she had done with Manson moments earlier, she took her cohorts up the stairs towards the fourth floor. Once there, Linda took the initiative and knocked on the wrong door. Eagerly preparing for the rush of death, Sadie and Clem hid around the corner, waiting for the call. As Linda nervously waited, she hoped that no one would answer. However, a voice from behind the wood asked, 'Who is it?' Linda called out her name and the door opened slightly ajar. Seeing the bemused tenant, Linda quickly remarked, 'Sorry, wrong door', and moved away. Linda went back to tell Sadie and Clem that the actor seemed to have moved on.

Such was her disappointment at the lack of action, Sadie took a shit on the floor of the landing. Symbolic ablution out of the way, the trio left the apartment block to make their way back to Spahn Ranch. There has never been any report about how Manson reacted to the trio's lack of success that night, but it seems likely that he would have been furious. How was Helter Skelter to play out if he couldn't rely on his troops?

It wasn't until late into Sunday evening that the bodies of Leno and Rosemary LaBianca were discovered. Rosemary's son Frank had returned from Lake Isabella, and was dropped off at the house at around 8.30 p.m. Approaching the drive, he was surprised to see that the kitchen lights were still on. Additionally, the car and boat had not been put away in the garage; something Leno would have done either the previous night or that morning. Frank went round the back of the house and tried the door. Finding it locked, he went to the opposite side of the house, and noticed that the side louvre doors had been left open. There he called out for his mother and Leno, but there was no reply. Sensing something was wrong, he walked away feeling agitated. He called his sister Suzan from a nearby phone box, and explained the mysterious situation. Equally concerned, she got her fiancé Joe to drive over to help check the place out, while she herself made her way over independently. The trio met at a nearby hamburger stand, and then drove the short distance over to Waverly Drive, arriving there at 10.25 p.m. Telling Suzan to hold back, Frank and Joe approached the property. After finding the keys to the back door in the couple's car, they entered the house from the rear. Walking into the lounge, they found Leno's bloody corpse on the sofa. Suzan, her curiosity duly pricked, had also entered the house, but boyfriend Joe prevented her from going into the lounge. Still in shock, the trio ran from the house to a neighbour's and begged them to call the police.

chapter 10
Run

'I was a squatter with a stubborn jaw,
My nose is droopy red and my whiskers grey,
Cause the magical mystery tour has taken me away.'

From *Arkansas* by Charles Manson

IT was only when the police arrived at Waverly Drive at around 1 a.m. that a quick search of the rest of the house led to the discovery of Rosemary's butchered body in the bedroom. The dead couple's dogs were also found, alive and well but with their masters' blood matted into their hair.

Police swiftly sealed off the LaBiancas' Waverly Drive house as the murder investigation began. Although just twenty-four hours after the Cielo Drive massacre, investigators held back from making any snap connections. Others hungry for sensationalism were, however, quick to make an equation between the two nights of savagery, linked with bloody inscriptions. For the media, it was a huge news bonus in the otherwise sleepy 'silly season'. Even in Britain the *London Evening News* reported the LaBianca killing. With a front-page headline declaring 'COUPLE DIE IN NEW HOLLYWOOD "HOODED" MURDER', it appeared that everyone other than the police were in a rush to unite the crimes.

Temperatures were certainly running high in the aftermath of the murders, and police were forced to face the television cameras. Lieutenant Dan Cook, acting as spokesman for the LAPD, attempted to allay any fears of a connection. 'There are some things there that were of similar nature,' he agreed, 'but actually, the homicides are not connected. I think the public and a lot of the media have picked up the fact that they were similar in nature, possibly because of the blood and the inscriptions, but this is rather a common type of thing in homicides. We've had many cases before where a suspect has written in blood, or in lipstick, various things of that nature.'

The composure Cook displayed for the cameras, was in stark contrast to the serious rumblings about the lack of communication between the various police departments. Separated by a few feet of office space, detectives attached to both the Cielo Drive and LaBianca murders set to work independently of each other. Because of the high-profile nature of the Sharon Tate murders, the police department's most senior detectives were allotted to handle the crime. Slightly lower down the hierarchy were the personnel attached to the LaBianca case. However, these detectives were younger and considerably more tenacious. They began looking beyond the evident horror of the murder scene for clues.

Elsewhere, local Sheriff's Department detectives were independently engaged in unravelling Gary Hinman's murder. The lack of communication on the three cases was heavily compounded by the structure of the sprawling Los Angeles law enforcement agency. Policing for the region was effectively split into two, the city led by the Los Angeles Police Department, while the outer area was handled by the Sheriff's Department. On this occasion, it appears that none of the teams were aware of the advances the others were making.

To the tabloids' delight, the grief-stricken Roman Polanski landed at Los Angeles Airport on the Sunday evening following the Cielo Drive massacre. With sections of the media already concocting murky tales about Sharon Tate and her celebrity friends, a press statement was hastily composed on the flight over, in the hope that it might deter any wild inaccuracies. The statement, penned by Polanski's business colleague Gene Gutowski and Playboy executive and club owner Victor Lownes, talked of the 'storybook couple, deeply in love and expecting a much-wanted baby'. Also within the text was an attempt to pre-empt any salacious rumours about the state of the couple's marriage: 'Mr. Polanski wishes to make it very clear that there was no rift between his wife and himself as some irresponsible journalists here have suggested even before the tragedy.' Once on the ground, Polanski was driven over to secure accommodation within the Universal Studios lot, where he was treated by a physician for shock.

The team working on the Cielo Drive murders were headed up by Robert Helder and a team of five detectives. Since caretaker William Garretson was still the only suspect, his claims of innocence were put to the test using a polygraph lie-detector. The polygraph session took place on the Monday afternoon after the murder spree. With Garretson giving his own version of events, police managed to build up a picture of his movements that night.

The polygraph proved Garretson's innocence, and by the Monday morning the nineteen-year-old had been released, with all charges against him dropped. Although detectives hedged on making any association with the LaBianca murders, because Garretson had been in custody on the Saturday night, he was eliminated from any putative connection. The following Monday, with a lawyer by his side, the stunned teenager faced the world's press. Although Garretson was ruled out of the inquiry, for reasons best known to himself he failed to tell detectives anything about the mysterious lift he'd had on the evening of the murders. Bizarrely, it would take a further twenty-five years before he went public with this and several other key facts that he'd failed to mention during questioning.

With Garretson free, police were now left with no tangible leads to pursue. Roman Polanski, whilst still under heavy sedation, offered himself up for questioning. The police had heard the whispers concerning the director's string of affairs. Adding further intrigue, Jay Sebring's close proximity to Sharon was starting to raise question marks. Another angle the police were looking at was the freakiness of the killing, and whether it might in some bizarre way be connected to Polanski's last film, *Rosemary's Baby*. Under interrogation, Polanski revealed that he had received some disturbing mail following the release of the picture, and hadn't dismissed the notion that the killers might well have been after him.

Like Garretson before him, Roman Polanski consented to a polygraph test, undergoing a session just days after landing back in Los Angeles. A tape of Polanski's test still exits and it is obvious that the slightly spaced-out dialogue was presumably a result of heavy tranquillisers. 'The whole crime seems so illogical to me,' he mused. 'I'm looking for something which doesn't fit

your habitual standard in which you used to work as police ...
I'd look for something much more far out, and that's what I am
going to do. I am devoted now to this, and I am going to do it. I
wouldn't be surprised if I was the target.'

Although a mass of information was piling into police in-trays,
there were numerous hindrances to the detective work. Forensic
officers based at the Cielo Drive house had their task badly
disrupted as overzealous police personnel caused innumerable
disturbances to the evidence left behind. In particular, police
had trailed Frykowski's blood on the stone porch back into the
living room. Parts of the shattered gun grip from Tex's revolver
had been mistakenly kicked under a table by one of the police
officers. Additionally, various law-enforcement personnel had
smeared their fingerprints all over the house. This overexcitement
and ineptitude delayed the emergence of any possible leads in
those vital first weeks.

With a brief to fillet the entire house for any clues, detectives
checked every nook and cranny for evidence. Secreted in loft
space directly above the murder scene, a roll of videotape was
discovered. The tape was an intimate, single-lens shot of Roman
and Sharon making love. Discreetly, the tape was returned to the
loft.

Elsewhere, police scientists, their senses seasoned by years of
similar investigations, discovered the potpourri of chemicals that
had been left in the house. In addition to the small package of
MDA tablets that had been delivered before the evening's horror
began, seventy-five grams of hashish were found in a living-room
cabinet, and thirty grams in Frykowski and Folger's bedroom.
Additionally, stray marijuana deposits were found in Sharon and
Roman's bedroom. Later, the cars were swept for clues. Bolstering
the growing suspicion that the killings were drug related, inside
Sebring's Porsche a gram of cocaine and numerous traces of
marijuana were discovered.

While the house and cars were systematically checked, the
grounds and surrounding areas were also meticulously swept.
Sus-pended by rope, agents painstakingly searched the plunging
hillside around the house. However, despite scouring every inch
of the property, nothing of any relevance was found outside of the

house itself. However, the autopsies confirmed police suspicions about a narcotics angle, with both Frykowski and Folger's blood containing traces of the drug MDA.

However, over in the Sheriff's Department, more imaginative approaches to the murders were being explored. Detectives attached to the Gary Hinman murder, Paul Whitely and Charles Guenther, were intrigued by the similarities between the cases, especially the bloody writings on the wall. Their investigations had easily revealed Bobby Beausoleil's fraternisation with Manson and the Family at Spahn Ranch. Although Bobby had kept his counsel when questioned, the style of Hinman's killing convinced officers that it wasn't just a solitary individual involved in the murder. With the Family connection established, intelligence from officers monitoring Spahn Ranch was passed to Whitely and Guenther. The detectives presented these similarities to LAPD officers working on the Cielo Drive killings; however, they were ignored, with detectives still keen to pursue the drug angle. As a result of these dismissals, any progress in those first few weeks was painfully slow.

A police report on the Cielo Drive investigation highlighted some other possible motives for the crime. The first of these, mentioned a bungled robbery that had turned nasty. The other, more cogent theory, given the evidence, suggested that the killings were connected to a drug turf war. Adding weight to this, several shady characters connected to Sebring and Frykowski were starting to surface, spinning lurid tales about their dealings with the victims. Whilst a lot of these allegations came from criminals looking to make some sort of bargain, police did rope in a few dealers whose names kept coming up. What was becoming singularly apparent was Frykowski's burgeoning involvement with drug dealing; not least his interest in securing a large patch of the fast-growing MDA market.

These investigations also uncovered a sickening litany of violence attached to the Hollywood drug-supply chain. In addition, tales started to surface of sadomasochistic parties held within Hollywood society. These salacious reports revealed connections with the inhabitants at Cielo Drive. In particular, the free-range sexual antics of Jay Sebring began to cause interest at police headquarters. After questioning Sebring's numerous partners, tales of the hairdresser's preference for bondage began to prompt suggestions that the killings might have been the result of an orgy that had turned nasty.

Not surprisingly, these juicy revelations soon seeped out of police interview rooms and into the hands of ravenous journalists. With the possibility of ritualised murders driven by exotic drug use and sexual deviancy, editors ran an interminable number of seamy stories allegedly connected to the Tate murders. This wave of sleaze even permeated magazines not normally noted for muck-raking. *Time Magazine* was just one authoritative journal that garnered snippets from the rumour mill. Evidently not checking with the police's explicit photographic evidence, the magazine declared that 'Sharon's body had been found nude ... and one of her breasts had been cut off.' Further inaccuracies appeared, such as that 'Sebring had been sexually mutilated and his body bore X marks.' *Time* claimed that Sebring's trousers 'were down around his ankles.' *Newsweek* also picked up on the sleaziest rumours, proclaiming, 'Hollywood gossip about the case was of drugs, mysticism and offbeat sex – and for once there may be more truth than fantasy in the flashy talk around town. The theme of the melodrama was drugs. Some suspect the group was amusing itself with some sort of black magic rites.'

Whilst media and rumour-mongers were having a field day, police and detectives were careful to leave the victims' families alone to bury their dead. As expected, hundreds turned up to pay their respects to Sharon Tate when her funeral took place on Wednesday 13 August. The couple's unborn child was placed alongside Sharon in her coffin. The tiny, eight-and-a-half-month male foetus was given the name Paul Richard.

Sharon Tate's service at Culver City's Holy Cross Memorial Cemetery was attended by a large celebrity contingent: Peter Sellers, Warren Beatty, Joan Collins, Kirk Douglas and Yul Brunner were among the 200 guests who paid their respects. Noticeable by his absence was the Polanskis' close friend, Steve McQueen. Like many others, he'd intended to call in on Cielo Drive that fateful night; since the murders, he had been carrying a loaded pistol at his side. Despite his understandable fear, Polanski was livid that he didn't come to Sharon's funeral.

Although press and curious onlookers were shepherded back from the chapel's limits, a few paparazzi still managed to get close to the funeral. What their lenses captured was a truly harrowing scene. Barely able to walk under the emotional strain, Roman Polanski was supported by Sharon's mother, Doris, herself inconsolable with grief. Behind, were Sharon's two sisters, Debra and Patti, closely followed by their father Paul. Jay Sebring's funeral took place a few hours later at Forest Lawn Memorial Park, with most of Sharon Tate's retinue in attendance. Steven Parent's funeral was a small, family affair in El Monte, while Abigail Folger's body was flown back to San Francisco for a private ceremony. Voyteck Frykowski was later cremated, his ashes sent back to the Polish city of Łódz.

The press seemed to hold very little respect for the grief-stricken widower Roman Polanski, and he was constantly having to fend off implications that his left-field filmmaking had in some way influenced the killings. Partly in an attempt to halt these wild inaccuracies, Roman arranged to go back to Cielo Drive on Sunday 17 August with photographer Julian Wasser and Tommy Thompson, a reporter from *Life Magazine*.

'My urge to visit Cielo Drive,' recalled Roman, 'grew stronger as the days went by ... I was drawn to the house by a strange nostalgia – an illusory feeling that something of Sharon might be lingering there.'

Senses still dulled by tranquillisers, Polanski consented to the additional presence of Peter Hurkos, a Dutch psychic of some note and a friend of Jay Sebring, who was eager to come along to see if any residual energy might offer up a clue to the killers.

Past the heavily guarded gate, Roman walked through the grounds, trailed by reporter, cameraman and psychic; their brief, to record Polanski's emotional response on seeing the house for the first time since the murders. Passing the spot where Abigail Folger had been slain, Polanski noted the sheet that had covered her dead body was still lying on the lawn. Walking over to the stone porch, he knelt down close to where his friend Voyteck had finally died; the brickwork was still spattered with blood. Behind him, and still visible on the door of the house, was Sadie's daub 'pig', written with Sharon's blood.

Once inside the house, the scene was total chaos. In the lounge, furniture had been moved around, and upon every conceivable surface, forensic powder lay in great clusters, while the carpet was heavily stained with pockets of dried blood. Roman wandered around, tearfully reacquainting himself with his and Sharon's possessions. On leaving the lounge, Roman walked down the corridor and entered their bedroom. Once inside, he saw the cot he and Sharon had bought together, lying on top of the wardrobe, still wrapped in plastic. In a drawer, Roman discovered a collection of Sharon's publicity shots. With the weight of the tragedy now bearing down on him fully, he collapsed, imploring, 'Why?' Cameraman Wasser attempted to detach himself from the ordeal, and he took a few Polaroid shots to test the light inside the house. He discarded some of them in the lounge fireplace, although curiously they'd reappear later on.

Despite the emotional trauma Polanski was undergoing, he was later accused of milking the situation by doing the *Life* interviews, and criticised for allegedly taking money for the exclusive photographs and story. Although the allegations were swiftly denied, they had distressing ramifications. Landlord of the Cielo Drive property, Rudi Altobelli, was reportedly incensed with the idea that Polanski had profited from the feature, and sued Roman for all manner of reparations ranging from depreciation of the house's value to 'trespassory conduct'. Included was a charge for his own 'emotional distress' and 'damage to carpets'. In an attempt to level matters, both Polanski and Sharon's father Paul, returned to the house at a later date to clear up; both attempting vainly to remove the bloodstains off the carpet.

While Polanski attempted to compose himself after the ordeal of returning to Cielo Drive, psychic Peter Hurkos convened an immediate press conference. Declaring that the vibrations he'd received at the house gave him a clear view of what had happened, Hurkos claimed that three men killed Sharon and her friends whilst high on LSD and marijuana. Even going so far as to mention possible suspects, Hurkos reported his beliefs to police. Given that the psychic had some credibility after assisting detectives on the Boston Strangler case, his observations were given considerable credence. Soon after, Hurkos started hawking Julian Wasser's Polaroid photos of his visit to Cielo Drive to the press. Furthermore, he promoted his involvement with 'the current Sharon Tate massacre' on a series of public appearances.

Another speculative view on the case came from an altogether more noteworthy source, Truman Capote. In the wake of his 1959 book, *In Cold Blood*, Capote had proved himself a respected authority on the twisted psychology of murder. Whilst appearing on the top-rated *Johnny Carson Show* shortly after the murders, Capote revealed his theories, based on information he'd sourced from the plethora of news reports. Believing the killings were the work of a single person with a considerable grudge against the residents, Capote noted: 'Something happened to trigger a kind of instant paranoia.'

While Truman Capote's observations did at least appear reasonable, a murky spectrum of witches, oracles and amateur sleuths presented their own slants on the grisly events. Hollywood's Satanist-in-residence, Anton LaVey, was perversely well placed to comment, yet his declaration that the slaughter was a 'lust murder' was evidently drawn from his own psyche rather than anything more concrete . Others, too, were quick to leap on the bandwagon: cinemas and drive-ins began immediate reruns of Sharon Tate's films. Although Tate had only received a co-star credit on the likes of *Fearless Vampire Killers* and *Valley of the Dolls*, in the wake of the murders, her name was prominent on billboards and hoardings around Los Angeles. Even Jay Sebring's minuscule contribution to the documentary *Mondo Hollywood* lead to it being shown in a few theatres.

In response to the murder of their fellow celluloid star, members of Hollywood's celebrity clique began to fear for their own safety. Within days, gun shops were cleared of their stocks, while security firms were inundated with requests for additional protection. Many celebrities, their fragile sensitivities crushed by the murders, left town. Equally, those who had had chemical dealings with Frykowski and Sebring, quickly got rid of their stashes. 'Toilets are flushing all over Hollywood,' remarked one industry insider. 'The whole sewer system is stoned.'

Dominic Dunne recollected that 'it was amazing. Everyone's got a piece of the story. Everywhere you went, there was somebody talking about it ... The shock waves that went through the town were beyond anything I had ever seen before. People were convinced that the rich and famous of the community were in peril. Children were sent out of town. Guards were hired ... '

In a desperate attempt to pre-empt any more scandalous reports about Sharon, Roman Polanski decided to face the press head-on. Just ten days after the murder, the diminutive Pole cut a sombre figure in the function room of the swish Beverly Wilshire Hotel. Dressed in a black suit and tie with his fringe nudging his eyebrows, Polanski faced a legion of press microphones and cameras trained in his direction.

Given his first opportunity to respond to the media, Polanski assumed a determined stance. 'It is not my reputation that is at stake, but it is the memory of [the] only person who loved me truly,' Roman asserted through his tears. 'We'll make ashamed, a lot of newsmen, who for selfish reasons write unbearable, for me, horrible things about my wife ... All of you know how beautiful she was, and very often I have read and heard statements that she was one of the most, if not the most beautiful woman in the world ... But only [a] few of you know how good she was.' Drawing on his own experience revisiting Cielo Drive, he challenged the press to go over and visit the murder scene. 'The house is now open,' he implored. 'You can now go and see the orgy place. You will see the innumerable books on natural birth, which she was planning ... You will see the baby's clothes. You will see the room which she was painting. You will see a lot of blood all over the place.'

Amid the accusations and finger-pointing, Polanski had set about performing his own detective work. Although police had questioned the widower about the couple's large coterie of friends, Polanski began his own investigations. He utilised a variety of methods to qualify his suspicions, some not altogether sound, but his actions show a desperate intent to determine who was behind the killings.

Roman's list of possible suspects included John Phillips, one quarter of the Mamas & the Papas. Polanski had had a brief fling with Phillips's wife Michelle while he was in London. Despite the fact that they'd remained superficially friends, Roman feared that there might have been some stray resentment regarding the indiscretion. To try and clarify his suspicions, Polanski crept over to Phillips's house one evening to scrutinise the singer's cars for any possible clues. On finding nothing untoward, he nevertheless tagged the musician for a few days. At one point, he arranged a car ride with Phillips. When the singer momentarily left the vehicle, Polanski pocketed some of Phillips's handwritten documents. Convinced that the handwriting style was similar to the 'Pig' inscription on the Cielo Drive door, he sent them off to be analysed, but there turned out to be no connection. Out of his mind with paranoia, Polanski continued to pursue Phillips. At one point, Polanski held a knife to Phillips's throat demanding he confess to the murders.

Alongside his amateur sleuthing, Polanski kept in close contact with the head of the Cielo Drive investigators, Robert Helder. The detective fed Roman as much information as was permissible, often revealing interesting leads as they came in. During one of these informal chats, Helder told Polanski that among the many leads flying about was a report concerning a group of hippies living at a ranch 'with this guy they called Jesus Christ'. Helder mentioned that sheriff's officers had sent over a report that drew some parallels between the death of Gary Hinman and the Tate massacre. Polanski reportedly scoffed at the suggestion, saying, 'Come on Bob, you're prejudiced against hippies.' Helder replied, 'You should suspect everyone. Don't dismiss it so easily.' Despite the detective's words, the report was filed away, and no one followed up on the 'hippie' lead.

In fact, this information from the Hinman detectives had a considerable history attached to it. Prior to any suspicion of murder being levied, Sheriff's officers had been focusing considerable attention on Manson's clan, albeit on a much more mundane level. For weeks, a whole raft of cars, notably Volkswagen Beetles, were being reported stolen around the Chatsworth area. Somewhere along the line, an informant had been supplying police information on the activities of the Family. Having the unenviable task of monitoring the movements of biker and gang fraternities, Sergeant Bill Gleeson of the Sheriff's Department, was fully aware of the position Charlie held within the Family's ranks. Whilst he'd been briefed on Manson's alleged divinity, and his vision of an impending apocalypse, Gleeson had focused his attentions on the stockpiling of stolen vehicles at Spahn's. Gleeson had conferred with a number of his associates on ways to close down operations at Spahn's, and a raid on the ranch had been scheduled.

Whoever fed the information regarding the stolen vehicle business was certainly correct; no one other than the myopic George Spahn could have failed to see the mass of motor parts littered around the ranch. The police had tangible evidence as well, having previously engaged a helicopter to buzz over the ranch to gather reconnaissance photographs. Charlie, too, was picking up signals that something was about to break. 'I was constantly watching the roads,' Manson would later recall. 'I couldn't shake the feeling that, any minute now, a bunch of police cars were going to come racing into the ranch to gather us all up and book us for the slayings.'

Plans for the desert retreat were stepped up. Dune buggy production went into overdrive and, for once, Mason green-lit the use of amphetamines to maintain constant work on the vehicles. By the morning of 16 August there was, however, an even more pressing problem. Straight Satan biker, Danny DeCarlo, had found staying with the Family far more appealing than the leather and grease of his biker chums. This might have pleased the Family, but his pals were less than delighted, as Danny was an important link in their chain of command. While Danny partied hard at the ranch, his fellow bikers had made no bones about the fact that they wanted him back. In an attempt to retrieve their errant 'brother' from Manson's clasp, members of the Straight Satans went over to Spahn's on Friday 15 August 1969, threatening all sorts of violence if Danny wasn't released. By all accounts, it was a heavy scene, with guns and knives raised in anticipation of a blood bath. Manson managed to smooth things over in his customary fashion, and had offered to die in place of any other

Family members. By way of a further peace offering, Charlie instructed the girls to come and lower the bikers' temperatures for the evening. The approach worked, and with gargantuan amounts of liquor and drugs, tensions soon eased. The gathering stretched into the early hours when most of the bikers finally left and everyone else succumbed to fatigue.

Any notion of an extended lie-in was summarily dashed at 6 a.m. when the sound of approaching helicopters broke the silence. With whirling blades conjuring up the cacophony of an impending Armageddon, it was as if they'd woken up on the other side of Helter Skelter. Adding to the confusion, blue strobes cut through the dawn's early mist. Twenty squad cars and over a hundred police and special enforcement officers burst into the shacks and cabins, guns aloft. Manson grabbed his bed-mate Stephanie Schram and headed out by the rear, where they hid themselves under a wooden porch. With the whole area illuminated by massive searchlights from the helicopters, there was little chance of escape. Tellingly, though, the secretive nooks and crannies the Family had earmarked for such a raid were comprehensively searched.

Although police were equipped with automatic guns and body armour in anticipation of a possible retaliation, there was no resistance. Evidently working on prior information, the question, 'Where's Jesus?' became a repetitive chant as police hauled Family members into a crude semi-circle outside the ranch's buildings. The raid was particularly thorough, and it soon became apparent that the police wouldn't leave until Manson was found. Eventually, police located Charlie's bolt hole under the porch, and he was brought out handcuffed and at gunpoint. Eyebrows were raised as several of the police exclaimed, 'So that's Manson?' Perhaps they had expected a more imposing-looking nemesis. As Manson was manhandled out of the building, a cache of credit cards fell out of his shirt pocket.

With the Family squatting on the dusty ground outside the shacks, police began to deliver the charges. For the Cielo Drive and LaBianca cognoscenti, it seemed inevitable that 'murder' would be top of the charges. For the most part the charges were received in silence, albeit with a few stifled giggles. Although charges of firearms possession, grand-theft auto and handling stolen credit cards were levied against Manson and some of the men, their leader just smiled and looked around knowingly. Preliminaries over, a police photographer took a few images of the raid; several with Charlie sitting with some of his co-conspirators on the back of a trailer. Leaving some of the officers behind to take a full inventory of the ranch, the arrested were ushered over to a large municipal bus. Only Squeaky showed any distress, wondering who would look after old George and the dogs while they were gone. Although the women were separated from the men on the bus, it did nothing to dull their spirits, and they broke into a sing-along, delivering the Beatles' song 'Piggies' in celebration of their apparent omnipotence.

Hours later, the Sheriff's Department fed reports of their smashing of the car-theft ring to newspapers. They even supplied a few photos of the raid for the press to publish. It was good publicity for the law enforcers, scoring a high-profile feature in the *Los Angeles Times* on 17 August, with the headline 'POLICE RAID RANCH, ARREST 26 SUSPECTS IN AUTO THEFT RING'. With excited hyperbole, police relayed that the Family had been 'living like animals' when they were found. George Spahn was also roped in for a quote, hiding any potential culpability by claiming that, although he suspected that people were living on the sets, he 'couldn't get around and was frightened of them'.

Proving highly embarrassing for detectives later on, on the same page was a feature entitled 'NIGHT OF HORROR – ANATOMY OF A MASS MURDER IN HOLLYWOOD,' which examined the police investigations into the Tate murder. Also on the same page, and further piling on the irony, was an article detailing the funeral arrangements for Leno and Rosemary LaBianca.

The Family's apparent impregnability was confirmed three days later at police headquarters in Malibu. Despite the careful planning to smash the car-theft ring, the administrative paperwork had been so sloppily prepared, that arrest warrants were wrongly dated for 13 August, three days before the raid was to take place. Seeing as they were only good for that date, all charges were effectively rendered null and void. With all now free to leave, an atmosphere redolent of an end-of-term party ensued as Manson and girls ecstatically flitted out of the courthouse. If ever there had been any doubts amongst the Family about their own divinity, they were now fully quashed.

Manson and his fellow arrestees hitched their way back to Spahn Ranch, but their levity at avoiding all charges was short lived. As the shambling caravan of Family members arrived back at the ranch, they were confronted with the pathetic sight of their furniture, bedding, and other personal possessions strewn around the dusty ground. While to the outside world, the Family had maintained a blithe attitude, in reality, they prided themselves on their ability to live in fairly organised environment. In the wake of the police operation, their quarters resembled something more akin to a derelict shantytown. In addition to the stolen vehicles, police had removed the few cars that were legitimately acquired; most worryingly for Charlie, the car used on the nights of the murders. Additionally, tools and other domestic implements had also disappeared. Worst of all, all seven of the Family's children had been taken into social service care.

The upset caused by the actions of the police soon turned to rage. Initially, the Family attempted to get back some of their possessions, but police employed stalling tactics, demanding proof of purchase for every item before it could be released. Given that a lot of their possessions were stolen in the first place, little could be retrieved, and of course no one had kept receipts for the legitimate purchases. 'Our natural contempt for the police turned into a unanimous "fuck you, you bastards", Charlie later recalled. ' "We'll get it all back and then some!" '

But the police weren't finished. They revisited the ranch a few days later, and this time, it was Manson they were after. Breaking into the cabin he was sharing with young Stephanie Schram, they searched his clothing and found a half-smoked joint in a denim shirt. As Stephanie was semi-naked when police entered, she was charged with indecency. The pair were then driven back to Malibu to be booked; the second time in a week. As they left the ranch, Manson screamed out of the police car for someone, anyone, to call him at the police station, his plan being to push the charge of possession on to someone else. But yet again, the gods were evidently on Manson's side. Stephanie's supposed indecency was not considered illegal, seeing as she was technically 'at home'. Fortuitously for Manson, the 'joint' turned out to contain no noxious substances. It later came to light that Sadie had dropped the reefer into Manson's shirt by way of a peace offering. She'd been led to believe it was marijuana; however, it turned out to be some rogue substance, not in any way related to any marijuana plant or derivative. Charges against the couple had to be dropped.

Stephanie and Charlie were released on the afternoon of 25 August 1969. However, given Stephanie Schram's age, she was placed on probation and ordered to return to her parents' house in Anaheim. Manson swiftly made his way back to Spahn's, having had plenty of time to fester over the possible identity of the informant who'd snitched to police.

Tex Watson and Dianne Lake missed out on the arrest. Both were engaged on an errand for Charlie that took them out to a ranch in Olancha, on the fringes of Death Valley. Uncharacteristically, Tex was up early each morning, buying up reams of the day's newspapers, which he'd then study intently. During the couple's stay in Olancha, Dianne Lake was picked up by police while ferreting for food in a supermarket garbage skip. For this misdemeanour, she was briefly held in custody. When she returned from her incarceration, Tex, his paranoia over her arrest now at fever-pitch, went ballistic, showing Lake a pertinent headline from the Tate–LaBianca massacre. 'See this stuff in the paper?!' he barked at Lake. 'I did this!'

As police began cracking down on the Family, stuntman Shorty Shea had been royally strutting his stuff around Spahn Ranch. With Charlie incarcerated twice in a week, and the Family's activities broken up by a raid, Shea resumed his position as top dog around Spahn's.

With Stephanie Schram heading back to her parents, Manson arrived back at Spahn's alone on the afternoon of 25 August, now convinced that Shea was the police informant, and it appears that Manson was not alone in this assertion. Steve Grogan remembered how they all felt: 'It was through his actions that he caused us this trouble ... There was, you know, a feeling almost of hatred toward the guy because of what he made us go through, the children and stuff. Like we had held the children in really almost the highest position. They were home-delivered and breast-fed. Our feeling for the children was really the highest thing we felt. This was mostly the whole reason we was all together, to put the children in a good environment, free from social indoctrination and stuff, try to raise them as natural as we could. And then to have someone come along and form a false story and have them put in foster homes, it was really a blow to the women and men that were at the place at the time.'

By evening, the atmosphere at Spahn's was charged in Shea's direction. The stuntman was already aware that something major was afoot, and had confided to an associate that he believed that the Family were intending to kill him. On the eve of Manson's return, ranch-hand-in-chief, Ruby Pearl, recalled that Shea had asked a favour as she prepared to go out for the evening. 'Gee, I would like to stay down at your house tonight,' he nervously told Pearl. 'These people are giving me the creeps. They're acting awful weird . . . They're out to get me.' As Pearl drove away, she saw in her rear mirror, Manson, Tex, Clem and Bruce all bearing down on Shea.

As befits nebulous Manson Family folklore, ascertaining the exact details of Shorty Shea's demise is a nigh on impossible task. What is abundantly clear, though, is that his death was a savage one.

According to evidence Clem gave during a parole hearing in the late 1970s, the murder occurred the day after Manson's release from his incarceration in Malibu. Charlie had woken him up and told him he was going to take a ride with Shorty. Tex was now back from Olancha and, under the pretence that he was to locate some discarded vehicle parts that someone had dumped not far from the ranch, was also up fairly early that morning. Manson then handed Clem a pipe wrench and instructed him to hit Shorty on the back of the head as soon as Tex gave him a signal.

The car duly set off with Clem in the rear, Tex driving and Shea in the passenger seat. A few hundred metres along from Spahn's, the vehicle pulled off the road into a small lay-by. Tex got out and pretended to look around the bushes in search of the motor parts. With Shorty focusing elsewhere, Clem was having difficulty in mustering the willpower to strike Shea from behind. Tex was now looking back and throwing pointed looks. He'd also pulled out a knife and was brandishing it. With the pressure building, Clem finally struck Shorty on the back of the head.

The blow stunned Shea, knocking him forward with such ferocity his head hit the steering wheel. Shorty was resilient, though, and even in a daze he attempted to get out of the open car door. Tex hadn't secured the brakes of the vehicle, so the weight of Shea's large frame rolling around started the vehicle moving towards a nearby ditch. As Clem attempted to put the handbrake on, Tex moved in and began stabbing Shea with his knife.

When Manson arrived on the scene with Bruce Davis, Shorty was lying on the ground in a semi-conscious state. Although Charlie had arrived with a machete, as usual he was reluctant to do any of the actual stabbing himself, leaving Clem, Tex and Bruce to weigh into Shea's body with knives and bayonets. When it was apparent that Shorty was dead, Charlie ordered Clem to drag Shea's body into some bushes, cover it up and then return later to bury him. Charlie, Tex and Bruce then left, leaving Clem to hide the body as best he could. Clem reportedly returned later that night and transferred Shea's body into a shallow grave he'd dug.

Despite the strict secrecy that surrounding their previous killings, Charlie made little secret of the fact that Shea had been done away with. To Manson, two birds had been killed with one stone. While Shea's death had silenced the Family's fieriest critic, it also sent out a terrifying message to anyone else thinking of dissension.

Biker Danny DeCarlo was startled by the candour shown by those involved. 'Bruce [Davis] said they cut him up in nine pieces. They cut his head off, then they cut his arms off too, so there was no way they could possibly identify him. They were laughing about that.'

Barbara Hoyt was another who tuned into gossip about Shorty's death. However, she has always maintained that she actually heard it happen on 25 August, the night of Manson's return, and that Shorty was killed at the creek-bed to the rear of the ranch. Like a lot of the peripheral Family members, Hoyt had been privy to the mutterings about Shorty's uncertain allegiances. In particular, she'd overheard key personalities claiming that Shorty would 'be taken care of' as a result of his alleged snitching. Hoyt had served Shea dinner that night, and claims that was the last she saw of him.

'I went to go to sleep in one of the trailers at the back of the ranch overlooking the creek-bed below,' she later said. 'At about 10 o'clock at night, just as I laid my head on the pillow, I heard a long, loud, blood-curdling scream, which came from about fifty to seventy-five feet away from me, from upstream . . . I recognised the screams of Shorty's voice. I can still hear those screams today, exactly as I heard them that night. Then it was quiet for a minute or so, and then the screams came again, and again, again, again . . . They seemed to go on for ever. I have absolutely no doubt that Shorty was being murdered at that time.'

The next morning, Hoyt asked around if anyone else had heard Shorty's cries during the night, only to be met with a stern silence. However, later in the day she heard Charlie bragging to Danny DeCarlo about how Shorty had committed suicide the night before 'with a little help from us'. Bruce Davis was also heard to remark that, 'We just stabbed him and stabbed him until Clem cut his head off. And we buried him under some leaves.'

According to Hoyt, on the morning of 26 August, Charlie had been quizzing various people about whether lime or lye would best decompose Shea's body.

The rumours concerning Shea's death gathered momentum as the days progressed. If the reports are to be believed, the stuntman's death was a collective act, everyone, however peripheral, having a part to play in his murder and disappearance. Aside from the bloody killing, Family members were engaged in removing all traces of Shea's presence from Spahn's. Anything of value he owned was either shared out or sold. Charlie bagged Shea's most prized possession, a pair of ornate Colt .45 revolvers he'd kept in an attaché case, embossed with his name. It was not altogether an efficient clean-up, though, and several key items of evidence were later identified and used in convictions. As personnel attached to the ranch began to notice Shorty's absence, Family members told the curious that he'd 'gone to San Francisco' in search of acting work.

While Shea's death might have silenced some, it tested loyalties within the Family. As a result, a harder vibe of self-preservation replaced the 'oneness' that had been so apparent during the Family's early days. While the singing, drugging, and lovemaking continued, the passion that fuelled it had a more acerbic edge. As always, Charlie's evening raps were still a mainstay, and yet some of the after-dinner antics were becoming more questionable. Bloody re-enactments had started to become commonplace, with Family members reportedly acting a pantomime of their crimes, often accompanied by spirited laughter.

While the weirdness served to galvanise the Family's hard-core in the wake of the killings, some of the more peripheral members of the clan fled. With paranoia running rampant, the disappearance of anyone – however low in the Family's hierarchy – gave considerable cause for concern. The most prominent of these escapees was Linda Kasabian, who disappeared four days after the Tate/LaBianca slayings. Such was her desire to escape Manson's clutches, she left her baby Tanya behind. Kasabian made her escape following an order from Charlie to visit Sandra Good, Mary Brunner and Bobby Beausoleil in their respective jails in a borrowed car. Reconnecting with her husband Robert in New Mexico, she spilled out the horror that had occurred during her time with the Family. With baby Tanya still in Charlie's stewardship, a series of convoluted games had to be played to retrieve her.

Others too, it appears, were planning their own escape, even Sadie – once Manson's most vociferous supporter. Sadie had met a man from Hollywood and, unbeknown to Charlie, had begun to hang out with him more and more, often spending days at a time away from the ranch. Her young son was still in the arms of the Family, but she explained to her new man that she desperately wanted to take back her child. With her friend in tow, Sadie approached Spahn's with the intention of retrieving her son, and, it appears, taking off more permanently.

Susan Atkins explains: 'I met this young man from the Hollywood area, and he realised that I wanted my son, and he

A distraught Roman Polanski pictured outside his Cielo Drive residence eight days after the murder of his wife. Still visible on the door is the word "PIG", written by Susan Atkins in Sharon Tate's blood.

Saturday, August 9th, 1969. Sharon Tate and Jay Sebring lie butchered on the lounge floor at 10050 Cielo Drive.

Voyteck Frykowski finally succumbed to death on the lawn of Cielo Drive after taking two shot wounds, numerous blows to the head, and fifty-one stab wounds.

18-year-old Steven Parent; murdered in Cielo Drive in the early hours of August 9th, 1969. Parent would be shot four times by Tex Watson and then stabbed.

Leno LaBianca as found by police on August 10th, 1969. Patricia Krenwinkel scored the words "War" on Leno's dead body. She'd later attempt to validate her actions by claiming, "He won't be sending any of his children off to war."

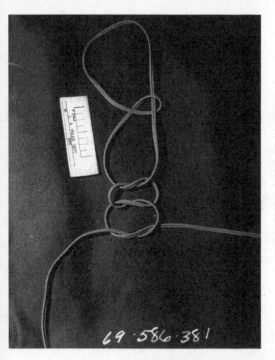

The Los Angeles Police Department photographed every possible smidgen of evidence relating to the deaths of Leno and Rosemary LaBianca. Published for the first time, this is the electrical chord that had secured the pillowcase over Rosemary LaBianca's head.

Here, they capture the pathetic scene in the bedroom just hours after the slaughter. Poignantly, the LaBianca's pet dog sits patiently on an empty bed.

Manson's edict to leave something 'witchy' was carried out by the Family during the LaBianca massacre. Among other graffiti, "Death to Pigs" was daubed across the couple's living room wall in Leno LaBianca's blood.

Written on the LaBianca's refrigerator, the legend "Healter Skelter" was part of Charlie's 'grand plan'. Not that police knew it at the time, keeping this vital detail out of the public domain.

Peter Hurkos searches for inspiration from the floor of Cielo Drive, 17th August 1969. A celebrity psychic, Hurkos visited the murder scene to check for any extrasensory clues that might be present following the slaughter.

Biker Danny DeCarlo and Charlie under arrest at Spahn's Ranch, August 16th 1969.

Manson in handcuffs on his way to court. Such was the fear that the Manson Family instilled in Los Angeles, it was deemed appropriate that Charlie be escorted by seven armed police to and from the courtroom.

Tex Watson arriving in court, March 1971. Watson would fight extradition for nine months before being brought to Los Angeles to face seven counts of first-degree murder.

Acolytes of Charles Manson would maintain a heavy presence outside Los Angeles' Halls of Justice during the trials. Almost inevitably, they would mimic the antics of the defendants inside the courtroom, carving "X's" into their foreheads, and shaving off their hair.

Official arrest photos of Charles Manson, as preserved in Los Angeles' Police file. Despite having no direct participation in the Tate/LaBianca murders, by dint of his messianic celebrity, Manson would find himself as principal suspect.

Family member Bruce Davis, pictured here as a spectator during the Tate/LaBianca trials. Davis's shady and undetermined movements have been the subject of considerable debate since his arrest in December, 1970.

The Talgarth Hotel, Hammersmith, west London, scene of Joel Pugh's death in December 1969. Much has been said of Pugh's relation to the Manson Family, and the circumstances behind his demise.

Joel Pugh, seen here with Sandra Good in December 1967. Pugh's association with Good would ensure that his untimely death would forever be linked with the activities of the Manson Family.

said, "I will go back with you to get your child." I feared for this man's safety, and I told him, "You stay out in the car, and I'll go in and get my boy and I'll be back out." And I went back in to get my son. I picked him up. I had him in my arms, and I was walking out the door and Charlie came down, and he stood in front of me and he said, "Before you leave, I want you to go into that bedroom and I want you to look at Mary Brunner. She tried to leave and take her son Michael with her and I want you to look at her. If you try to take your baby, the same thing will happen to you." And I went in, and Mary Brunner was lying on the bed. Her jaw was half broken. She had a black eye, and she had two cracked ribs.'

Although no one was yet pointing fingers, Charlie saw that the race war he'd predicted following the killings was not materialising. Other than the familiar stand-offs between black youths and police, there was nothing to back up Charlie's talk of the impending Armageddon. Given the vehemence of his predictions, Manson was acutely aware that his judgement would soon come under scrutiny if it didn't kick off. Sensing a seismic implosion within the Family, Charlie's options were severely limited. With the move to the desert now beckoning, Manson made a last few calls in a vain attempt to raise finances for the Family's relocation. It's evident that Charlie (or another Family member) also decided to pay a call on Terry Melcher's Malibu house following the murders. Either late at night or when Melcher was momentarily absent, Melcher's beach property was 'Creepy Crawled', the producer losing an ornate telescope in the process.

While Dennis Wilson had made every effort to keep out of Charlie's way, he wasn't surprised when Manson's keen radar eventually tracked him down at his friend Gregg Jakobson's house. A small gathering was taking place that evening and, despite the spectre of the Tate–LaBianca murders, the vibe was cool until Charlie burst into the gathering, wearing an oversize sombrero.

'Electricity was pouring out of him,' recalled Jakobson later. 'His hair was standing on end. His eyes were wild. He was like a cat that was caged. He was like an animal.'

When Dennis asked his unexpected visitor where he'd been

of late, Charlie replied that he'd 'been to the moon'. Charlie reiterated yet again the debt that Wilson and the Beach Boys owed him concerning his songwriting credits, and demanded $1,500 in cash. When Dennis told him he had no money, Charlie left.

It wasn't to be the last time that Charlie attempted to touch Dennis for favours. He turned up again at Gregg Jakobson's house hoping for a private audience with Wilson. With Dennis on tour with the Beach Boys in Canada, and Jakobson himself absent, Stan Shapiro, a friend of both Dennis and Gregg's, was house-sitting. Manson was in no mood for compromise and, taking out a revolver, he opened up the chamber and threw one of the bullets on the floor. The gesture was explicit: one bullet for Dennis, and a message that he also had one for Wilson's son, Scott.

Adding considerable weight to Charlie's threat, Wilson's son went missing that night, and Dennis and his family endured a traumatic night worrying about Scott's fate; in fact the boy returned safe the next morning, having spent the night at a friend's house without bothering to call home. Whilst there was considerable relief at the child's return, Manson had nonetheless left his terrifying imprint. The bullet incident soon swept through the Beach Boys' circle of friends. Terrified, Dennis started sleeping with a revolver under his pillow, and instructed all house-guests to have some kind of weapon with them when they went to bed.

Meanwhile, Charlie was preparing to leave Los Angeles for good. With the advance party already ensconced in Barker Ranch, a shuttle service of goods and supplies were being transported to the desert on a regular basis. In honour of the Family's new home, several of the girls designed a special jacket. Based on the style of the biker gangs that had frequented Spahn's, they were denim creations with the logo, 'Devil's Witches, Devil's Hole, Death Valley' written in a crescent on the back. By late September, the final nuts and bolts of the relocation had been mostly completed. Manson was evidently in battle mode, and had been witnessed parading around Spahn Ranch with a pump-action shotgun and Shorty Shea's pistols. At this point, old George Spahn had finally had enough, and he ordered Charlie out. Whilst there was little to keep Manson at Spahn's, he initially left Squeaky, Cathy Gillies and Leslie Van Houten behind to keep an eye on things while he moved to the desert.

While the Family were coordinating their relocation back to Death Valley, detectives in Los Angeles were continuing their blind fumble for the Tate and LaBianca murderers. Still harbouring the belief that the deaths were drug-related, they managed to overlook some choice clues – some handed to them on a plate. On 1 September 1969, ten-year-old Stephen Weiss discovered the revolver used by Tex at Cielo Drive at the rear of his family's house in Sherman Oaks, Los Angeles. The boy's father, Bernard, had phoned the Los Angeles Police Department, and carefully detailed the gun's distressed condition, including the missing grip. A policeman came to pick up the weapon from the Weiss's and it was duly logged and filed away. Something of a crime buff, Bernard Weiss followed the ongoing investigation into the Tate/LaBianca murders on television, harbouring a suspicion that the gun was in some way related to the crimes.

Incredibly, forensics had already determined from bullets and the broken gun grip recovered from Cielo Drive that they were looking for a Hi-Standard .22 calibre 'Longhorn' revolver – an unusual weapon. Meanwhile the Hi-Standard .22 calibre 'Longhorn' revolver that Bernard Weiss had handed over was being kept a short distance away in a police repository section in Van Nuys. Adding further embarrassment, a photo-flyer had been sent out to police personnel across North America, describing the weapon and its relation to the Tate crime. By late August, police were still investigating the narcotics lead, with Canadian Police being engaged to check on the movements of certain shady characters who had passed through the Frykowski/Sebring circles.

Amongst the suspects who were called in for questioning were Harris 'Pic' Dawson and Billy Doyle. Aware of the rumours about Sebring's public whipping of Doyle, and the openly hostile threats Dawson had made to Frykowski, detectives hoped to add a personal angle to their theory of a drug-related killing. Police had quickly honed in on Dawson's connection to Cielo Drive; his name had come up during caretaker William Garretson's polygraph test just two days after the murders. However, Dawson had a cast-iron alibi for his movements that weekend, as had Doyle. While there was little doubt that both men had been involved in narcotics, and had been frequent visitors to Cielo Drive, alibis and other circumstantial evidence eventually absolved them of any involvement. Detective Mike McGann, who worked closely on the Tate case, later described to author Greg King the realisation that they were barking up the wrong tree. 'We looked at the drug angle long and hard,' recalls McGann. 'In the end there just wasn't anything there.' The detectives had seen their investigations take them to Hawaii, Mexico and Canada. Meanwhile, right under their noses, Manson and the Family were barricading themselves into their new desert home.

Despite their lack of progress, figures supplied by Los Angeles Police Department show just how exhaustive the Cielo Drive investigations were. During the first month of investigations they had checked the few fingerprints they had against 41,034 records they had on file. Four thousand five hundred individuals had been interviewed. A detailed description of the spectacles found at Cielo Drive had been sent to more than 18,000 opticians, and yet no positive identification had been made.

With Hollywood still in a state of shock, close friends of the Polanskis began to rally around in a show of unified defiance. A consortium of actors comprising Peter Sellers, Warren Beatty, Yul Brunner, and other associates close to Polanski and Tate, stumped up a reward of $25,000 for help in tracking down the murderers. They made it public via a full-page advertisement in the *Los Angeles Times* on 10 September 1969.

'Roman Polanski and friends of the Polanski family offer to pay a $25,000 reward to the person or persons who furnish information leading to the arrest and conviction of the murder or murderers of Sharon Tate, her unborn child and the other four victims.'

To reiterate their desperation, actor Peter Sellers gave an emotional address to the media. The actor's plea for assistance summed up the dismay that had been felt around Hollywood since the murders occurred. 'It's inconceivable that the amount of blood on clothing would have gone unnoticed,' implored an emphatic Sellers. 'So where is the blood-soaked clothing, the knife, the gun, the getaway car? Someone must be able to help, please!'

Addresses by the likes of Sellers only served to bring more pressure on police to deliver some semblance of a breakthrough. Others, though, were working independently to crack the case. Sharon's father, Paul Tate, had resigned his post in Army intelligence the day after the murders at Cielo Drive. Flying back to Los Angeles, Paul Tate began his own investigation into who could have killed his daughter. To fully assimilate himself in the hippie underworld, he grew a beard and let his hair grow, hoping he'd hear any buzz circulating on the network. This small subscript to the tragedy would be picked up later by filmmaker Paul Schrader, who'd commit the story to celluloid in *Hardcore*, the tale of a distressed father seeking revenge on his daughter's seedy killers.

Meanwhile, officers working on the LaBianca case were making considerable progress in their efforts to track down the killers. A report from early September contained the following passage, and in itself showed how close detectives were to Manson.

'Investigation revealed that the singing group, the Beatles', most recent album, no. SWBO 101 [the 'White Album's serial number], has songs titled 'Helter Skelter', and 'Piggies' and 'Blackbird'. The words in the song 'Piggies' make reference to the knife and fork in the bacon [sic]. The words to the song 'Blackbird' frequently say 'Arise', 'Arise', which might be the meaning of 'rise' near the front door.'

Pertinently, this information was not fed to the press. If indeed a Beatles connection had been mooted at this point, it's possible that one of the many people who'd been privy to Manson's Beatlemania might well have made the connection. LaBianca detectives were even closer with their next progress report, naming Charles Manson as a possible suspect on information they'd gleaned from the Sheriff's officers. Remarkably no one, it seems, saw any need to explore the angle further.

chapter 11
Shadows

'Where the eagle flies
We will lie under the sun
Where the eagle flies
We will die, Die to be one
Nights are so dark,
And the winds so cold,
Love's fire is burning
And you can't grow old
Living with the poison ones
Sun-in with the Devil's sons'

From the Charles Manson song, 'Die To Be One'

UNAWARE of the turmoil over at Spahn's Ranch, Brooks Poston had maintained a fairly constant presence in Death Valley since the spring of 1969. Life there had been enlivened considerably by the arrival of twenty-three-year-old student teacher Juanita Wildebush. She was new to the Family, enticed in by Charlie with talk of the abundant possibilities of life at Barker Ranch. In addition to her other charms, Juanita contributed a large quantity of money – $3,000 – to the Family coffers, which was swiftly used to buy two dune buggies. Obediently, she also handed over her Dodge camper van to Manson.

Although Manson assumed the Family had now taken exclusive tenancy of the ranches, they still remained a popular rest point for the occasional prospector or desert voyager who passed by their door. Given the freak weather changes that occurred within Death Valley's microclimate, these visitors often sought sanctuary at the ranch, and were not turned away.

Gold miner Paul Crockett was one of those who'd dropped

into Barker's in search of shelter. Ultimately, he'd play an important role in the unravelling of the Family and, in particular, the deprogramming of Charlie's closest male confident, Paul Watkins.

Crockett had led an eventful and varied life for his forty-four years. He'd begun his working career as a navigator in the US Army Air Corps, and had seen considerable action, flying more than fifty combat missions in the South Pacific. Disturbed by the futility of war, Crockett had begun to seek out a deeper meaning to his life. As a result, he immersed himself in a plethora of philosophies ranging from Christianity through Scientology to the esoteric doctrines of Rosicrucianism. Additionally, he read up on many technological sciences, gaining practical knowledge that would stand him in good stead.

With a keen ability for determining precious metals, Crockett had scoured the mines and valleys of south-west America. Hearing tell of the abundance of minerals to be found in Death Valley, he headed over to check things out for himself. During the summer of 1969, he formed a loose alliance with Bob Berry, a fellow prospector and desert scavenger. Not surprisingly, Barker Ranch became a familiar bolt hole on their excursions throughout the area.

Crockett and Berry first encountered Manson's advance party during April of 1969. With Paul away on one of his numerous errands for Charlie, Brooks Poston and the lusty Juanita Wildebush happily accommodated the prospectors in the ranch. Juanita soon became enamoured with Crockett's mining partner, Bob, and, seeking some privacy, the pair moved into the vacant Family bus at the front of the ranch. As life at Barker's was largely uneventful, Brooks began to join the prospectors on their daily mining expeditions.

During the long evenings at Barker Ranch, Crockett tended to keep to himself, whiling away the time playing Solitaire. During these moments of repose, he'd occasionally eavesdrop on the conversation between Brooks and Juanita. It was only a matter of time before their talk of 'Charlie' this and 'Charlie' that awakened his curiosity. Given his interest in all things mystical, he was intrigued to hear this Manson described in almost religious terms, and he listened intently to the youngsters' colourful tales. Being seasoned to all sorts of cult mumbo-jumbo, Crockett easily figured out the situation. Beneath their reverential attitude, he saw that they were frightened of Charlie. Crockett also gathered from Brooks and Juanita's exchanges, that Paul Watkins was fairly high up in the Family's hierarchy.

Intrigued, Crockett waited until Watkins returned from his trip to Spahn Ranch and then broached the subject of Charlie with him. Given the prospector's weathered appearance, Watkins was initially suspicious of Crockett, assuming he was nothing more than an ignorant miner. However, as Crockett seemed genuinely interested in the enigma that was Manson, Watkins soon poured out his own take on the Family's credo. 'I laid out my rap on Helter Skelter,' Watkins would reveal later. 'Trying to convince Crockett what I felt was "the truth". The shit was coming down, that we were on the verge of an all-out race war, and that the survivors would wind up in Death Valley.'

Regardless of his own interest in mind-expansion and esoteric doctrines, what Crockett heard from this nineteen-year-old spooked him considerably. 'I'd never run into a stranger situation; talking to this kid disturbed me. He kept telling me about life and love and to be free you had to submit to love: he talked about karma and psychic balance, and a lot of what he said was perfectly true and beautiful ... But the words he spoke were not from him, they were from another source. They were from a man he called Charlie.'

While Crockett had only planned to stay a few weeks in Death Valley, the much-anticipated arrival of the Prophet Manson seemed like too great an event to miss, and he abandoned all plans for moving on. 'It seemed like I had found another gold worth mining,' Crockett remarked later.

To try and gauge how deep Charlie's theories ran with Watkins, Crockett started to include young Paul in his daily mining expeditions. Amid the blistering heat of the desert and the deadening routine of hard work, Crockett slowly began to chip away at Watkins. He discovered that – even from a distance – Manson was controlling every thought, word and action of his impressionable acolytes. 'It seemed hard to believe that anyone could be so heavily programmed,' Crockett reflected. 'He [Watkins] told me about the Family, the girls, and about this holocaust, this Armageddon that was going to happen, Helter Skelter.'

At one point, Crockett took Poston and Watkins over to the far reaches of the desert to mine some particularly fertile territory. As the area required some serious attention, they pitched up in a local motel. After work, the trio met to watch TV together. The news was still dominated with the ongoing saga at Cielo Drive, and all three watched the reports intently. When Watkins and Poston mentioned that they recognised the property, Crockett mumbled over the commentary, 'Wouldn't it be somethin' if old Charlie did that.' Watkins dismissed the suggestion as a freak remark, but still he found it hard to completely throw it off.

Crockett sensed a challenge. During his chats with the youngsters, he began to gently query some of Charlie's beliefs, comparing them to his own New Age interests.

Basing his views on metaphysics, Crockett talked at length about the sphere of astral realities and kinetic energy. Crockett was careful to stress the scientific basis of his beliefs, as he was gathering that Manson appealed to his followers' imaginations, rather than their reason. To this small group, Crockett's theories made infinitely more sense than Manson's fantastical prophecies, none of which had yet come true. Crockett's approach found considerable favour with young Paul Watkins. 'Paradoxically, what drew me to Crockett was his indifference,' recalled Watkins. 'He wasn't really trying to influence me or convince me. He didn't tell me anything unless I asked him.'

It wasn't long before Paul, Brooks and Juanita began looking to Crockett as an alternative leader. Sensing their fear of Charlie and for once using the kind of theories favoured by Manson, the miner told them that he'd engineered a psychic force field over the desert to protect them from any destructive forces. As a result, their tongues began to loosen, and Manson's hold over them seemed to be weakening. However, for someone as integral to Charlie's organisation as Watkins, Crockett's words caused great confusion. Lost amid a whirl of loyalties, Paul decided that he had to rejoin Charlie at Spahn's and get involved once more in the preparations for Helter Skelter. Feigning indifference, Crockett presented Watkins with a challenge; suggesting Paul ask Charlie to release him from all his 'agreements'. That way Paul would be able to see what his relationship with Manson was based on: mutual respect or coercion.

During the twelve-hour drive from Barker Ranch to Spahn Ranch, Watson thought over what Crockett had said. In the end, he decided to present Manson with the challenge, and see how he'd respond. Leaping out of the truck at Spahn's, Watkins asked Charlie to be released from any agreements he had with him. First bemused, then angry, Manson couldn't believe that his right-hand man appeared to be in the throes of defecting. He laughed scornfully at the news that Crockett had placed a psychic energy field over the entrance to the desert to repel negativity. Sensing Charlie's fury, Watkins shot out of Spahn's and headed back out to the desert.

Manson was extremely curious to see what powers this Crockett had that enabled him to win over his loyal followers. With renewed energy he began to rally his forces towards the desert. Hard-liners Bruce Davis, Tex Watson and Brenda were sent ahead as an advance party; their mission was to inform Crockett that Manson wanted a meeting with him. With his minions leading the way, Charlie followed behind in a dune buggy.

Despite Watkins' fears of a confrontation, Crockett was eager to meet up with Charlie and see what all the fuss was about. Manson's advance party soon made its way to Barker Ranch. With Manson's tongue evidently doing the talking, Bruce Davis coyly asked Crockett if any psychic force fields could be lifted momentarily for Charlie's expected arrival. Crockett agreed and, with all astral barriers lifted, Manson was clear to approach the ranch.

Manson soon arrived with a gaggle of girls riding in the rear. With his usual effusive charm, Charlie bounded into the ranch and greeted everyone (including Crockett) with considerable warmth; although it was obvious that Charlie's purpose was to check out the miner and his rival powers of persuasion.

While Crockett quietly weighed up the scene, Charlie started on his familiar ravings about Helter Skelter. While his coterie of admirers listened in awe, the miner appeared unmoved, and occupied himself playing Solitaire. Sensing that Crockett was engaged in his own mind-game, Manson took a knife to Brooks Poston's throat, and threatened to kill him. Although this sort of stunt had become familiar in Family circles, it was startling to those unused to such theatrics. Crockett, however, was unfazed.

Once Charlie had finished threatening Brooks, he sat down next to Crockett and attempted to quiz the miner on his beliefs. Crockett revealed little. At first Manson was intrigued, but then Crockett's taciturn stance began to make him angry. Leaping up, he took Watkins outside, and told him of the Helter Skelter murders that had happened in LA since he'd moved to the desert. Watkins was unsure whether this was bluff. Watkins could see that Crockett had failed to be rattled by Manson's histrionics, so now Charlie had to up the stakes. One thing Watkins was increasingly aware of, however, was that Charlie had already gone to an extreme place with his behaviour. 'By that time,' Watkins later recalled, 'Charlie had created a void around himself; he had fallen "into the hole" of his own madness. He could only grow if he were challenged, and by then, there was no one to do this – just a band of followers programmed to heed his every whim. Just how far they were programmed to go (and had gone), I had no idea.'

To tempt the male dissidents at Barker's, Charlie would send the occasional sensual army of girls over to tempt them back, and yet, under Crockett's quiet command, no bait was ever taken. In a further attempt to drag Paul Watkins back to Charlie's side, he was invited over to hear tapes of the music they'd made together, but Watkins refused the offer.

Manson's followers even attempted to unsettle the Barker Ranch tenants by Creepy-Crawling onto their premises. One particular night, Charlie, Tex and Bruce Davis clambered into the others' sleeping quarters on all fours. With Crockett managing events with his customary cool, Charlie was forced to leave before any fun could be had. As his rage increased, Manson started brandishing guns and other weaponry in and around Barker Ranch, and yet the dissidents still remained unimpressed.

To prevent these threats escalating into violence, a brief ceasefire was brokered, allowing Crockett and Manson to meet up and look for some common ground. While Crockett was deeply sceptical of what lay behind Charlie's bluster, Manson respected the miner's 'no-fear' approach to life. During this brief respite, Crockett and Manson walked off to engage in deep discussion, which by all accounts lasted a couple of days. Despite Manson's offer to Crockett to weld their considerable powers into one, Manson's angry outlook clashed heavily with Crockett's gentler nature.

A deal of sorts was brokered, and with the tension cooling between the two parties, Charlie could now start his new desert life in earnest. The last of the Family stragglers had now been bussed into the desert, and Manson began to move towards his vision of oneness, trying to penetrate deeper into the Family's collective psyche. In an attempt to get his followers to assimilate themselves fully with their new environment, Charlie took small groups out to the desert and forced them to allow scorpions and snakes to crawl over them. As Manson had always favoured animals over humans, the few dogs that had come with them to the desert were fed first, with Family members having to wait until the animals had finished before they themselves could eat. On other occasions, he'd lecture to the group about detaching themselves from pain. To demonstrate this, Manson spent a whole night stark naked, as the cold desert winds battered his body. He emerged the next morning, barely dented by the experience. Also during this time he sent Kitty Lutesinger, a pregnant Family member on a three-day survivalist hike across the desert. Remarkably, she survived, but, like a few of the others, came back determined to escape at the earliest moment. Lutesinger had become something of a whipping post for Manson; he had repeatedly threatened her because of her loyalties to Bobby Beausoleil and was deeply suspicious that she'd transfer her allegiances to Crockett.

Manson's nightly lectures around the desert campfire made frequent references to his oneness with desert animals; in particular, the coyote. As Manson was fast assuming a feral appearance to match his already wild psyche, he drew numerous parallels with the desert dog, attempting to validate his own splintering paranoia. 'Have you ever seen the coyote in the desert?' he asked his followers. 'Watching, tuned in, completely aware. Christ on the cross; the coyote in the desert. It's the same thing, man. The coyote is beautiful. He moves through the desert delicately, aware of everything, looking around. He hears every sound, smells every smell, sees everything that moves. He's in a state of total paranoia, and total paranoia is total awareness.'

Despite his increasingly fraught behaviour, Charlie still wasn't beyond a bit of smoke and mirrors. One day, he took a group out to one of the farthermost reaches of the desert for one of his assimilation practices. En route, they happened upon a dying bird. According to those present, Charlie picked it up and blew over it. Within seconds the bird came back to life and flew off.

Such divine acts aside, there were other darker practices taking place. With the revolution imminent, the murder classes first inaugurated at Spahn's were continued in the desert. Manson's favourite, Stephanie Schram, recalled that those present were given a knife and tutored by Tex on the correct way to dispatch any advancing forces.

According to Stephanie, it appears Manson was fully involved in these tutorials as well. 'Charlie held classes for the girls on how to kill people, and had asked different girls if they could kill the "Pigs" from the city. Then Charlie showed them how to stab people in the neck and stated if they were going to stab someone, they should try to cut the person from ear to ear; also to stab them in either ear or eyes and then wiggle the knife around to get as many of the vital organs as possible.'

Absolutely terrified by this turn of events, and of the numerous beatings Charlie was inflicting on the girls, Stephanie began to plot her own escape from the desert.

Barbara Hoyt was another young follower harbouring severe doubts about her life in the desert. Initially, her enquiring nature was excited by the retreat to Death Valley, yet after a few weeks with little to occupy her mind, she began to tire of the monotony. Now that the Family had drained their food supplies, they were living predominately on the scant pickings the desert had to offer. Soon, the predominant menu of figs and pomegranates began to wear down their metabolisms, making the most basic of tasks impossible. Hoyt had bonded with the other young girls of the tribe, and they all agreed that Charlie was heading off towards decidedly darker zones.

'In the desert, [this] group of young girls became quite close, because we got more afraid of Charlie … ' Barbara later said. 'He was getting demanding. He was doing things like making us chant. He'd have us sit in a circle and chant "Om!" He'd walk around the circle and if you weren't doing it the way he wanted, he'd let you have it in the head with a stick.'

Adding to the growing disharmony, the fragile peace brokered between Manson and Crockett had now broken down. Not surprisingly, at the core of this was Charlie's paranoia, now raging hideously out of control. Of late, he was prone to explode at the slightest challenge to his authority, and Crockett's presence maddened him beyond all reason. In those months after the killings, there was an ever-present sense that something was going to break. Adding to the tension, sections of Charlie's flock had started looking for an escape route.

Barbara Hoyt recalled: 'We were hungry and we were irritable and we were hot, and we were thirsty, and there was nothing to eat … So people were starting to get irritable. I was certainly losing any love I felt … The fantasies seemed to disappear … Things weren't fun … It didn't feel like a Family any more, it felt like a prison.'

With between thirty and forty Family members shuffling between the ranches, Charlie had been keen to isolate the killers in the Tate–LaBianca massacres as best he could. Tex had initially made his way up to the desert, but only maintained a intermittent presence. Evidently, the brazen stance he'd assumed following the murders faltered as his psyche began to crash around him.

'I was losing myself,' he later admitted. 'My individual thinking, like I was becoming Charles Manson and I was becoming the girls. I remember we could look into each other's face and it would be the same face; my face would be Manson's and the girls' faces would be Manson's and just have one face.'

Sadie had initially avoided the desert retreat, instead spending time in Venice carousing with some bikers. High on the promise of lawless isolation, she'd brought a couple of these new friends over to the desert to party. Following an audience with Charlie, they promptly disappeared. According to Sadie, they were 'done in.' Adding to the intrigue was the fate of a young backpacker who'd stopped in at the ranch partway through a hike across the valley. After allegedly spending a few nights with the Family, the hiker mysteriously disappeared; his backpack left behind. When Clem was quizzed on the lad's disappearance, he reportedly replied, 'He got homesick.' Another, anonymous female who happened upon the encampment had attached herself to the Family. Her presence had allegedly heightened Charlie's paranoia; according to one witness, she went for a walk with Tex and Manson and was never seen again.

Resting one afternoon, Barbara Hoyt overheard Sadie revealing in graphic detail to Ruth Ann Morehouse her role in the Cielo Drive murders. On hearing Morehouse sigh, 'I can't wait to get my first piggy, I can't wait,' Hoyt took her chance and ran off with Sherry Cooper, another youngster on the edge of the Family. When Manson discovered that the two girls had escaped, he took off in search of them. The runaways spent a torturous few hours crossing the desert, and eventually found their way to a nearby town. Manson discovered the pair the next morning having breakfast in a local diner. In front of a room of witnesses, the women told Charlie they wanted to leave. In an act of false generosity, Charlie handed them $20, and told them they were welcome back at any time. However, in reality their cards were marked: Charlie told all and sundry that they would pay heavily for their defection.

Inyo County police wasn't used to dealing with rogue elements like Charlie and the Family. A few park rangers were employed to monitor comings and goings in the area, and they kept in close contact with the police in case there was any serious trouble. Despite Manson's strenuous efforts to keep a low profile, word of the caravan of vehicles making their way in and out of desert created quite a buzz. Although the odd hippie had been known to pitch up in the area, they'd normally move on without too much resistance. However, the rumblings about Charlie and Co. soon propelled both the park rangers and police into action.

As environmentalism was one part of Charlie's rage against society, he'd take every opportunity to attack anything he considered an enemy of the planet, blissfully ignoring the damage the Family's own vehicles had wrought on their desert home. Given that the arid temperatures in Death Valley could precipitate terrible fires, the authorities used a large earth-moving machine to dig huge gullies to prevent any blaze from spilling out. Additionally, when the ferocious storms hit the desert basin, the machine could score emergency channels to drain the water. In Manson's skewed logic, these deep trenches were not just an environmental abomination, but also a deliberate attempt to stop the Family's trucks reaching their hideouts.

On one balmy afternoon in mid-September, Manson drove down to where the machine was situated. With him were Tex, Gypsy and Kitty Lutesinger. The car they were driving was a Toyota four-wheel drive, which Brenda had rented and then conveniently forgotten to return. When they arrived, Manson ordered the girls to fill one of these ditches. Meanwhile, Charlie and Tex busied themselves stripping the earth-loader of its fuel and parts. When they'd scavenged anything useful, Charlie tossed a match in the remains of the fuel tank, setting off a massive explosion.

When Park Ranger Richard Powell discovered the charred remains on 19 September 1969, he was saddened to see it was damaged beyond repair. The machine had been the pride of the park authorities, bought for $30,000. As Powell scanned the area around the wreckage, he seized on a matchbox that had evidently been discarded, as well as spotting 4x4 tyre tracks pointing east, in the direction of Barker Ranch. Whilst scouring the area, Powell conferred with the locals about who might be responsible. The tight-knit community had long been aware of the Family's presence in the desert. Of late, they'd become suspicious of their activities, and intimidated by their increasingly anarchic behaviour.

Strongly suspecting arson, Powell reported his findings to local police. On his own initiative, a few days later, Powell decided to return to the area to check for any further clues. On his way there, at a point in the desert known as Hail and Hall Canyon,

Powell pulled over a red Toyota. Inside he found three 'scantily clad' women and a 'hippie-type' male. Sensing they were up to no good, he would normally have run a check on the car, but they were deep in the valley and his radio was out of signal, so he'd had to let the party go. Nonetheless, he made a note of the car's plate: California, 36309.

Back at base, Powell checked out the registration and found it belonged to Gayle Beausoleil, wife of murder-suspect Bobby. Powell duly reported his findings to Dennis Cox, the deputy of the local Sheriff's Department. Powell and Cox went on their own independent recce of the area, and talked to some local prospectors who'd run into the Family. On discovering that large groups of hippies were intimidating the locals, Cox lobbied for a major operation to assess the situation. However, the authorities weren't interested in allotting considerable funds to investigate arson and car theft. Undeterred, Powell doggedly continued with his investigations.

Powell soon found an ally in highway patrol officer, James Purcell. He accompanied Ranger Powell to check on both Myers and Barker Ranch on 29 September. They found two of Charlie's girls sitting out front, who told them that the owner of the property had gone on a shopping errand and would be back later. As they left the ranch, officials came across a group of seven women, hiding in bushes at the rear of the ranch. Most were nude. On further inspection, they also found what appeared to be a graveyard of old, ransacked vehicles.

The officers made their way back to file reports at police headquarters. On their way they met Paul Crockett and Brooks Poston. They had agreed to Charlie's request to retrieve a truckload of vehicle parts that had been dumped at the edge of the desert. Quizzed by police, Crockett seized the moment, spilling the whole pot of beans on Manson and the Family. In addition to tales of drugs, sex orgies and brainwashing, they revealed that an enormous armoury of weapons was being stockpiled in preparation for a bloody war. This Armageddon was to be styled on Rommel's desert campaign of World War Two, with dune buggies replacing Panzers as the preferred vehicles. Leading this advance was Manson, who was calling himself Jesus Christ, and was anticipating hordes of new followers.

It may seem out of character that Crockett would side with police over Manson and the Family, but by this point Crockett was frightened for his life, and the safety of his young cohorts. Once back at base, the officers disseminated and passed on their information. This included reports of the mass of stolen cars they'd witnessed dumped around the ranches; many of them with their number plates all switched round.

The grand auto-theft investigations also threw up other disturbing clues, not least the discovery of a blue Volkswagen tipped over a cliff. The owner, Phillipo Tenerelli, was listed as a missing person from the Culver City area. On 1 October 1969, he was found in a motel at Bishop, dead from shotgun wounds in what looked like a suicide. It later transpired that Tenerelli had partied with the Family on occasions, earning himself the name 'Dago' on account of his Latin descent. Allegedly, he'd been part of the Family's narcotics dealing and was also linked to the 'Gypsy Joker' biker gang fraternity. The fact that Tenerelli's car was found spattered with blood threw his 'suicide' into question.

Back at the ranch, Paul Watkins was worried he might be next. On hearing Bruce Davis brag about Shorty Shea's bloody murder, Watkins prepared to take his leave. Bagging a ride over to Las Vegas with Bruce, the pair hit the road; ostensibly travelling to collect a large consignment of petrol paid for with stolen petrol cards. Once in Las Vegas, Watkins managed to lose Davis long enough to call police officer Don Ward back in Inyo County, and arrange a rendezvous with Crockett and Poston. Manson had already declared a fatwa on Ward for investigations he'd made into the Family's dealings during an earlier trip to Barker Ranch.

Under interrogation, the trio handed over key information concerning Charlie and the Family's movements, including the details of Shorty Shea's death they'd heard from Bruce Davis. Watkins was most voluble under interrogation, identifying many Family members, their pseudonyms and the depth of their involvement with Manson. This collusion with police didn't stop Watkins from hooking up again with the Family soon after, but ultimately his betrayal would cost him dearly.

Working on information fed to them by Watkins, Crockett and Poston, Sheriff's officers and park rangers made their way up towards the desert ranches. They didn't need to wait long to gather some collateral evidence. As was their style, some of Manson's girls were out basking naked in the sun in the hills surrounding the homestead. On seeing uniforms, they scattered into the distance. Further along the track, the rangers saw what appeared to be Manson roaming towards one of the ranches. Manson saw them too. Sensing an intrusion, Charlie grabbed a shotgun and blasted four shots in the direction of the officers. Mindful of what they'd heard earlier about his huge arsenals of weaponry, the officers decided to retreat back to base. With news of Beausoleil's murder charge now in the police domain, there was a sense that this was to be a much more serious task than evicting a gang of crazy hippies.

Manson would later claim that, prior to the rangers' arrival, a large coyote had come up to him and warned him of the advancing police. 'He stopped just in front of me and was looking at me dead ahead with no fear,' Charlie reported. 'He kept it up for maybe half a minute, and a few times he kept looking back over in the direction he had come. And then I was looking out that way and I saw some rangers. They were coming across the desert floor. The big coyote was warning me.'

Whatever the merits of Charlie's story, it was evident that Manson was in no mood to be arrested, and he hot-footed it out of the desert. With him was Bruce Davis and five other men, all eager to avoid what looked like being a major raid. Nonetheless, in his absence, Manson instructed his followers to maintain a twenty-four-hour watch over their plot, and to retaliate if necessary. Later, one of the girls revealed that Charlie left instructions that, if a small party of police arrived, they should attack their faces and ears with knives.

Manson was right. A comprehensive raid was planned on Barker Ranch for early in the morning of 10 October. With forces drawn from rangers, sheriff's officers and the highway patrol, a team of over thirty men were briefed on what to expect. Armed with information from sheriff's officers in Los Angeles, they were all suitably equipped for what they believed might well become a pitched battle. With a twelve-mile trip through the winding corridors of the desert, it was decided that a dawn raid would be the best way to take the Family by surprise.

Drawing on reconnaissance assembled from a vast array of maps and photographs, officers easily penetrated the lookouts that were scatted around the hilltops overlooking the ranches. Although Manson had commandeered a night watch to keep an eye out for police, his sentry guards were poorly equipped, both mentally and physically, for the task. Officers first happened upon Clem and another character by the name of Rocky fast asleep in a gully some distance from the ranch. Despite being in possession of a sawn-off shotgun, they offered no resistance when arrested. In one of the ramshackle lookout points overlooking the ranch, Katie, Leslie and Gypsy were apprehended, and in their bleary state, they turned themselves in fairly easily.

Regardless of the sloppiness of Manson's first defences, officers were impressed with how advanced these observation points were, as radio telephones, telescopes and other surveillance equipment were uncovered. With the lookouts now secure, police began an assault on both ranches. Again, there was little resistance from Family members, and police easily apprehended ten girls and three males. They didn't seem much like hardened desert warriors. The girls giggled and shed their clothes in front of the officers. In an attempt to unnerve them further, several others decided to urinate in front of the police, just as Manson had directed them to do. On inspection, the inhabitants seemed to have been badly weathered by the harsh environment; most sported huge sores and wounds that had failed to heal in the desert sun. Most upsetting for the officers was the condition of the two children in Family care, both suffering from sunburn and malnutrition.

With those arrested handcuffed to each other, police began a search of the area to retrieve any incriminating evidence, and to look for any clues that might lead them to Manson. As expected, they found a mass of stolen cars and parts, as well as a small armoury of weapons, but nothing relating to Charlie's whereabouts. By dusk, the tribe was escorted under police supervision through Golar Wash and towards police headquarters.

The group was charged with a variety of offences, but there was still the matter of Manson, highly conspicuous by his absence.

As the first contingent of Family members was being charged at Inyo County headquarters, somehow a message made its way through to Charlie. However, after being told that the charges were car theft, possession of firearms and other petty crimes, Manson was more irritated than anything else by the raid. Aware that any operation in the desert took a considerable amount of manpower, he assumed that it would now all be over and he would be safe to return to the ranch. Furthermore, nearly two months since the killing spree in LA, Charlie was feeling as if he'd already got away with murder.

Feeling invincible, Charlie set off back to the desert. However he was wrong about the local police. Despite having a good dozen of his followers in custody, Manson was still their prime suspect for the earth-mover arson, and several other offences relating to car theft and arms possession. Unbeknownst to Charlie, a further raid was planned for the evening of 12 October.

Charlie arrived back at the ranch in the early afternoon of 12 October. By 6.30 p.m., he'd gathered together eleven members of the Family. Several who'd escaped capture had already drifted back and were eager to fill Charlie in on the raid. After the debriefing, Manson and a few die-hards sat round a table in the lounge, while others retreated outside to the surrounding hills.

Knowing that the desert acoustics would quickly signal their arrival, the second battalion of police officers made the majority of their journey on foot. Arriving at dusk, they surrounded Barker Ranch and waited to make their move. In a two-pronged attack, officers entered from the front and rear of the ranch simultaneously. With guns trained on those around the table, they easily apprehended this second contingent of Family members, including Bruce Davis and Dianne Lake. Manson's feral sense of imminent danger had seen him leap into the bathroom before the police had even entered the property. Despite careful police searches of the ranch and surrounding buildings, he couldn't be found. It seemed that their main quarry had escaped again.

Officer James Purcell was not, however, prepared to give up that easily. He'd already invested a lot of time on this case, and he couldn't shake his hunch that Charlie was somewhere on the premises, so he embarked on one last, meticulous sweep of the property. Working his way through the ranch house, he went through to the tiny bathroom at the back. With the only light coming from a candle lit in a small jar, Purcell scanned around the bare area with his torch. At the back of the room was a heavily distressed cupboard, measuring no more than three-feet square. Despite the gloom, Purcell, caught sight of a straggly piece of hair coming out of the door. On further inspection, the officer saw two fingers attempting to hold the cupboard shut. Purcell stepped back and waited. Wrongly anticipating that the coast was clear, a small, ragged man crept out of the cupboard. On seeing armed Officer Purcell, Charlie greeted him with a flippant 'Hi', before being handcuffed and led away.

Charlie and those arrested at the ranch were charged with a variety of offences, ranging from possession of firearms and auto theft to the destruction of the earth-mover. Despite the lengths he went to avoid arrest, Manson joined the rest of those captured fairly peaceably. However, before they were carted off, Manson begged to go back and retrieve a rucksack that was still inside the ranch. In it, he claimed, were various essential items of his. Despite his pleas, the request was denied. When police located the bag in their searches, its contents proved highly illuminating.

Charlie and the others were handcuffed together and driven to the entrance of Golar Wash. Taken through the hazardous canyon on foot, they were then driven over to Independence to join the first posse already in custody. As star captive, Manson was afforded a large retinue of police to keep watch over him during the trip. To while away the long, bumpy journey, Manson took the opportunity to spill his Helter Skelter theory to officers keeping watch. While Charlie's ravings about black uprisings and Armageddon were of little interest to his captors, what startled them was hearing Manson's acolytes muttering 'Amen' every time Manson paused for breath. Equally disturbing to police was the power Charlie held over his followers, especially when one happened to speak out of turn. As one of the arresting officers noted, 'Charlie would simply look at them and immediately they would fall silent . . . the amazing part was how obvious the results were without a word being spoken.'

On arrival at police headquarters, this second contingent of Family members was processed and sent down to the cells. Officers, working off the myriad of information supplied to them, were taking no chances with Charlie's splintered persona, and booked him variously as 'Manson, Charles M', 'Benson' (a pseudonym Charlie was known to use) and 'Jesus Christ, God'. As before, the mood amongst the prisoners was convivial, with most believing that they'd be free before long. During the Family's incarceration, the women did their utmost to make their warders blush. During the day, they'd shamelessly remove their clothing in the prison yard, while by night they'd yell like coyotes from their cells. Hearing them, Manson would howl back in gleeful response. In their cells, the woman demanded a supply of peanut butter and honey, for what they described as a 'purification ceremony'. This anarchic larking was wholly engineered by Manson, convinced that, within hours, the doors to their cells would be thrown open. Bolstering this belief, ten of those arrested over the two raids were released the following morning without charge. However, for the fourteen charged on twenty felons, a total bail of $263,000 was set. Suddenly it wasn't a game any more; with such an impossibly high figure, Manson and the others stood little hope of release.

Although the raid had proved successful in capturing Manson, two of the youngest Family girls, Bobby Beausoleil's ex, Kitty Lutesinger, and Charlie's favourite, Stephanie Schram, had fled. They'd witnessed first-hand Manson's accelerating rage and, having both been threatened by Charlie, they were terrified that he would hurt them soon. Both girls were also pregnant. The chaos of the raids gave the girls the opportunity to run away, and they'd trekked overnight to a nearby freeway, albeit with Clem and another Family member in hot pursuit.

The following morning, exhausted and dehydrated, the girls flagged down a routine patrol, and begged to be taken into custody. They were driven to police headquarters at Independence, and questioned by detectives about Manson and Barker Ranch. As a formality, Inyo County Police checked wanted lists for both of the girls. On 13 October, word was relayed from Los Angeles that Lutesinger had long been sought by LA sheriff's officers to see if she could give them any leads on the death of Gary Hinman. When Lutesinger confirmed her connection to Beausoleil, all hell broke loose.

Within hours of Lutesinger's revelation, officers attached to the Gary Hinman case, Paul Whitely and Charles Guenther, were driving the 200-odd miles to question the girl. During a four-hour interview, Lutesinger revealed to the detectives that she'd heard that Manson had sent Sadie and Bobby Beausoleil over to Hinman's house to call in a debt. Once there, a fight had ensued. Lutesinger also claimed that she'd overheard Sadie boast that she'd been involved in a fight with a man who'd pulled her hair, and that she'd retaliated and stabbed him in the legs. It was soon confirmed that Sadie was in fact Susan Atkins, and had already been booked under the pseudonym, 'Donna Mae Powell'. Lutesinger also implicated Mary Brunner in the murder.

Initially, Kitty Lutesinger's comment about Sadie 'stabbing' a man 'in the legs' confused police, as Hinman's body bore no evidence of a leg wound. In fact, the gossip Kitty had heard referred to Sadie's attack on Voyteck Frykowski during the massacre at Cielo Drive. Nonetheless, Lutesinger's revelation was enough to have Sadie thoroughly investigated.

Although she was initially guarded, detectives skilfully manoeuvred Sadie into talking about life with the Family, engaging with some idle chitchat about their glory days at Spahn's and the people she met there. Eventually, they steered the conversation towards Gary Hinman. Working on information supplied to them by Kitty Lutesinger, detectives lied to Sadie, claiming that Bobby Beausoleil had implicated her in Hinman's killing. In addition they claimed that, on searching Gary's Topanga Canyon property following his death, a fingerprint of hers had been found. Sadie retaliated, stating she'd heard that some black men had killed Hinman. Tired of her evident lies, one of the detectives snapped, shouting, 'Stop kidding us, Sadie. You killed him!' Cornered, Sadie retracted her initial story; claiming that, although she and Beausoleil had been at Hinman's house to collect some money he'd inherited, she didn't know who actually killed him.

Whilst she continued to plead her innocence, detectives nonetheless booked Sadie on suspicion of being involved with his murder. This prolonged her custody, and gave them ample time to investigate the other leads that were now starting to emerge. In Inyo County, Manson, Leslie Van Houten and several other Family members were still being held; the other members of the Family were released, however, and swiftly scattered. Although several Family members had by now informed on Charlie, police were still no closer to making a connection with the Cielo Drive murders.

Awaiting his chance to walk free yet again, Charlie still felt invincible. 'At the time of the arrest,' Manson recalled later, 'I thought most of us, including myself, would be back on the streets in a matter of days. But the worm had finally turned.'

chapter 12
Game

'I am not allowed to be a man in your society. I am considered inadequate and incompetent to speak or defend myself in your court. I have "X'd" myself from your world. The words you have used to trick the people are not mine. I do not accept what you call justice. The lie you live in is falling and I am not part of it. You have murdered the world in the name of Jesus Christ. I stand with my X with my life, with my God and by myself. My faith in me is stronger than all your armies, governments, gas chambers or anything you may want to do to me.'

Statement by Charles Manson, 24th July 1970

'The only performance that makes it, that really makes it. That makes it all the way, is the one that achieves madness.'

Mick Jagger as Turner, from the film *Performance* (1970)

ON 13 October 1969, a four-seater plane transported Sadie back to Los Angeles and into the secure custody of the Sybil Brand Institute for Women. Arraigned for her involvement in Gary Hinman's murder, she'd now have to wait while the case was prepared against her. At that time, the prison had quite a reputation. As one journalist noted, 'The lesbians of southern California love it. Thirty days at Sybil Brand compares favourably to a free, all-expenses-paid romantic ocean cruise for the heterosexual world.'

Since the Family had a long history of wheedling their way out of charges, Sadie believed that her imprisonment would only be temporary. In a remand cell awaiting transfer to a prison dormitory, Sadie soon made the acquaintance of Nancy Jordan, a stunning redhead doing time for heroin possession. As Jordan was put in the next bed, the pair chatted to each other through the long nights. Within a short while, Sadie begun to trust Jordan; and started imparting details about her involvement in the Tate massacre. Not surprisingly Jordan was intrigued, but kept the information close to her chest, remarking, 'In jail, if you don't want your throat slit, you don't snitch.' There were others that Sadie spilled the beans to, but they were either too scared or too incredulous to take it further.

Following processing, Sadie was transferred into the general prison population. There, she soon made the acquaintance of thirty-one-year-old Ronnie Howard, a seasoned prostitute with a history of drug use and a string of aliases. This time Howard was back in jail for forging a prescription, but was pleased to find herself in the same wing as Virginia Graham. The self-styled 'celebrity hooker' was in for trying to pass bad cheques and a violation of her parole conditions. The pair had built up a friendly relationship, making their joint incarceration that little bit sweeter.

Even for hardened carousers like Howard and Graham, Sadie's carefree behaviour around the prison dormitory was astounding. Someone charged with murder would usually cut a solemn figure, yet Sadie seemed amused by it all. In among the hardened jail population, she made for a peculiar sight. Constantly dancing to the sound of own beat, she'd bend over, proudly showing off her naked nether regions – underwear long having been banished as an unnecessary restriction. According to reports, Atkins freely shared her body with many of the female prisoners, earning herself the nickname 'Crazy Sadie' in the process. When the shock-value of her behaviour wore off, Crazy Sadie was left very much to her own devices. Sensing her alienation, Graham and Howard befriended her.

'When I first saw her, she was doing cartwheels up and down the aisle,' recalls Graham. 'She was in a total state of happiness. Truthfully, I thought she was in for a drug bust.'

It wasn't long before Sadie's tongue became as loose as her sexual morals. With a childlike innocence, she began to put all her trust in these older women, who had taken her under their wing.

In return, Ronnie and Virginia were curious to see what motivated this complex creature. Early in November 1968, Virginia Graham and Sadie were employed to perform some messenger duties for prison officials. While waiting for assignments, the pair began to talk about the circumstances of their imprisonment.

While Virginia imparted the relatively mundane tale of her arrest, the story she got in return was highly illuminating. Sadie coolly revealed that she was charged with Gary Hinman's murder, and described her active role in his death. She then began to talk about Manson, explaining Charlie's 'Christ meets Satan' persona, and the bonds of free love within the Family. Graham's eyebrows shot up even further when Sadie confided, in reverent tones, how Manson was going to lead the Family to the hole in the desert, where they would prepare to rule the new world following Helter Skelter. Whilst psychedelic hippie-chatter wasn't uncommon in late-1960s California, Graham was intrigued by the way Sadie talked about Manson as if he were a god.

Amidst these ramblings, a confidence soon emerged, with Graham's genial understanding drawing more and more out of the excitable Sadie. As their chats became more frequent, Sadie began to give more details about Hinman's killing, becoming visibly excited as she spilt the gory details. Although aggrieved at the thought that Beausoleil might have implicated her in the murder, Sadie was confident that if she acted crazy enough, she'd be excused of all charges. As their chats continued, Sadie coyly hinted to Graham that she was also involved in some other murders that were far, far more sensational.

Intrigued, Graham conferred with Howard, and they both agreed to pump Sadie for more information. During the night of 6 November 1969, with the attentions of the guards elsewhere, Graham tried to draw Sadie into a discussion about the crimes she'd been hinting at. Graham was careful not to appear too keen, but Sadie was only too happy to boast about her celebrity murders.

Virginia Graham said later: 'I told her that I didn't care particularly what she had done, but I didn't think it was advisable for her to talk so much. She told me that she wasn't really worried about it. And she also told me that she could tell by looking at me, my eyes, that I was a kind person; and that she wasn't worried about it anyway. And that the police were on the wrong track about some murders. And I said, "What do you mean?" And she said to me, "The murders at Benedict Canyon." And just for a moment I didn't quite snap to what she meant, and I said, "Benedict Canyon?" And she said, "Yes. The Tate murders." And she said, "You know who did it, don't you?" And I said, "No, I don't." And she said, "Well, you are looking at her."'

With excruciating candour, Sadie revealed exactly what had occurred at Cielo Drive on the night of 8 August. Such was her excitement, Graham had to tell Sadie to lower her voice, lest she alerted the guards. With Graham vainly attempting to contain her shock, Sadie's descriptions became more and more graphic. 'You have to have real love in your heart to do this for people,' Sadie told a stunned Graham, as she described each killing with increasing relish. Becoming more and more animated, she recalled how she'd held Sharon Tate down, and assisted in her death. Following the slaughter, Sadie described how she'd tasted Tate's blood and had wanted to cut out the victims' eyeballs and squash them against the walls of the house but 'didn't have time'. Sadie offered no expression of remorse, saying that after the slayings she'd felt 'at peace' with herself.

Sadie told Graham that she wasn't concerned that she'd lost her knife in the fracas, or that she might have left prints at Cielo Drive. 'My spirit was so strong that obviously it didn't even show up or they would have me by now.' As motivation for the crime, Sadie mentioned Terry Melcher's brief courtship of Charlie's musical talents, claiming that the producer was far too interested in the money side to work with the likes of Manson. If these revelations weren't enough, she informed Graham that following the massacre at the Tate house, the gang had gone on to commit the murders at the LaBianca house the following night.

Shocked at her frankness, Graham asked Sadie why she'd got involved with such horrendous crimes. Parroting Manson's credo, Sadie replied, 'We wanted to do a crime that would shock the world [so] that the world would have to stand up and take notice.' Still agog at the confession, Graham asked what drove her to kill a pregnant woman. Sadie was unequivocal, reiterating her position. 'I thought you understood?' she told Graham. 'I loved her, and in order for me to kill her I was killing part of myself when I killed her.' Later, Sadie told Graham that the brutal stabbings 'would help release the souls of the victims.'

Still not sure whether to believe Sadie's lurid stories, Graham conferred with Ronnie Howard, and together they decided to employ some subterfuge to check whether Sadie really had visited Cielo Drive. Coincidentally, Graham had previously visited the house and was familiar with its layout. When Graham asked her specific questions about the property's decor, Sadie was able to reply in such convincing detail that it seemed certain she really had visited the Polanski-Tate house.

Oblivious to her listeners' misgivings, Sadie continued with her gory narration. Revealing a shopping list of celebrities that had been lined up for execution, Sadie was happy to reveal to Graham who they were planning on targeting next. Whether this was just bravado, we may never know, but evidently considerable thought had gone into compiling the list.

Actress Elizabeth Taylor was one celebrity signalled out for annihilation, as was her then husband, Richard Burton. Although Sadie was in awe of the Taylor's movie-idol looks, she believed she 'deserved to die' in a particularly gruesome fashion to 'bring out the real beauty in her'. To facilitate this 'beauty', Sadie planned to poke out her eyes, and then take a knife, heat its blade, and impress the legend 'Helter Skelter' on the side of her face. Once done with the couple, the Family proposed to send Taylor's ex, Eddie Fisher, Burton's penis and Taylor's eyes in a glass bottle.

Although never a fixture on the Family's musical play-list, Sadie admired Welsh crooner Tom Jones's sexual physique enormously. However, other Family members were upset at the amount of fame someone like Jones had acquired, especially after Charlie's musical talents had been ignored by the music industry. To correct this, they'd planned an explosive finale to the Welsh singer's life, with Sadie naturally at the helm.

Ronnie Howard remembered the details: 'She wanted to make love to him [and] right in the midst of the climax while he was making love to her, she wanted to stab him; she wanted to see the look on his face. She said, "Wow, that would be something to see."'

However, it appeared that the Family were going to vent their depravity most fully on Ol' Blue Eyes, Frank Sinatra. According to Sadie, the plan was to hang Sinatra up by a meat hook, and then skin him alive whilst his music played in the background. Once dead, they then planned to take his skin and manufacture purses, which they'd in turn sell to hippie shops in Los Angeles, so that 'everyone could own a piece of Sinatra'.

Not surprisingly, once these claims were aired publicly, they made for frenzied headlines. Given her frazzled demeanour, it's possible that Sadie may have concocted the dark scenarios herself. However a list of thirty-four businessmen and celebrities were found in the wake of the Barker Ranch raid. Some were names that Sadie had bragged about; others were music industry personnel like Gary Stromberg, Terry Melcher and Dennis Wilson, who'd actually gone out of their way to help Charlie with his musical ambitions. Tellingly, the name of recent collaborator, Paul Watkins, was reported to have been included. This grizzly 'Death List' was found – along with a host of tawdry movie-magazines and military journals – in the rucksack that Charlie had been so intent on retrieving after his arrest in the desert.

Unaware of Sadie's kamikaze confessions, Los Angeles' Sheriff's officers had a strong suspicion that the LaBianca murders were somehow connected with Gary Hinman's death. Although still working independently of the Tate investigations, they were focusing heavily on the antics of the Family. Not surprisingly, the association with biker gangs soon began to surface. Fortuitously, some members of the Straight Satans motorcycle club had been pulled in on 15 October for marijuana and motor-related charges. Two of these characters would prove pivotal in the breaking of the case.

On 12 November, biker Al Springer was interviewed by detectives about his involvement with the Family. Despite only visiting Spahn's a few times, Springer's limited association with the Family allowed him to speak freely, and his testimony helped link the bloody murders together. Although unaware of the Cielo Drive massacre, Springer had overheard Charlie bragging about 'knocking off five piggies' during one visit to the ranch. Springer also recalled that Manson had mentioned that the killers 'wrote something on the fucking refrigerator in blood … Something about pigs or niggers or something like that.' The detail had scared Springer, and he'd kept his distance from the Family ever since.

After speaking to the likes of Springer, it was only a matter of time before detectives reined in fellow 'Straight Satan', Danny DeCarlo. He'd been tracked down via one of Gary Hinman's vehicles – the payoff from the mescaline deal turned sour. Given DeCarlo's close association with the Family, detectives were confident he'd have far more telling evidence than the other bikers.

Initially, DeCarlo was reticent. As he was still in with the Family, he knew only too well their attitude to snitches. Paul Watkins had, after all, already made it on to Charlie's Death List. Nonetheless after police struck a deal, DeCarlo began to open up; revealing, bit by bit, more about Charlie and the Family and their associates, such as Gary Hinman and Shorty Shea. Whilst the biker was unaware of the Tate massacre, he had explicit detail concerning the death of Shorty Shea, a man he'd known and liked.

'They stuck him like carving up a Christmas turkey … ' DeCarlo reported. 'Bruce [Davis] said they cut him up in nine pieces. They cut his head off, then they cut his arms off too, so there was no way they could possibly identify him. They were laughing about that.'

Whilst DeCarlo was right to be concerned for his own safety, his information enabled police to identify key Family personalities, and helped form the case against Bobby Beausoleil, shortly to be tried for Gary Hinman's murder. In custody, Beausoleil had remained tight-lipped. His firm stance could well have won his freedom, but when DeCarlo's testimony was read out in court, it resulted in a hung jury. Beausoleil was held until March 1970, by which time the whole Manson case had blown wide open, leaving him little room for manoeuvre.

Confirming their earlier suspicions, Sheriff's officers were now convinced that the Manson Family were responsible for all the atrocities in Los Angeles linked by bloody inscriptions. Again, they made their findings known to colleagues over at LAPD, but consumed by their investigations that had already involved vast amounts of man-hours from more than a hundred personnel; the information was, yet again, filed away.

Back at Sybil Brand, Sadie continued to incriminate herself and the Family. Given the magnitude of her confessions, Howard and Graham felt compelled to inform police. Despite both asking leave to contact detectives, the prisoners were denied access to a phone. Then, hampering matters somewhat, Virginia Graham was transferred to another prison. There she tried to put a call through to detectives, and yet again the request was denied. However, Ronnie Howard's persistence finally paid off and, following a call to the LAPD, police detectives came over to Sybil Brand on 17 November to take a statement. Following her revelations, Howard was moved into solitary confinement for her own protection, where she went under the pseudonym of Shelley Nadel. Virginia Graham was also called on to confirm Ronnie's allegations. Sadie soon twigged that her confidence had been breached. Later, she managed to get a letter through to Howard and, although laced with bitter invective, it made for sad reading:

'When I first heard you were the informer I wanted to slit your throat. I snapped that I was the real informer and it was my throat I wanted to cut ... In killing someone physically, you are only killing their soul ... Death is only an illusion. Well that's over with now as I let the past die away from my mind. You know it will turn out OK in the end anyway. "M" or no "M", Sadie or no Sadie. Love will still run for ever. I am giving up me to become that love a little more every day.'

Checking Howard and Graham's information against their own intelligence confirmed that Sadie had been at the Tate house on the night of the murders. She'd soon be taken into solitary confinement to await further questioning. Placed in a cold isolation block, Sadie's fragile world began to cave in on her. 'A yawning, pulsating sickness filled my stomach,' she'd recall years later. 'I knew I had dug a big hole, so big and so deep, that I'd never be able to crawl out. My mind turned to blackness.' Ascertaining Sadie's true mental state at this time is a nigh on impossible task, and as her later testimony would reveal, her emotions and allegiances changed frequently.

The evidence against Charlie and Family was now so strong, that by 18 November, the three police investigations were finally unified. With collated information from Ronnie Howard, Virginia Graham, Danny DeCarlo, and Sadie herself, a case against Manson and the Family could begin to take shape.

With the help of this new intelligence, detectives started putting names and faces to those implicated in the murders. With the media's ear finely tuned towards the police, news stories were starting to appear linking Manson and the Family to the investigations. As this buzz became louder, members of the Family who were still at large began to scatter.

Katie, now using the name 'Marnie Reeves', had already gone back to live with her mother in Mobile, Kentucky. Tex Watson had left even before the desert raids. He claimed that his mother had somehow managed to get a message to him, and he'd returned home to Texas. For a while he attempted to revert back to his former self, helping out in the family store and maintaining a low-key presence. According to his recollections, he battled with his memories of Manson and the killings. In an attempt to escape his demons, Tex travelled to Mexico and Hawaii, before the pull of the Family drew him back to Death Valley. With the Family either in custody or elsewhere, Watson returned to Texas and, according to his own account, fell into a deep void.

'My mother tried to take charge of things,' recalled Watson later. 'She got me to the doctor, talked to me, worked to pick up the frayed ends of our family life. But it was obvious that something had happened to me, something that it would take more than good sense and home cooking to make right. I slept most of the time, ate little – and threw up, whenever I tried to please her by downing one of her huge Texas meals. I didn't wash, just lay around, watching television blindly with the shades drawn, screaming at my parents to shut up if they tried to speak to me.'

Other Family members found life outside the Family equally challenging. Mary Brunner, Ruth Ann Morehouse and Barbara Hoyt all fled to their family homes. Others, like Bruce Davis and Brenda McCann initially pitched up in Los Angeles before spreading their wings in other directions. Ever-loyal Squeaky and Sandy Good holed themselves up in a motel close to Charlie in

Inyo County, and busied themselves running numerous errands for him. Paul Watkins and Brooks Poston found themselves pulled in different directions. For a while, Watkins vainly attempted to stick with the Family, yet his extensive collaboration with the prosecution meant he was branded as a snitch.

By this point even Charlie was sensing that he would be facing more serious charges than arson or theft. Sadie's wagging tongue had already heavily implicated him, yet he kept his own counsel, hoping that some legal loophole would set him free. Whilst loyalty or fear kept some tongues still, there was an increasing number of Mansonisms coming back to haunt Charlie.

With sections of Los Angeles still in a state of paralysis following the Tate murders, the pressure was on to bring the case to a successful conclusion. On 18 November 1969, Vincent T. Bugliosi and Aaron Stovitz were chosen as joint prosecutors for the Family trials. The county of Los Angeles was looking for top personnel with the stamina to handle what would be a very demanding case. Forty-five-year-old Stovitz was then head of trials at the downtown division of LA, and an experienced, tenacious lawyer. Although still in his early thirties, Bugliosi too had an impressive reputation, having lost only one of the 104 criminal cases in which he'd been prosecutor. Bugliosi was something of a celebrity in legal circles; his driven personality used as the model for the character of Robert Conrad in the television series, *The DA*.

Dismayed at the lack of communication between the Sheriff's Department and LAPD, Bugliosi took on a vast amount of the research himself. Within hours of his appointment, he'd travelled over to the Spahn Ranch to search for any traces of evidence to aid the prosecution. Bugliosi roped in Danny DeCarlo to act as tour guide. DeCarlo was initially reluctant to accompany police – with Charlie patently still orchestrating events from jail, the biker was terrified of the possible repercussions. A sinister death had taken place in a Family bolt hole in Venice just days before, and DeCarlo didn't fancy being next. As a compromise, he agreed to be handcuffed during the trip to give the impression he'd been forced into this reconnaissance mission. Shortly after the visit to

Spahn's, Bugliosi and his team went out to the desert hideouts to collate any other useful pieces of evidence.

Despite the sudden wave of new information, the prosecutors' task of linking the crimes together still proved extremely arduous. To date, the case's most telling evidence was based on hearsay and gossip, presented by a rogue's gallery of informants, many with lengthy criminal records themselves. Additionally, Bugliosi had to successfully prove Manson's guiding hand in all the events, whilst conceding his absence during the actual Tate and LaBianca slayings.

Vincent Bugliosi explained: 'You have to realise that I viewed Manson as the main defendant, so to convict his co-defendants and have him walk out of court, I think, would have been an unsuccessful prosecution. The problem was that Manson was not at the murder scene, he did not physically participate in these murders, so I had to connect him with the murders, and bring him in by way of circumstantial evidence and the law of conspiracy, which states that each member of a conspiracy is criminally responsible for the crimes committed by his co-conspirators ... There's no way in the world that these people would have gone out on their own, and committed some of the most horrendous murders imaginable without his direction and guidance, because he controlled their daily activity.'

There was also serious doubt about whether any of the core Family members would be willing to publicly testify against Manson. Ironically, the one person who appeared happy to oblige was Sadie. Her statements had been peppered with details that were vital to the prosecution. Already heavily implicated in the Hinman murder, she was now facing additional charges relating to the massacres of 9 and 10 August. As was her right, Sadie had been allotted the services of county-appointed lawyer, Richard Caballero. Faced with the enormous challenge of defending someone so eager to display her guilt, Sadie's lawyer made a bid for a reduction in her charges if she assisted with the prosecution. Caballero managed to strike a deal where the prosecution would not seek the death penalty against his client in any future court action. Moreover, she would be free to rescind every word of her testimony if she so wished. With Caballero's guiding hand,

Sadie, at this point lost in an eddy of confusion, began to assist the prosecution.

After surreptitiously removing her from Sybil Brand, detectives got their informant to retrace the route to and from the Tate house. Since finding the weaponry and clothing was vital to the prosecution, Sadie pointed out some of the winding ravines she thought the bloodied clothes, knives and gun had been thrown into. In response, teams of policeman – helped out by a group of Boy Scouts – began combing the area. Despite strenuous efforts over the following two weeks, nothing was found.

Bugliosi implored court officials to hold back on setting an immediate court date. With a mass of hard evidence still to be recovered, and hopes of convicting Manson still looking tenuous, Bugliosi argued that it was far too early to announce that the case had been broken. However, with Los Angeles still reeling from the crimes, there was a real need to announce some sort of a breakthrough.

Despite the prosecution's pleas for a postponement, at 2 p.m. on 1 December 1969, with banks of the media present, Los Angeles police-in-chief, Edward Davis, announced that the Tate–LaBianca murders had been solved. As a result, warrants for the arrest of Linda Kasabian, Patricia Krenwinkel and Charles (Tex) Watson had been issued. They were all charged on seven counts of murder and one count of conspiring to murder. The following day Charles Manson was included in the roll call. Leslie Van Houten, still in custody after the Barker Ranch raid, was also indicted. The clamour to bring the suspects to court saw police asking for both cases to be heard together – an unusual step, especially as one of the accused was known to have been present on only one night. Despite opposition from the defence, the courts agreed to try the cases simultaneously.

Linda Kasabian, living in fear since the two nights of murder, had voluntarily handed herself into custody in Concord, New Hampshire. Now with her involvement in the murders confirmed, she was shuttled over to Los Angeles for questioning. The warrants for Tex Watson and Katie were acted on immediately. Krenwinkel, living under the assumed surname of Montgomery, was arrested on the day of the announcement, Tex the day before, taken into custody in Texas by his second cóusin. However, it would take nine months, and an appeal to the Supreme Court before Tex was successfully extradited and sent over to Los Angeles to face trial.

With news of the arrests breaking, Charles Manson and the Family started to enter the public's consciousness. *Life* magazine devoted an enormous eight-page feature to the case in its 11 December 1969 edition. Titled 'The Wreck of a Monstrous Family', it pieced together the whole saga with some choice photographs and stories cobbled together from various sources. In the wake of *Life*'s spread, the media stepped up its coverage of the case, ensuring copious column space was given to any aspect of the Manson story, regardless of whether it was based in fact or speculation. These sensationalist reports by turns captivated and terrified the American public.

On 5 December 1969, Sadie was brought before the Grand Jury to instigate the prosecution of the accused. If the press had been hoping for some juicy detail, Sadie's testimony managed to surpass all expectations. Although she looked like any other shy, pretty twenty-one-year-old, Sadie's heartless recounting of the two nights of indescribable horror swiftly shattered that illusion. One juror fled the courtroom to vomit at the horrendous detail she coolly imparted. Even at this preliminary stage, Prosecutor Vincent Bugliosi paid particular attention to the huge influence Charlie had on the Family's mindset, and how he underpinned their every move.

During this precursor to the main trial, Sadie played to the gallery. Such was her candour that on 8 December 1969, the jury had little difficulty in passing down guilty indictments on the suspects for the seven murders. Sadie's shocking evidence notwithstanding, there had also been a few advances in the area of hard evidence. The Longhorn revolver that Tex used on the night of the Tate killing was eventually retrieved from police storage. Bernard Weiss, father of the young boy who'd found the weapon over three months previously, had seen a news report showing the type of revolver that forensics believed had been used in the killing. Weiss informed police that the weapon they had been looking for was probably already in their hands.

Remarkably, it wasn't until 16 December 1969 that they made the association.

Behind the scenes, negotiations were being conducted for the rights to Sadie's sensational confessions. Her lawyer, Richard Caballero, had allowed the deal to go ahead, hopeful that it would elicit some sympathy for Sadie by revealing how far she'd sunk into Manson's nightmare world. To the anger of pre-trial judge William Keene, an expanded version of Sadie's testimony was published in the *Los Angeles Times* on Sunday 14 December. Judge Keene attempted to block publication by ordering a news blackout. However, this was easily circumvented, and tawdry publications worldwide soon followed the *LA Times'* lead. Britain's *News of the World* scooped the European rights, paying $40,000 for the privilege. Soon after, cult publisher, New English Library, issued a gaudy one-shot paperback entitled, *The Killing of Sharon Tate*, selling at a dollar a copy. The book raked in a cool $100,000 in the first few weeks of publication.

Not surprisingly, Los Angeles' news crews had kept close tags on any developments. Taking note of Sadie's vivid descriptions of the murders, newscasters began their own trawl for any paraphernalia from the massacre. Performing their own detective work, a TV crew from ABC7 news discovered the ball of bloody clothing, some two kilometres from Cielo Drive. After handing the evidence over to police forensics, the TV bosses publicised their findings to the world.

Buoyed by their discovery, the news team began further searches, also recovering one of the knives used in the slaughter. Despite these embarrassments, police were making their own advances. A lone fingerprint Tex left at the Cielo Drive property was successfully matched up with prints he'd given to police earlier in the year, when he was arrested whilst tripping on belladonna. In time one of Katie's prints was also found on the property. Meanwhile, Barker and Spahn ranches were again minutely filleted for clues. Pertinently, a door at Spahn's with 'Helter Skelter' scrawled over it was taken to police headquarters for tests.

Although Sadie's evidence was invaluable to the prosecution, there were severe reservations about the deal struck for a reduced sentence. The dilemma worsened when she requested to confer with Charlie in the run-up to the trial. Sadie travelled over to see Manson in jail, and her leader easily persuaded her to renege on her testimony. Following her meeting with Charlie, she fired her lawyer and cut off all links with the prosecution, claiming that her Grand Jury statement was nothing more than 'a magical mystery tour'.

Whilst Bugliosi and his team shed no tears at Atkins's retreat back to Manson, with no credible witness the prosecution's case was looking anaemic. On 6 January 1970, Linda Kasabian was arraigned on charges relating to the murders, to which she pleaded not guilty. Kasabian's return to California handed the prosecution a golden opportunity for a star witness. Intelligence from all quarters confirmed that she'd been the most reluctant participant on both nights, and had merely acted as driver and lookout. Furthermore, she looked much more like a reliable witness than Crazy Sadie. Keen to testify in an attempt to 'get it out of my head', an immunity deal was struck with her lawyer. In return for her testimony, Linda would be cleared of all charges against her. Until the trial she'd be placed in solitary confinement, as many were out to silence her. Furthermore, she was heavily pregnant and in a fragile condition. She readily agreed to offer her full assistance. Despite her delicate state, she had to endure a tearful trip back with detectives to Cielo Drive to ascertain key details.

With no funds for a lawyer of his choice, Charlie was allotted the services of public defender, Paul Fitzgerald. The thirty-three-year-old lawyer had gained some notoriety, having previously represented Senator Robert Kennedy's assassin, Sirhan Sirhan, in 1968. Despite his legal credentials, he did have some insight into youth culture. Most importantly, he'd taken LSD, and was aware of the frequency that the defendants were tuning into. With his defendants likely to be found guilty, Fitzgerald was aware that his main brief was damage limitation. He conferred heavily with Charlie and the Family members, and was impressed by their devotion.

'With Charles they found happiness; with Charles they found light; with Charles, believe it or not, they would look me in the eye and tell me, they found love,' Paul Fitzgerald reported. 'And when they looked into his eyes, they saw love. They told me that over and over and over again. They would do anything for him, not out of power, but of love.'

Despite Fitzgerald's attempts to bridge the enormous gulf of cultural understanding, Charlie began to talk about standing as his own counsel, a right upheld by the constitution of the United States. On 17 December, Manson fired Fitzgerald; although the lawyer remained in the fray, later picking up duties for Katie. In preparation of his own defence, Charlie had done his best to apprise himself of some basic law. Manson was savvy enough to realise that by representing himself, he'd have access to everything one would expect of a defence lawyer. Most importantly he'd have the opportunity to question prosecution witnesses – a terrifying prospect for anyone thinking of testifying against him. Buoyed up by these prospects, Charlie formalised the decision on 17 December 1969, in the presence of Judge William Keene.

'Your honour,' he said, 'there is no way I can give up my voice in this matter . . . If I can't speak in my own defence and converse freely in this courtroom, then it ties my hands behind my back, and if I have no voice, then there is no sense in having a defence. Lawyers play with people, and I am a person and I don't want to be played with in this matter. The news media has already executed and buried me . . . There is no attorney in the world who can represent me as a person. I have to do it myself.'

After this explosive request, Judge Keene appointed the eminent Joseph Ball to assess Manson's ability to represent himself. After meeting Charlie, Ball, a former president of the California State Bar Association was upbeat, and reported that if the defendant was given the opportunity to represent himself, 'they will realise he is not the kind of man who would perpetrate horrible crimes'.

Hands tied, Judge Keene had no other option than to allow Charlie his own defence status. 'In this court's opinion,' Keene relayed to Manson, 'it's a sad and tragic mistake you are making by taking this course of action, but I can't talk you out of it . . . Mr Manson, you are your own lawyer.'

With his self-representation status now confirmed, Manson (now calling himself 'Jesus Christ, Prisoner') swiftly fired off a habeas corpus motion to the Los Angeles court authorities, claiming that he'd been denied sufficient space to exercise his rights as a lawyer, and that he should be freed immediately. Unsurprisingly, given the gravity of the charges against him, the motion was thrown out. In another bizarre move, Charlie attempted to have defence prosecutors Vincent Bugliosi and Aaron Stovitz jailed to match his own status. Although Charlie had little joy with his requests, other members of the Family took his lead and began to fire their own state-appointed representatives, causing chaos. Even locked in jail, Manson was still evidently in charge of the Family's movements.

In the wake of Manson's string of ludicrous requests, Keene revoked Charlie's self-defence status on 5 March 1970. To represent him, Charlie appointed Richard Hollopeter, a public defender. With little room to manoeuvre, Hollopeter immediately put in a request to have Charlie given a psychiatric evaluation. This enraged Charlie, and he immediately fired his lawyer.

Next Charlie opted for Ronald Hughes, a character who had previously socialised with the Family. As a UCLA student, Hughes had been over to Spahn Ranch to attend LSD parties the year prior to the trial. However, Hughes was an inexperienced lawyer who had never tried a case before, not to mention one of the magnitude of the Manson trial. Hughes's status as 'hippie' lawyer found little favour with Charlie and, as a consequence, Hughes only lasted a few days. The 250-pound, balding lawyer remained in the frame, though, later defending Leslie Van Houten. His loyalty to his client would ultimately cost Hughes dearly.

While Manson battled with the judge and his own lawyers, he at least enjoyed some light relief thanks to the indiscretion of co-prosecutor Aaron Stovitz. Stovtiz had been far too open with the press; in particular, he was censured by the trial judge for remarks he made to *Rolling Stone* magazine in March 1970. A later quip concerning Sadie's court performance as being worthy of 'Sarah Bernhardt' was picked up by reporters and sent out to news desks across the world. As a result Stovitz was removed from the trial, leaving Bugliosi as sole prosecutor.

With 'pre-trial' preliminaries now completed, Manson filed a request for a change of judge, principally on account of Judge Keene's refusal to allow him to defend himself. On 13 April a weary Judge Keene agreed to step down. Judge Charles Older moved in to oversee the main part of the trial. An air-force veteran, Older had seen action in both World War II and in Korea. In his time, he'd become something of a legend within air-force circles, renowned for having shot down eighteen enemy aircraft during conflict. Once demobbed, he'd turned his attentions to law, and swiftly rose through the legal ranks to be given a place on the LA Superior Court Board in 1967. Whilst firing bullets and dodging missiles was familiar territory for Older, presiding over the Manson Family would present him with new, equally wily enemies to contend with.

Yet again without a lawyer, Manson was forced to seek further representation. He reportedly screened more than sixty circuit lawyers before opting for Irving Kanarek. Fifty-seven-year-old Kanarek was notorious within Californian court circles for his obstructionist behaviour. Already gilded in legend was one trial where the cantankerous lawyer objected to a defendant saying their own name, claiming it was hearsay because they'd heard it first from their mother. It appears that Charlie was fully aware of Kanarek's 'celebrity' as a legal *agent provocateur*. In fact, he'd been at pains to inform Judge Older that, after being denied self-representation, he'd been forced into having to 'cause you as much trouble as possible'.

On Friday 24 July 1970, with Watson still battling his own extradition, the trial was ready to start in earnest. Manson, Atkins and Krenwinkel faced seven counts of murder relating to both the Tate and LaBianca murders. Leslie Van Houten was charged with two counts of first-degree murder in relation to the deaths of Leno and Rosemary LaBianca, and with conspiracy to murder. If the preliminaries had been littered with legal mines, the actual trial pushed California's court system to the absolute limit. Aware that Manson and his tenacious legal team would be looking to exploit any cracks in the prosecution's case, they continued their research right up to the start of the trial. The prosecution called an unprecedented number of witness to support their claims of Manson's extraordinary power over his charges.

As expected, the anticipation in Los Angeles for the first day of the trial was at fever pitch, with over a hundred news crews descending on the Los Angeles Halls of Justice. While the trial predated television coverage inside the courtroom, the press was nonetheless well represented. In keeping with the media's demands, fifty-five reservations were put aside for the press. In the corridor outside courtroom number 104, a bank of telephones and fax machines was primed to deliver the fates of Manson and the defendants to the outside world.

With space inside the courtroom strictly limited, hordes of reporters and film crews had set up residence outside on the corner of Temple and Broadway. Legions of overseas journalists had also flown in to capture the unfolding drama. With the guarantee of horrific revelations aplenty, the press was determined to catch every sensational sound bite as it occurred. Noted Associated Press reporter Linda Deutch remarked that, had there been cameras inside the courtroom, the whole country would have come to a standstill for the next ten months. Networks were so desperate to maintain a presence that they hired 'seat sitters' to ensure they didn't lose their places in the gallery. Sandi Gibbons, a reporter from City News Service in Los Angeles, was witness to the unfolding drama.

'There was a huge number of spectators who showed up, and tons of media both inside and outside the courtroom,' recalls Sandi Gibbons. 'But being Los Angeles, there were other things going on ... At the same time as the Manson case there was a woman down the street dressed in mermaid costume protesting against the Federal Government.'

With the press and public galleries bursting at the seams, Manson and the girls were led into court. As decreed by statute, the jurors had not been told which case they were due to rule on. Given the amount of pre-publicity the trial had generated, the five women and seven men sitting on the jurors' bench were soon aware that this was to be a unique case.

Juror William McBride recalled his utter dismay when he first saw Charles Manson being led into court. 'The first time I walked into the courtroom and saw there was Charles Manson and the three girls and the courtroom was cram-packed with people I thought, "Oh brother, what am I doing here?"'

From the outset, events inside the courtroom tested everyone's mettle. Knowing the enormous publicity value of a visual statement, Manson had scored an 'X' into his forehead the night before he entered court, a graphic sign of his removal from society. Within days, many of Charlie's followers copied his bloody statement, all more than happy to declare their social exclusion. In solidarity with those being tried, Manson's supporters outside on the street corner unanimously declared that they would maintain a presence at the Halls of Justice until Manson and the defendants and, by extension, everyone within the prison system, were set free.

Charlie accompanied his first appearance in court with a press statement, read out by Squeaky to waiting reporters in the hallway outside. 'I am not of you, from you, nor do I condone your unjust attitude toward things, animals, and people that you do not try to understand . . . I stand opposed to what you do and have done in the past . . . You make fun of God and have murdered the world in the name of Jesus Christ . . . My faith in me is stronger than all of your armies, governments, gas chambers, or anything you may want to do to me. I know what I have done. Your courtroom is man's game. Love is my judge.'

A hush descended on the courtroom as Vincent Bugliosi took to the floor. Despite an exhausting schedule of eighteen-hour days spent preparing the evidence, he was raring to go; driven by his commitment to winning the case for the state of California. Despite the charges being spread over four defendants, Bugliosi wasted little time in going straight for Manson's jugular with his opening statement.

'A question you, ladies and gentlemen, will probably ask yourself at some point during this trial,' he began, 'and we expect the evidence to answer that question for you, is this: "What kind of a diabolical mind would contemplate or conceive of these seven murders?" "What kind of mind would want to have seven human beings brutally murdered?" We expect the evidence at this trial to answer that question and show the defendant Charles Manson owned that diabolical mind. Charles Manson, who the evidence will show at times, had the infinite humility, as it were, to refer to himself as Jesus Christ. Evidence at this trial will show defendant Manson to be a vagrant wanderer, a frustrated singer–

guitarist pseudo-philosophiser, but, most of all, the evidence will conclusively prove that Charles Manson is a killer, who cleverly masqueraded behind the common image of a hippy.'

Despite Bugliosi's emotive prologue, Manson and girls remained detached from the rhetoric. Instead they giggled, laughed and made eyes – both sensual and threatening – at anyone who came into their line of vision.

The first witness on the stand was Paul Tate, father of murdered Sharon. He'd maintained a low profile following his daughter and grandson's murders. Now Tate had emerged from his own investigation into Los Angeles' underworld, and was ready to see justice delivered. Rumours had circulated on the grapevine that the ex-military chief was out to exact revenge for Sharon's death. As a result, he was thoroughly searched by police on entering the courthouse.

Trained up by years spent in Army Intelligence, Tate calmly picked out daughter Sharon and her friends from the graphic crime-scene photos taken on the morning after the massacre. Tate's appearance as first witness was a skilled piece of scheduling by the prosecution team, focusing the jury on the personal loss suffered by the victims' families.

It was at 2 p.m. on the afternoon of Monday 27 July that star witness, Linda Kasabian, was transported from secure custody to face questions from the prosecution. With her hair bunched in ponytails, and her cheesecloth dress accentuating her innocent appearance, all eyes focused on Kasabian as she entered the courtroom.

Linda had barely begun the perfunctory process of being sworn in when Manson's lawyer Kanarek rose from his seat. 'Objection, Your Honour,' Kanarek interrupted, 'On the grounds that this witness is not competent and she is insane.'

Aghast at the defamatory slur directed at their most valuable asset, the prosecution leapt to their feet. Bugliosi led the charge to Judge Older's table, shouting, 'Your Honour, I move to strike that, and I ask the court to find him in contempt for gross misconduct. This is unbelievable!'

Judge Older agreed, and verbally censured Kanarek for the indiscretion. It would be the first of numerous objections and interjections. Focusing on Kasabian's relatively modest LSD usage (reportedly 'fifty trips'), Kanarek would utilise every available tool to unseat her composure and query her mental health status. If the result was to test Kasabian's fragile sensitivities, then Kanerek succeeded in scoring a point when he confronted Linda with photographs from the crime scene, causing her to break down. Pulling herself away from the photo of the butchered Sharon Tate, the heavily pregnant Kasabian looked across at the defendants and asked, 'How could you do that?' The girls just laughed. Never one to miss an opportunity, Irving Kanarek stepped in to ask Kasabian whether because of her LSD usage, she might well have been involved in the savagery. Kasabian adamantly refuted his suggestion, insisting, 'I don't have that kind of thing in me, to do something so animalistic.'

There were other threats to Linda during the trial, some more obvious than others. At one point during her testimony, Sadie hissed to Linda across the court: 'You're killing us!' Unfazed, Kasabian broke away from her thread to retort, 'I am not killing you. You have killed yourselves.'

While Kanarek did his best to disrupt Kasabian's testimony, Manson began his own personal war of attrition towards Linda. On numerous occasions, Charlie loudly poured scorn on Kasabian's revelations; at others, he'd mimic a knife being drawn across her throat.

Thoughout this all, Bugliosi maintained a steely determination to guide Linda through the evidence. The prosecution knew only too well that Linda's first-hand experience of both nights of murder was invaluable, and took considerable steps to shield her from any outside interference. Nonetheless, the Family still attempted to make contact with her. In the early stages of the trial, Sandy Good managed to get a letter to Kasabian, much to the chagrin of her defence team. The note was explicit in its content: 'Are you trying to kill us, Linda? Tens of thousands of pretty young people. The X you see on Charlie's forehead is now being worn by hundreds of people. Look at the faces of the people you are cooperating with.' Driving the subtext home further, outside the courtroom placards reading 'A Snitch in Time' were starting to appear.

With Bugliosi at the helm, Kasabian constructed a vivid picture of the Family's lifestyle, underpinned by Charlie's all-encompassing control. Considerable amounts of Linda's evidence involved recounting the group's copious drug use, criminal activity and, most tantalising for media watchers, their licentious and free-range sex life.

'There was this particular girl,' recounted Kasabian under questioning – I don't remember her name – she was fairly young, I'd say maybe sixteen, and she was very shy and very withdrawn, and I remember she was lying in the middle of the room, and Charlie took her clothes off and started making love to her and kissing her and, you know, she was trying to push him off, and he just sort of pushed her back down and kissed her. And at one point she bit him on the shoulder, and he hit her in the face, and then she just sort of let go and got behind it or whatever. Then he told Bobby Beausoleil to make love to her, and he told everybody to touch her and to kiss her and to make love to her, and everybody did.'

Despite the constant barbs, Kasabian endured eighteen days of testimony. Bugliosi then steered the likes of Danny DeCarlo, Juan Flynn and Paul Watkins through the mire, drawing a grubby picture of Manson's ethos. Watkins, at that point teetering between both camps, was instrumental in confirming the prosecution's belief that Charlie's Helter Skelter theory was the prime motivator for the crimes. He'd recently survived a fire in the camper van he'd been living in and, although the arson was never proved to be the work of the Family, under questioning he was in uncompromising mood.

Vincent Bugliosi: 'During your association with Charles Manson, did he frequently discuss "Helter Skelter" with you?'
Paul Watkins: 'Constantly.'
Vincent Bugliosi: 'He used the word "Helter Skelter" constantly?'
Paul Watkins: 'I wouldn't go so far as to say constantly. He did not say, "Helter Skelter, Helter Skelter, Helter Skelter." But he did quite a bit, yes, it seemed to be the main topic.'

With Beatles' lyrics adding an enigmatic backdrop to the proceedings, it transpired that Manson wanted to call John

Lennon to court to support his reading of 'Helter Skelter'. In fact, Charlie was wrong to credit Lennon with the song, as it was actually Paul McCartney's composition. Nonetheless, someone from the Family obtained the London number of Apple Corps, the Beatles' London headquarters. As chief messenger, Squeaky made a series of calls with a view to talking to one of the group.

'One of the Family, Squeaky, called the Apple press office,' remembers Apple press office assistant and 'House Hippie', Richard Di Lello. 'Not wanting to get involved, I do remember that we passed that call on to Peter Brown [Apple Corporation head]. The call from Squeaky did not get very far. We wanted nothing to do with them, and we didn't.'

But the Family didn't give up on the Beatles so easily, not after they'd help kick-start their bloody rampaging. Gypsy, one of Manson's most loyal supporters, collared reporters during the trial, armed with a message to be passed on to the Fab Four. 'What can I say to the damn Beatles?' Gypsy begged journalist David Felton visiting Spahn Ranch. 'Just get in touch, man. This is their trial. And all the things they've been hearing – there's something happening here; they should see it by now. It's hard to see through the negative, but just tell them to call. Give them our number.'

While the members of the Family tried to contact the Beatles through the world's press, it seems that defence lawyers were attempting to officially subpoena John Lennon, who was currently in LA.

'We want John Lennon to testify,' a defence spokesperson revealed at the time. 'We feel he may want to explain his lyrics . . . He's the most articulate and philosophical of the Beatles, and he understands his social and political effect on the world.'

Lennon understandably went to strenuous efforts not to be embroiled in the case, and, as defence counsel noted, 'there is an unbelievable wall surrounding him.'

Lennon, along with the other Beatles, did not want to comment on the Manson case. However, during Lennon's famous interview with *Rolling Stone* in 1970, he appeared to share some of Charlie's viewpoints, although also conceding that he thought Manson was 'barmy', 'I just think a lot of things he says are true, that he's a child of the state made by us. And he took their children in when nobody else would, is what he did. But he is cracked.'

Whilst the defence had little luck in snaring England's rock royalty, events of 3 August 1970, would see the Manson trial reaching the highest echelon of America's government. As the case had become a nightly fixture on the news stations, there was a queasy sense that Manson was garnering a dangerous amount of publicity. Manson himself was pleased that he and his followers' struggle had succeeded in winning support from unexpected quarters. While events like the US Army's massacre at My Lai in southern Vietnam divided public opinion, Manson's flimsy plight was momentarily championed by the counterculture. Famed hippie and notorious thorn in the side of the Establishment, Jerry Rubin, gained an audience with Manson in custody, where they chattered happily for hours.

Far-left agitprop publications like *Tuesday's Child* named Charlie as 'Person of the Year'. *Rolling Stone* magazine was so convinced that Charlie and the girls had been set up, they planned to emblazon a cover of the magazine with 'Charles Manson Is Innocent'. Even the radical Black Panthers, themselves targets of Manson's unashamed racism, declared 1969 as 'the year of the pig' in honour of Tex and the girls' creative stabbings. With Charlie's profile in the ascendancy, there was a sense that – despite an inevitable guilty verdict – the momentum from the case would continue to make him a celebrity.

Indeed, such was the coverage that was afforded to Charlie and the girls during the trial that voices from the highest levels of society began to echo down in discontent. One such voice belonged to none other than the President of the United States himself. Unanimously seen by the counterculture as the most despised individual in the country, Richard Nixon offered his own slant on the Manson phenomena. The President had been visiting a government building in Denver, Colorado on 3 August, where he'd convened a press conference. Evidently working without notes or prior consultation, Nixon made an enormous gaffe in front of the assembled media.

'Now, as we look at the situation I think the main concern that

I have is attitudes that are created among our younger people and also people as well, in which they tend to glorify and to make heroes out of those who engage in criminal activities,' he began. 'This is not done intentionally by the press. It is not done intentionally by radio and television, I know. It is done perhaps because people want to read or see that kind of story. I noted, for example, the coverage of the Charles Manson case when I was in Los Angeles, front page every day in the papers. It usually got a couple of minutes in the evening news. Here is a man who was guilty, directly or indirectly, of eight murders without reason. Here is a man, yet, who, as far as the coverage was concerned, appeared to be rather a glamorous figure, a glamorous figure to the young people whom he had brought into his operations.'

Declaring Manson 'guilty' just a few weeks into his trial was an astonishing error, especially for someone like Nixon, who had himself trained as a lawyer. Nixon's words were swiftly relayed across the world. Closest to the action, the *Los Angeles Times* had a headline four-inches deep across their late evening edition proclaiming, 'MANSON GUILTY, NIXON DECLARES'.

As Nixon and his aides battled with a retraction on their flight back to Washington, it was clear that the President's blunder could have serious ramifications for the trial. Paul Fitzgerald, then representing Patricia Krenwinkel, led the charge for the defence: 'If the President of the United States says you're guilty, what recourse do you have?'

That night, Nixon put out the following statement: 'I have been informed that my comment in Denver regarding the Tate murder trial in Los Angeles may continue to be misunderstood ... The last thing I would do is prejudice the legal rights of any person in any circumstances. I do not know and did not intend to speculate as to whether or not the Tate defendants are guilty, in fact, or not.'

Despite the apology, Nixon had caused severe problems for the LA court. There was a very real belief that if the jury became aware of the President's verdict, grounds for a mistrial could be levied. To prevent this, Judge Older went to extraordinary lengths to ensure the jury didn't catch sight of Nixon's remarks. Kept in secure hotel accommodation for the duration of the trial, the jury had to have the windows of their court shuttle bus whited out, so that no one could catch a glimpse of a newsstand. But the judge hadn't counted on Manson's anarchic influence.

More than anyone, Manson knew that the slip-up could seriously derail the prosecution's case. With Nixon's words dangling tantalisingly in the atmosphere, the courtroom was in a state of high anticipation the following day. While Irving Kanarek continued his finicky cross-examining of Linda Kasabian, Manson waited until after the lunchtime recess to make his move. With the prosecution lawyers in a huddle by the judge's desk, Manson shuffled a pile of legal papers and books at his side, to reveal the day-old copy of the *Los Angeles Times*, its headline screaming Nixon's blunder. In an instant, Charlie was brandishing it to the members of the jury.

Although Manson only held the paper towards the jury for a few seconds before court officials snatched it away, the damage was done. Incensed, Judge Older called the lawyers together and effectively put the trial on hold. While the jury was buzzing at what they had just seen, the assembled press corps was ignited into fevered action, sensing a crisis approaching.

While Irving Kanarek pleaded his innocence, Daye Shinn, Susan Atkins' current lawyer, owned up to bringing the paper into court. Shinn, at one time a used-car salesman, was duly sentenced for contempt, and taken into custody for three days. With Shinn out of the way, the business of assessing what influence the headline might have had on the jury began. In turn, jurors were quizzed on what they had seen, and what effect, if any, it might have on their judgement. Unanimously, they returned it had little or no influence on their potential decision, and the trial continued.

The controversy wouldn't die, though, and on the morning of 5 August, as Linda Kasabian was being led into court, Atkins, Van Houten and Krenwinkel stood up as one, and in unison delivered, 'Your Honour, the President said we are guilty, so why go on with the trial?' The judge ordered them to sit down. As with the other interruptions, this had been stage-managed by Charlie, a point that Patricia Krenwinkel was keen to emphasise some twenty-five years later.

'The entire proceedings were scripted by Charlie. Each day

348

we'd meet, and he'd decide, "Well today, I want you each to stand up and hold your hands in some stupid symbols; you're going to get up and scream." And each day was scripted ...With Manson he believed that everything we did was creating some picture that was going to go out into the universe and somehow change it towards his will.'

As if wading through the Family's women outside the court wasn't stressful enough, the witnesses had to endure testifying in front of Manson and the Family. For some it was an opportunity to level the score, while for others it proved to be a deeply unsettling experience. Terry Melcher, allegedly the main target of the night of slaughter at Cielo Drive, made a nervous appearance in the stands. For Melcher, the trauma of his association with Manson was so colossal that he'd end up in therapy for two years.

On 5 October, Charlie took his courtroom antics even further. Aggrieved at events taking place without his input, Charlie contested his own defence's decision not to cross-examine Paul Whitely, one of the Sheriff's officers attached to the Gary Hinman investigation. Asking to question him personally, Judge Older ruled that Manson could not. Glowing with anger, Charlie bellowed at Older, 'You are going to use this courtroom to kill me ... I am going to fight for my life one way or another. You should let me do it with words.'

As he had done on frequent occasions, Judge Older remonstrated with Manson, adding, 'If you don't stop, I will have you removed.'

Manson swiftly reflected the message back. 'I will have you removed if you don't stop. I have a little system of my own.'

Judge Older then ordered the next witness to be called, leading Manson to do a double-take. 'Do you think I'm kidding?' he added incredulously.

There was a split-second of silence before Manson continued his attack on the judge. 'In the name of Christian justice someone should cut off your head!'

From nowhere, Manson leapt into action. With a sharpened pencil in his hand, Charlie used the defence table in front of him as a springboard, and leapt ten feet through the air in the direction of Judge Older's bench. A temporary wave of shock allowed Manson to reach the base of the judge's platform. Before he could hurl himself at Older, Manson was tackled from behind and knocked to the floor. With two other bailiffs weighing in, he was finally subdued and led out of the courtroom. As if on cue, the girls rose from their chairs and began delivering a nonsensical chant, 'Moem be oro decaio', adding to the mad cacophony. They too were led out of the courtroom to a secure antechamber.

While Older had faced many an enemy fighter jet in his time, Manson's gravity-defying leap left him visibly shaken. The shock was evident as he told the court, 'If he had taken one more step, I would have done something to defend myself.' From that day onwards, a loaded pistol was kept within his reach. Outside the courtroom, Older was taking no chances with his safety, and was allotted the services of a bodyguard and round-the-clock security at his home. This privilege was extended to the trial's twelve jurors, and preventative measures were taken, in Older's words, 'to protect them from harassment and to prevent their being exposed to trial publicity'.

Nonetheless, somewhere along the line, the identities of some of the jurors' families had been revealed, and several malicious calls were made. Members of the prosecution team were also threatened. Stephen Kay, one of the prosecutors, was trailed back to his car by Squeaky and Sandy Good one evening. Their threat was chilling, he remembers. 'Sandy Good and Squeaky Fromme snuck up behind me one night as I was walking to the parking lot, and they indicated that they were going to do to my house what was done at the Tate house. These were very dangerous people – very unpredictable.'

It wasn't just those intimately connected to the court that were now under threat. Pretty eighteen-year-old Barbara Hoyt found her wavering loyalties were about to be dramatically challenged. She'd heard talk of the murder of Shorty Shea, and had fled Barker Ranch as the heat had started to be turned up. As part of his comprehensive sweep of the Family members, Bugliosi had honed in on Hoyt's revelations, and with her parents' encouragement, she nervously agreed to testify for the prosecution. As with many of these peripheral personalities, Hoyt still maintained a connection with the Family at large, and was happy to socialise with them whilst the trial took place. As luck would have it, one of the girls,

Ruth Ann Morehouse (Ouisch), had obtained a couple of plane seats over to Hawaii, courtesy of Dennis Rice, a Family supporter who'd leapt in to the fray following Charlie's incarceration.

Sweet-talking Barbara into going on holiday rather than testifying was easy enough; Hoyt was so nervous, the opportunity to escape the trial was hugely attractive. Additionally, there had been veiled threats made towards Hoyt that her family would be in danger if she took the stand. In early September, Barbara took off with Ouisch, to spend some quality time away in the sun. The pair checked into a swish hotel in Honolulu, although, despite the sun beckoning outside, Ouisch warned Hoyt to stay hidden away.

After a few days, Ouisch told Hoyt that she needed to return urgently. Although she was explicit that Barbara should stay on in Hawaii, she asked for her company on the trip to the airport. Once there, the pair went over to the snack bar. Ouisch claimed she wasn't hungry, but encouraged Hoyt to buy a cheeseburger. While Hoyt stumped up the bill, Ouisch took the burger outside and loaded it with ten hits of LSD, which she then took to the waiting Hoyt.

Barbara Hoyt recalled: 'She begged me to eat the hamburger, and she was getting ready to board the plane. She took a swipe with her finger across the ketchup and then sucked on her finger. She was about to get on the plane and she remarked to me, "Just imagine if there was ten tabs of acid on that hamburger," and I went, "No way, that couldn't be!" Then she got on her plane.'

Barbara happily waived Ouisch off back to sunny LA. It was only when she wandered away from the airport that the effects of the psychedelic burger took hold. Thrashing through two lanes of traffic, she finally collapsed and was taken to hospital. While ten hits of LSD would be enough to send most into a state of intense hysteria, an overdose of the drug is rarely, if ever, fatal, and Barbara was soon stabilised. However, the emotional nature of the experience took the young girl to the brink of insanity.

Once the prosecution got wind of this attack on their witness, they immediately ordered that a charge of attempted murder be levied against those responsible. When Hoyt finally recovered her composure, she testified with a renewed vigour for the prosecution. Despite calls for attempted murder, Squeaky,

Ouisch, Clem, Gypsy and Dennis Rice – the five implicated in the hamburger caper – served only three months for witness interference. Ouisch, who administered the acid burger to Hoyt, escaped prosecution by fleeing California before the case started.

Despite all this drama, after nearly six months of damning evidence, the prosecution rested their case on 16 November 1970. They now waited with bated breath to see what the defence counsel would present in return. Three days later, they got to see for themselves. Collectively, the defence lawyers had allotted Paul Fitzgerald as their spokesperson. Fitzgerald had so far vainly attempted to champion his clients, even while they were freely admitting their guilt. Although one of the only lines of defence left would be to prove that the others were acting under Charlie's spell, Manson clearly had other ideas. Fitzgerald soon began to hear whispers that, in an attempt to save his own life, Manson had instructed the women to take responsibility for masterminding the whole series of crimes themselves.

Leslie Van Houten recalls Manson's justification: 'Charlie suggested that we, meaning the three women, try to carry the load of the case so that he could be released, so that he could further carry on his work to save the world.'

Aware that the women were now preparing to fully exonerate Charlie during the cross-examination, the girls' lawyers succeeded in trumping him. Following the judge's invitation, Paul Fitzgerald rose from his seat at exactly 4.27 p.m. on the afternoon of Thursday 19 November. With anticipation heavy in the air, the defence's presentation carried with it enormous expectation, especially as the prosecution's case had been so comprehensive.

'Thank you, Your Honour,' Fitzgerald begun. 'The defendants rest.'

For a courtroom that had at times resembled a battlefield, the silence that permeated the air was tangible. Even Judge Older was visibly shocked and called an immediate recess so that he could meet with the defence team behind closed doors to listen to the reasons behind their decision.

Summarising their decision, counsel for the defence conceded that with those accused planning to fully exonerate Manson, their involvement would be like 'aiding and abetting a suicide'. While counsel for the defence had hoped to show the defendants being caught in Charlie's web, with the women intent on writing him out of the murders, the only option was to deny them the rope to hang themselves. For once, the prosecution agreed with the defence lawyers. As a considerable part of their evidence had hung on Manson's ability to control their every action, the girls' declaration could have seriously undermined their case.

On being denied the chance to testify, Charlie and the women protested vociferously. Aware that every nuance of legal protocol was being observed, Judge Older forged an unprecedented ruling, whereby the defendants could testify, but not in the presence of the jury. This would allow any inadmissible evidence to be later expunged before it reached the jurors. Furthermore, it would remove the threat that Charlie would try to brainwash the jury with his hypnotic words.

To the defendants, this compromise was the work of the devil. All three girls refused to speak. As befitted his contrary personality, Charlie unexpectedly took the opportunity to testify. Five months into the trial, Manson took the stand on 20 November 1970 to put forward his side of the story.

Manson began: 'There has been a lot of charges and a lot of things said about me and brought against the co-defendants in this case, of which a lot could be cleared up and clarified ... I never went to school, so I never growed [sic] up to read and write too good, so I have stayed in jail and I have stayed stupid, and I have stayed a child while I have watched your world grow up, and then I look at the things that you do and I don't understand ...

'You eat meat and you kill things that are better than you are, and then you say how bad, and even killers, your children are. You made your children what they are ...

'These children that come at you with knives. They are your children. You taught them. I didn't teach them. I just tried to help them stand up ...

'Most of the people at the ranch that you call the Family were just people that you did not want, people that were alongside the road, that their parents had kicked out, that did not want to go to Juvenile Hall. So I did the best I could and I took them up on my garbage dump and I told them this: that in love there is no wrong . . .

'I told them that anything they do for their brothers and sisters is good if they do it with a good thought . . .

'I was working at cleaning up my house, something that Nixon should have been doing. He should have been on the side of the road, picking up his children, but he wasn't. He was in the White House, sending them off to war . . .

'I can't dislike you, but I will say this to you: you haven't got long before you are all going to kill yourselves, because you are all crazy. And you can project it back at me . . . but I am only what lives inside each and every one of you.

'My father is the jailhouse. My father is your system . . . I am only what you made me. I am only a reflection of you.

'I have ate out of your garbage cans to stay out of jail. I have wore your second-hand clothes . . . I have done my best to get along in your world and now you want to kill me, and I look at you, and then I say to myself, You want to kill me? Ha! I'm already dead, have been all my life. I've spent twenty-three years in tombs that you built.

'Sometimes I think about giving it back to you; sometimes I think about just jumping on you and letting you shoot me . . . If I could, I would jerk this microphone off and beat your brains out with it, because that is what you deserve, that is what you deserve . . .

'If I could get angry at you, I would try to kill every one of you. If that's guilt, I accept it . . . These children, everything they done, they done for the love of their brother . . . If I showed them that I would do anything for my brother – including giving my life for my brother on the battlefield – and then they pick up their banner, and they go off and do what they do, that is not my responsibility. I don't tell people what to do.'

Charlie then turned to the female defendants.

'These children were finding themselves. What they did, if they did whatever they did, is up to them. They will have to explain that to you . . . It's all your fear . . .

'You expect to break me? Impossible! You broke me years ago. You killed me years ago . . .

354

'I have killed no one and I have ordered no one to be killed. I may have implied on several different occasions to several different people that I may have been Jesus Christ, but I haven't decided yet what I am or who I am ... You can do anything you want with me, but you cannot touch me because I am only my love ... If you put me in the penitentiary, that means nothing because you kicked me out of the last one. I didn't ask to get released. I liked it in there because I like myself.'

Charlie then turned to the chief prosecutor in the case.

'Mr Bugliosi is a hard-driving prosecutor, polished education, a master of words, semantics. He is a genius. He has got everything that every lawyer would want to have except one thing: a case. He doesn't have a case. Were I allowed to defend myself, I could have proven this to you ... Helter Skelter is confusion. Confusion is coming down around you fast. If you can't see the confusion coming down around you fast, you can call it what you wish ... Is it a conspiracy that the music is telling the youth to rise up against the establishment because the establishment is rapidly destroying things? Is that a conspiracy? The music speaks to you every day, but you are too deaf, dumb, and blind to even listen to the music ... It is not my conspiracy. It is not my music. I hear what it relates. It says "Rise", it says "Kill". Why blame it on me? I didn't write the music ....

'I don't recall ever saying "Get a knife and a change of clothes and go do what Tex says." Or I don't recall saying "Get a knife and go kill the sheriff." In fact, it makes me mad when someone kills snakes or dogs or cats or horses. I don't even like to eat meat – that is how much I am against killing ...

'I haven't got any guilt about anything because I have never been able to see any wrong ... I have always said: Do what your love tells you, and I do what my love tells me ...

'Is it my fault that your children do what you do? What about your children? You say there are just a few? There are many, many more, coming in the same direction. They are running in the streets – and they are coming right at you!'

There was a brief silence. Judge Older, sensing that Manson

had come to the end of his soliloquy, asked him if he wanted to add any more thoughts.

'No. We're all our own prisons, we are each all our own wardens and we do our own time. I can't judge anyone else. What other people do is not really my affair unless they approach me with it. Prison's in your mind ... Can't you see I'm free?'

On that note, Charlie brought his testimony to a close. Convinced that the rambling testimony was innocuous, Judge Older offered him the opportunity to repeat his statement to the jury. Manson was unmoved. 'I have already relieved all the pressure I had,' he said before leaving the witness stand to resume his seat. As he walked past his three co-defendants, all visibly weeping, he motioned to them and said, 'You don't have to testify now.'

Manson's dramatic soliloquy effectively brought the curtain down on the main phase of the trial. Despite the defence offering no supporting evidence, Judge Older ordered a short recess for both sides to prepare themselves for the closing statements

Charlie's cast-off lawyer, Ronald Hughes, was having a tough time. Despite occasionally showing his admiration for Manson, he had fought vainly for his client, Leslie Van Houten. Hughes was about as close to a hippie lawyer as you could find, and his insight into the counterculture helped him sympathise with Van Houten's slide into Manson's murky world.

Like his colleagues on the defence bench, Hughes had been keen to pursue the angle that Van Houten was totally dependent on Manson, and as a result was not acting on her own volition on the night of the LaBianca murders. Above all else, Hughes was aiming to avoid the death penalty for his client. Supporting the defence counsel's spectacular decision to offer no defence, Hughes had been vociferous in protecting Leslie's interests.

'I believe that it is clear,' he said, 'that this court has, on the one hand, wanted the defendants to hurtle [sic] themselves out of the window, but has always demanded that someone be there to push them as they go. Your Honour, I refuse to take part in any proceedings where I am forced to push a client out of the window.'

While this action may well have endeared him to the more

sensitive members of the jury, it would ultimately send damning signals to Charlie. Hughes had twigged that Manson was leaning heavily on the women to take responsibility for the killings, and had no qualms about making it public. For Manson, this was the final straw from this lawyer with hippie pretensions. At the time, Hughes confided in several colleagues and press representatives that he was seriously 'afraid' of Manson. As it turned out, he had good reason to be.

Prosecutor Stephen Kay recalled an ominous moment on the Friday before the weekend recess. 'I remember the last time I saw Hughes in the courtroom. After the judge excused everybody, Manson pointed his finger at Hughes and said, "Attorney, I don't ever want to see you in this court ever again."'

If Manson's antagonism was draining Hughes' nervous system, his finances were also suffering. He'd taken to sleeping on a mattress in a friend's garage, where, poignantly, he'd appended his framed legal certificate to the wall. If time allowed, he liked to get away from LA to some remote part of the county to soothe his troubled soul. The short recess between trial stages allowed such a visit, and with two young friends – James Forsher and Lauren Elder – he drove the 100 miles from Los Angeles over to Ventura County, home of the famous hot sulphur springs at Sespe Creek. Crammed into a VW camper van, the trio planned to stay over for the weekend.

What happened over the next two days is still for the most part a mystery.

Hughes and his two companions had pitched base halfway up the Ojai Mountains; a notoriously unpredictable region that is prone to flash flooding. The previous year, seven Boy Scouts had been lost in the area without a trace. By all accounts, the weather on the Friday night of Hughes's arrival was horrendous, and it rained well into Saturday morning. Compounding matters, Hughes' VW camper had got stuck in the horrendous terrain. Forsher and Elder decided to make for base on foot, while Hughes opted to ride out the storm in the comfort of the camper van.

Weather conditions that weekend had deteriorated so badly that four hikers were helicoptered out of the region. By Sunday night, with Hughes still absent, friends were starting to worry for his safety. When the court resumed business on the Monday morning, Hughes's non-arrival wasn't initially seen as a major cause for concern. The lawyer was often late. On one occasion, he'd failed to show after being pulled over by traffic police on account of his car's shabby condition. However, by midday, there was a feeling that Hughes's absence might be due to something more serious. With news of the torrential weather, and learning of Hughes's trip to Sespe during the weekend, an immediate recce of the area was ordered.

When the floodwater had retreated sufficiently, a twenty-two-man team searched the mountain, but with no success. Reports suggested that Hughes had been seen wandering around the area as the storm took hold. Back in Los Angeles, with discontent still bubbling about the decision to silence the women, there was a palpable suspicion that somehow the Family had got their revenge on Hughes.

Adding to this atmosphere of suspicion, anonymous phone calls were made to court officials claiming that Hughes had been murdered by the Family and buried at Barker Ranch. An immediate search was convened in the desert but no trace of Hughes's body was ever found.

Manson and the girls seized on Hughes's disappearance to lay on a further display of contempt for the court. In unison, the girls accused the judge of 'doing away with Hughes'. This created a buzz within the press circles, who were already linking Hughes's disappearance to irate Family members. Van Houten was allotted the services of co-counsel, Maxwell Keith, to represent her in Hughes's absence. With Manson presumably pulling the strings, Van Houten objected vociferously to the appointment, but to little avail. Ironically, Keith's help would serve to secure Leslie's temporary release some seven years later.

On 15 January 1971, the case for the prosecution began to draw to a close, and the opportunity came to make closing statements to the jury. In his summing up, Bugliosi summarised the mass of evidence he'd presented. While moments of the trial had presented the Manson tribe as a psychedelic version of *The*

Partridge Family, Bugliosi brought the focus back fully on to the victims.

'Ladies and gentlemen of the jury, Sharon Tate, Abigail Folder, Voyteck Frykowski, Jay Sebring, Steven Parent, Leno LaBianca, Rosemary LaBianca are not here with us now in this courtroom, but from their graves they cry out for justice. Justice can only be served by coming back to this courtroom with a verdict of guilty ... The plaintiff at this trial is the people of the state of California. I have all the confidence in the world that you will not let them down.'

With closing arguments out of the way, the jury deliberated the verdict. Outside the courtroom, loyal members of the Family maintained a constant presence. On the rare occasions that events inside the courtroom were uneventful, the media trained their cameras on these young, wayward girls on the corner.

The inclusiveness of the Family lifestyle seemed appealing to many lost souls across America. Many gravitated to the corner of Temple and Broadway to hook up with the Family. For a while, sympathetic elements of the counterculture embraced them with offers of food and supplies. Letters poured into the courthouse, many simply addressed 'Charles Manson, Los Angeles', often filled with questions about how to join the Family. Joining the girls on the steps was the occasional disaffected youth, eager to buy into the unity of the Family ethos. While the protests against Vietnam continued throughout the early 1970s, the far-out aims of the Manson Family offered an appealing alternative for those seemingly alienated by everyone.

The girls on the street followed the courtroom proceedings, either through first-hand dispatches, or via transistor radios. In between listening for nuggets of information, they'd sing Manson's songs, and tell anyone who cared to listen that Charlie and Co. would soon be free. When Charlie and the girls on trial carved an 'X' into their foreheads, outside their faction did the same. For the world's press, these sweet, gentle girls' association with what was perceived as outright evil, created a shocking duality.

At times when the case dragged, the girls engaged in publicity stunts to keep Manson in the news. One day, the girls decided to crawl for Charlie, wending their way through the streets of Los Angeles on all fours, with television news crews following the scene. At night, the girls slept in the bushes around the courthouse, until they managed to acquire an old white van. They lived off various handouts from the concerned and the plain curious – and money from their welfare cheques.

Just ten days after the prosecution rested its case, the jury reached a unanimous verdict. While there was to be no leniency for Manson, Atkins and Krenwinkel, Leslie Van Houten's fate was somewhat more complicated. Although she'd been proven to have a less important role than the others, her steadfast loyalty to Manson ensured that no mercy could be shown. All four defendants were found guilty of murder in the first degree. Charlie led the volley of cries towards the judge and jury. 'You're all guilty. We weren't allowed to put on a defence.' Turning towards Older, Manson screamed, 'Old man, you won't forget it in a long time.'

When the guilty verdicts were announced inside the Halls of Justice, the girls on the street corner offered their own responses. Huddled around a transistor radio with the world's press scrutinising their every move, Sandy Good, the most verbally adroit of the Family women, was swift to offer her reaction, proclaiming, 'There's a revolution coming and you are next!' This, and other threatening statements from the women made for excellent copy in newspapers already crammed with Manson stories. However, there were still a couple more legal rounds to endure before the trail came to a close.

The penalty phase was the stage of the legal process in which the court determined the appropriate sentencing for the crime. It also gave the defendants another chance to present their case. In a last-ditch attempt to unseat the prosecution's charges against Manson, the women accused Linda Kasabian of masterminding the murders, and called upon other members of the Family to support their claims. Gypsy testified, although she now maintains that Manson threatened to drag her behind a car at Spahn Ranch until her body was broken if she failed to do so. The jury did not rise to this obvious ruse, and sat unmoved as Manson's loyal followers attempted to absolve their master.

With little chance of overturning the prosecution's case, the death penalty was looking more and more like a certainty. While Manson had few supporters, the fate of the women was harder to determine. However, prosecutor Vincent Bugliosi had no doubts regarding the death penalty, and made his feeling abundantly clear to the jury. 'I told the jury, "If this [was] not a proper case of imposition of the death penalty, no case ever would be." I even challenged the jury. I said, "If you're not willing to come back with a verdict of death in this case, then we should abolish the death penalty in the state of California. How many people would you have to kill to get the death penalty?"'

The twenty-ninth of March 1971 was the day the Family members on the street had decreed as 'Judgement Day'. With death sentence notices anticipated, security was at an all-time high in the courtroom lest any attempt be made to derail the hearing. For the sentencing, Manson had shaved his head, commentating to waiting journalists, 'I am the devil and the devil always has a bald head.' Once more, the girls followed suit. Their shorn procession made for a pitiful sight, despite their smiles and garish costumes.

Inside the courtroom, it came as no real surprise that Manson was the first to receive the death notice. Charlie's presence had cast an enormous shadow over the whole trial, and he had become the main protagonist of the case. As the words left the judge's mouth, Charlie began shouting that his constitutional rights had been encroached. 'You don't have any authority on me,' Manson spat at Judge Older. 'You're not nearly as good as me.' On cue, the girls then spat out their own reactions.

Katie: 'You have just judged yourselves.'

Sadie: 'Better lock your doors and watch your own kids.'

Leslie: 'Your whole system is a game. You blind, stupid people. Your children will turn against you.'

Following the outburst, Judge Older ordered the girls and Manson out of the courtroom so that the formalities of the jury's decision could be presented. On the counts of first-degree murder, the order was for Manson and the three female defendants to be put to death in the gas chamber.

Outside, the girls on the street corner, their heads shaven in sympathy with those inside the courtroom, were aghast at the decision. They'd previously announced that they would pour petrol over their bodies and set themselves on fire if the death penalty was announced. With television cameras trained to capture their reaction, Sandy shouted, 'Death? That's what you're all going to get!'

After the necessary period of due deliberation, on 19 April 1971, Manson and the girls received formal confirmation of the death penalty. Judge Older rubber-stamped the decision, adding his own stipulation to the verdict: 'Not only is the death penalty appropriate, but is almost compelled by the circumstances of this case.' As was their right, Manson and the girls were present to hear the judge's verdict. Typically, Charlie offered his own idiosyncratic reaction: 'I have always lived in the truth of your courtroom. I have always done what I was told. Sir, I invented this courtroom. I accept this court as my father.'

Following the handing down of the sentences, the girls especially had to process what it really meant to them. In some ways, the severity of the sentence offered a perverse way of coping with the magnitude of their crimes.

Leslie Van Houten remembers her reaction: 'I was more than willing to go to the gas chamber. The death penalty for me at the time seemed ... it almost justified my not having to deal with what I had done. It was the "eye for an eye"; "they're going to kill me; I don't have to deal with it."'

In summing up, Judge Older praised the jury for their remarkable commitment. 'To my knowledge,' Older remarked, 'no jury in history has been sequestered for so long a period or subjected to such an ordeal.' He then walked over from his bench and shook each juror's hand. With these final actions, the curtain was drawn on the most incredible murder trial of the twentieth century.

For the victims' families, the guilty verdicts seemed cold comfort. All had seen their lives irreversibly damaged by the killings. Following the decision to put the defendants to death, it was hoped the healing process could begin. Paul Tate, Sharon's father, summed up the mood of the relatives of the deceased on hearing the guilty verdicts. 'That's what we wanted. That's what we expected. But there's no jubilation in something like this, no sense of satisfaction. It's more of a feeling that justice has been done. Naturally, I wanted the death penalty. They took my daughter and my grandchild.'

While there were many who heaved a sigh of relief at the conclusion of the trials, for the counterculture, the Manson saga had brought the 1960s to a deeply unhappy close. For the majority of peaceful hippies, the revolution that had once sought to free mankind and build a world based on peace and love had ended in horror, courtesy of Charles Manson. As if to confirm the death of the hippie dream, a disastrous free concert by the Rolling Stones in Altamont, San Francisco on 6 December 1969 had turned hideously sour. By the concert's end, four people were dead, including Meredith Hunter, a young black male who was murdered by a Hell's Angel while the Stones were playing. Despite sections of the counterculture being eager to extend the party into the next decade, there were few winners at the end of the Sixties, just a lot of broken dreams.

chapter 13
East

'The crimes are just the fruit of the tree. The crimes are just the part
you can see. Although they are the most tragic consequences, inner,
personally, they're not the most threatening part of the situation.
The most threatening part is what causes that, the destruction. And
what we saw was the destruction. But that's not as important as what
caused it.'

　　　Bruce Davis, 1993

IN between the capture of the Family and their subsequent
trials, dark events continued to occur in and around their shattered
circle. Contrary to popular opinion, Manson's sinister influence
would travel far beyond the vicinity of California. In fact, one of
the most intriguing chapters of Family history happened in the
United Kingdom – a suspicious death in a dingy West London
bedsit. We may never know for sure what really happened that
day in West Kensington, but it is certain that, a world away from
Charlie's desert hideout, two very different young men – both
with connections to Manson's inner circle – made the journey to
England, and only one came back alive.

During an exhaustive interview with the BBC's Bill Scanlon
Murphy in 1994, Manson let slip a small, yet highly significant
nugget of information concerning Family member Bruce Davis.
Although it was known that Bruce, one of the more mobile of
the Family members, had maintained a presence in California
during the Family's heyday, a number of trips Bruce made to the
UK during 1968 and again in 1969 remain, to this day, shrouded
in mystery. Not surprisingly, the spark behind these voyages
was Charlie, keen as ever to forge closer links with the Process
Church, Scientology and other darker elements connected to 'the

occult'. Additionally, Manson was determined to alert the Beatles to his presence following their 'White Album' revelations. As he explained to Murphy, 'I sent some people to England, I couldn't go myself, but I sent some people there, to do some certain things to make an effect, to cause an awakening of an awareness ... Bruce was just one person that went in that direction. There were some people riding motorcycles that was doing some other things ... You know how the occult is. You get involved in all kinds of darkness. It would take too long to explain it all.'

Undoubtedly, Bruce Davis's role within the Family is less clear cut than that of many of the others. Whilst most of the Family seemed content to follow Charlie, it appears Davis was concentrating his efforts on higher targets. Family member Barbara Hoyt had noted Bruce's ambitious streak.

'Bruce was older and vying for a leadership role in the Family, or at least a second in command to Charlie. He was the only other male to have worn Charlie's embroidered vest. He lectured like Charlie when Charlie was not there. We had more fear of Bruce than we had of Tex or Clem or anybody. He was scary. He obviously wanted to be head of the Family.'

Born on 5 October 1942, Bruce McGregor Davis first saw light in the town of Monroe, the eighth largest city in Louisiana. His parents were of working-class stock: father Bert was a pipe-fitter and welder, and mother Marguerite a housewife. He had an older sister, Judy. Bruce led a transitory early existence, moving first to Mobile, Alabama and then to Kingston, Tennessee. While securing considerable affection from his mother, Davis's relationship with his father was particularly tempestuous. A whipping boy for his father's frustrations, Bruce would find himself the constant butt of his anger. Davis's father was an alcoholic, and through the mist of alcohol came numerous beatings.

As Davis grew older he began to develop what would become a raft of physical health problems, possibly compounded by an alleged molestation by a family friend. While adept in the creative field, his father's constant abuse made any thoughts of following a career virtually impossible for Bruce. At school things weren't much better; as an adolescent, Davis was sexually abused by a schoolteacher and after that appeared happy to drift along, more than likely in an attempt not to draw any further attention to himself.

Despite these massive obstacles, Bruce graduated from high school in 1961. After an aimless summer, he secured a place at the University of Tennessee the following autumn. Davis attended classes only sporadically, however, and eventually he dropped out of college altogether at the age of nineteen. Over the next four years, Bruce wandered in and out of various menial jobs, and, despite repeated attempts to 'turn over a new leaf', he was never able to finish his education.

Finally Davis, perhaps accepting that academia just wasn't for him, left Tennessee altogether and headed off to California, where manual work was plentiful. Regardless of the tensions between parent and son, Bruce's father Bert had passed on some pipe-welding skills to aid his son's chances of getting work, and it was these skills that would later prove invaluable to Manson and his dune buggy assembly line.

Davis first arrived in California in 1962. His burgeoning affection for narcotics chimed beautifully with the anti-establishment attitudes of the time, and it was these two things that almost immediately led Bruce into contact with a string of like-minded recalcitrants. He very quickly established himself, funding his lifestyle with income from engineering work and indulging in various illicit substances, notably marijuana and LSD. His relocation to California proved to be a deeply empowering experience, and he was consumed by the enormity of his own 'prospects of personal power'. Like many of Manson's gang, acid proved an important factor in his new-found sense of self: '[Acid] enlarged my sense of what was permissible for me,' recalled Davis in 2000. 'It was all baby steps. The unthinkable became the thinkable. Then the thinkable became the do-able.'

It was during November 1967 that Davis would first come into contact with Charles Manson and the fledgling Family, during a trip to the Nevada desert. Soon after, he cemented his connection with a stay at one of the tribe's Topanga Canyon bases. Manson immediately sensed Davis's emotional vulnerability, and Davis very quickly came to adopt Charlie as the understanding father he had never had.

With the full range of Family delights at his fingertips, Davis began to indulge in Manson's version of Paradise. He'd elaborate on these first auspicious meetings in an interview with *World Magazine* in March 2000. 'I was very self-involved. Manson had a vision, and a group of ambitionless subjects. He understood what people needed and gave it to them . . . I thought what I was getting was acceptance, love, and respect.'

In the spring of 1968, soon after meeting Manson, Davis was picked up twice on charges of marijuana possession. The charges were dropped due to insufficient evidence, but he still spent ten days in the LA county jail. 'I got put in jail for something that I was innocent of,' he'd later recall. 'So I am in LA county jail, scared, disgusted with everything around me, don't know what's going to happen and I was in a lot of self-pity, feeling sorry for myself about [what] all these terrible people had done to me.' It was during this short time behind bars that Davis decided to 'commit himself to rebellion'.

After his release, Davis wholeheartedly swallowed Charlie's unique brand of sex, drugs and rock 'n' roll and, despite the Family's penchant for free love, it appears that Davis found a soul mate in Sadie. They connected on a level that went deeper than just sex, and managed to maintain a relationship – a rarity in Family circles – well beyond their days in the Family.

At nearly twenty-six years of age, Davis was one of the oldest members of Manson's followers. By dint of his age, gender and numerous abilities, he was afforded a significant amount of deference by other members of the Family. Buoyed up by their respect, Bruce quietly began to plot his own ascendancy. He shared Charlie's interest in the works of L. Ron Hubbard and, while the Family was in the process of moving themselves over to Spahn Ranch, Davis was reportedly often seen entering Thetan Manor. The manor was a communal, three-storey, fourteen-room Scientology house on South Bonnie Brea Street, and reports around the time suggest a bus, similar to the Manson Family vehicle, would regularly be seen parked outside. During his stay there, Bruce admitted to 'being intimate' with no less than nine residents of the house. One of these residents was a nineteen-year-old student called Doreen Gaul. According to papers later released by police, Davis broke off the relationship when he discovered that Gaul had also been seeing a black man. Gaul was later the victim of one of the most horrific murders California had ever witnessed.

An epiphany of sorts occurred in 1968 when his sister Judy tracked Bruce down to inform him that his father had died of a sudden heart attack. Davis was reportedly completely unemotional when told the news. Although he deliberately missed his father's funeral, Davis did return to Tennessee to collect his share of the will. There, his family noticed a change in him, one relative remarking: 'Something had happened to Bruce. He was involved in something. There was a "glaze" over his eyes ... He was blowing in from outer space.'

In December 1968, just days after the Beatles had released their much-anticipated 'White Album', Bruce – funded by his sudden windfall and the sale of his black BMW motorcycle – decided to take himself off on a prolonged trip overseas. Manson was happy to rubber-stamp the trip, especially as he knew that Davis was keen to drop in on London. Charlie's rap sheet would have prevented him applying for a visa, but having an emissary as keen as Davis was the next best thing. Charlie was eager to inform the Fab Four that he had received the messages apparently coded into their new album. Additionally, the Process Church's 'open-house' policy at their premises in Mayfair would allow Davis to mingle and promote Charlie's own brand of Processian magic.

Davis, however, did not travel alone on the trip; two unnamed men went with him (Manson refers to them as 'bikers'), and Charlie gave them a cache of stolen gold coins to sell. Manson was seemingly aware of 'Spinks', the noted coin dealers in London, and had advised Davis to drop in there as soon as he got into town. According to Davis, his travels took him through Spain and Portugal, North Africa and Gibraltar before he finally landed in England.

Once in London, Davis hooked up with the Scientology movement, ostensibly to further his knowledge of its disciplines. In his own words, he was 'attracted by their hospitality'. Such was his involvement with the movement that Home Office officials contacted Davis's family to confirm his student status and to ensure that he had some means of subsistence. From reports supplied by the Home Office, at some point Davis travelled thirty-odd miles out of London, and down towards East Grinstead on the Surrey/Sussex border. This trip into English suburbia was a well-trodden pilgrimage for all students of Scientology: East Grinstead the Mecca for all those wishing to trace L. Ron Hubbard's footsteps.

On the surface, East Grinstead appeared nothing more than a sleepy, though modestly wealthy enclave of suburban Britain. Over the years it has gained a reputation as the cult capital of the UK, hosting a variety of alternative religious organisations, which for reasons indiscernible, have all been drawn to the region. From Rudolph Steiner's Anthroposophists, to New-Age Pagans, to Mormons, Rosicrucians and many others, this seemingly unremarkable area is littered with the alternative. L. Ron Hubbard was sufficiently impressed with East Grinstead to buy Saint Hill Manor, a quintessentially English property set in fifty-nine acres on the edge of the town. Hubbard lived there from 1959 to 1966, personally taking many of the classes at the Manor. The once close-knit, largely agricultural community was unprepared for the massive influx of soul-searchers into the town during the late 1960s, and for a while there was a visible tension. Local Conservative MP Geoffrey Johnson Smith drew battle lines in July 1968 when he declared that the Scientology movement, 'direct themselves deliberately towards the weak, the unbalanced, the immature, the rootless and the mentally or emotionally unstable.'

Mr Smith's comments barely dented the Scientology's popularity, and accommodation for the many students that flocked to the area was at a premium. In 1969, to help alleviate the need for room-space, Dormer Cottage, a small, detached property on Woodcock Hill in nearby Felbridge, was commandeered to accommodate those wanting to be close to Saint Hill. During Davis's first trip to the UK, he gave this address as his place of residence. Here he'd hang out with several fellow students, starting a sexual relationship with one of his more attractive fellow students. It was during their time together that Davis would impart crucial details of the lifestyle he shared with Charlie and the Family.

To supplement his coursework, Davis found employment in the Scientology mail-room as part of their Foundation Staff team. Regardless of the movement's zero tolerance to narcotics, Davis's drug habits continued unabated and he only lasted a few weeks before being fired.

After the East Grinstead adventure, Davis returned to London, and hooked up with the Process Church and other left-field groups. Reports also suggest that some years later Davis collided with a decidedly murky organisation known as the Fraternity of Lucifer. The group, which boasted a worldwide network of like-minded dabblers, had been visible in Haight-Ashbury during the mind-explosion of the mid-1960s, and may well have crossed Manson's path. With London, at the tail end of the Sixties, a melting point of every conceivable kink and cult, Davis would have found many willing to dabble in the dark side of free love.

Following his five-month odyssey, Davis headed back to the States at the tail end of April 1969. Once back in Los Angeles, Davis was met by Charlie and one of the Family's women, Ella Jo Bailey. The trio travelled over to Spahn Ranch, allowing Bruce to be welcomed back into the mercurial, timeless world of the Family. Here his adventurous spirit and advanced technical skills were soon put into service, building Charlie's dune buggy and planning the organisation's next strike. Davis was to have more murky business to conduct in England later that year, but for now California was where the action was.

Within weeks, Bruce was involved with the killing of Gary Hinman, and was likely to have joined Charlie on his return trip to Cielo Drive following the massacre of its inhabitants. Bruce would further dirty his hands with Shorty Shea's bloody death. Despite the bloodshed, from all available information, Bruce's love for Charlie barely faltered. However, in the interview he gave in 2000, Davis claimed that on one occasion he was driven close to taking Manson's life.

It was shortly after the Tate–LaBianca killings when, wandering around Spahn Ranch, Bruce had discovered Manson sleeping in one of the barns. Apparently, Charlie had been suffering from the after-effects of some strong marijuana, and had dozed off, leaving a pistol lying in his lap. According to Davis, he was suddenly overcome with a desire to kill his leader. 'I could see with sudden clarity that killing Manson would be a good thing,' recalled Bruce. 'I could've easily made it look like a suicide.' Despite his momentary conviction, Davis balked at the task and walked off. Even asleep, Charlie's charismatic appeal was powerful enough to save his life.

Despite this momentary blip, Davis followed Manson to Barker Ranch in late September 1969. His stay there was brought to an abrupt end on 12 October when he was arrested (along with the rest of the Family) on a variety of auto-theft offences. On 3 November 1969, he appeared in court with John Phillip Haught, who stood under the pseudonym 'Christopher Jesus'. Haught's re-assignment as 'Jesus' had put Inyo County Officers in a quandry of sorts, as information they'd received had labelled Manson as 'Jesus', and not twenty-year-old Haught.

Born 20 April 1949, in Missouri, Haught had dropped into the Family as they were making their way to Death Valley in September of 1969. Despite his five-foot eight-inch frame, Haught was thickset and imposing. On his left arm was tattooed the words 'Little Devil', and a little further down 'Zero', a nickname which was soon adopted by Family members. By all known reports, Zero was drawn to the Family by the promise of sensual satisfaction, and he reportedly indulged heavily in the free-flowing sex that Manson encouraged amongst his followers. Given the fleshly pleasures of Family life, prison seemed like a particularly unappealing prospect for both men.

This time they were lucky. Davis and Zero were discharged from the courts due to insufficient evidence and fled in the direction of Venice, Los Angeles. There, they visited a house that was leased by an actor named Mark Stephen Ross. Ross had come late to the Family, but was sufficiently enamoured with the group to allow some of them to stay in his rented house, at 28 Club House Avenue. This was known territory for the Family, as a few doors down from Ross's pad was situated a popular meeting point for The Straight Satans motorcycle gang. Bikers, actors and Manson followers were all seemingly part of the scene at Club House Avenue.

Family members found their host Mark Ross an attractive

entity. The actor had been playing the role of a latter-day Christ figure in a low-budget film, and had retained many of the messianic trappings of the part. Such was Ross's fascination with the Family, he discussed the tribe's charisma with his friend, the film director Robert Hendrickson. As a result of Ross's tip-off, Hendrickson began to formulate plans for a documentary on the cult of Charlie and the Family.

As police investigations were edging closer to ascertaining the Family's involvement in the Tate–LaBianca slayings, Manson's followers nose-dived further into bloody madness. On 5 November 1969, Mark Ross was out at an acting class, leaving desert exiles like Zero, Bruce Davis, Cathy Gillies, Susan Bartell (aka 'Country Sue') and Manson's old prison buddy, Bill Vance, to skulk around and smoke hashish in the lounge. Inside one of the bedrooms that night was twenty-three-year-old Madeline Cottage, a.k.a. 'Little Patti'. At some point, Zero left the others to join Little Patti on her mattress. Given the heady atmosphere of free love, no one batted an eyelid. Little did they know that that was the last time they'd see Zero alive.

At around 7.30 p.m., Country Sue was in the bathroom adjoining the bedroom, and heard noises coming from Zero and Little Patti's direction. Minutes later, the soundtrack of grunts and moans was interrupted by the crack of gunshot emanating from the bedroom. Little Patti then fell out of the bedroom babbling, 'Just like in the movies, just like in the movies.' Bruce Davis and the others swiftly made their way to the bedroom to see what had happened. There they saw Zero, lying on the mattress, blood pouring from a gunshot wound to his temple. Country Sue held Zero as he lay dying, then covered him with a sleeping bag. Little Patti told the others: 'I touched the barrel of the gun.' At that Davis reportedly picked up the revolver, wiped it clean of prints, put it back in its leather holder and placed it near Zero's right hand.

In the heat of the moment, Little Patti escaped from the house and, using the pseudonym Linda Baldwin, called the police. When officers from a local division arrived at 7.45 p.m., they found the still-warm Zero lying on the mattress, with blood on the pillow and a bullet wound to his head. Police routinely questioned those present on what had occurred. Even by Manson Family standards, the story they presented was suspiciously tall. According to those present, Little Patti had been sleeping on the mattress when Zero walked in and got into bed with her. He apparently woke her up to ask her when she was going to fix dinner. He then began hugging her. As he was doing this he noticed Mark Ross's .22-calibre pistol lying on the night stand. Zero reportedly picked up the revolver, saying, 'Oh, here's a gun.' He then spun the cylinder, Russian roulette-style, remarking, 'Hey, there's only one in the chamber!' before pointing the gun to his head and pulling the trigger. Somehow Zero had been unaware that the pistol was fully loaded and, not surprisingly, died from a gunshot wound to the right temple.

Under separate interrogation, each member of the house confirmed the story, remarking that Zero wasn't 'apparently disturbed' in any way. With no one else present at the time of Zero's death, police were then left in a quandary, especially as the gun, and the leather wallet it was housed in, revealed no fingerprints. As a result they were forced to go along with the Russian roulette story. A police spokesman at the time remarked, 'We had to list it as suicide. The gun was fully loaded. He would have been blind not to have seen that.'

With the Manson connection to the Tate–LaBianca scenario still to be verified, no further investigations were undertaken. However, it was only later that police discovered that those present during Zero's death were full-blown members of the Family. Not surprisingly, everyone involved that evening quickly left the Club House Avenue residence that night; some making their way back to the Death Valley area, others disappearing into the ether.

Shortly after Zero's death, police roped in Danny DeCarlo for questioning. Although detectives were primarily fishing for information about the Tate–LaBianca killings, the biker identified Zero from a gallery of Family members' photos. The exchange was telling, DeCarlo reporting that, during his time with the Family, Zero, along with another young member, clearly 'didn't fit in'. Some weeks following Zero's untimely death, an anonymous individual contacted journalist Jerry Cohen of the *Los Angeles*

Times. He claimed to have been present during the night of the shooting, and evidently wanted to get something off his chest. On meeting Cohen, the anonymous informant revealed that it was 'one of the chicks that killed Zero'. This 'slight young man' told Cohen that he had run into the bedroom to find the girl holding the gun lightly by the trigger guard. She had reportedly told him that, 'Jesus shot himself.' Clearly shocked by the incident, the informant told Cohen, 'She had this strange faraway smile on her face, as if she was saying to me: "His time has come, time for me to shoot him."' Adding some insight to how those present could collectively twist events, the source told the reporter, 'You have to understand that those people believe, that "you are me, and I am you" to realise how their minds interlock, how she could have killed him and then said he did it.'

Cohen's source was said to be a fairly new member of the Family, who'd joined soon after the arrests in Death Valley. However, in that short time he had gained the group's confidence and had been given key information concerning their activities. Following Zero's killing, he had become, 'scared to death'. Among other peripheral details he passed on to Cohen, he declared that 'the Family is a whole lot larger than you think', and that there were, 'many more murders than the police know of'. Cohen paid his informant $25, and kept a line of dialogue open with him, with a promise of further cash incentives. At one point, the youth indicated that he was prepared to testify in court to substantiate his allegations, but following a planned trip to the north of California, he was never seen or heard of again.

With the news of Zero's spectacular demise hot on the Family grapevine, Country Sue Bartell popped over to Sybil Brand Institute for Women, to pay a courtesy call to Sadie, who was in custody on charges relating to Gary Hinman's death. Reportedly, Bartell imparted the whole story concerning Zero's death to a visibly excited Sadie. Country Sue apparently claimed that the hapless Zero had wanted to die and had 'rouletted' himself in the process. Sadie would later repeat the story to fellow inmates Virginia Graham and Ronnie Howard, sparing few details. If we are to believe Sue's story, there was a dark aura surrounding Zero's untimely demise. During the making of the film *Manson,* an incredulous Ronnie Howard would recount what she had heard. 'He said he was going to kill himself anyway, and she thought it would be a groovy experience. So he had the gun in his hand . . . and he told her, "When you start to reach your climax, tell me when." As soon as she started reaching her climax she said "OK, now", and when she said "now", he just took the gun to his head and "Bang", and killed himself, right in the head. And she said it was really groovy.'

If Zero's death had aroused suspicions, further deaths in Los Angeles would suggest a connection with the Family's bloody activities. On 17 November, deep in the winding brushwood ravines of Mulholland Drive, the mutilated body of a young teenage girl was found among the undergrowth. It was just two days after Zero's death, and this time had all the nightmarish hallmarks of a Family murder. The style of the 157 ferocious stab wounds to her neck and throat were horribly consistent with the Tate–LaBianca slayings. Disturbingly, the blade strokes included her right eye, a detail that would be repeated in further atrocities. The girl's clothing and jewellery denoted that she was every bit the hippie child, yet with no evidence confirming her identity, her name would remain a mystery. The leather belt she was wearing had originated from one of the Process Church members in Haight-Ashbury, and one of her rings had esoteric hieroglyphics dotted over it.

The girl's face and body were so badly disfigured that police were forced to issue an artist's impression of the victim, which was duly circulated to local press. As a result, reports suggested that she had been seen occasionally over at Spahn Ranch, and may well have been present at the Venice house where Zero had died. With the timing of her murder so close to Zero's killing, some heavy suspicions were raised. To this day, she has never been identified. 'Jane Doe 59', as she was referred to for police purposes, remains one of the saddest enigmas of the Family's saga.

Two weeks later the bludgeoned bodies of James Sharp, fifteen, and Doreen Gaul, nineteen, were discovered in an alleyway close to the Santa Monica Freeway. It was just before midnight on 21 November 1969 – sixteen days after Zero's bizarre death. The way they had been gruesomely butchered defied belief. Indeed, the ferocity with which they were killed led police to believe they were victims of shotgun blasts. They had taken some sixty knife wounds between them and, chillingly, both had been stabbed in the right eye, just as Jane Doe 59 had been. It soon became apparent that Gaul, who was naked on discovery, had also been raped. Forensics discovered that the pair had been killed at another location and then dumped in the Santa Monica alleyway. The last known sighting of the teenagers had been at 7.30 that night, when they were seen hitchhiking, reportedly heading for a Scientology lecture at Bruce Davis's old haunt, Thetan Manor, on South Bonnie Brea Street.

Both Gaul and Sharp were connected with the Scientology movement, and in fact it was at the manor that Gaul had first met Davis. According to newspaper reports at the time, despite Gaul attaining the status of 'Clear', she had become disenchanted with the religion, and had gone on to work in an insurance company. It was not known whether she kept up her stormy relationship with Davis in her new, straight life. Doreen Gaul was said by her father to be a 'good kid, an emotional kid. She was always looking for green grass and rainbows.'

It wasn't a safe time to be young and idealistic in LA. Less than a year later came the grisly discovery of the corpse of seventeen-year-old Marina Habe, found close to the spot where the 'Jane Doe 59' body was uncovered. Again, she'd suffered numerous lacerations and stab wounds to her eyes, but had also been burnt with cigarettes. Later, there was a suggestion that Marina had been fraternising with the Family at Spahn Ranch.

Already stretched by the Tate–LaBianca killings, Los Angeles detectives didn't have enough manpower to determine who was responsible for this new batch of downtown murders. Nonetheless, police were convinced that the links between these killings and the Tate–LaBianca crimes were too strong to ignore. Police Lieutenant Earl Deemer's first words on seeing the bludgeoned bodies of Gaul and Sharp were, 'The same ones that did Tate did these kids.' Deemer, who had been involved in the investigations into the killings at Cielo Drive, further noted that the knife wound patterns were almost identical to those in the massacre that occurred on 9 August 1969.

However, with the main players already in jail, police had little in the way of physical evidence to connect the killings with members of the Family. The press, in their own sensationalist way, were quick to add the murders to the litany of other senseless, seemingly motiveless murders that had occurred that year. They dubbed them 'thrill murders', and reported on the slayings in gruesome detail.

While no one was ever charged over the deaths, the rumours regarding Bruce Davis's involvement with the 'thrill murders' of Gaul and Sharp would not go away, and he was later interviewed about the pair's deaths. Although offered a promise of immunity, Davis was unwilling to cooperate, denying that he'd ever met Doreen Gaul, or knew anything about the killings.

Despite the fact that there were startling similarities between the string of LA murders, at the time police had no hard evidence to connect the crimes to Bruce and his fellow Family members. On 23 November 1969, just two days after the Sharp/Gaul murders, Davis flew back to the UK. A few weeks previously, during a journey through Death Valley to pick up fuel supplies, Davis had mentioned that he was off to London to study Scientology, adding that 'Helter Skelter would stun the world.'

Once back in the UK, Davis first spent time in London, where reports suggest he picked up a few girls. He then headed north, ostensibly to Liverpool to 'meet up with the Beatles' as per Manson's instructions. If Davis had indeed wanted to touch base with the Fab Four, he was around two hundred miles off course. The Beatles had long since forsaken the kitchen sink of Liverpool for the bright lights of London, and by 1969 were living in wealthy suburbia, while their Apple headquarters nestled in stuccoed affluence at 3 Savile Row in the heart of London's West End.

Seemingly badly informed, Davis travelled north anyway. While he might have had Penny Lane in his sights, Davis ended up in Manchester, some thirty miles adrift from the Beatles' home turf. Nonetheless, he found the city a fairly receptive base for his meanderings, and took out lodgings there; at the time Manchester was picking up a quiet reputation as an occult hotbed. During the late 1960s, 'Father of British Witchcraft' Alex Sanders was based in the city, and several groups had sprung up in his wake. Scientology was attempting to gain a foothold in the city, and now so too was the Family.

Davis's ramblings through the north of England weren't entirely without witness. C. P. Lee, founder member of the satire band Alberto y Lost Trios Paranoias was based in his native Manchester during the late 1960s. Despite being hip to the city's alternative scene, an experience with an individual matching Davis's description deeply unnerved him.

'I used to work at a "Head" shop in Manchester called On the Eighth Day,' he recalls. 'One of the girls who worked there was called Juliet, and she said that she'd met this American guy who was really "witchy". He was staying in Manchester, and was trying to persuade her to go to Liverpool, and then back to America with him. Anyway, she asked if I would check him out. Americans were very infrequent visitors to Manchester in those days, particularly American freaks. The guy was staying with a group of girls in the city ... His trip with the "chicks", it seems, was to give them acid, make love to them and pretend that he was their father. Anyway, we arranged to meet this guy in the boutique-cum-café bar in the House of Fraser department store. He was clean-shaven, had long hair, and was dressed in a suede fringe jacket with beads. He was more like a cowboy than a New Yorker. He was kind of witchy, and he appeared to be playing head and mind games. I remember that his hands were always busy. He was constantly making finger shapes like an Indian dancer. He said that he had to get to Liverpool to give the Beatles a message.'

It seems that the 'witchy' Davis was unsuccessful in tracking down the Beatles. There, the trail goes cold. Presumably, Bruce would have headed back to London and spent some time there before flying back to Los Angeles. Ostensibly, the Manson mission to London had failed. Yet the history of the Family in the UK has one last twist in its tail, involving an idealistic young American who'd end up forever entangled in the Manson Family web.

It seems that twenty-seven-year-old Joel Dean Pugh came loosely into contact with the Manson Family some time during March 1968. Joel was born 7 June 1940 to Marjorie and David Pugh; his father was a physician at Minnesota's Mayo Clinic. After serving time in the US Army, Joel had moved to northern California in the mid-1960s. He had taken up a job as a lab technician in a university in San Francisco, putting to good use his degree in Zoology and his interest in natural sciences. Joel was an original, if slightly off-beat character, who combined quirky passions with a great sense of humour.

'Joel was a very funny guy,' recalls his brother Daniel today. 'It was just nifty being with him at any time. I sort of admired him so much. He always had this great imagination ... When he was little, people would ask him what he wanted to be when he grew up. Joel had two answers: one was "to be a pirate". The other was, "to be a little boy".'

It was in San Francisco that Joel met Sandra Good, a student at San Francisco State College. She and Joel mingled in various collegiate circles, and being similarly aged, had hit it off. For a while, things appeared promising. Their happiness can be seen from a smiling photograph taken over Christmas 1967 at the Pugh household, Joel evidently proud of his petite, glamorous girlfriend. Despite being in his mid-twenties, it was Joel's first serious relationship.

His brother Daniel recalls the happy scene. 'She seemed like a very nice girl when she was staying with us ... Joel had never gone with a girl before, and we were very happy that things were looking up for him.'

Joel's closest confidante at this time was Jim Balfour. He was privy to all of Joel's movements around Sandy Good, and yet he shared none of his friend's affection nfor her, as he recalls today. 'I was very disturbed by her most of the time. She was probably charming when she needed to be. I thought she was a very loose cannon.'

The couple's joy was short-lived though. After a life-changing meeting with Manson in March 1968, for Sandy everything, including Joel, suddenly took second place. Depressing as it was for Joel to lose his first real love, the fact she'd run off with Charlie's strange gang added a large measure of insult. For a while, it appears Joel kept up contact with Sandy and even tried to steer her away from her new chapel of friends, especially Charlie.

Daniel Pugh remembers his brother's reaction. 'When she started hanging around with Manson, Joel was extremely embarrassed about it. He regarded Manson as a phoney, who was very full of himself and a sort of embarrassing character. He didn't want Sandy to have anything to do with a guy like that; sort of uncool by association ... Manson was what Joel, in his own words, would have called "a Gnarl".'

Evidently, Sandy's complete immersion in Manson's all-encompassing world placed an enormous strain on her and Joel's relationship, and they eventually broke up, putting paid to any wedding plans. As Los Angeles Deputy District Attorney Stephen Kay tells it, Manson couldn't have planned it better himself. 'Charlie wanted very much for Sandy Good not to be married, because her father had been very wealthy. He left a trust find that paid her two thousand dollars a month, which was the money the Manson Family lived off most of the time; that was their biggest source of income ... Joel was an irritant, and Manson didn't want anyone getting in the way of him and the trust fund.'

Ironically, it seems that Sandy herself held on to an idea of marrying Joel, despite no marriage certificate ever being recorded. During the 17 August 1969 auto-theft raid on Spahn Ranch, Sandy was booked as 'Sandra Collins Pugh'. In later arrests she would again refer to herself as Mrs Pugh. While it is well documented that the Manson girls used a plethora of pseudonyms when arrested, her choice of name seems significant. A rumour has gathered momentum over the years that Good became pregnant as result of her liaison with Joel. If there was any truth in the allegations, this would have pointed to their relationship lasting until late 1968. During the Barker Ranch arrest of 10 October 1969, Sandy was quizzed on the paternity of her small baby. She has since claimed that to save her child from being put in care, she used Joel's surname as a stalling device. However, despite the crowd of potential suitors, and the interminable sex orgies, Sandy also used Joel's name on the baby's birth certificate. This clearly records Ivan S. Pugh born to Sandra Good on 16th September 1969.

At one point during late 1969 when the fortunes of the

Manson Family were on the decline, Sandy returned to San Francisco to catch up with her old coterie of friends. In addition to informing people that, 'a lot of shit was going to come down', she reportedly made another attempt to cajole Joel into marrying her. Joel's freind Jim Balfour recalls the scene: 'She was visiting, and she was pregnant, and she wanted Joel to either marry her or say they were married, because she was going to use his name as the father, and that's what she did . . . My understanding of it is that she probably thought that with things that Manson's people were being charged with, it would look better if Manson weren't the father of the chld, and that she would use Joel as a respectable person . . . However, Joel's response to Sandy's request was clear; "no way"'.

By 1969, Joel's mental health had started to take a slide. Putting a strain on his fragile psyche, Joel had been dabbling with LSD and, as a result of one bad trip, he'd withdrawn inside himself, believing that he could never be happy again. Joel's wacky, off-beat persona was in itself an unwitting foil to his inner turmoil and also prevented him gaining any proper help.

His brother Daniel recalls this upsetting duality. 'I totally missed the fact that he was losing it . . . I didn't realise he was being as serious as he was about a lot of things. He decided that he was schizophrenic as a result of reading stuff by R. D. Laing and, like Laing, he thought it was some sort of a spiritual gift or something . . . The last time I saw Joel he remarked, very wistfully, that it would be nice if there was "something you could take that would let you be happy".'

Joel had maintained contact with various friends he'd met in high school who had also moved to California. They kept up a close alliance with him, and shared an interest in soul-searching. These friends were aware of his slide into depression, and rallied around as best they could. Being open to all the new psychological slants on offer, they freely offered their own opinions on his melancholy.

In a tape recorded message at the time of his son's death, Joel's father David recalls: 'When Joel was in trouble out there, his friends were all aware of it. And they were either having him read this kind of crap, or else they were quoting it to him. And they were trying to give him psychotherapy with the stupid information they had obtained from this way-out type of clinical psychiatry that these people read. Some of the others in the group wanted him to get professional help, but others felt they could talk him out of the problems.'

As a result of his mental decline, Joel stopped working in the laboratory and returned to his parents' home. There he read a book on rainforests, and became obsessed with South America. Pleased that his son finally seemed interested in something other than his own psychological state, Joel's father funded a trip for him to visit the region. Despite a considerable amount of time spent wandering around, Joel never found the rainforests of his dreams, and in the end he returned home.

Despite his disappointment, Joel's wanderlust was unabated, and he decided that he wanted to go to Morocco, North Africa. Landing in Marrakech, his hopes of authentic Middle Eastern promise were swiftly dashed. On seeing the legions of Western travellers in various hedonistic states, he turned away disgusted, and moved northwards towards Spain. There, he ran into some friends of his who were also travelling through Europe, and together they continued their journey. It was during this period that Joel convinced himself that he could predict the future from reading comic books, a game he'd become increasingly obsessed with. One female in this travelling party was schoolteacher, Harriet Smith, who recalled Joel saying that he'd deduced from the comic strips that 'she would become his wife'.

Despite his crazy predictions, Joel was taken under the wings of his travelling buddies and tagged along with them to London. Once there, Joel found lodgings in West Kensington, an area which, despite the swanky name, had long been a cheap base for peripatetic wanderers. The room he rented was at the Talgarth Hotel, situated on the busy Talgarth Road, a main artery that links London with the west of England. The title 'hotel' was a somewhat grandiose one, as the property was nothing more than a collection of basic, self-contained rooms, available for long-term rent. It was a far cry from the glamour of the Amazon rainforest or the Moroccan deserts.

According to the Talgarth's records, Joel moved in on 27

October 1969 – a month before Bruce Davis made his second trip to the UK. With him was a female, 'a hippie' who never gave her name. Joel and his live-in partner took out weekly terms on a single room, and were allotted a ground-floor flat overlooking the rear of the property. Manager Joseph Falk was impressed with his guest, noting Pugh as being a 'very nice person . . . Very clean in his ways and quite a gentleman.' From time to time Joel's travelling friends would pop over and try to encourage him to visit various sights around town with them. Depressed once more, he'd tell them that he was 'unworthy of London' and was content to stay in his room. At one point during his stay, he told Harriet Smith about the breakdown of his relationship with Sandy Good. Clearly, it was still on his mind. Smith, like other members of Pugh's travelling group, was more concerned about Joel's slide into depression, and tried to get him to seek professional advice. Joel refused, telling her that his quest was to 'find out who I am'.

Once in West Kensington, Joel began to ensconce himself in his room with his female companion. However, the joy was to be short lived. Joel's partner would leave after three weeks. The manager, Joseph Falk, noted 'Mr Pugh became more withdrawn and stopped eating. Eventually he was only drinking coffee.'

Despite his enforced isolation, Joel would always keep his door unlocked, and would while away the hours playing the guitar and reading. His most consistent visitor during those days was the seven-year-old son of the manager, who'd occasionally pop by to see him. The young boy evidently enjoyed Joel's company, especially as Pugh shared his beloved comic book stories with him. He also showed the little boy backwards writing, a process that Joel himself found fascinating. Much to the child's delight, Joel would reflect whatever was written in the mirror to make it legible, scribbling jokes and fragments of nursery rhymes. Meanwhile, his fascination with comic books would start to overwhelm Joel; alone for so many hours of the day, he felt that he was being sucked into their fantastical tales.

The day of 1 December 1969 would prove pivotal in the fortunes of the Manson Family. In Los Angeles, relieved police finally announced they'd broken the Tate–LaBianca case by finally connecting it to the Family's nefarious activities. For Joel Pugh in London, the day would signify a much darker and finite conclusion to his personal troubles. The only known movement of Joel that day was to pop down to reception to fix himself a coffee. There, he met the hotel manager and exchanged some small talk. Once his coffee was sorted, Joel swiftly retreated back to his room. That was the last time he was seen alive.

The following morning the hotel's cleaner was performing her usual duties, and wasn't unduly perturbed when she found Joel's door locked. At around 6 p.m. that evening, manager Joseph Falk knocked on Joel's door to check he was OK. On getting no response, Falk attempted to gain entry using his passkey. However, on unlocking the door, Falk sensed a weight keeping the door shut, and could only partially open it. Putting his hand around the door, he felt 'what seemed like an arm' hanging limply on the inside.

Police were immediately called; a few minutes later, PC Wright, a constable from the local Hammersmith Police Station, arrived at the premises. Forcing his way into the room, he saw Joel lying on his back, with a couple of razor blades lying about two feet away from him. He was naked, save for a sheet covering the lower part of his body. There was blood everywhere. On inspection, Joel's throat had been slit twice, there were razor cuts to his wrists and a bruise was on his forehead.

On searching the room further, a pipe with traces of cannabis resin was discovered. Police also found the comic books and the mirror writing that so captivated Joel's young friend. Pugh's body was taken away to await a coroner's inquiry, although the job of notifying Joel's family was passed to the American consulate.

With no immediate clues to Joel's death, a thorough and comprehensive autopsy was ordered. Metropolitan Police pathologist, Richard Pearce, made the following observations: 'The body is thin, there are bruises on the forehead and left shin. There are incised wounds in either side of the neck (three inches long) parallel to the sterno-mastoid muscles and extending deeply to the muscle; the external jugular veins are divided. Trial cuts are present. There are a number of slashes of both wrists in the long axis of the forearms, and a superficial cut across the front of the elbow.' Adding to his belief that Joel had inflicted the wounds on himself, Pearce noted that Pugh had a nick in his left hand from holding a razor blade.

Later in his report, Pearce would note, 'There was no wound not capable of being self-inflicted,' and that there was no evidence of a struggle or violence.

Following the completion of autopsy and psychiatric report, the coroner declared Joel's death a suicide at West London Magistrates' Court on 9 December 1969. Joel's emaciated state, the length of time he'd spent isolated in his room, and the residue of the cannabis resin found in his bedroom, along with the fact that his door was locked from the inside, all made it look as if he'd taken his own life. There was a smattering of press there to hear the verdict, although with no foul play recorded, the story was not deemed worthy of any national interest. However, both the *West London Gazette* and the *Fulham Chronicle* made some mileage out of the reverse writing and the comic strips. The *Fulham Chronicle*'s headline, 'Death Notes in Mirror' would later fuel erroneous rumours that the backwards writing had been written on the mirror in blood.

Following the coroner's hearing, police immediately suspended any further investigations into Joel's death; their paperwork was duly filed away, and later destroyed. At that time, Scotland Yard wasn't in the slightest bit aware of the dead man's connection with Manson, through Sandra Good. Equally, they had no inklings as to Bruce Davis' movements; believed to have been in London around the time that Joel died.

When Joel's parents were informed of their son's death, they allowed his body to be cremated in England, and waited for his remains to be sent back to the family home. Whilst the tragedy hit the Pugh family hard, Joel's father (himself a sufferer of depression, as well as a psychiatrist) was familiar with the landscape of mental illness. Having charted his son's slow slide into melancholy, he had no cause for suspicion over his death. A couple of years later, Joel's father and brother Daniel travelled over to the UK to retrace Joel's last footsteps. They visited the Talgarth Hotel and talked with the owner about Joel's unhappy end. At that time they had no idea that police investigators back in American were starting to raise questions about Joel's death.

On the surface, Joel's death appeared nothing more than the tragic demise of an intelligent young man with everything to live for. For the Manson Family, with their eyes sharply tuned to signals from anyone who'd crossed their path, news of Joel's death came quickly, and in a manner that would intrigue generations of investigators to this very day.

Following the arrest of Manson and his cohorts at Inyo County during October 1969, Joel's ex, Sandy Good, and Squeaky were holed up inside a motel on the fringes of Death Valley; their brief was to keep close contact with Manson and act as a communication line between him and the disparate strands of the Family. With news of Manson and his clan now out in the public domain, police were keeping tabs on anyone connected to the Family. As Charlie's prime emissaries, Sandy and Squeaky's movements were kept under close surveillance. Aware of this, and equally aware of their rising accommodation costs, the pair decided to flee their motel room early in January 1970. As expected, police jumped swiftly in, and filleted the room for clues. Among the detritus left behind was a letter Sandy had recently received from an associate called Joanne, whom Joel's father recalled was a close friend of his son's.

The contents of this letter have assumed legendary status. In late 2008, after being presumed lost, the letter resurfaced in a university archive in Nevada. The full contents of Joanne's note have never been publicly revealed before, and offer a fascinating perspective on Joel's untimely death.

Although the letter was written without any forwarding address, much of what is said appears to follow previous conversations. Reading between the lines of the text, it is abundantly clear that Joanne was very close to Joel. The letter's first references to Joel's recent death occur early in the letter. All the references to Joel are reproduced here verbatim; no words or phrases have been changed.

Pugh! Sandy, I'm changing and changed so much since. I'm pulled, twisted-my body and my mind have gone through so many changes in the last two weeks, feeling one part of me pulling towards Joel- so strongly I took (A)[7] to attempt to reach him, and even thought of killing my own self- all these- or some sort of experience and things replaced by a high of feeling his presence- his nearness- a new strength because I have a friend, a lover, who knows- and he told me the day before he left that he'd either come back or send for me if he were in a good place. I've got to find out what to do, and yet I can't let what happened to Joel, happen to me – or should I?

... I'm not sure if its help I need or a lover, or a purpose or new friends. I'm not so sure anything will help, but I'm ready to try anything- first off a move- a move- far away- maybe Europe- anonymity- God, sounds like Joel. Jesus what can I say.

Police in Inyo County greedily scanned the letter for any coded information. Not surprisingly, alarm bells rang when they found out that Joel Pugh had recently died in mysterious circumstances. The passage of Joanne's letter reading, 'I can't let what happened to Joel, happen to me' was swiftly copied over to police working on the Tate–LaBianca cases in Los Angeles. Inyo County District Attorney Frank Fowles, whose department had let Bruce Davis slip through the net in the wake of the Barker Ranch raid, was quick to act.

Recently discovered papers reveal that Fowles's investigations went to the highest level of authority on both sides of the Atlantic. Initially, Fowles went to Interpol to confirm whether Davis was in the UK at the time of Pugh's demise. The enquiry was soon disseminated to police over at Scotland Yard. British police confirmed that Davis's movements in the UK had been tracked earlier in 1969, but couldn't confirm his whereabouts in December 1969. However, local police believed that Davis had made a return trip to England later that year.

Whilst the coroner's report of suicide ensured that the file on Pugh's death was closed, detectives working on the numerous Family investigations in the States were amazed that a case for murder wasn't explored. As reported by Ed Sanders in his book, *The Family*, LA Sheriff's detective Paul Whitely recalled, 'That thing just stunk to high heaven ... It was handled just by a routine patrolman and they kissed it off as suicide.'

Despite being consumed by the Tate–LaBianca case, prosecutor Vincent Bugliosi was alarmed by the details of Pugh's death, and would later add it to the list of deaths that he felt could be attributed to the Manson Family. District Attorney Stephen Kay, privy to all the data flying around in Manson Family case files at that time, recalled an atmosphere of deep suspicion once news of Joel's death made its way back to Los Angeles. With Pugh's strong association with Sandra Good, the likelihood of Bruce Davis being in UK at the time, and – not least – the strange circumstances of his death, Kay was wholly sceptical of the suicide verdict. He still is. 'When people over here ask me, "Do you think that the Manson Family committed any more murders than they were prosecuted for?" I say, "Well, the one we always thought was the most suspicious was Joel Pugh being murdered in London."'

Despite the considerable interest in Joel's death from police in California, no attempt was made to contact the Pugh family to ask pertinent questions regarding Joel's history of mental illness. Likewise, Joanne's letter was also kept out of the public domain for many years. In fact it was not until the publication of Vincent Bugliosi's book *Helter Skelter* in 1974 that Joel's family and friends became aware that he was being talked about as another possible victim of the Manson Family.

Meanwhile, the enigmatic Bruce Davis – who at the end of 1969 seemed to have fallen off the map – eventually reappeared in the Death Valley area during February 1970. On 17 February he was picked up and held on other charges relating to the Barker raids. While officers had been investigating Bruce's trip to England, and the controversy caused by Joel Pugh's death, there was no hard evidence to hold him and Bruce was released.

Bruce scuttled back to Los Angeles and, once there, he hung around Spahn Ranch and even attended a few of the court hearings for Charlie and the girls. With documentary maker Robert Hendrickson training his cameras on Spahn's during this period, Bruce took the opportunity to don Charlie's ceremonial vest. If ever there was a sign that Bruce was assuming de facto leadership in Manson's absence, it was at this moment. The sight of Davis confidently strutting his stuff around Family HQ, in the intricate vest that 'only Charlie could wear' was more than just a vain display: it was a statement of intent.

Davis again fell foul of the law a few months later when it was discovered that a firearm he'd purchased the previous summer had been obtained with false identification. Although arrested on the felony, someone stumped up $10,000 bail, and he walked free, with little intention of answering the charge. It was later discovered that the pistol Davis had been charged over was used in the notorious murder of Gary Hinman.

With so much Manson Family activity pouring through the courts, Mary Brunner was able to cut a deal with police to give her immunity on charges relating to Hinman's death. During questioning, she had implicated Bruce Davis in the murder, and as a result, a warrant for Davis's arrest went out on 14 April 1970.

Aware that he was a wanted man, Davis swiftly went underground. The night before his disappearance, he'd brazenly appeared at a Family party at Spahn's, which had been captured on film by Robert Hendrickson. Mindful of his wanted status, Davis hung back in the shadows, well out of the glare of the lights and cameras. It was a bold move to attend, as police were monitoring the activities at Spahn Ranch on a daily basis by car and by helicopter. Confirming his fugitive status, Sheriff's officers compiled a 'wanted' poster detailing some of the many guises that Davis operated under.

For the next seven months, Davis led a hunted life. Passing through a succession of Family safe houses, he made clandestine meetings to keep up to date with the diminishing fortunes of the Family. Joining him on the latter part of his enforced sojourn was Brenda McCann, herself fleeing a charge for forgery. Together they hiked around the hinterlands of California, dropping in on Death Valley. Inyo County police were rightly concerned about reports that Bruce and Brenda were revisiting the area, and a search party of over twenty police personnel was employed to scour the area for the couple. Taking no chances, they even commissioned a desert gamekeeper to try and snare the feral couple.

After Death Valley, Bruce and Brenda moved to Los Angeles, and the city's labyrinthine storm-drain system. Police had been informed that Davis and Brenda were living an outlaw existence under the earth, and had sent officers to try and flush out the pair. Although police came close to locating them on several occasions, it appears the slippery pair's knowledge of the pipelines' layout enabled them to evade capture.

Towards the end of the year, the couple's trail ran cold. There were reports that the pair had embedded themselves in Ventura County, about 130 miles outside central Los Angeles. This happened to be the site of defence lawyer Ronald Hughes's last known movements. With Hughes's disappearance logged on the morning of 30 November 1969, suspicions were ignited when Bruce and Brenda sent word they were ready to hand themselves in – just a few days later. Reportedly, this was on Manson's order. With word that some sort of deal could be struck, the pair appeared outside the Halls of Justice just after midday, to be met by a posse of screeching Family members, press and police personnel. Manson had asked defence lawyers Daye Shinn and Paul Fitzgerald to be present when the pair arrived, and to accompany them into custody. Charlie's lawyer Irving Kanarek was also waiting on the courtroom steps; the suited solicitor looking highly incongruous amongst the squealing throngs of Manson's girls.

Being on the run for nine months hadn't dented Davis's spirit, and he laughed as he emerged with Brenda out of a truck and into the limelight. Even the driving rain didn't dampen their spirits. The pair, with newly scored Xs on their heads, gleefully tripped barefoot across the junction of Temple and Broadway, arm-in-arm. As befits the enduring celebrity of the case, Brenda and Bruce were allowed to meet the press before being taken into custody. Once in the media scrum, they introduced themselves as 'Mr and Mrs Davis', claiming they had tied the knot in Las Vegas. They grinned out at the journalists, looking for all the world like a hippie version of Bonnie and Clyde.

It was later discovered that Bruce had dropped a tab of acid prior to their arrest. Looking at the footage today, Davis's chatter is as cosmic as the gold lamé clothes he'd worn especially for the occasion.

'I'm here to get my father out of the tower,' he claimed. '...They want to kill bodies don't they? I'm here if that's what they're after.'

While reporters battled unsuccessfully to get coherent quotes from Davis, he did impart one intriguing morsel of information. On being told by a reporter that he'd face charges relating to the deaths of Gary Hinman and Shorty Shea, Davis cocked his head quizzically and retorted, 'Is that all?'

While police were happy to strike a deal with Brenda over her forgery charge, this time there was no way out for Davis. In fact, given the spate of deaths that seemed to occur wherever Davis went, LA lawmakers went to extraordinary lengths to ensure Davis's convictions. Despite the fact that Shorty Shea's body had yet to be discovered, Davis was charged with the murders of both Shea and Gary Hinman and sentenced to life in jail.

Over the years, and despite his convictions, the enigma surrounding Davis has endured. Did he have a hand in the deaths of Joel Pugh, Jane Doe 59, Doreen Gaul and James Sharp, or any of the other unsolved 'thrill murders' that plagued California during those heady years? Or is that all just, as he claims, wild speculation? Although imprisoned for the murder of Gary Hinman and Shorty Shea, recent parole hearings have offered the man some hope of freedom. However, Stephen Kay, who successfully tried Davis back in 1971, has strong opinions on his suitability for release. 'Bruce Davis is a very dangerous person. He was the number two in the Family. Whenever Manson left to go on a trip or something he'd leave Bruce Davis in charge ... I'm afraid he may get out at some time, but it would certainly be over my objection and the objection of the Los Angeles District Attorney's Office.'

Dr Howard Davies has even more serious objections. Over twenty years of research have led him to believe that, in addition to deaths ascribed to the Family, Davis may well be the infamous Zodiac mass murderer who terrorised California throughout the 1960s. In support of his shocking theory, Dr Davies wrote, *The Zodiac/Manson Connection*, an exhaustive account of Bruce Davis's movements before his arrest in Death Valley on 12 October 1969. If the book is correct, the unsolved murders that have been outlined in this chapter would represent only a small part of Davis's bloody campaign of terror.

Given Bruce Davis's long silence, it is tempting to look elsewhere amongst the Manson followers for clues that might link Joel Pugh's death with the cult of the Family. Sandra Good, to this day still loyal to Manson and his aims, sternly refused to comment on the fate of her former partner for the best part of forty years. However, on a website she hosted for Manson during the late 1990s, she wrote: 'Pugh is usually described as the husband of Sandra Good. In fact they were never married. Although Pugh is also described as a "former Manson Family member" in [Bugliosi's] *Helter Skelter*, he never met Manson or any of the other so-called Family members. After Joel Pugh's death his parents journeyed to London to satisfy themselves with the official verdict of suicide. After checking all the medical records and the files at Scotland Yard they were satisfied that the death was, indeed, a suicide.'

For Joel's father David, the spectre of his son's demise weighed heavily on him. In happier days he had got into the habit of keeping in touch with his children by means of tape-recorded messages. When Joel died, his father put his thoughts regarding his death on to tape, which he then sent over to his remaining sons. The tape survives to this day, and reveals his sense of loss: 'It hurt all of us terribly [that] Joel destroyed himself,' David Pugh reflected. 'I think that worse things could have happened to him. We loved him dearly. I don't know if Joel realised how much we loved him. But I think he did recognise the deep affection that we had, and I think he had great affection for us.'

In the years after his death, Joel started to appear in his father's dreams on a regular basis. Upon waking, he'd have to face the sad truth that his son was dead. To distract himself, Joel's father would often stay up late, translating texts from Japan; a country whose culture and language fascinated him. While poring over an anthology of haiku late one night, he came across a brief poem that moved him deeply, and seemed to resonate with the loss of his son. It is a bittersweet reminder of the human cost of all this soul-searching gone awry: 'I wonder in what fields today, He chases butterflies in his way, My little boy who ran away.'

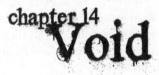

chapter 14
Void

'If I'm not paroled
And I don't get a chance
To get back on top of this dream
You're going to lose all your money
Your farms ain't going to produce
You're going to win Helter Skelter.
You're going to win your reality
You're going to get everything you want.'

Charles Manson 1992

CHARLIE had always wanted to be a rock star and, now that he was a convicted murderer, it looked as if he might finally get the chance. With tales of his musical pretensions leaking out of court, it wasn't surprising that tapes of Charlie's early recordings began to surface. Courtesy of Manson's earliest musical champion, Phil Kaufman, an album of twelve songs was cobbled together from a 1968 session to capitalise on the Family's notoriety. Shamelessly lifting Charlie's picture from the December 1969 cover of *Life* magazine, two thousand copies were pressed, under the ambivalent title, *Lie*.

Squeaky, Brenda and a few of the girls held a press conference at Spahn Ranch to launch the record. The presence of a film crew and a smattering of journalists did little to help propel the album up the charts. Finding suitable outlets for the disc was clearly going to be difficult, so a mail-order scheme was devised. However, only a few leftist and fringe publications were prepared to take the advert. Regardless of the effort involved, initial sales only totalled a few hundred.

Undaunted by the album's dismal showing, Charlie green-

393

lighted the recording of a collection of his songs by Family members still at large. Entitled, *The Manson Family Sing the Songs of Charles Manson*, it succeeded only in turning Manson's twisted tunes into a girl scouts' sing-along. Only the cult magazine *Crawdaddy* dared to afford it review space, and promptly crushed its appalling pretentions underfoot.

'This is banal in the proper sense of the term,' read the review. 'Mediocre talentless hippies, an artefact that only a really sick puppy would want to own. Nasty people, shit record.'

The Family's 'shit record' was at least fairly innocuous. However, there were other, far more deadly plans afoot at Family Grand Central. Indeed, if anyone believed that the death penalty sentences would bring an end to the Manson Family saga, they were soon proved wrong.

Whilst Charlie's supporters outside the courthouse were relying on hope that those imprisoned would soon be free, behind the scenes a more concerted effort was being cooked up. Front-liners Mary Brunner and Gypsy had formed a rogue cell with newcomers Dennis Rice, Chuck Lovett, and Lawrence Bailey. With them was Kenneth Como, a charismatic thirty-three-year-old prison escapee who shared a charismatic similarity with Charlie. In honour of his fearlessness, Como had been nicknamed 'Jesse James' by fellow convicts. Como had hooked up with Manson while both were in custody, and discovered they had a lot in common.

Adding to his notoriety, Como was a member of the infamous prison mob, the Aryan Brotherhood. Wanting to befriend the 'World's Most Dangerous Man', Como and members of the Brotherhood began to fraternise with Charlie behind bars. Since his own philosophy was deeply racist, Charlie easily engaged with the Brotherhood's neo-Nazi sympathies. In return for protection from the other prisoners, Charlie had offered the accommodating services of his harem of females on the outside to exiting Brotherhood members. Additionally, some of Manson's girls were smuggling in contraband to the men inside.

Pre-empting his own release, Kenneth Como escaped from jail in Los Angeles, and swiftly made his way over to one of the Family safe houses. The Como/Family alliance was quick to bear fruit, and they quickly relieved an off-licence of over $2,500. Eight days later, the faction embarked on a much more ambitious plot. If their plans had worked, it would have offered an even more frightening codicil to an episode that has already rewritten criminal history.

In an attempt to get Manson and the others out of jail, Como, Mary Brunner, Gypsy and Co. had allegedly planned to hijack a 747 airliner. Once this was done, they'd kill one passenger at a time on an hourly basis, until Charlie and other Family members were freed. Even by Manson Family standards, the plot was fantastical; but, given their devotion and scant regard for the law, perhaps they could have pulled it off. With international terrorism in its ascendancy during the early 1970s, hijacking became an emotive bartering tool. Charlie was evidently looking for something from his followers on this sort of scale. He told newcomer Dennis Rice, 'Don't come to get me, unless you can take out the whole jail.'

Needing considerable weaponry for the task, the six-strong gang earmarked the Western Surplus Store in Hawthorne, Los Angeles, as a suitable target. The day they chose to relieve it of its stock was Saturday 21 August 1971. The store was open late but, being a weekend, was fairly quiet as it ran towards closing time. Just before 9 p.m., a white van appeared in an alleyway at the side of the premises. Bursting in at the rear, the gang secured the store, holding two customers and a female assistant at gunpoint. The van was then loaded up with over 150 guns and a range of ammunition. At some point, the shop assistant managed to trip a silent alarm, and within minutes a stream of police vehicles arrived and sealed off the area. Cornered, the tribe dismissed an idea to hold shop staff and punters as ransom, and fled out through the rear exit.

Dennis Rice takes up the story. 'We came out of the back of the store. We opened fire on the police car. We blew out the front window of the car with a shotgun . . . They'd gotten out of their car and were hiding behind a wall on the other side of the alley, so as soon as we got back in our van they opened up on us. They put so many holes in our van, it looked like Swiss cheese; I felt bullets creasing my scalp.'

With the gang surrounded and their hopes of escape remote, they gave up. For their efforts, those involved in the Hawthorne shoot-out were sentenced on charges ranging from five years to life imprisonment. Taking the chance to politicise their actions, the tribe cobbled together a press release, and leaked it out to the media. 'We were and are determined to free as many of the victims of the Criminal System as we possibly could and to build and spread this thought to others.'

Whilst awaiting sentencing, the mercurial Como yet again broke out from his cell in the Halls of Justice. He escaped in the courthouse girls' white van, driven by Sandy Good. However, police easily outdrove the van and arrested the pair. For his troubles, Como saw his sentence extended yet again, whilst Sandy served a six-month sentence for assisting him. However, the Aryan Brotherhood link with the Family lasted beyond Como's recapture, and others would wend their way towards Charlie's girls on their release.

With drama occurring outside the courtroom, Tex Watson, the main hatchet man of the August 1969 murder spree was engaged in his own separate trial. Despite every conceivable objection from his defence counsel, Watson had been brought to Los Angeles to stand trial. Since his arrest, Tex had fallen headfirst into a pit of psychosis, and was refusing to eat. As a result, his weight had dropped to a little over fifty pounds. By all accounts, Watson spent his days curled up in a foetal position, babbling nonsense. He lost control of all bodily functions and his condition steadily deteriorated into what specialists called 'an acute psychotic state'. Tex was removed to Atascadero State Mental Hospital for a ninety-day assessment. Despite his sorry state, rumours persisted that Watson was faking his condition in an attempt to escape an inevitable death sentence. Hearing of Tex's condition, Manson offered to 'straighten him out in twenty minutes' with his dazzling array of mind-control techniques. Prosecutor Vincent Bugliosi, mindful of tales of Manson's superhuman powers, acknowledged the offer, but didn't want Charlie performing any miracles with Tex. 'I'm sorry,' reported Bugliosi, 'I can't afford to take that chance. If you cured him, then everyone would believe you were Jesus Christ.'

More conventional specialists in mental health decreed that

Watson was fit to stand trial, and so he took the stand in the first week of August 1971. With the prosecution's tales of a satanic, knife-wielding predator preceding him, there were gasps of incredulity as the gaunt, preppy boy sat down in the dock.

Ex-Family member Barbara Hoyt was there to give testimony against the Texan. She was shocked by his transformation. 'He painted the picture of a young Republican, like a college student from the 1950s ... He was a striking contrast from when I knew him before, when he was flamboyant, happy-go-lucky ... Now, he was solemn, moody. He seemed a little bit disconnected to everything going around.'

Despite recovering most of his equanimity, Watson entered a plea of 'not guilty' on account of insanity. With much of Watson's case covering the same ground as the other defendants, Watson vainly battled to present himself as being under Manson's spell when committing the murders. Furthermore, he downplayed his own involvement in the crimes. Aware that a case for diminished responsibility was being cooked up, the prosecution wheeled out a succession of psychiatrists and psychologists to verify their claims that Watson was fully in control of his actions during the murder spree. Their observations were telling.

Dr Joel Fort stated: 'Watson probably had no mental illness at the time of the crimes that would prevent him from forming a specific intent to perform murder. He demonstrated the mental capacity to deliberate, to premeditate, to hyper malice and to meaningfully reflect upon the gravity of his actions to the extent that he knew what the result would be for his victims and what it would be for himself to be caught.'

Watson's trial concluded after twelve weeks on 12 October 1971. The jury needed little prompting, to convict Tex on seven counts of first-degree murder and conspiracy to murder. On 14 October, he was sentenced to death and sent to San Quentin to sit on Death Row.

There were other notable casualties of the Family trials; lawyer Ronald Hughes's fate being perhaps the most sinister. Leslie Van Houten's lawyer had gone missing during the first round of murder trials, after refusing to let his client sacrifice herself for Manson. Now, in between the verdict and penalty phase of Tex's trial, the court received news that Hughes's naked body had been discovered by fishermen trawling through Sespe Creek, some six miles from his last reported location. The lawyer's corpse had badly decomposed in the months following his disappearance, and was found wedged between two rocks. It took dental X-rays to ascertain it was indeed Hughes's body.

First reports drew a blank over the cause of Hughes's death. In certain quarters though, his death was regarded as deeply suspicious. Prosecutor Bugliosi strongly suspected foul play, and demanded an immediate inquiry. However, as the coroner had reported that there was no tangible evidence to suggest outside interference, the request was denied. Nonetheless, with whispers starting to gather momentum, Bugliosi heard through a third party that Hughes's death was one of the first 'retaliation killings' ordered by Manson. This was confirmed by a phone call Bugliosi later received. 'I got a call a couple of years later from a former, young male associate of the Manson Family who wanted to remain anonymous. And he said, "I want to tell you that Ronald Hughes was murdered by the Manson Family."'

Although it's possible that the Family capitalised upon the sensational timing of Hughes's death, several key questions remain unanswered. In preparation for his weekend away, Hughes had taken reams of written testimony related to the trial to peruse while he relaxed. With him also were several tape-recorded interviews with Charlie and other Family members. During a comprehensive sweep of the area, only a few of the documents were ever retrieved. Tellingly, a postcard emanating from Cielo Drive was later discovered floating downstream. It has also since come to light that the enigmatic Bruce Davis and a couple of other Family members were in the area that weekend.

With Hughes's death casting a shadow over proceedings, Charlie, along with Bruce Davis and Clem Grogan, were due to face charges relating to Gary Hinman and Shorty Shea's deaths. Both cases of murder were heard together.

With Bobby Beausoleil's conviction for murder in the first degree confirmed in April 1970, evidence relating to the Hinman killing was simple enough to re-present. The case regarding Shorty Shea's murder was much more complicated, although the prosecution succeeded through sheer dogged diligence. Having no witnesses to the murder, it was a remarkable effort to bring these charges to bear; and only the third time in American history that a murder conviction had been upheld without a body. For some reason Tex Watson escaped prosecution, despite testimony pointing to his active involvement in Shea's death. While Bruce Davis and Charlie received guilty verdicts, the judge commuted Clem's death sentence to life imprisonment, claiming that 'Grogan was too stupid and too hopped-out on drugs to decide anything on his own.' Shea's missing body continued to mystify detectives for many years. Not one to miss an opportunity, Charlie used Shea's trial to further the notion that he'd 'chopped off Shorty's head'. This announcement served to instil greater fear in the wider community, and raise Charlie's sinister profile even further.

Manson's 'front-street' girls maintained their loyal presence on the corner outside the Halls of Justice – for a while. Despite Charlie being moved to await execution at San Quentin Prison, he'd sent out an edict requiring the girls stay outside the courtrooms 'until all of us are free'. Ultimately, their dedication waned, and they moved on. Even Squeaky, Charlie's most loyal foot soldier, packed up and left. Manson was reportedly livid with her for this. This guilt weighed heavily on her mind until a few years later, when she sought to counter her 'disloyalty' with the most sensational of acts.

While the male Family members sat on Death Row, Sadie, Katie and Leslie had been removed to the California Institute for Women at Frontera to await their own executions. With them, on charges relating to the Hawthorne shoot-out, were Mary Brunner and Catherine Share. Clearly the authorities were taking no chances. Indeed, such was the fear of an escape attempt that a heavily fortified wing at the prison was especially constructed to house the Manson women. With the hoopla of the trials over, the harsh reality of the girls' future began to hit home. Sadie, whose loose tongue had kick-started proceedings, had to cope with inordinate amounts of guilt, as well as her imminent execution. 'I had no expectation of survival. I was scared and confused, but not about the gas chamber. It centred on my aloneness. I had betrayed humanity, I had betrayed my colleagues, and I had betrayed myself. There was no one left. I had betrayed myself.'

Whilst Barker Ranch became a living monument to the Family's last stand, the rotting shacks at Spahn Ranch's mysteriously burnt to the ground during November of 1970. For the stragglers keeping watch on the ranch, the inferno took on the appearance of Charlie's apocalypse. As the flames took hold, the women danced merrily amid the smoke and embers chanting 'Helter Skelter is coming down'. Following the blaze, the aged George Spahn was seen preparing to leave, asking reporters for donations to rebuild the ranch. Spahn lived to be eighty-five; no one, least of all himself, could have predicted such a whirlwind finale to his last years.

By the early 1970s, the more fantastical elements of the Manson case were already starting to manifest themselves. For writers and filmmakers possessing a keen sense of the bizarre, the Family's story had already begun to assume mythical status. As a result, many were looking to capitalise on what had already been dubbed 'the crimes of the century'. Even before the guilty verdicts had been handed down, the film rights to the Manson story were already being discussed. With violent films like *Straw Dogs, The Wild Bunch* and *Easy Rider* making inroads into conventional cinema, the time seemed right for the Family saga to hit the screen.

Up-and-coming actor and producer Jack Nicholson had attended several of the court hearings, taking copious notes. Nicholson's friend Dennis Hopper was also an occasional visitor to the courtroom, and word soon leaked out that Manson wanted an audience with the actor. Reportedly, Manson had been impressed with the actor's résumé, particularly an episode of the TV show, *The Defenders*, where Hopper had killed his screen father in retaliation for beating his mother. Aware that the rights to his life story were under discussion, Charlie was keen to have some sort of involvement.

As Hopper had been a close friend of Jay Sebring's, he initially turned down the chance to meet Charlie. However, his inquisitive nature got the better of him and he finally agreed to meet with

Manson and talk over the proposed film. Despite some spirited discussion, Hopper's movie plans never got past the talking stage.

Filmmaker Robert Hendrickson would be more fortunate. Through his friend and Family cohort, Mark Ross, he found himself at the centre of the Manson hurricane with a 16-mm movie camera in his hand. Hendrickson's plan to record the activities of the Family-at-large was met with tacit approval from Charlie. The resulting movie, simply entitled *Manson*, succeeded in capturing the trippy atmosphere that surrounded the group. Regardless of Charlie's brief involvement with the finished product, it was more successful than any of the other cinematic interpretations in putting the Family on the big screen. The film was nominated for an Academy Award in 1974.

The movie's producer, Lawrence Merrick, had gained the confidence of several members of the Family during the making of the film. Being close to both camps, he shared some telling information with prosecutor Vincent Bugliosi, including the alleged fate of lawyer Ronald Hughes. He also flagged up a raft of further killings allegedly committed by the Family. In 1977, Merrick was hit by an unknown assassin's bullet following a lecture at a film school. Whether coincidence or not, the fact remains that when Merrick interviewed Squeaky during the filming of *Manson*, she proclaimed, 'Snitches will be dealt with.'

Whilst relatives of the victims waited patiently for the executions to take place, the system that had brought the murderers to justice handed them their lives back. On 18 February 1972, California's Supreme Court voted to abolish the death penalty. Following a landmark court ruling, all 115 Death Row prisoners in California had their sentences immediately commuted to life imprisonment. Calling the death penalty 'cruel', 'unusual' and 'unconstitutional', the judge ordered that the ruling should be made retroactive, effectively sparing the lives of all the Manson murderers. In their new status as life prisoners, it also ensured that they would have the opportunity to apply for parole after seven years.

Inside the California Institute for Women at Frontera, Katie, Sadie and Leslie awoke excitedly to news of the death penalty being lifted. Susan Atkins revealed the scene several years later.

' "They can't kill me," ' I said to myself. "They can't kill me! I've got a whole life ahead of me. What will happen now?" '

After spending two years of his life in pursuit of the guilty verdicts on Manson and his cohorts, prosecutor Vincent Bugliosi reacted very differently to the news. It struck an ominous chord with the prosecutor, as Manson had shown little upset at the prospect of returning to prison.

Vincent Bugliosi recalled his own feelings. 'I'm driving my car, 1972, the car radio is on and I hear that the US Supreme Court had set aside the death penalty, making all of their rulings retroactive. And the first thing that came into my mind is what Manson had told me, that they were sending him back to where he came from. He doesn't mind prison life, most of his life has been spent behind bars; he's totally institutionalised . . . In a sense, and I hate to say this, but in a sense, Manson's beaten the rap.'

With the lives of the guilty effectively spared, everything changed. Without the constant drip-feed of Manson's words moulding their consciousnesses, the convicts began to come to a bitter awakening. They were still only in their early twenties, with a lifetime in jail now stretching out grimly before them.

On the outside, Manson's most vociferous representatives, Squeaky, Brenda McCann and Sandy Good remained as dedicated as ever. With Barker Ranch under close scrutiny, and Spahn Ranch burnt to the ground, the girls flitted around Los Angeles. In their wake trailed ex-cons, enjoying the deal brokered by Charlie to party on the outside. With Manson's blessings ringing in their ears, Squeaky, Brenda and Sandy welcomed their new brothers, and remained faithful to Charlie's rule of female subservience, much to the delight of the newcomers.

During late 1972, a Family base at 720 West Flora Street, Stockton, was established. With Charlie in jail some ninety miles away at San Quentin, they could keep tabs on Manson's progress, and run any errands he might require. With the gang was a retinue of strange newcomers, drawn by the opportunity to share in the Family ideals. Two of these new followers were James and Reni Willett, a freewheeling couple who'd tagged along with their young daughter Heidi. They'd met Manson's women on the courtroom steps in Los Angeles during the trial. James had previously seen service in Vietnam and, on his return, had turned his skills to tutoring deprived children. A right-on acceptance of all lifestyles meant the couple were all too happy to mingle with the Family and their ex-con cohorts.

Predictably, money was soon required to finance the house's partying, so some of the male occupants began a burgling spree across the locale. By now the Willetts were having second thoughts about being embroiled in this orgy of lawlessness, and had began to talk of leaving. With paranoia running high, three of the men connected to the Manson women's circle, William Goucher, James Craig and Michael Monfort, sensed a potential snitch in James. One night, the trio lured Willett to a local wood. Forcing him to dig his own grave, he was shot and then beheaded. The tribe then buried his body and absconded with his wallet and ID. Later that night, Monfort and Goucher attempted to rob a liquor store. However, their raid was unsuccessful, and they were swiftly captured. With one of the murderers using Willett's name, they managed to get released on bail.

Three days later, Willett's wife Reni was shot in a similar style to her husband. Although still alive, she was buried in a shallow grave in the basement of the house. The couple's little child, Heidi, thankfully too young to know what had happened, was looked after by the women of the house.

Hikers discovered James Willett's body three weeks later. A routine patrol discovered the Willetts' truck parked outside the Stockton property. As police were aware of dubious goings-on in the commune, they raided the house, and discovered Reni's body in the basement. Police dismissed the Family's ludicrous claim that a game of Russian roulette had ended the girl's life. The story had worked for Zero's death but, since a considerable amount of effort had gone into burying the body, no one was buying it this time. Despite their objections, Goucher, Craig and Monfort, along with Brenda, Squeaky and Family newcomer Priscilla Cooper were all arrested and charged in relation to both deaths.

When the cases came to court in April 1973, four of the five suspects entered guilty pleas. Predictably, Manson's girls acted out. With their trademark crosses re-scored into their foreheads, the women were clearly still under their leader's influence. In the end Brenda served a lengthy term for her involvement, and swiftly faded away into obscurity. Squeaky received a lesser sentence, as it was proved that she was out of the house when Reni's murder took place.

On her release, Squeaky moved up to Sacramento with Sandy Good. Despite the authorities forbidding any direct contact with Manson, written communication was maintained. During this period Charlie would send out hundreds of cryptic notes, often directing his rapidly diminishing flock towards some new theory he'd come up with.

One such proclamation was to christen his scattered followers after colours, a throwback to the practices of Krishna Venta and the Process Church, who had both applied the paintbrush effect to their members' auras. As a result, Sadie became 'Violet'; Katie, 'Yellow'; Brenda, 'Gold'; and Leslie was 'Green'. Charlie's prime emissaries, Squeaky and Sandy were also given colours: Squeaky became 'Red', and was given a mission to save the giant redwoods of northern California. Sandy became 'Blue', her steely, cobalt eyes reflecting her love of the sea. Another edict sent from Manson contained a more direct, 'back to basics' approach. 'No meat; no smoking; no make-up,' the dispatch read. 'No fornication or showing your ass . . . Morality is the highest on earth.' To fully qualify his new approach, further down the letter Charlie added, 'No movies with violence that sets thoughts to death and confusion.'

In response, Squeaky and Sandy began wearing nuns' habits in their respective colours. The pair had holed themselves up in a maisonette at 1725 P-Street, Sacramento. With renewed vigour, they began to plot the next chapter of Manson's campaign. Charlie had begun to send out signals reaffirming his love of the planet, coining the acronym ATWA (air, trees, water, and animals) in the process. Buoyed up at the prospect of being Manson's rainbow warriors, the pair bombarded local media, attempting to garner support for Charlie's environmentalism. Despite making themselves visible around various news desks and TV stations of northern California, there was little interest in their cause.

Alongside his new status as incarcerated eco-warrior, Charlie remained keen to keep tabs on the world of rock and roll. Feeling a kindred alliance with these pop 'messiahs', he vied for the attentions of two of the scene's prime movers, who were both British, and both highly idiosyncratic in their personas.

Charlie decreed that Led Zeppelin's Jimmy Page and the Who's Keith Moon were ripe for infiltration, and both celebrities were approached. As both bands were gigging across the States during the early Seventies, it wasn't difficult to track them down.

According to Stephen Davis's authoritative book, *Hammer of the Gods*, Squeaky honed in on Led Zeppelin at the Hyatt House Hotel during the Californian leg of their 1973 tour. With Charlie's hand seemingly guiding her every move, Squeaky had managed to bypass the band's security, and get to their tour manager, Danny Goldberg. Demanding an audience with Page, she imparted a premonition that a terrible fate was going to befall the guitarist and warned him that the last time she'd had this thought, the person in her mind had been shot dead. After failing to impress Goldberg, Squeaky left in a huff. It was scant consolation to the Family when that night Page was hit on the head by a toilet roll thrown by an overenthusiastic fan.

A more sustained attempt was made to recruit Keith Moon, the anarchic drummer of the Who. As the group had trodden a similar allegorical line to the Beatles during the late 1960s, they were very appealing to the Family. Although the heady operatics of the group's album *Tommy* had seemingly passed Manson by, it's likely that the Beatles' demise in 1970 had led Charlie to seek out other potential avatars.

According to roadie Dougal Butler in his illuminating memoir, *Moon the Loon*, Keith Moon was approached by 'six nuns' dressed in red during the San Diego leg of the band's US tour in 1973. By all accounts, Moon and Butler twigged early on that these weren't your everyday groupies, and hastily beat a retreat on hearing their impassioned plea to help spread Manson's word. Undeterred, the girls followed the Who's entourage towards Oregon. It was in Portland that the girls managed to access the group's hotel suite in order to confront the errant musician. Seizing their moment, the girls laid the full Manson trip on to the startled drummer, declaring that 'Charlie is the sun and you will be the moon.' Although not usually fazed by weirdness, a visibly terrified Moon excused himself, leaving hotel security to escort Charlie's flock of nuns off the premises. The Who concluded their American tour that night, and Moon was no doubt relieved to return to the UK.

During these adventures, Squeaky and Sandy desperately tried to hold the fragmented strands of the Family together. With those in jail realising that Helter Skelter might not be 'coming down' any time soon, there was a growing sense of closure. For Squeaky, the inevitable collapse of the Family was going to be a bitter pill to swallow. As one of the first to leap aboard Charlie's magic caravan, she could only watch its demise with sad incredulity. Compounding matters, the jailed women started questioning her loyalty: how could she be happy to wander freely while they were imprisoned? Fromme and Good canvassed the incarcerated girls girls' attorneys, only to be told that any chances of parole would be heavily compromised if they maintained contact with Manson, or any of his active supporters. Furthermore, their attempts to gain visitation access to Charlie were constantly being blocked. As a result, the mood inside the camp began to turn increasingly more desperate, as Squeaky explains. 'We're waiting for our Lord, and there's only one thing to do before he comes off the cross, and that's clean up the earth. We're nuns now; our red robes are an example of the new morality . . . They're red with sacrifice, the blood and the sacrifice.'

It wasn't just the end of an era for Squeaky and Co. On 9 August 1974 the counterculture's nemesis and Sixties icon Richard Nixon was forced to resign as President in the wake of the Watergate scandal. The large swathes of America expecting a sea-change in policy were disappointed when Nixon's successor, Gerald Ford, granted Nixon an unconditional pardon for any of the acts committed whilst in the Oval Office.

Squeaky and Sandy liked to keep a keen eye on world events. After Ford's indenture, they sent out a press release with a chilling threat barely covered by hyperbole. 'If Nixson's [sic] reality wearing a new face, [Ford] continues to run this country against the law, your homes will be bloodier than the Tate–LaBianca houses and My Lai put together.' To drive the message home further the pair convened a small press conference in a Sacramento graveyard with local journalists. The location was pertinent because the women said they 'identified' with the dead. With their cryptic words resonating against the surrounding tombstones, they told reporters that Ford, 'Would have to pay for what he's doing. Ford is picking up in Nixon's footsteps and he is just as bad.' Cryptically, Squeaky then added that, 'Something very big is going to happen.'

In the end this big 'something' managed to outstrip all expectations. Meanwhile, Squeaky began to plot her own renaissance. Along with Sandy, she revisited San Francisco, the Family's birthplace, and attempted to persuade the likes of Jefferson Airplaine and the Grateful Dead to stage a benefit concert to raise awareness for Manson and the girls. They also attempted to lure newcomers to the rebranded Family, but without Charlie's silver tongue there were few takers. Whilst in San Francisco, Squeaky canvassed a government official about the fate of Sacramento's giant redwoods that were in danger of falling. Unsuccessful in her advances, she returned home to Sacramento deflated.

Squeaky's return home coincided with an important event for the city: a visit from President Gerald Ford. As was typical for all visiting dignitaries, a walkabout was planned prior to a meeting with the governor of the district. On the morning of 5 September 1975, a crowd of well-wishers turned out to welcome the new President on his first visit to Sacramento. In amongst the throng was Squeaky, dressed in her customary red robes, and waiting by a nearby magnolia tree for the cavalcade to approach. She later claimed that she was there to give Ford a message from Manson about the fate of the giant Californian redwoods. Whilst her passion for the environment was strong, the fact that she and Sandy had been constantly denied access to Charlie in San Quentin was also weighing heavily on her mind. She later recalled her feeling at that point, saying, 'You know, when people around you treat you like a child and pay no attention to the things you say, you have to do something.'

However, there were more than just words in her armoury. Secreted in a holster secured on her thigh was a Colt .45

automatic gun. Squeaky had charmed the weapon off sixty-six-year-old Harold 'Mani' Boro, a 'sugar daddy' she'd been seeing on and off. However, whilst four bullets were found on the gun's clip, none were in the firing chamber. Squeaky did her best to look inconspicuous as the presidential party began to approach at 9.57 a.m. As Ford arrived, she lifted the gun, and with only two feet between them, she pointed it in the President's direction.

She recalled what happened next. 'Ford had his hands out and he was waving. He looked like cardboard to me. I got two feet from him and I could have shot twice, had I put the bullet in there ... To me his life didn't mean more than the redwoods.'

Secret Service agents quickly leapt on Squeaky, and wrestled the weapon from her grip. As Ford was swept away by his bodyguards, Squeaky was restrained, handcuffed and held against the tree. She was screaming, 'The country is in a mess! This man is not your President! He's not a public servant! He's not a public servant!' A nearby journalist also reported her saying: 'It didn't go off. Can you believe it? It didn't go off.' Although later it transpired that she had been pleading against the painful way the agents had restrained her, shouting, 'Easy guys, it didn't go off!'

Regardless of her objections, Squeaky was carted off to police custody and charged with the attempted assassination of the President. Squeaky had the dubious honour of being the first person convicted under the new law instigated after Kennedy's murder in November 1963. In the wake of the attempt, reporters who'd served on the front line during the Tate–LaBianca trials swiftly put two and two together. With the Manson element added to this already sensational incident, the news made headlines around the world.

Squeaky's trial began two months after her arrest. As expected, she utilised the opportunity to challenge the establishment, just as Charlie and the girls had done some five years previously. While interest in the case was muted in comparison to the Tate–LaBianca trial, Squeaky still managed to enliven proceedings with her continual breaches of court protocol. It was little surprise that she also attempted to have Charlie and the girls testify on her behalf. 'Your Honour,' she implored on one occasion, 'it's going to get bloody if they are not allowed to speak.'

Whilst President Gerald Ford gave his side of the story via a video-link, Judge Tom MacBride refused Squeaky's request to subpoena Manson to expand upon his ideals and injustices. Squeaky's lawyer, John Vira, argued that, despite having the gun on her person, she wasn't intent on shooting Ford, and had just wanted to highlight the plight of the environment. This rhetoric failed to move the court. When prosecutor Duane Keyes described her as 'full of hate and violence', Squeaky threw an apple at his head, knocking his glasses off in the process.

Charlie's reaction on being told about the Ford incident was to exclaim, 'Oh my God!' Whatever the cost to herself, Squeaky's action served to raise Charlie's profile again and, by association, align him once more with the highest level of United States authority.

With most of Charlie's main players now in jail, it was left to Sandy Good to rattle the sabre for the Manson Family ethos. With Squeaky's sketchy environmentalism effectively silenced, Sandy continued alone. Following Squeaky's arrest, Good held a press conference to announce that 'a wave of assassins' was to engage in a comprehensive sweep of anyone guilty of polluting Mother Earth. Good's words made for a chilling reminder of the terror that had gripped Los Angeles following the Tate–LaBianca killings. 'We're going to start assassinating Presidents, Vice Presidents and major executives of companies. I'm warning these people they better stop polluting or they're going to die.'

To consolidate this message, Sandy and Family newcomer, Susan Murphy, composed a formal letter that was to be sent to corporate executives of large multinationals. Between them, the pair managed to mail over 3,000 copies of the letter.

'*Your products are poisoning our world. <u>STOP!</u> Or many with <u>Knives</u> come to butcher bodi [sic]... If you chose a self-destructive course I will help you reach that goal in a way that will save the rest of us from the mad men and women selling death to my children.*

The letter was signed,

International People's Court of Retribution/Manson.

Sandy's threat reached corporate heads across the length and breadth of the United States. Although the text itself was written by Good, there was little doubt who was really calling the shots.

Given the high-profile way they'd conducted their activities since Squeaky's arrest, it wasn't long before Good and her assistant were arrested and charged for the poison pen campaign. As a result Sandy spent ten years inside, characteristically waiving her right to parole and release programmes until the entire length of her sentence had been served.

With the majority of the Manson Family protagonists now in jail, over time the concept of 'Charles Manson' morphed into a popular metaphor for unbridled horror. By the mid-1970s, the 'innocence' of the previous decade was out of favour. With Republican opportunists keen to portray the 1960s as a vulgar and indulgent aberration, sensitivities all around started to harden. The punk rock culture of 1977 trampled these last few buds of optimism underfoot, and replaced it with a starker world view. Not surprisingly, with all the bile coughed up, Manson's anarchism was embraced by a few of the punk bands, although most wanted little to do with any Sixties' figures, regardless of their iconic status.

During this period of readjustment, it was perhaps inevitable that Charlie's former cohorts would begin to reassert their own identities. Severed from Manson's umbilical cord, their stunted consciousnesses began to recover their equilibrium. With the help of their families and prison counsellors, they began to see beyond the world of Charlie and the Family. By the mid-1970s, Krenwinkel, Van Houten and Atkins had all publicly renounced Charlie.

Leslie Van Houten reflected: 'I've had a lot of different women I've met who have been inside who tell me they are really glad that they didn't run into Charlie, because they too would have been taken in. I feel like I was a pawn in whatever his scheme was. I think that at one point I believed he was Jesus Christ.'

In 1977, some eight years after her capture, friends and sympathetic lawyers were pointing to Van Houten's transformation from unapologetic murderess to contrite prisoner. A retrial began to look like a real possibility, especially since the original trial had been disrupted by Ronald Hughes's disappearance. In the end, Hughes's replacement, lawyer Maxwell Keith, successfully argued for her case to be heard again. However, not everyone was in the mood for forgiveness.

Stephen Kay, a prosecutor who came into the fray partway through the Tate–LaBianca trials, continued to monitor the fate of the Manson Family. He opposed Leslie Van Houten's release; and in fact continued to counter the Family's bids for freedom for the next twenty-five years. With impassioned pleading on both sides, the trial ended with a hung jury, and Van Houten was offered parole while the case was prepared again. Despite opposition, a bail bond of $200,000 was raised by friends and relatives. As a result, Leslie enjoyed freedom for the first time since the raid at Death Valley in October 1969. Once released, she kept a low profile, resuming her former career as a legal secretary. Although the prosecution marshalled their resources to re-convict her, hopes remained high for a permanent release.

What was in fact Leslie's third trial commenced in March 1978. Her defence lawyer, Maxwell Keith, argued for diminished responsibility due to her heavy use of psychedelics at the time, deeply underscored with Manson's mind control. With prosecuting attorney Stephen Kay countering with a highly emotional call for justice, the jury reaffirmed the original first-degree murder charge, and Leslie was sent back to jail.

Stephen Kay wasn't the only thorn in the Family's side. Whilst Manson and Co. tried to put their crimes behind them, it wasn't so easy for the victims' families. The Family had cast a permanent shadow over their lives. By dint of her celebrity, Sharon Tate's family shouldered most of the morbid interest, and for years Sharon's mother Doris struggled to come to terms with the brutal reality of her daughter's murder. Shielding her two remaining daughters from the press, she'd attempted to operate under a cloak of anonymity, until the unwelcome spectacle of her daughter's killers seeking parole forced her to take a public stand.

Sharon's mother had kept in contact with prosecuting attorney Stephen Kay. In 1982, Leslie Van Houten had gathered 900 signatures to support her parole hearing, and once more stood a good chance of release. Stephen got wind of this, and called Doris to explain the situation. 'I got home, and I picked up the phone right after I got through the door, and I called Doris, and I said,

"We have a problem." I told her about the 900 signatures and said, "Doris, I think we can do better than that." And her answer to me was, "You bet we can honey."'

The National Enquirer, heading up America's gutter press, was more than happy to champion Doris Tate's crusade. In a nationwide sweep, a total of over 350,000 letters came through objecting to the release of any of the incarcerated Manson Family.

Energised by her new direction, Doris, with Stephen Kay as legal mentor, successfully blocked Van Houten's parole hopes. As a result of her success, Tate began to wield considerable influence in the field of victims' families' rights, reshaping California's penal laws in the process. In 1982, Tate established a caveat in the law to allow victims' families to attend parole hearings and make 'impact statements' on any projected release. For Doris Tate, this was a defining moment – she would now be able to confront her daughter's killers face to face.

In 1985, the Tate family got their first chance to face Tex Watson, the man who led the slaughter of her daughter. Doris let her husband talk to the parole board, since she could barely contain her anger, claiming afterwards that she 'could have killed him'.

Watson was refused release for five years, the maximum denial a parole board could give. Whilst Leslie Van Houten and Patricia Krenwinkel had appeared to come to terms with the gravity of their actions, Tex Watson and Susan Atkins deflected a lot of their guilt into high-profile conversions to Christianity. Despite the scepticism of Doris and others, they nonetheless took to their newly found convictions with considerable gusto. Tex's awakening led to him establishing his own prison ministry titled, 'Abounding Love Ministers'. This turnaround afforded him considerable privileges in jail, and the opportunity to minister at various locations on the prison circuit.

By this stage, Tex had published an account of life under Charlie's spell under the title. *Will You Die for Me?* Sadie too, following her monumental Christian awakening, rewrote her memoirs, as *Child of Satan, Child of God*. Although both became best-sellers, neither did anything to deter Sharon's family from their quest to see them rot in jail. At Tex's next parole hearing in

1990, Doris Tate got her own chance to confront her daughter's killer. After all the preliminaries, Doris laid into Sharon's murderer, releasing years of pent-up resentment.

'What mercy, sir, did you show my daughter when she was begging for her life? What mercy did you show my daughter when she said "give me two weeks to have my baby and then you can kill me?" When will [Sharon] come up for parole? Will these seven victims and possibly more walk out of their graves if you get paroled? You cannot be trusted.'

Tate's speech convinced the board of Watson's unsuitability for parole; but the day's emotional rollercoaster was far from over. Suzan LaBerge, the daughter of murdered Rosemary LaBianca, had come out very publicly in sympathy with Watson. LaBerge, herself a born-again Christian, had acknowledged Watson's religious conversion, and had openly declared that she forgave him for slaughtering her parents. She'd met with Tex behind bars in 1987 and shouted his corner at the parole hearing.

'It has taken time, information, knowledge and God's love for me to come to the opinion and conclusion that I have reached,' she said. 'I don't think any kind of fear is justifiable for keeping Charles [Tex] in prison. For Charles, I believe twenty-one years of imprisonment, and his having to live with the memory of what he did, is punishment enough. It is my belief that Charles could live in society, peacefully. And should be given a parole date.'

Suzan got short shrift from Doris Tate, who left the courtroom the moment LaBerge began to speak. Undeterred, LaBerge continued to put Tex's case to Tate in the car park after the hearing. Despite the confrontation being captured by TV cameras, Tate brushed off LaBerge's theory that Watson was a changed man.

'To think she can sit there knowing that this man stabbed her mother forty-two times in the back!' Doris Tate said incredulously. 'And she wants him out? That is beyond human forgiveness.'

Doris Tate began to attend all the parole hearings of those charged with her daughter's death, stressing the devastation wrought by the terrible crimes, regardless of the passage of time. Tate's crusading further highlighted the incongruity of Watson (and others, such as fellow Mansonite Susan Atkins, and even mass-murderer Ted Bundy) enjoying conjugal rights. Watson had married Kristin Joan Svelte in 1979 and, thanks to the use of the conjugal trailer on prison grounds, the couple now had four children. Doris Tate fought for this privilege to be removed and, before her death from a brain tumour in 1992, she changed the statute books.

Others were more fortunate than Leslie and Tex. Steve Grogan, who as 'Clem Scramblehead' completely succumbed to Manson's stewardship, underwent a miraculous transformation. Having escaped the death penalty, he'd buckled down into the prison system and left all traces of his misspent adolescence behind. He'd been commended by the parole board for assisting in a programme to deter youths from entering into crime. After serving eight years of his life sentence, in 1977 Grogan offered to help police find Shorty Shea's body. Despite strenuous efforts over the years, Shea's remains had never been recovered. In a bid to aid his parole, Grogan drew a map, directing authorities to Shea's body; as a result, the stuntman's remains were recovered close to Spahn Ranch. Shea's family were relieved, the fact that the body was found virtually intact nailed rumours that Shorty had been butchered into many pieces. For his assistance, and excellent behavioural records, Grogan stood a good chance of parole. In November 1985, he was finally awarded his freedom, and under cover of darkness was released back into society. For a while this act of clemency offered hope for the other Manson Family members still rotting in jail.

While Tex and the women hoped against hope for a possible release, Charlie continued his fractious relationship with prison officialdom. After coming off Death Row at San Quentin in 1972, Charlie was bounced between various institutions – as he had been all his life. For a while he was placed at the California Medical Facility at Vacaville, a secure unit that specialised in monitoring convicts with psychiatric conditions. Ironically, Charlie was put in a cell next to another perceived enemy of the establishment, LSD guru Timothy Leary. Remarkably, given his complex relationship with Christ, Manson was allowed to hold a position of 'clerk' at the facility's chapel.

For a while, all seemed to be going well and Charlie was even allotted the use of an office. Despite the benefits, Manson was reportedly expanding his role beyond clerical duties. With tales of Charlie ministering several hard-line inmates in his own brand of religion, the authorities undertook a comprehensive sweep of the chapel. Searching Manson's office, a trap door was discovered which led to a secret chamber. There, guards found a home-made weapon, wire cutters, a tape recorder and several bags of marijuana. Of particular concern were the discovery of a phial of noxious liquid, and a catalogue detailing hot-air balloons for sale.

Some years later, Manson found himself under physical attack, this time at the hands of another prisoner. Inmate Jan Holmstrom was a Hare Krishna devotee imprisoned at Vacaville on a charge of second-degree murder. During the afternoon of 24 September 1985, Charlie was in the institutions' hobby room, where Holmstrom was also present. Tiring of the devotee's interminable repetition of the 'Hare Krishna' chant, Manson directed a tirade of abuse towards him. In return, Holmstom unloaded a bottle of paint thinner over Charlie and set fire to it. Manson suffered burns covering eighteen per cent of his body, the majority of them concentrated on his head and hands. Following this incident, and many other infractions, Manson was moved back to the secure environment of San Quentin.

Whilst there was little sympathy for Charlie's fate, the story of the assault on Charlie made it to the press; Manson was evidently still newsworthy. Original trial prosecutor Vincent Bugliosi had inadvertently gone a long way to gild Manson's notoriety with the book *Helter Skelter*, first released in 1974. An exhaustive account of the trials, the book succeeded in transforming Charlie's fireside raps, bizarre schemes, and supernatural powers into a hugely marketable package. The public certainly lapped it up, and in turn it became the best-selling crime book of all time. Following in its wake, in 1975 a TV mini-series based on Bugliosi's book spread word of Charlie's antics even further. The series became America's most watched mini-series, though to those who witnessed events first hand, it didn't even come close to showing what life with Manson was like.

Bobby Beausoleil said: 'Most of what has been written has been exploitation – the events and the people seen through the eyes of fear and sold to a public with an insatiable lust for vicariously experienced violence and excitement ... For me, it is like seeing the events and the people I knew reflected in a fun-house mirror. This has deprived a great many people of an opportunity to understand what happened.'

Charlie's cult credentials were given further validation on 18 November 1978, when he became associated with the death of over 900 members of Jim Jones's People's Temple in Guyana. Two years later, the murder of John Lennon by deranged fan, Mark Chapman, on 8 December 1980 threw the spotlight back on celebrity killings, and twisted interpretations of the Beatles' songs. Predictably, the name Charles Manson came back into the public domain.

While media contact with Charlie during the 1970s had been sparse, Manson did consent to a coast-to-coast interview for NBC's top rated *Tomorrow* show in 1981. The programme's host, Tom Snyder, had become something of a legend in media circles for his ability to soft-shoe shuffle with his guests. Ironically, he was the last person to interview John Lennon on television before his murder. Although Manson proved an enormous media coup, Snyder's strong-arm pretensions had little effect on Charlie when they met.

Tom Snyder: 'How old are you in your world?'

Manson: 'Er, for ever. Since breakfast. I can't remember.'

Tom Snyder: 'I don't know what that means, come off the space shuttle, Charles.'

Manson: 'Yes, off the space shuttle.'

Tom Snyder: 'How old are you in your world?'

Manson: 'How old am I? I'm as old as my mother told me. How's that?'

It's evident that from the offset Charlie had decided to evade Snyder's questions with his trademark abstract flow. Snyder, evidently acting for the prosecution, had little chance of entering Charlie's labyrinthine mind. Over a painful fifty minutes, the conversation darted around several mental universes, with Manson revealing little of any relevance. Despite Snyder's lack of success, the interview won enormous ratings and put 'Manson the Maniac' back into America's consciousness.

During the 1980s, Charlie also took on other chat-show luminaries – Charlie Rose and Geraldo Rivera – for more futile mind-mashing. The interview with Rivera was an unsettling confrontation, as both men fought for their own piece of the small screen.

Geraldo: 'This show's about murder Charlie, you're the issue.'
Charles Manson: 'OK, I killed everybody since day one. I've murdered them all. I'm God and I've killed everyone, now what? It doesn't improve your issue any. I'm working for your position just as well as I'm working for mine. I got dealt the hand, "Hippie Cult Leader". What the hell is a hippie cult leader?'

Later in the show Manson taunted Rivera, claiming he could send for his head in a box if he so wished. Geraldo retorted that he had friends inside jail that could easily take care of Charlie. All in all, it was a deeply unsavoury piece of television, with no points scored on either side. However, like Snyder before him, Rivera got enormous audience figures, and saw his show syndicated around a world hungry for a piece of Manson.

With their leader's television appearances descending into pantomime, Squeaky and Sandy Good vainly attempted to bat in Manson's ideological corner. Imprisoned since her spectacular assassination attempt on President Ford, Squeaky maintained her support for Charlie, disdaining those who had since moved away from Family. She'd spent her time inside happy in the knowledge that she was still sharing in Manson's thought-line. Aside from one violent incident where she attacked another inmate with a claw hammer, she kept herself to herself, tending mainly to her past life with the Family.

In 1987, Squeaky heard a false rumour that Manson had been diagnosed with advanced testicular cancer. In response she absconded from Alderson Federal Correction Institute in West Virginia, on 23 December 1987. While embarrassed prison officials attempted to track her down, America was thrown into a renewed panic. With Manson's 'number two' escaped, the media went on high alert about this crazed assassin on the run. Over a hundred officers, many with bloodhounds, scoured the area close to the prison, and Squeaky was eventually arrested some two days later, suffering from exposure. She was later charged with the escape, and during the trial took the opportunity to reaffirm her unswerving dedication to Manson. 'I got word that [Charlie] had cancer,' she'd tell the court. 'He needs a relative, somebody to check on him. [Charlie] was my husband, my brother, my father, my son, the man who's been my friend . . . My access to him is so limited, I've been feeling helpless for years.'

Squeaky's mirror image, Sandy Good, was eventually released from jail in 1985. By her own admission, her loyalty to Manson had been unwavering, and she'd stubbornly opted to see out the entirety of her sentence. Seeing that her probation required her to be housed far away from Manson, she took herself off to Bridport, Vermont, where she settled in a small, remote property. There, she kept up contact with Charlie as best she could through letters dropped in by sympathetic friends.

Despite his mercurial passions, Manson's environmentalism had remained something of a constant over the years. The popularisation of the Green movement during the 1980s made saving the planet a fashionable pursuit. Good (using the name Sandra Collins) was quick to seize the ecological nettle when it appeared in her own backyard. An ongoing dispute against a local paper mill company in Vermont saw Sandy join ranks with the locals to protest against the mill pumping their waste products into a nearby lake. With the press on hand to monitor events, she was captured waving a placard outside a local court. Inevitably, someone recognised her face when it hit the press, and her notoriety stole the headlines. Sandra retreated from active campaigning to see out the term of her probation, but once it was completed, she headed to California to be close to Charlie once more. By now in her forties, Sandy's faith in Manson was as strong as ever.

In 1992, with sections of the media keen to mark the twenty-fifth anniversary of the murders, Charlie's music underwent a minor renaissance. Since the release of the *Lie* album in 1970, he'd gained a sort of curiosity value, and bands with an anti-establishment slant began exploiting his sparse catalogue.

Pneumatic punkster Henry Rollins, and his band, Black Flag, swallowed a large dose of Mansonisms during the early 1980s. He'd named his early gigs 'Creepy Crawls' in honour of the Family's after-dark adventures in Los Angeles. In fact such was Rollins' fascination with Manson that he planned to record an entire album's worth of Charlie's music – although following much controversy, nothing appeared. Across the pond, British oddities, Psychic TV, led by the enigmatic Genesis P. Orridge, reworked Manson's 'Never Say Never To Always' in their own strange fashion. To add to the cult rockers' left-field kudos, they later released the track 'Roman P,' as a single in 1984, with several controversial references to Sharon Tate.

Over the years, many others would release music either written by Charlie, or in tribute to the cult of the Family. Ozzy Osbourne leapt into the Manson mire to come up with a predictably dark, 'Bloodbath In Paradise'. Neil Young, once fascinated by Charlie, penned an oblique tribute to wasted promise in 'Mansion On The Hill'. He'd later put together a darker paean to the Family on 'Revolution Blues'. 'I played it for [David] Crosby' recalled Young in 2008. 'And he said, "Don't sing about that, it's not funny."' Punksters Sonic Youth commited their own tribute to the cult of Manson with 'Death Valley '69', while Evan Dando's Lemonheads tackled Manson's 'Clang Bang Clang'. Summing up the feelings of his generation, Dando explained: 'Charlie was just a good symbol of the beginning of my life in America, and how messed up things were getting.'

However, these recordings were small fry compared to the musical tributes to come. In November 1993, neo-metal renegades Guns N' Roses tried to take Charlie's music to the top of the charts. Mansonism had evidently been simmering in the Roses' camp for some time; lead singer W. Axl Rose had taken to wearing a T-shirt of Charlie's face, with the words 'Charlie Don't Surf' plastered over the rear. This Manson-authorised shirt had already assumed cult status in the surfer regions of LA, its oblique motto lifted from the film *Apocalypse Now*. During sessions for the band's uneventful covers album, *The Spaghetti*

Incident, Manson's song 'Look At Your Game Girl' was slipped in as the final track. Perhaps anticipating a furore, the track's credit was left off the album sleeve.

Speaking with writer Tommy Udo following the release, Axl Rose claimed that he was unaware initially that the song was written by Charlie. 'I was played this track and I though it was really good ... really great. I'd never have guessed who it was.' It was a limp excuse, and with news hitting the tabloids, the Tate family were fired into action. Patti Tate, Sharon's sister, had taken over torch-bearing duties following her mother Doris's death in 1992. Bearing a striking likeness to her famous sister, Patti entered into the front line to stop any possible revival of the Manson phenomena. With projected global sales of the Guns N' Roses album set to rake in $60,000 in songwriter royalties for Charlie, Patti took her campaign direct to the album's sponsor, Geffen Records, and to the world's press.

Patti Tate recalled: 'I wanted to go in there and state exactly where I stood and that I would continue on with the boycott. I needed to touch them with my story, with my sister's story, with her memory ... It was necessary for me to sit down with them, face to face and ask them, "Do you realise what you are creating here?" This isn't about whether or not Manson is making money or who is making money. This is about Manson still profiting by becoming a cult hero, an idol to a lot of young kids out there who will buy the album. And that's where violence and crime is hitting us the worst right now, with our kids.'

Patti Tate's valiant efforts to thwart the release drew conciliatory responses from both band and record company. With a promise to remove Charlie's offending track from all future pressings, the royalties of the song were passed to Bartek Frykowski, who'd won a landmark court ruling against Manson following his father Voyteck's murder.

Despite the Tate family's intervention, Manson's influence on popular culture continued unabated. Trent Reznor, the man behind the 'industrial' sound of Nine Inch Nails, took 'method recording' to a new level. With few wanting to occupy the Cielo Drive property, Reznor took out a lease on the long-vacant property. Once inside, Reznor installed a studio in the lounge that had hosted the killing of Sharon Tate and Jay Sebring which he christened Le Pig, in homage to Susan Atkins' bloody scrawl on the front door. Although Reznor claimed it was quite by chance that he took the property on, celebrity watchers were quick to make the association. 'I looked at a lot of places, and this just happened to be the one I liked most,' he told reporters at the time, presumably with his tongue firmly in his cheek. Reznor and the band recorded the album *The Downward Spiral* in the house, as well as filming a couple of promotional videos inside the lounge. Reznor's friend and fellow artist, the larger-than-life Marilyn Manson (né Brian Warner), also recorded several tracks for his first album in the studio.

Someone else keeping tabs on the activities at Cielo Drive was Patti Tate. With access to celebrity circles, Patti angrily confronted Reznor at a society gathering. Reznor related details of the embarrassing confrontation to *Rolling Stone* magazine in 1997. 'I met her [Sharon's] sister . . . And she said, "Are you exploiting my sister's death by living in her house?" For the first time, the whole thing kind of slapped me in the face. I said, "No, it's just sort of my own interest in American folklore. I'm in this place where a part of history occurred." I guess it never really struck me before, but it did then. She lost her sister from a senseless, ignorant situation that I don't want to support. When she was talking to me, I realised for the first time, "What if it was my sister?" I thought, "Fuck Charlie Manson." I went home and cried that night.'

With Charlie's music in a perverse ascendancy, a clamour began to hear his own recordings. With industrious friends on the outside, tape recorders had already been smuggled in and out of prison over the years, allowing Manson to lay down some fragmentary music and poetry from inside. Over the course of a decade, three albums, *Commemoration*, *Way of the Wolf* and *Live at San Quentin* surfaced. At moments during these primitive recordings, Manson seems sanguine and folksy; at others he's away with his demons, spitting bile for the tape. From the optimistic 'So Today Has Been A Good Day' to the brutal 'I Got A Tough Bastard Child Want to Become Into A Samurai', these albums present a disturbing record of Charlie's schizophrenic state.

With Manson's signals still seeping out into the universe, it was predictable that his twisted idealism would find favour with a new generation of dissenters. With the Manson legend propped up with indiscriminate racism, unapologetic violence and frenzied environmentalism, Charlie unwittingly armed a slew of neo-Nazi bands with his extreme manifesto. This flirtation with the far right led to an unlikely alliance between Manson and James Mason, self-styled 'American National Socialist'. As a reflection of his commitment to extremism, Mason had been thrown out of the official Nazi Party of America. Mason had gleefully taken on Charlie as a figurehead for his proposed new party, declaring Manson, 'the foremost revolutionary leader in the world today'.

Under Charlie's patronage, the 'Universal Order' party was born. While Manson could obviously not assist in the party's everyday activities, he did submit a logo, replete with swastika and Justice scales for promotional purposes. Manson had few takers in the mainstream, but the 'Universal Order' did raise Charlie's ideological stance among the far right.

Apart from the skinheads and rock stars, Sandy Good was the Family's last champion on the outside. During the 1990s, with the explosion of the Internet, it was obvious to her that Charlie's message would best be shared through this unregulated digital domain. Manson had already become a major player in the Internet crime scene and, by the mid-1990s, typing his name racked up over eight and half million hits on one search engine alone. Inspired by the possibilities, Sandy Good and her partner (and Manson advocate) George Stimson inaugurated 'Access Manson', a wholly digitised version of Manson's 'Air Trees Water and Animals' manifesto. As close to an 'Official' Charles Manson website as one could get, its preamble left little to the imagination:

'The purpose of this website is to begin to lift the shroud of lies and distortions that have been used for almost thirty years by self-serving individuals, the mass media, and certain California state departments and offices to cover the reality that is Charles Manson. The purpose is also to begin the process of correcting the wrong done to Charles Manson by the denial of his constitutional right to defend himself during his trials, a denial that resulted in his illegal convictions and incarceration.'

Additionally, the site included a discography, several photographs of Charlie, and examples of his artwork. Whilst there was little anyone could do to curtail Manson's rampant voyage through cyberspace, his acolytes were upbeat about the amount of interest shown. Website coordinator George Stimson described the response to Richard Metzger, editor of *DisInformation* magazine.

'A lot of different kinds of people from different walks of life have contacted us. We've heard from students, lawyers, blue-collar people, people who are still affected by the counterculture, all kinds. And yes, we hear from a lot of young people, many who are not familiar with Manson and his case from their own memory of the time. Kids are fine. The people who were with Manson in 1969 were mostly kids.'

By 2004 however, the site disappeared; reportedly, on Manson's insistence. Allegedly, Charlie wanted more control over the content, which given his environment was impossible. It has since been reported that Sandy Good has apparently severed all ties with Manson. If Sandy has indeed withdrawn her support, Squeaky Fromme remains his sole champion from the Family's 1960s heyday.

If Manson or his former followers believed that the new millennium would offer a relaxation of attitudes towards them, they were to be sorely disappointed. The metaphor they collectively carved out for unspeakable terror means that the chances of any of them getting parole appears as remote as ever.

In 2007, both Leslie Van Houten and the enigmatic Bruce Davis were up for parole. Despite Van Houten's spirited reiteration of her innocence, the fifty-eight-year-old nonetheless received her eighteenth parole denial, the board – yet again – citing the cruel and odious nature of the crimes.

At Bruce Davis's hearing, Sharon Tate's sister Debra appeared on the witness stand – despite the fact that Davis had not been directly involved in her sister's murder. There too, was district attorney Patrick Sequaria, filling the shoes of the recently retired Stephen Kay. Their case against Davis was successful, and Sequaria drew in some terrorist frisson to bring the forty-year-old Manson saga up to date. 'Is it any different from any other terrorist organisation?' he asked. 'No, it's just back then we weren't attuned to domestic terrorists the way we are today. But that's what they were; they were domestic terrorists, they were trying to start a race war.'

Charles Manson declined to attend his last parole meeting on 23 May 2007. It was his eleventh hearing to date. Aware that he will never be released, Manson has remained unapologetic. When asked if he was interested in attending, he reportedly replied, 'What for?' With his chair unoccupied, it was left to officials to list his miserable record of obstinate resistance to prison authority.

'The inmate indicated that he was not interested in being interviewed for the psychological evaluation. The inmate spoke in a tangential manner, and attempted to manipulate the process of the interview . . . He has failed to follow the recommendations of the previous panel. He has not upgraded himself educationally, vocationally and has also failed to participate in any self-help programme.'

Post Script

Forty years on from the days when 'Manson' first entered the world's consciousness, what is left? Whilst the main protagonists in the saga see their lives dwindle away behind bars, Manson's legend remains most vivid in the properties that hosted the Family's revelry and their terrible atrocities.

Spahn Ranch, once the Family primary home, is now a barren piece of wasteland. During the fire in 1971, the film sets and rambling shacks burnt to the ground. Across the road from where the ranch once stood, a thriving church community has been established. In 2004, 'The Church at Rocky Peak' announced plans to reclaim what was once Spahn Ranch and turn it into something more optimistic for the future. Following the church's acquisition of the land, 600 young believers engaged in a cleansing ritual of sorts, when they took over the ranch area for the day. 'We had sharing about the Lord,' recalls church elder Pastor MacKerron. 'The total opposite of what Manson was selling . . . It's gone from evil to sharing that Jesus is the answer, not Satan. Jesus changes lives for the better; Satan changes lives for the worse.'

Five hundred miles away from Spahn's, Barker Ranch, the Manson Family's desert hideout, is pretty much as they left it in October 1969. The guest-house is still used by the occasional traveller seeking shelter, whilst legions of the curious still drop in to see the place that formed the backdrop for the last days of the Family. A guest book records the thoughts of some of these visitors, and the comments range from the ridiculous to the disturbingly grisly. Whilst the Family bus was dragged away and dynamited in a nearby mine in the late 1970s, some of the vehicles the Family bought up to the ranch lay scattered around the property's outer limits, gradually disintegrating in the arid heat. On a hill overlooking the ranch, one of the look-out points the Family constructed still maintains a ramshackle presence. Currently, the Death Valley authorities own Barker Ranch, and they keep a watchful eye lest anyone outstay their welcome. Entering Death Valley requires a permit these days.

There were rumours of dead bodies buried in the desert around Barker Ranch, which gathered momentum in the decades following the murder trials. In 1998, a loose associate of the Family called 'White Rabbit' claimed he knew where some bodies were buried, and was offered immunity if he could pinpoint the exact locations. Despite some digging and a lot of publicity, nothing was found. It would take a further ten years before a more reliable source, albeit of the canine variety, would prise the mystery open again.

In early 2007, Sergeant Paul Dostie, a police sergeant specialising in forensics from the Mammoth Lakes Police Department, grew curious about the legends of bodies hidden in the desert. That February, Dostie visited Barker Ranch with several other colleagues and a dog by the name of Buster. Dostie's pet had been trained in human remains detection, and possessed what was described as an incredible sense of perception. While most cadaver dogs are used to trace the recently deceased, Buster had proved able to trace bodies buried for over forty years. Raising much excitement, Buster pinpointed five possible sites around the ranch that might contain bodies. Having had their fingers burnt before, officials from Inyo Country were apprehensive about funding further excavations, and about raising the grisly spectre of the Manson Family once again

Undeterred, Dostie engaged some specialists in body detection to visit the site. With them were three more cadaver detection dogs. To further his suspicions, Dostie had sent soil samples off to be analysed for possible human traces. Behind the scenes Dostie claimed that former members of the Family had given him information concerning bodies buried in the desert. Additionally, Dostie mentioned to a journalist that Charlie himself had made some oblique references to murdered individuals. As the body-hunt gathered pace, Sharon Tate's sister, Debra, entered into the fray. She accompanied Dostie and a cameraman over to the ranch area to add some emotional gravitas to the story.

'I would love to see this go forward,' Tate revealed to the media. 'There are so many stories from Manson Family members about these areas. I would like to help some other families come to closure . . . there are kids at the Barker Ranch that need to go home.'

With pressure mounting, Inyo County officials consented to a brief dig on the places identified by Buster and the other dogs during May 2008. With the world's press camped out on the fringes of the desert, a party consisting of police and science experts began what was described as a 'limited excavation'. In addition to the cadaver dogs, they were to use ground-penetrating radar, magnetometers and more traditional spades and shovels.

After two days, however, the dig was called off. All the investigators had for their toils were some animal bones and a bullet casing pre-dating Manson's era. With little hope of future successes, police who monitored the area were somewhat relieved at Dostie's failure. 'It's a good thing that there weren't bodies to be found,' revealed County Sheriff Bill Lutz to the media, adding that, 'I think we're all glad not to have more victims having been murdered by the Manson Clan.' Later, a press release served to close the episode once and for all, stating that, 'Inyo County Sheriff's Department will not conduct further testing or excavation at Barker Ranch.'

Despite the failure to locate anything, original prosecutor Vincent Bugliosi told me he does not believe all the victims have been found. 'I am very confident that there are bodies out in the desert. The fact that they didn't find them where they looked at Barker Ranch doesn't mean the bodies are not out there. The Manson Family is not a group that we can ignore, especially as they murdered people. So my view is that there are bodies out in the vast area of the desert.'

Not surprisingly, Cielo Drive still seems like a haunted place. Following the Tate slayings, the house at 10050 passed through a variety of tenants, all of whom swiftly tired of the stream of ghoul watchers and freaks that gravitated there. Following Nine Inch Nails' Trent Reznor's very public occupation of the house, landlord, Rudi Altobelli had enough and ordered the property to be demolished. An enormous Mediterranean manor was built on the site that bore no resemblance to the modest property that once stood among the pine trees. Despite a gradually descending price tag, few dared take it on. After years of vacancy, Hollywood film producer Jeff Franklin bought the house, now called Villa Bella. Despite the property additionally having a new house number, 10066, it hasn't deterred the curious from wanting to see where the bloody deeds took place. This fascination gathers considerable momentum each year on 8 August, when legions of Manson fanatics from all over the world make a dark pilgrimage up the hill to the gates of the house.

These, and other locations allied to Manson's Family are now part of a grim tourist trail. Both *Lonely Planet* and *Rough Guide* list the main Manson locations, but for those wishing to be shepherded around in style, the unwieldily titled 'Hollywood Helter Skelter Tragically History Tour' bus trip has been established. The tour takes in the predictable locations such as Cielo Drive and the LaBiancas' residence, as well as Family bolt holes around Los Angeles. The three-hour ride strives to remain controversial throughout its murky circuit, and for those in need of a toilet break, it stops at the public convenience where pop singer George Michael was arrested for 'lewd acts' in 1998. At the end of the tour, each participant is given a small piece of the fireplace that originally dominated the lounge in Cielo Drive. The tour's leader, Scott Michaels, obtained a large quantity of these bizarre keepsakes during the demolition of 10050 Cielo Drive in 1994. The idea for the business came from his own fascination with the murders.

Scott Michael reports: 'It's doing OK; I'm never going get rich, but I'm happy ... Some people collect coins, some people collect memorabilia about the Presidents. My thing is death certificates and obituaries.'

Closer to home, Charles Manson still continues to cast a dark shadow over those who once crossed his path. Whilst the families of the victims continue to grieve over their loved ones' untimely deaths, those imprisoned have to face up to their own terrible crimes. Whilst Tex Watson, Susan Atkins and Bruce Davis have found solace in Christianity, Bobby Beausoleil, Patricia Krenwinkel and Leslie Van Houten appear resigned to the dismal fact that their connection to Manson is irreversible. As the parole hearings come and go, their statements of regret and sorrow do little to sway parole boards. Patricia Krenwinkel – who, after Tex Watson, was the Family's most prolific killer – seems to have come to terms with the fact that she may never experience freedom again. Despite having kept a flawless prison record for nearly forty years, she knows nothing she does will ever erase the brutality of those two insane nights. 'I wake up every day knowing that I'm a destroyer of the most precious thing, which is life; and I do that because that's what I deserve, to wake up every morning and know that.'

As Manson's chief hatchet man, Tex Watson's chances of release appear as remote as Charlie's. His rebranding as 'Forgiven' would convince few observers of the case. Watson has a website, www.aboundinglove.org, where he ministers to many across the lively prison fraternity with monthly updates, mostly drawn from scriptures. Watson's online biography offers little hope for his release, and he writes that, 'He expects Christ will return for His church way before then.'

The mercurial Susan Atkins remained a conundrum from the day she was brought into custody in November 1969. Barely confinable under Manson's spell, she struggled hard to assimilate herself among the prison population; not least among the co-conspirators she'd helped convict. The lifting of her death penalty in 1972 left her splintered psyche in limbo, and in 1974 she opted for a life following Christ. Whilst shouting loud her conversion, she immersed herself in prison work, and earned several commendations for helping other inmates in coming to terms with prison life. With the nickname 'Crazy Sadie' finally dispatched, Atkins began to desperately rebrand herself. However, her impetuous nature led her into many scrapes, the most badly judged of these being a marriage to fifty-two-year-old Donald Lee Leisure, a larger-than-life Texas 'billionaire'. The union was short-lived. Leisure, who claimed to have been married some forty-seven times, fled from Atkins, saying that she'd attacked him while the pair shared an intimate moment during a conjugal visit.

Six years later, Atkins married again, this time to an attorney named James W. Whitehouse, some seventeen years her junior. Although Whitehorse's legal skills were swiftly called into duty for his wife's parole hearings, Whitehouse had little success in championing his wife's cause, and Sadie continued to receive lengthy deferrals.

In 2002, Atkins and Whitehouse filed lawsuits against the state of California, claiming that the notoriety of the case was keeping her as a 'political prisoner'. Despite the case reaching the higher echelons of officialdom, it was dismissed; again the Manson tag and the heinous nature of her crimes overrode any legitimate right to appeal.

Members of Sharon Tate's family have consistently attended Atkins' parole hearings to oppose any release. With Atkins' loud protests on her prison status designed to sway the parole board, the normally taciturn Paul Tate was spurred into action in November 2000. With wife Doris and younger daughter Patti both having died, Paul Tate broke a thirty-five-year silence in a letter to the parole board.

Paul Tate wrote: 'Thirty-one years ago I sat in a courtroom with a jury and watched with others. I saw a young woman who giggled, snickered and shouted out insults, even while testifying about my daughter's last breath, she laughed. My family was ripped apart. If Susan Atkins is released to rejoin her family, where is the justice?'

Atkins wasn't released. However, during the summer of 2008, it emerged that she was suffering from a terminal illness. The prognosis was poor; she had been diagnosed with brain cancer, and one of her legs had been amputated. Additionally, she was bedridden and could barely talk. Doctors had given her just six months to live.

Whilst officials at Atkins' jail conceded that in her condition she no longer posed any real threat, there were still numerous hurdles, both emotional and otherwise, to negotiate before she could have any chance of receiving her long-desired freedom.

In the run-up to the parole hearing, Atkins discovered an unusual champion in Vincent Bugliosi, who as chief prosecutor fought for her to receive the death penalty back in 1971.

Vincent Bugliosi argued: 'She has paid substantially, though not completely, for her horrendous crimes. Paying completely would mean imposing the death penalty. But given that she has six months to live, and the loss of her leg, I don't have an objection to her being released.'

Atkins' hearing was scheduled for Tuesday 15 July 2008 before The California Board of Parole at Sacramento. The ninety-minute hearing was a highly charged, emotive affair, with representatives from both Atkins' family and relatives of the dead present. James Whitehouse, Susan's husband, implored officials to release his dying wife, pointing to the fact that in jail her healthcare was costing the state's taxpayers over a million dollars.

James Whitehouse went on, 'The real question is why we should continue to incarcerate her at this point in her life. She literally can't sit herself up in bed, she has suffered paralysis on her right side, she's lost her left leg.'

Ultimately, Atkins' request stalled, with the parole board unanimous in their decision to refuse her freedom on compassionate grounds. Adding his own voice to the mass of people opposed to her release, Governor of California, Arnold Schwarzenegger, offered his own slant on the controversy a few days before the hearing. 'You know, I think that they have to stay in. They have to serve their time. And I think that it's something, if someone is about to pass away. But those kind of crimes are just so unbelievable that I'm not for that compassionate release in that case.'

If the Governor of California wouldn't sanction Atkins' release in these pathetic circumstances, then the fate of all of the other imprisoned Family members appears similarly decided.

Others connected to the Family have long since forsaken the madness of the times, and gone on to continue their lives with varying fortunes. Linda Kasabian, who turned state's evidence to ensure the successful conviction of her Family cohorts, fled California following the trials and returned to New Hampshire, where she lived among a commune with her husband and children. Despite giving evidence against Manson, the FBI kept her under close surveillance long after her trial. She has surfaced publicly just once, for the coast-to-coast TV show *A Current Affair*, some twenty years after the Tate–LaBianca killings. These days, with Linda incognito and impossible to trace, the hip British band Kasabian reflects her past notoriety; many of their young following are unaware of the origins of their favourite band's name.

In time, young Family members Barbara Hoyt and Dianne Lake returned to their families, and tried to put their misspent youth behind them, albeit with deep scars from their time under Charlie's dominance. Catherine Share, who as Gypsy, prided herself on her unswerving loyalty, eventually freed herself from Manson's grip. Like others connected to the Family, she changed her name and immersed herself in the teachings of Christ. Steve Grogan, once the acid-fried Clem, successfully reassimilated himself in California following his parole release in November 1985. During 2008, it was revealed that he'd joined a swing band called 'Rhythm Town Jive' under the name 'Adam Gabriel'. Damned by his temporary association with the Family, the talented Bobby Beausoleil carried on making music inside prison walls, and finally finished the long overdue soundtrack to *Lucifer Rising*. He is now a very different man to the cherubic youngster Kenneth Anger hexed back in San Francisco.

Mary Brunner, Charlie's first convert, eventually pulled away from the Family. Following her lengthy sentence for the botched raid on the Hawthorne weaponry store, she returned to her native Wisconsin. With her was Manson's son Michael, long since free of the 'Pooh Bear' moniker. Paul Watkins, who had survived an arson attack in the run-up to giving evidence for the prosecution, emerged defiant, and back in control of his destiny. Settling in the Death Valley region with his wife and children, he penned his memoirs under the title, *My Life with Charles Manson*, published in 1980, and drew on his experiences of his time under Manson's spell to travel and lecture on cult psychology. He reflected, 'I know why I was in the Manson Family. The young people who came into the Manson Family were there because they have this personality, and Charlie was able to play on each person's dysfunction and if you had a hatred for women, he could bring that out, or a hatred for men, he could bring that out. A general acting out a hatred for society, he could bring that out, and as this deteriorates, it deteriorates into a scene like the Tate–LaBianca murders.'

Sadly, Paul died from leukaemia in 1990. Other, less pivotal members of the Family fled California into obscurity, hoping that their notoriety wouldn't catch up with them.

As for Charlie ... at the time of writing (September 2008), he is currently spending one of his frequent spells in the Secure Housing Unit (more commonly known as 'The Hole') at the California State Prison in Corcoran. Even at the venerable age of seventy-four, Manson continues to cause trouble, with a long list of attacks on prison guards and fellow prisoners racked up over the years. It's been reported that Manson has been suffering with breathing problems, and has of late taken to using a wheelchair to get around. To date, Manson has been offered the chance to apply for parole eleven times; all eleven times parole has been denied whether he turned up or not. In 1978 he told the court, 'I'm not unsuitable for the world out there.' He went on to reiterate what was fast becoming his mantra, that he 'didn't kill nobody and didn't order nobody to be killed.'

While even he knows that chances of a release are zero, Manson's occasional appearances in front of the parole board are always eventful. At one hearing he claimed that, if released, he'd head off to Iran to see the Ayatollah; in another he expressed a desire to go to Mars. With television cameras trained on him, Manson has been happy to play his part – a cross between innocence lost and a psychedelic court jester.

Despite his play-acting, Manson's words are still littered with dark allegory, and rage is never far from the surface: 'We're in pawn four, bishop four and seven, let's see. How do I finesse that?

You say in your minds that I'm guilty of everything that you've got on paper. So therefore, it would run logic that I would need to have remorse for what you think is reality, and if that be true, then all the oceans' contents, if it were my tears, there would not be enough to express the remorse that I have for the sadness of that world that you people live in ... You've been using me ever since I was ten years old. You used to beat me with leather straps, you know. It's like, does anyone have any remorse that I've spent twenty-five years in a solitary cell and even on Devil's Island, you didn't keep anyone over five years. You broke every record that they've ever set in the planet earth. You only kept Christ on the cross three days.'

Acknowledgements

As may be imagined, gluing together this hugely disparate story has been something of a daunting task. However, I have been aided in no small way by the many who've shared my vision of presenting something less hysterical than has been presented previously. Despite this, numerous individuals have been reticent to talk about what is clearly Hollywood's darkest chapter. Manson's enormous notoriety has served to seal the lips of many people who once passed his way. However, for those who have acquiesced to share thoughts and memories, I offer my immense gratitude.

Primarily, I'd like to thank Manson's original trial prosecutor, Vincent Bugliosi, for sharing some of his valuable time for an interview in the middle of a hectic schedule. Equally, District Attorney Stephen Kay, was considerate enough to share several aspects of the Manson case never covered before. Much gratitude must also go to Gary Stromberg, for breaking four decades of silence regarding his early championing of Manson's musical talents. Thanks too to Dr. David Smith of Haight Ashbury's legendary Free Medical Clinic, for building a vivid picture of San Francisco in the mid-1960's. I am also grateful to Bobby Beausoleil who was kind enough to answer a few questions regarding Manson's early musical prowess via email. Additionally, I would like to thank Tony Bramwell and Richard Di Lello, two former employees of the Beatles Apple Records, who came forward with new information. Equally, I am heavily indebted to Sandi Gibbons at Los Angeles Police media relations, for processing my numerous requests with great professionalism.

My immense gratitude goes to Daniel and David Pugh, who bravely revisited memories of their much-loved brother Joel. I do trust that we have been able to build a more complete picture of your remarkable brother. Equally, I am indebted to Joel's best friend James Balfour, who came forward at the eleventh hour to share memories and key details of his best friend.

I am eternally grateful for the efforts of Jacqueline Sundstrom, archivist at the University of Reno in Nevada. Through her efforts, a file of papers relating to the Manson Family's activities in the United Kingdom was discovered buried deep in a library repository. The fruits of her assiduous work are revealed here for the first time, and fill in some important gaps in the case.

"Cats", "Coroner" and everyone from truthontatelabianca. com; the most informed and reasoned site in Mansonia cyberspace. Thanks also to websites charliemanson.com and mansonfamilytoday.com for their estimable on-line resources.

Special thanks must go to Dayan Ballweg for invaluable photo research in Los Angeles. Equally, I am grateful to Josine Meijer for her expert handling of these hugely sensitive photos once they touched down on British soil. My thanks also go to librarians at Los Angeles and San Francisco public libraries for sourcing original news features for me, and to librarians at Berkeley University for checking some key facts for me, and staff at the Metropolitan Police headquarters in London for sourcing items through the Freedom of Information Act.

Additionally, I have been blessed with the good services of the British Library and Westminster, Hammersmith and Kensington and Chelsea public libraries. Special thanks to librarian Peter Grimwood for his extraordinary research skills.

On a personal note special thanks to my agent David Luxton for guidance and support; Ben Dunn for his enthusiasm in this project from the start; Paolo Hewitt for his inspiring words and words of wisdom; Mark Lewisohn for opening some doors I'd long considered closed and Gary Lachman who guided me through the convoluted activities of the Process Church. Additionally, special thanks for their invaluable assistance must go to Keith Altham; Keith Badman; the late Mick Cox of the band Eire Apparent (RIP); David Dalton; Sgt. Paul Dostie; Joss Hutton; Gerard Jones; Phil Kaufman; C.P. Lee; and Inyo County District Attorney Art Mallet.

There are several people who provided more than just tea and sympathy when dealing with harrowing tales of mind control and mass murder. Thanks then to Adam Smith and Mark Baxter for being first-class fellows; Phillip, Robert and Melanie for being the best family support team ever; Michael Collins; Joanna Cronin; John Mason (RIP); Tim Poulter; Sara Rennison; Kilmer Varient; Phillip Watson; and many others too numerous to mention. Rest assured though, I value all of your input along the way.

Simon Wells. Sussex, March 2009.

Picture Acknowledgements

Corbis;1, 7 below left, 8 below, 13 below. Getty Images: 2, 3, 7 above, 9, 14. Courtesy Los Angeles Police Department: 4, 5 above, 11, 15. Los Angeles Public Library: 5 below, 6, 16 above. Courtesy Daniel Pugh: 16 below. Rex Features: 13 centre. All other pictures courtesy the author.

Every reasonable effort has been made to contact the copyright holders, but if there are any errors or omissions, Hodder & Stoughton will be pleased to insert the appropriate acknowledgement in any subsequent printing of this publication.

Bibliography

Books

Andrews, Frank Earl (ed.): *Prose and Cons*. Pyramid Books, 1976.
Anthony, Gene: *Magic of the 1960's*. Gibbs-Smith, 2004.
Atkins, Susan. Schiller, Lawrence: *The Killing of Sharon Tate*. Signet, 1970.
Atkins, Susan, Slosser, Bob: *Child of Satan, Child of God*. Bridge-Logos, 1977.
Badman, Keith: *The Beach Boys*. Backbeat, 2004.
Bergan, Candice: *Knock Wood*. Linden Press/Simon & Schuster, 1984.
Bishop, George: *Witness to Evil*. Nash Publishing, 1971.
Bravin, Jess: *Squeaky: The Life and Times of Lynette Alice Fromme*. St. Martin's Press, 1997.
Bugliosi, Vincent: *Helter Skelter*. W.W.Norton, 1974.
Butler, Dougal: *Moon the Loon: The Amazing Rock and Roll Life of Keith Moon*. Star, 1981.
Capote, Truman: *Music for Chameleons*. Random House, 1980.
Davis, Howard: *The Zodiac/Manson Connection*. Pen Power Publications, 1997.
Davis, Stephen: *Hammer of the Gods: Led Zeppelin Unauthorised*. Macmillan, 2005.
Didion, Joan: *The White Album*. Simon and Schuster, 1979.
Dilello, Richard: *The Longest Cocktail Party*. Popular Culture Ink, 1977.
Emmons, Nuel (with Charles Manson): *Without Conscience: Manson in His Own Words*. Grafton, 1987.
Faith, Karlene: The *Long Prison Journey of Leslie Van Houten: Life Beyond The Cult*. Northeastern, 2001.
Felton, David: *Mindfuckers: A Source Book on the Rise of Acid Fascism in America*. Straight Arrow Books, 1972.
Freedland, Nat: *The Occult Explosion*. Michael Joseph, 1972.
Gains, Stephen: *Heroes and Villains: the True Story of the Beach Boys*. MacMillan, 1986.
Gilmore, John, Kenner, Ron: *The Garbage People*. Amok Books, 1995.
Gorightly, Adam: *The Shadow over Santa Susana*. Writers Club Press, 2001.
Harrison, George: *I Me Mine*. Simon & Schuster, 1980.
Hoskyns, Barney: *Hotel California: Singer-songwriters and Cocaine Cowboys in the L.A. Canyons 1967-1976*. Fourth Estate, 2005.
Hoskyns, Barney: *Waiting For the Sun*. St. Martin's Griffin, 1999.
Kaufman, Phil, White, Colin: *Road Mangler*. White Boucke Publishing, 1993.

King, Gregg: *Sharon Tate and the Manson Murders*. Mainstream Publishers, 2000.
Lachman, Gary: *Turn Off Your Mind: The Mystic Sixties and the Dark Side of the Age of Aquarius*. Sidgwick & Jackson Ltd, 2001.
Lewisohn, Mark: *The Complete Beatles Chronicle*. Hamlyn, 1995.
Livesey, Clara (M.D): *The Manson Women: a Family Portrait*. Richard Marek, 1980.
McCartney, Paul. Miles, Barry. *Many Years From Now*. Holt, 1998.
McDonough, Jimmy: *Shakey: Neil Young's Biography*. Random House, 2002.
Murphy, Bob: *Desert Shadows*. (Self Published) 1986.
Nelson, Bill: *Manson Behind the Scenes*. Pen Power Publications, 1997.
Parker, John: *Polanski*. Victor Gollancz, 1993.
Polanski, Roman: *Roman by Polanski*. William Morrow & Co, 1984.
Quantick, David: *Revolution: The Making of the Beatles' White Album*. Unanimous, Ltd, 2002.
Sanders, Ed: *The Family: the Story of Charles Manson's Dune Buggy Attack Battalion*. Dutton, 1971.
Schreck, Nikolas (editor): *The Manson File*. Amok Press, 1988.
Stebbins, Jon: *Dennis Wilson: The Real Beach Boy*. ECW Press, 2000.
Udo, Tommy: *Charles Manson: Music, Mayhem, Murder*. Sanctuary, 2002.
Wall, Mick: *W.Axl Rose: The Unauthorised Biography*. Sidgwick and Jackson, 2007.
Watkins, Paul, Soledad, Guillermo: *My Life with Charles Manson*. Bantam, 1979.
Watson, Charles "Tex": *Will You Die For Me?* Fleming H. Revell, 1978.

Audio Sources

Rice, Dennis: web-broadcast on *"Focus on the Family"*. June, 2008.
Barbara Hoyt: in conversation with Bill Nelson. CD release, (uncredited) 1994.
Cease to Exist: The Rock and Roll Story of Charles Manson. BBC Radio One,1994.
Dianne Lake: in conversation with Bill Nelson. CD release, (uncredited) 1995.
Family Jams: Transparency Records, 1970.
Charles Manson: Lie: The Love and Terror Cult. Awareness Records, 1970.
The Manson Family Sing the Songs of Charles Manson. ESP Disk, 1970.

Visual Sources

Among several hundred hours of film sourced for this book, the author would like to credit the following items which were of particular use.

ABC: Raw News Footage, 1969-
All Eyes on Sharon Tate. MGM, 1967.
BBC: *Twenty-Four Hours*. July, 1968.
CBS: Raw News Footage. 1969-.
The Hippie Temptation: CBS News, 1967.
Charles Manson: Journey into Evil. Biography Channel, 1998.
Charles Manson Superstar: Video Werewolf, 1989.
Dateline: The Devil's Business. NBC, 2008.
Dearly Departed Tours: Feature on Fox News. April, 2007.
Final Days of an Icon: Sharon Tate. Discovery Channel, 2008.
Geraldo: Manson Family Reunion. NBC, 1994.
Great Crimes and Trials of the 20th Century: The Manson Family Murders. Columbia Video, 2005.
Inside the Manson Gang (Film): (Dir. Robert Hendrickson). Tobann Productions, 2008.
ITN: Raw News Footage, 1969-.
Kasabian, Linda: interview on *Current Affair*. 20th Century Fox, 1988.
Lucifer Rising (film): (Dir. Kenneth Anger). Magick Lantern Cycle Films, 1970.
The Last Days of Sharon Tate: E! Entertainment Channel, 1999.
Manson (film): (Dir. Robert Hendrickson). Tobann Productions, 1973.
Manson Women (The): An American Nightmare. Biography Channel, 2002.
Mondo Hollywood (film): (Dir. Robert Carl Cohen). Omega-Cyrano Productions, 1967.

Murphy, Bill Scanlon: in conversation with Charles Manson. BBC/Channel Four, 1994.
NBC: Raw News Footage, 1969-.
Rose, Charlie: Interview with Charles Manson on *Nightwatch*. CBS, 1987
The Ramrodder (film): Dir. Ed Forsyth. EVI productions, 1969.
Rivera, Geraldo in conversation with Charles Manson. Raw footage, 1987.
Sharon Tate: Murdered Innocence. Biography Channel, 2002.
Something's Happening (film): *(AKA: The Hippie Revolt.)* Dir. Edgar Beatty. Belish-Freemont Associates, 1967.
The Tomorrow Show: NBC, 1981.
Turning Point: The Manson Women: Inside the Murders. ABC, 1994.
Watkins, Paul: *Larry King Live*. CNN, 1989.
Whicker's World: The Love Generation. BBC, 1967.
Will You Kill For Me: Charles Manson and his Followers. MSBN, 2008.
Witness: Charles Manson; The Man Who Killed The 60's.Channel Four, 1994.

Websites

The following websites have been helpful in the preparation of this book.

www.aboundinglove.org
www.ancestorylibrary.com
www.atwa.com (since defunct)
www.beausoleil.net
www.charliemanson.com
www.law.umkc.edu
www.mansondirect.com
www.mansonfamilytoday.info
www.mansonmurders.com (since defunct)
www.squeakfromme.org. (since defunct)
www.trutv.com
www.truthontatelabianca.com

Key Journals, Newspapers and Magazines.

I have researched numerous articles from newspapers and journals. Features and sources which were of particular interest are referenced below.

Dalton, David, Felton, David: *Year of the Fork, Night of the Hunter*. Rolling Stone, June 1970.
Dalton, David: *Into the Heart of Darkness with Dennis Wilson*. Mojo Magazine. September, 1999.
Family Jams: (Sleeve notes). Transparency Records, 1970.
Fulham Chronicle: 12th December,1969.
Hammersmith Gazette and Post: December 11th, 1969.
Journals of the Process Church (various). 1967-9.
Rose, Al, and (Dr.) David E. Smith. *The Group Marriage Commune: A Case Study*. Journal of Psychedelic Drugs, (published) September, 1970.
Life Magazine: *The Wreck of a Monstrous Family*. December 19th, 1969.
London Evening Standard (various).
London News of the World (various).
London Times (various).
Los Angeles Times (various).
Los Angeles Herald (various).
Manson, Charles. *Lie: The Love and Terror Cult*. (Sleeve notes). Awareness Records, 1970.
Moynihan, Michael: Interview with Bobby Beausoleil. Seconds Magazine. 1990.
New York Times (various).
Newsweek Magazine (various).
Noe, Denise: *The Manson Myth*. Crime Magazine.Com, December, 2004.

Reagan, Ronald: Remarks made at National Institute on Crime and Delinquency. 12ᵗʰ June, 1967.
Sanders, Ed: *Charlie and the Devil*. Esquire, November, 1971.
Smith, Dave: *Mother Tells Life of Manson as Boy*. Los Angeles Times, (circa) 1970.
Time Magazine: *The Girl Who Almost Killed Ford*. September 15th, 1975.
Tuesday's Child: *Man of the Year: Charles Manson*, (circa) 1970.
Vincent, Lynn: *Underestimating Evil?* World Magazine. March, 2000.

Parole Hearings, Police reports and trial transcripts.

By dint of the enormous amount of paperwork generated, the Manson Family case is evidently the most complex series of court cases ever held in America. I have found the following invaluable in the preparation of this book.

Susan Atkins: Grand Jury Testimony, 5ᵗʰ December, 1969.
William Garretson: Polygraph test, 10ᵗʰ August, 1969.
Barbara Hoyt: open letter to Bruce Davis' parole board hearing, 2ⁿᵈ February, 2000.
LAPD Homicide reports relating to murders at 10050, Cielo Drive and 3301, Waverly Drive, Los Angeles, 9ᵗʰ August,1969 & 10ᵗʰ August 1969.
Roman Polanski: Polygraph test, 11ᵗʰ August, 1969.
Psychiatric evaluation report on Charles "Tex" Watson, 7ᵗʰ August, 1971.

California Highway Patrol: Papers relating to the arrest of individuals at Barker Ranch, 12ᵗʰ October, 1969.
California Highway Patrol: Progress report on Barker Ranch arrests, 20ᵗʰ November, 1969.
Los Angeles Police Department: Papers relating to the death of John Phillip Haught, 5ᵗʰ November, 1969.
Los Angeles Sheriff's Department: Correspondence from interviews held at Inyo County, 20ᵗʰ October, 1969
District Attorney's Office, Inyo County, California. Papers relating to the death of Joel Dean Pugh, 13ᵗʰ May1970; 18ᵗʰ May, 1970.

Transcripts and case notes from the trial of Charles Manson, Patricia Krenwinkel, Susan Atkins and Leslie Van Houten; 24ᵗʰ July1970-19ᵗʰ April, 1971.
Transcripts and case notes from the trial of Charles Manson, Bruce Davis and Steve Grogan, 13ᵗʰ December 1971- 14ᵗʰ March 1972.

Note: As decreed by statute, all incarcerated Manson Family members have the right to apply for parole. Selected transcripts from the following hearings have been sourced for this book.

Susan Atkins: Parole hearings: July, 1978; September 1981; March 1985.
Bobby Beausoleil: Parole hearing: December 2005.
Bruce Davis: Parole hearings: June, 1993.
Steve Grogan: Parole hearing; October, 1981.
Patricia Krenwinkel: December, 1993.
Charles Manson: Parole hearings: April, 1992; March, 1997; May, 2007.
Leslie Van Houten: May 1998; June, 1999.
Charles "Tex" Watson: Parole hearings; January 1985; May 1990.

Index

The initials CM stand for Charles Manson.

447